Peter Ackroyd
The Ludic and Labyrinthine Text

Also by Julian Wolfreys

* APPLYING: TO DERRIDA (*co-editor with John Brannigan and Ruth Robbins*)

BEING ENGLISH: Narratives, Idioms, and Performances of National Identity from Coleridge to Trollope

DECONSTRUCTION • DERRIDA

THE DERRIDA READER: Writing Performances (*editor*)

THE FRENCH CONNECTIONS OF JACQUES DERRIDA (*co-editor with John Brannigan and Ruth Robbins*)

LITERARY THEORIES: A Case Study in Critical Performance (*co-editor with William Baker*)

LITERARY THEORIES: A Reader and Guide (*editor*)

READINGS: Acts of Close Reading in Literary Theory

* RE: JOYCE: Text–Culture–Politics (*co-editor with John Brannigan and Geoff Ward*)

* THE RHETORIC OF AFFIRMATIVE RESISTANCES: Dissonant Identities from Carroll to Derrida

* VICTORIAN IDENTITIES: Social and Cultural Formations in Nineteenth-Century Literature (*co-editor with Ruth Robbins*)

* WRITING LONDON: The Trace of the Urban Text from Blake to Dickens

* *From the same publishers*

Peter Ackroyd

The Ludic and Labyrinthine Text

Jeremy Gibson
and
Julian Wolfreys

Foreword by Peter Nicholls

First published in Great Britain 2000 by
MACMILLAN PRESS LTD
Houndmills, Basingstoke, Hampshire RG21 6XS and London
Companies and representatives throughout the world

A catalogue record for this book is available from the British Library.

ISBN 0–333–67751–X

 First published in the United States of America 2000 by
ST. MARTIN'S PRESS, INC.,
Scholarly and Reference Division,
175 Fifth Avenue, New York, N.Y. 10010

ISBN 0–312–22868–6

Library of Congress Cataloging-in-Publication Data
Gibson, Jeremy Sumner Wycherley.
Peter Ackroyd : the ludic and labyrinthine text / Jeremy Gibson
and Julian Wolfreys ; foreword by Peter Nicholls.
    p.   cm.
Includes bibliographical references and index.
ISBN 0–312–22868–6 (cloth)
1. Ackroyd, Peter, 1949–   —Criticism and interpretation.
2. Experimental fiction, English—History and criticism.
I. Wolfreys, Julian, 1958–   . II. Title.
PR6051.C64Z66   1999
828'.91409—dc21   99–43171
                                                          CIP

This book is printed on paper suitable for recycling and made from fully managed and sustained
forest sources.

10   9   8   7   6   5   4   3   2   1
09   08   07   06   05   04   03   02   01   00

Printed and bound in Great Britain by
Antony Rowe Ltd, Chippenham, Wiltshire

To friends at HEQC

Contents

Abbreviations   viii

Foreword by Peter Nicholls   ix

Acknowledgements   xi

Introduction: the 'ludicrous' Text of Peter Ackroyd   1

1   'A tiny light /seen in the mind's eye as a phoneme': the Poetry of
    Peter Ackroyd   35

2   'A bit of a game': the Styles of Peter Ackroyd I: *The Great Fire of
    London, The Last Testament of Oscar Wilde, Hawksmoor*   67

3   'A bit of a game': the Styles of Peter Ackroyd II: *Chatterton,
    English Music, First Light, Milton in America*   123

4   'Endless Variety': Writing the City in the Biographies, *The House
    of Doctor Dee*, and *Dan Leno and the Limehouse Golem*   172

5   Three Interviews with Peter Ackroyd
    • 26 August 1989   221
    • 4 January 1995   236
    • 21 December 1997   249

Bibliography   289

Index   304

Abbreviations

The following abbreviations for the works of Peter Ackroyd are used throughout the text. Full bibliographical details are given in the Bibliography at the end of the book.

B	*Blake*
C	*Chatterton*
CL	*Country Life*
D	*Dickens*
DLLG	*Dan Leno and the Limehouse Golem*
DP	*The Diversions of Purley*
DU	*Dressing Up*
EPW	*Ezra Pound and His World*
FL	*First Light*
GFL	*The Great Fire of London*
H	*Hawksmoor*
HDD	*The House of Doctor Dee*
ID	*Introduction to Dickens*
LL	*London Lickpenny*
LTM	*The Life of Thomas More*
LTOW	*The Last Testament of Oscar Wilde*
MA	*Milton in America*
NNC	*Notes for a New Culture*
O	*Ouch*
PP	*The Plato Papers*
TSE	*T. S. Eliot*

Foreword

Forewords are openings; this one, sadly, also marks a close. Jeremy Gibson, instigator of this book on Peter Ackroyd, died after a cycling accident in 1996. He was 29 and had recently completed his DPhil at the University of Sussex. He was a man of multifarious talents, and while working on his doctoral thesis he continued to develop as a musician, composer and creative writer. The thesis itself explored what Jeremy called 'Problems of Value in Literary Study, Critical Theory and Educational Politics', and in its wide sweep of reference it laid the foundations for his later work on Ackroyd's fiction. The enthusiasm for Ackroyd's novels was, however, an early one, and, as Jeremy's DPhil supervisor, I was aware that from the outset his interest in critical theory was motivated by a fascination with aspects of language and fictionality which his reading of Ackroyd had already provoked. With the thesis behind him, Jeremy promptly returned to Ackroyd's work and was generously granted several interviews, two of which are published here. At the time of his death, a manuscript had been submitted for preliminary assessment to Macmillan. Several chapters existed in draft form, along with a mass of speculative comments and extended citations from Ackroyd's writings. A book was clearly there in germ, though a daunting amount of work remained to be done. As reader for the publisher, Julian Wolfreys was enthusiastic about the project and accepted editor Charmian Hearne's invitation to bring it to completion.

Such is the history of the present volume, though as Ackroyd himself would be quick to remind us, mere facts are never adequate to events. 'The past can only really exist in the present,' he observes in one of the interviews included here, and this comment, so pertinent to his own fictional practice, provides, for me, one way of reading the words of someone whose lively and combative conversation I shall not be able to enjoy again. For this study – on the face of it just another work of literary criticism – is motivated by a critical imagination which – quite remarkably – is shared and developed by a co-author who never met his fellow writer. Somewhere in all this is something which our authors call 'the ludic and labyrinthine' – a shared sense of serious playfulness and an attentiveness to traces and memories which at once marks all of Ackroyd's fiction and establishes a textual network in which both absent and present voices speak. This responsiveness to what is past and shared – to a tradition which is active, pantomimic and not oppressive – is something which, the authors argue, characterizes much of Ackroyd's work and defines its sense of possible community. I will leave it to them to make that point in detail, noting here only that playfulness bespeaks a certain generosity, a lack of dogmatism, an openness of view, which both authors have admired in Ackroyd's fiction. Such intellectual generosity is certainly a quality for which I shall remember Jeremy, and it is something richly celebrated here, in Julian Wolfreys's own dedication to this project. In all of this, Peter Ackroyd's exploration of those complex and moving passages between past and present seems relevant indeed.

PETER NICHOLLS

Acknowledgements

I never 'knew' Jeremy Gibson. I put the verb in quotation marks to signal the fact that, while I never met Jeremy, I feel, having worked with his material for the past year, having spoken about him and his work with his parents, Charmian Hearne of Macmillan, and Peter Ackroyd, I know something of Jeremy Gibson, I know him, I know a particular Jeremy Gibson in a certain way, which this is neither the place nor the time to put into words.

This book is, inevitably, different in a number of ways from the book Jeremy might have written. Working with his material, in all its various forms, in varying stages of completion or incompletion, I have had to revise, rewrite or otherwise make editorial decisions. On occasions, I have felt, correctly or otherwise, that it was more important to go with the spirit of Jeremy's work, rather than the letter. This was particularly the case where all that was left to me were pages of citations from Ackroyd's texts, seeming to indicate some skeletal configuration of an anticipated chapter. Despite this, I hope this very different book might be neither unfamiliar nor unwelcome to Jeremy Gibson, and that it has become, if not the book he was going to write, at least one possible book he may have written, had he lived. Jeremy's work most immediately informs the opening pages of the introduction, Chapter 2 and the material on *Chatterton* from Chapter 3, along with the first two interviews.

My first acknowledgement and debt of gratitude is therefore to Jeremy himself. I would also like to thank Charmian Hearne for asking me to complete this book. I would like to thank everyone who read portions, drafts or complete chapters, those who criticized and commented, those who made remarks in passing about Peter Ackroyd's work, and those who gave me information and assistance over the nature and mythology of the golem, and other matters.

Finally, the greatest debt of gratitude, acknowledged as freely as possible beyond the bounds of conventional politeness, is to Peter Ackroyd. His receptiveness and generosity, his unstinting willingness to help in whatever manner, and his openness to questioning and discussion are, without question, the principal reason for the completion of this project. I would also like to thank Peter Ackroyd for granting permission to reproduce material from both his novels and his poetry.

JULIAN WOLFREYS

Introduction: the 'Ludicrous' Text of Peter Ackroyd

Peter Ackroyd: the Ludic and Labyrinthine Text addresses principally the novels and poetry of Peter Ackroyd. Aware as we are that this is one of the first full-length studies of Ackroyd's work,[1] we have nonetheless limited ourselves to considerations of *The Great Fire of London, The Last Testament of Oscar Wilde, Hawksmoor, Chatterton, First Light, English Music, The House of Doctor Dee, Dan Leno and the Limehouse Golem, Milton in America*, and the poems of *Ouch, London Lickpenny, Country Life*, and *The Diversions of Purley and Other Poems*, which is the most recent reprinting of poems selected from the previous three volumes.[2] Ackroyd's critical volume and cultural history of transvestism, *Notes for a New Culture* and *Dressing Up – Transvestism and Drag*, are considered briefly. The biographies are not discussed in any length, except where passages from these treat of London and support the reading of Ackroyd's visions of the city from the novels *The House of Doctor Dee* and *Dan Leno and the Limehouse Golem*, in Chapter 4 of this book. Specifically, the biographies of Dickens, Blake and More will be referred to in discussions of urban space and the mediation of the city in the text.

The biographies are not discussed in depth *as biographies* for a number of reasons. Practically, the biographies have not been addressed separately through lack of space in this study, which concerns itself throughout with questions of language, with text and with writing. In addition, *Peter Ackroyd: the Ludic and Labyrinthine Text* interests itself in the question of play and that of identity-politics – indeed, with both the play of identity-politics and the identity-politics of play. Another reason for the avoidance of the biographies as distinct from the novels is concerned with Ackroyd's own attitude towards the act of writing biography. Peter Ackroyd has asserted repeatedly that he wants to get away from conventional distinctions concerning the novel or the biography. He has also suggested that he regards himself primarily as a novelist, that he is unhappy with the limitations that the form of the biography imposes on him. In an interview in 1987, Ackroyd said 'I hate being called a biographer ...[this is] not only an insult but untrue' (*Publishers' Weekly* 1987). Glen Johnson points out that Ackroyd has always stated a desire to 'interanimate' the forms of fiction and biography and that, in attempting to achieve this, he has sought ways to install uncertainty into the biographical act by 'deliberately confusing the biographer's "act of interpretation" with the novelist's ability to "insist that things happen the way they ought to happen"' (Johnson 1996, 4; *D* 943). This is all part of Ackroyd's attempt to be as creative and inventive as possible when writing a biography. *Dickens* will be discussed briefly below in this introduction. The consideration of this biography is here, however, as part of the effort to situate Ackroyd's writing in relation to the critical response to his work, and, in response to issues raised by reviewers, to understand the playful and performative nature of Ackroyd's writing, regardless of genre, as it is given form in the biography of Dickens.

Finally, with regard to the self-imposed limits of this study, there is the question of Peter Ackroyd's output. He is still very much alive, he is still producing work and his output shows no signs of diminishing or stopping. To discuss all the work published so far would be to assume, however implicitly, a totality for 'the works of Peter Ackroyd'. Such a study would in effect create and propose a distorted canon. Therefore, this study seeks to introduce the reader to a limited number of interests in the texts of Peter Ackroyd. Specifically, these interests are not only those of this study but also concerns which occur throughout Ackroyd's career, which are read as being at work in the texts, albeit to greater or lesser extents, and with a constantly shifting focus. This introduction speaks to particular interests and the critical response to Ackroyd's work so far, as that response concerns itself with Ackroyd's play with narrative, with identity and the formal conventions of fiction, through the playful and labyrinthine movement of writing.

There is always a performative awareness on Ackroyd's part in the articulation of the texts of the available gambits in stylistic and formal play – in the double sense of that word of both torque and dalliance – along with those meanings to which the reader is directed in the introduction, above. Such strategies disarm the reader seeking to address style, form, and theme for the wholly conventional purposes of domesticating the texts of Peter Ackroyd, making them safe, homogeneous, so many offshoots of an organic whole, as we will see through a number of reviewers' responses to Ackroyd's publications.

Ackroyd's strategies achieve their effect through a deliberate display and deployment of artifice, role-playing, pantomimickry, palimpsest, parody, pastiche, intertextual referentiality, whether of a wholly conventional nature or in some other manner which is disconcerting, which disjoints ahead of the game all the conventional reader–text relationships. As Laura Giovannelli puts it, Ackroyd's texts have a 'chameleon' identity (1996, 20). Even history is open to 'falsification' in Ackroyd's writing. The past is always being rewritten so that, in the words of Luc Herman, whatever insights we may gain from Ackroyd's (per)versions of history, 'their epistemological value will inevitably be poor' (Herman 1990, 123). Indeed, to talk of 'style' singular with reference to Ackroyd's writing is to miss its own multiplicity within and from itselves, hence the plural indicated in the subtitles of Chapters 3 and 4. The question of stylistic experimentation arises, furthermore, out of Ackroyd's desire – paraphrasing Giovannelli – to subvert, albeit tentatively, a canonical and logocentric cultural system as manifested in its literary productions through the imperative to explore the potential of writing (Giovannelli 1996, 21).

Yet, despite what Giovannelli calls Ackroyd's 'indubitable faith' (21) in writing's subversive potential, such faith has hardly been acknowledged, unless frustratedly and, perhaps, fearfully, as in the case of reviewers such as Martin Dodsworth (as will be explored, below). Despite the occasional insistence on the part of reviewers over the past twenty years concerning Ackroyd's sense of literary and cultural national heritage through reference to past authors and dead literary predecessors, this expression of inheritance is not simply, unequivocally, straightforward. Given Ackroyd's attention to pastiche and parody, the relationship to literary culture and tradition expressed through his writing is yet one more game, one more ruse in the labyrinthine play of his texts. If the heritage is there, it is explored as being an improper and broken inheritance.

The filial relationship is, at best, problematic and equivocal. As readers of Ackroyd will no doubt be aware, the father is always and in some fashion lacking. Fathers and sons, literal or metaphorical, biological or symbolic are everywhere in Ackroyd's texts. Whether we consider Tim and Clement Harcombe, John Milton and Goosequill, the Old Barren One and nearly everyone in *First Light*, the strand of filiation never remains unbroken. The father fails, the father is lost, the father is absent, the father plays tricks, the father dissembles. The desire for a heritage, an inheritance, is always played off against that discontinuity, disjunction and disappointment (felt by so many of Ackroyd's narrators), along with that sense of frustration (felt by a few of Ackroyd's reviewers) which is the only imperfect and improper conduit between generations – of people, and of texts. The problem here then is one of filiation *and* betrayal, association and disassociation. It is the question of mourning *and* survival, of responding to a certain spirit, and yet acknowledging the tension in that act of responding.

Filiation *and* betrayal, association *and* disassociation: when one writes about a writer who is still alive, still producing, there is always the chance that the author will or could respond, in a manner which is, for the critic, wholly unpredictable, potentially troublesome. This opens a possible reciprocity based on equally potential tensions. While authorial intention is not everything, and while other contexts are to be taken into account, we are forced into recognizing that no context is exhaustible, finite or definable as such. Nonetheless, communing with the author, rather than simply with the author's texts – whether in the narrow sense of printed works, or in any broader sense[3] – we find ourselves as critics involved in a certain play, a very serious game. In this game, out of respect for the other, in this case the author for whom we claim respect, we find ourselves indebted and must pay attention to the writer's own considerations of what he does. The interviews which conclude this volume, having occurred over a period of nearly a decade, mark a certain reciprocity and, on occasion, amicable tension, as Peter Ackroyd enters into the debate concerning his texts, becoming part of the Ackroyd-text in a more general and broader comprehension of that word.

While it is not the purpose of this volume to suggest that Peter Ackroyd's intention is any more transmissible, or any more 'fully' comprehensible than any other author's, nevertheless the reader will encounter, from time to time, certain 'movements' between text and author's words in interview. Out of respect for the author's own desire, expressed in the interviews, to blur the distinction between genres as a principle of his writing, we have consciously refrained from attempting to connect between those statements which are found in the interviews and similar remarks to be found in the novels, the biographies, as well as in the poetry and criticism. Ackroyd is interested enough in making connections across texts and across forms, and it is not for the critic necessarily to force these, but, instead, to explain them. The boundaries dissolve themselves readily enough, and the astute reader of Ackroyd will have already noticed recurring, reiterating phrases, images, motifs and tropes. Again, it is not for the critic to raise these to the level of a theme, a programme for production, as we have suggested elsewhere in the introduction. Nor is it for the critic to impose on the reader certain concatenations as though these were, somehow, the keys to the 'truth' of either Peter Ackroyd or his writing.

Fiction and fact; commentary and narrative. It is impossible to tell where the discrete boundaries of these concerns are, supposing them to exist in the first place. This could well be something that Peter Ackroyd might want to transmit, whether in interview or in fiction; or, indeed, for that matter, in biography or poetry. Every new work that Ackroyd writes transforms the critical encounter with all his other works, with the readers' perceptions of Ackroyd's output, whether considered individually, as a series of singular, idiomatic works in the event of what we call an author's output, or whether considered as a whole. This can be seen to be the case with Ackroyd's *The Life of Thomas More*, the author's most recent publication as we write.[4] Each time a new work is published, it arrives relatively new and without what Derek Attridge has called 'the filter of commentary that so quickly surrounds a work when it enters the public domain' (Attridge 1996, 21). Yet, the relative newness inevitably gives way to that filter of commentary, and often with great force and speed. The transmission of the text is irretrievably altered. Its destination and reception cannot be assured. The question of the text becomes rewritten, and what we may think we understand about 'the works or text of Peter Ackroyd' undergoes transformation in incalculable ways.

The question of possible, if fraught filiation in Ackroyd's texts is one he acknowledges. He maintains that the poetry is the direct progenitor of his later novels, as is his one volume of critical thought (so far), *Notes for a New Culture* and his critical history of transvestism and theatricality, *Dressing Up*. In the poetry, Ackroyd's poetic language is frequently disengaged apparently from any immediate set of empirical meanings, and often from any conventional syntactical coherence. At its most extreme, the ludic dislocation of 'meaning' appears to figure what Horst Ruthrof has described as 'semiotic chaos' (Ruthrof 1997, 40). Often the words or brief phrases the poet employs will be literally dislocated from one another, extricated from the protective comfort of a conventional grammatical or traditional poetic form, and scattered over the page both to fend for themselves and to regard one another in separation. This practice at once highlights and undermines their conventional identities, even as it appears to allude to an alternative tradition in poetry, specifically that of the 'language' poets, such as John Ashbery for example. In some poems a fairly regular structure appears to be followed, but the sense of the lines is still fragmented, as if each line is slotted in from other poems, or is snatched from other works of prose. It is clear from the way that Ackroyd went about writing the poems that this formal fragmentation is, if not deliberate, then at least assured. Such an apparently arbitrary approach to composing poetry does not necessarily mean that Ackroyd is not making judgements about which phrases to place where. The poems can give fractured, fragmented glimpses of meaning which are suspended in a mood that is invoked without relying on apparently coherent narrative, however mannered, self-reflexively aware or stylized that narrative may be. All too often these ruins of the poetic force the reader to confront the word as word and not merely as some referent to the world within an unexplained textual network. Moreover, the words of the poems, in being unfixed, draw attention to their failed functions by being so playful, so ambiguous, so *ludicrous*. It is with the sense of the ludic that we must begin.

Notes towards etymological, semantic and cultural considerations

At the close of the twentieth century it appears that, in the English-speaking world, some of us have lost the ability to acknowledge the play in language. As we move towards the close of the millennium, things are getting serious.

There's little room and even less tolerance for ambiguity, polyvalence, play and sportiveness, especially when it comes to words and what they mean – or, more dangerously, what they might mean, given half a chance. Of course there is, or was, or, no doubt, will be that which is called 'postmodernism', whatever was, or is, or, no doubt, will be meant by that term. But, resisting categorization, if only so as to avoid the pat definition – thereby reducing the possibility of play to a controlled semantic and cultural horizon – we can suggest that the question of the word, of what the word means, is, above all else, a questioning of limiting what the word might mean. 'What do you mean?' has never seemed a more urgent, frantic question.

Words must mean one thing only: that's the prescription. At the same time, though, what that meaning is must remain somewhat vague. Necessarily. The only form of power over the word is to keep it at bay. Domesticating it doesn't mean bringing it into the house so much as keeping it in the yard, on a leash, in a definitive kennel we had already built for it before we had sought to bring it home. Or, to employ another metaphor (which, as we know from John Fowles, is the curse of western civilization [Fowles 1977, 339[5]]), the word is kept in questioning, a stranger at the border, no longer of or in another country, but not yet, not quite, allowed free and unobserved passage within our own.

There is an implicit paradox in attempting to restrict meaning while keeping that same meaning general: the more specific we are about 'what words mean', the more we delve and pry into their etymologies, their values, their histories and their contexts (and who, precisely, has time for that in an age of tele-technology, where the speed of the word's delivery is of greater concern?), the more the 'meaning' fragments into a number of meanings, all of which are slippery, and all of which are context-dependent – as, of course, is any meaning, even though, equally obviously, contexts are neither finite nor exhaustible. So, let's not get too specific with words and what they might signify. (A brief digression: you'll notice, if you pay attention to the historical frequency of words, that the verb 'to signify' – meaning 'to mean' – occurs in all its declensions often in literature and other forms of writing, at least from the early modern period to the nineteenth century with a more or less steady regularity and pulse. By the first half of the twentieth century, however, signification somehow has become a dirty and somewhat disused, discarded word, in English at least, only to be resurrected in the 1950s and 1960s by structuralist criticism.

Subsequently, in the passage of translation from French to English, from *Tel Quel* to the *Times Literary Supplement*, 'to signify' becomes a verb only employed within carefully defined contexts and discourses. Now a 'jargon' verb, 'to signify' signifies an operation indulged in only by those shadowy figures of what has become known as, referred to, defined as 'literary theory'.

In the Anglo-Saxon world people and words 'mean', they do not 'signify'. 'To signify' signifies nothing [borrowing momentarily from *Macbeth*] other than to signify a kind of unnecessary and inflated rhetoric, the verb having imposed on it the quality of a metonym with a somewhat ideological or ideo-phonological resonance. This, at least, is its 'meaning' for those who are fearful or distrustful of whatever it is all this literary theory supposedly does with words and texts [sorry, books[6]] and, specifically *English* texts: texts not only *in English*, but those taught in departments of English, which allegedly belong to an *English* heritage, a national culture, a national identity, and so on. You catch my drift. What this has to do with Peter Ackroyd will be already apparent to some, and will soon become apparent to others.)

As a possible result of not being specific, tiring perhaps of specificity, various meanings, no, entire words even, we allow or force to slip away from us, whence they become resigned to the pages of the full edition of the *Oxford English Dictionary*. It seems as if we cannot handle all the semantic slipperiness in words. Instead of the word being worn out, the word wears us out in its play. We let slide the multiplicity of values and usages, drying out words to keep their husks more clearly preserved (even though some residual trace is always there), using them with a degree of generality, calling specificity to our aid only when we want to score some pedantic point. (As, no doubt, I appear to have done in the parenthesis above; as David Lodge does in his review of Ackroyd's *Notes for a New Culture* [Lodge 1976].[7]) The last thing, or one of the last things (and last things are a concern of Ackroyd's), particular readers or reviewers seem to want, if the letter pages, certain reviews and opinion pieces in *The Guardian*, *The Times Literary Supplement*, the *New York Review of Books* and other locations are anything to go by, is a text where 'every word signifies the quiddity of the substance, and ... where every sentence signifies its form ...' (*HDD* 67). For – and paradoxically as has been stated – such signification only serves to worry meaning, revealing the movements of iteration and dissemination at the heart of the word. That which is unveiled in the play of meaning is the foreign within the familiar, the strange within the commonsensical.

As two examples, and as the means whereby to offer explanation as the rhetorical excuse for introduction, take briefly the subtitle of this introduction and the subtitle of this book (text): 'the "*ludicrous*" text of Peter Ackroyd'; 'the *ludic* and *labyrinthine* text'. Note particularly the words emphasized.

The immediate sense today of 'ludicrous' is almost wholly pejorative. It implies derisiveness, ridiculousness, allowing, for the moment, vague definitions. Is it the purpose then of *Peter Ackroyd: the Ludic and Labyrinthine Text* to suggest that Peter Ackroyd's novels, poetry, criticisms and biographies are ridiculous, laughable, open to derisive ridicule? Are they being dismissed out of hand before any reading has been sketched, any analysis offered? Alternatively, is this the reading which it is the purpose of this text to propose? Certainly there are reviewers who have been annoyed by the combination of what they perceive as 'ludicrous solemnity conspiring with grating frivolity' (Cropper 1989). Perhaps something else is intended entirely. Does the subtitle, 'the "ludicrous" text of Peter Ackroyd', seem to 'signify' one thing while being in effect a gambit, a play on meanings? Is the ploy to signify a number of possible meanings, no longer commonly associated with the term 'ludicrous'? The title may mean what it says while not exactly seeming to say what it might just mean.

This leads us to brief, etymologically derived considerations, certain notes on the possible play in meaning which seek to set the tone of this study. Doubtless, these are too hasty, but we will have to make do for now with the sketchiest of definitions. Because, before any designation, before discerning any design of a concept, a theme, a programme or model, the question is one of play.[8] The question of play, the questioning of play, is also a question put into play by the idea of play, in this case the *ludic* play in the play of words which the text of Peter Ackroyd plays with, puts into play, plays out – which, in short, is played, *performed*. (Some readers might discern a certain playfulness here, a certain play with 'style', supposedly that of Jacques Derrida; some will see this as pastiche, parody, others, doubtless, assuming the writer or the writing to be ludicrous; unquestionably they will have been correct, although in ways which they could not have foreseen.) Play puts into play the question of play, playing with the reader by asking the reader to play along, to consider what it means, to play.

The family of words, of which 'ludicrous' is today the most visible, derives appropriately not from one Latin parent but from two: *ludere* and *ludus* (the *OED* cites a possible third parent, ludicrously enough, in *ludicrum*), meaning to play or to sport. There are here the senses of game, gambit, acting, and performance even. *Ludic* signifies play which is spontaneous and without purpose, and behaviour which is undirected and spontaneously playful. In this range of parental possibilities we have to consider also *ludificare* meaning to delude, a deception; a mocking jest. Continuing in this vein, a number of family members – like so many apocryphal Chuzzlewits – have been lost to everyday use; they, and their play, are worth recalling: *ludible, ludibrious, ludibry, ludibund, ludicral, ludicrism, ludification*. They signify: playfulness, the subject of jest or mockery, derision or contempt, lightness, childishness, that which is intended in jest or one who is given to jesting, trifling, frivolity; more favourably, one who is sportive, witty, or who has a keen or lively wit (as in intelligence), that which, or someone who, is laughably absurd, a source of fun, a witticism, a sporting or theatrical show, burlesque.

With a little consideration it is possible to understand how any of these definitions, and any of the words which they define may be said to apply, carefully contextualized, to various aspects of the text of Peter Ackroyd, to particular formal and structural qualities, to certain concerns and interests which resurface. There is a constant sense of play and of gaming in Ackroyd's writings which numerous reviewers have noted over the last twenty or so years of Ackroyd's career as a writer, and which will be given further consideration in the next part of this introduction. Play is understood here to have to do with the historiographical, literary, epistemological and semantic engagement constantly at work in the texts in question. 'Strictly speaking,' suggests Horst Ruthrof, 'it makes little sense even to speak of "the meaning" of a sign. To do so suggests a static empirical basis for the production of meanings ...' (Ruthrof 1997, 39). This no doubt is believed by some to be the case and, perhaps desired as the ideal state of things by others. Yet, even in the most rigidly defined semiology, the indeterminacy of 'meaning' is acknowledged. The greater the fluidity of 'meaning "exchanges"', the broader the 'spectrum for negotiation. The more ludic, or playful, the discourse, the greater the spectrum' (Ruthrof 1997, 40).

Ackroyd plays constantly: within a given text, across his own texts, and between the texts which his name signs and those to which he alludes, from which he cites or otherwise borrows, often wittily, with knowing gestures of pastiche and parody, as much from a sense of fun or jest as out of a sense of respect and inheritance. He plays quite seriously between the conventional constraints of the novel and biography, so as to interanimate and contaminate the genres respectively. He plays too on expected values and meanings, toying with the commonsensical, with convention and received wisdom. Often his play involves characters, if not entire novels, histories or traditions. It is often the very act of ludicrous articulation which opens past into present, fact into fiction. Play is thus the means of articulation which simultaneously disarticulates, disjoints. Ackroyd's semantic or intertextual play is merely the configuration of ludic destabilization that is always already underway. Even the notion of 'history' is destabilized within itself, and from itself, as Katherine Kearns has recently shown (1997, 53–4). As Kearns makes plain, 'history' is always a double signification, signalling, as she puts it, 'what happened out there' and, at the same time, 'the story of those events' (1997, 54). Ackroyd's text puts this 'internal self-disidentification' into play through narratives which replay and reinvent history through historical narrative, through pastiche of writing styles which are consciously 'historical', and through the playful confrontation with the inadequacy of the fact in the face of the analytical or interpretive necessity.

In addition, his characters or, on occasions, caricatures: does Ackroyd not have fun with those? Are some of them not treated with derision or contempt, with mockery? Are not quite a few given to jesting or to theatricality? Are some not playful or childish? The author not only plays with his characters and their weaknesses, he also allows them what at times can seem like anarchic free play.

And, to take that last definition given above: burlesque. Is this not as suitable an adjective as 'ludicrous' for aspects of Ackroyd's writing? As is known, and as *Webster's* informs us, a burlesque is a literary or dramatic work that seeks to ridicule by means of grotesque exaggeration or comic imitation, mockery by caricature, and theatrical entertainment of a broadly humorous nature, consisting of short turns and sometimes striptease acts. Certainly, for as much as Peter Ackroyd indulges in 'dressing up' his writing in the clothes of others' texts and ideas, adopting a range of personae, he is equally happy to indulge in acts of literary striptease. He is quite happy to admit as much, in various interviews and through the narrator's acknowledgements towards the close of *The House of Doctor Dee*:

> And that at least is true – to the extent that I do not understand how much of this history is known, and how much is my own invention. And what is the past, after all? Is it that which is created in the formal act of writing, or does it have some substantial reality? Am I discovering it, or inventing it? Or could it be that I am discovering it within myself, so that it bears both the authenticity of surviving evidence and the immediacy of present intuition? *The House of Doctor Dee* itself leads me to that conclusion: no doubt you expected it to be written by the author whose name appears on the cover and the title-page, but in fact many of the words and phrases are taken from John Dee himself. If they are not his words, they belong to his contemporaries. Just as he took a number of mechanical parts and out of them constructed a beetle that could fly, so I have taken a number of obscure texts and have fashioned a novel from their rearrangement. But is Doctor Dee now no more than a projection of my own attitudes and obsessions, or is he an historical figure whom I have tried genuinely to recreate?
>
> (*HDD* 274–5)

This admission – confession is perhaps a better, more precise word – begins with the assertion of truth, and rapidly moves into self-questioning, through playful doubt concerning the propriety of words and words as property, which the narrator of the passage never seeks to remove or calm. Undecidability is the key to the playful disturbance within the field of identity and relationship between subjects. The play here is play of the most serious kind as there is unveiled through the theatrical gambit of the *mea culpa*, the acknowledgement of epistemological uncertainty in the face of competing theories of knowledge and possible interpretations. The question – and the play – remain open, the gesture seemingly spontaneous. And yet there is that discernible sense – is there not? – of parody here: a game within the game of 'postmodern' self-referentiality, where the text is all at once dressed up in another's clothing, and immediately stripped of those rags; or is there the hint of parodied or pastiched critical discourse, as if this writer had understood that unknown Derrida essay referred to by the silly Cambridge Don at High Table in *The Great Fire of London* (*GFOL* 90–1), whose unpunctuated speech is, in the contexts of that novel's relationship to *Little Dorrit*, a parodic reinvention of the speech patterns of Arthur Clennam's erstwhile fiancée, Flora Finching, née Casby ... ?

Given that Dickens's character is, herself, a source of mockery, the ludicrous subject of Dickens's own ludic structures, we can hardly say that either she, or the novel in which she is found simply are sources or origins. Ackroyd adapts that which is already manipulated by the parodist's art. The slightly fanciful scenario just painted above does serve to illustrate the playful intertext of Ackroyd's writing. Speaking of the fanciful and playfulness with reference to *The House of Doctor Dee* and *The Great Fire of London*, a perceptive reader will pick up on the repeated use of the family name Skelton. An Elizabeth Skelton, a member of the John Dee Society, appears briefly in the former novel (in Chapter Seven[9]), while Audrey Skelton, who believes she is possessed by the spirit of Little Dorrit (the character not the novel; she does not contain multitudes, and she does not do the police in different voices[10]), eventually sets the fire which consumes the film set. (Dee's house burns also.) Nothing other than a coincidental connection, no more in fact[11] than the recurrence of tramps with dogs (as in *Hawksmoor*). Is it even worth noting that the vagrant in the sixteenth-century passages of *Doctor Dee* names his dog Dickins? Connections are there if we read them as there, though in a number of cases, as in the one just given, once read do these amount to anything for the critical reader, or do such threads only serve to lead us deeper into a textual maze, where so many slight allusions, meaning much potentially, in the event mean little or nothing? This is typical of the density of Ackroyd's intertextuality which performs the weave and texture of much of his writing, whether at a now serious, or now playful pitch. Indeed, the serious and playful are not separable but slide – playfully – into each other, confusing the identities of each other as the text of Ackroyd burlesques seriousness and takes seriously textual play. This confusion is deliberate, acknowledged in the undecidability that haunts the passage quoted from *The House of Doctor Dee*.

But this is not a study of intertextual referentiality, except to note that the text of Peter Ackroyd is a text marked by the traces of affirmative resistance: text asserts its play while resisting through that affirmation the definition on the part of the reader or critic of a small range of themes which supposedly give the various novels an organic unity. *Peter Ackroyd* is not going to concern itself with the discussion of textual reference in any detail. As John Peck has pointed out in his astute discussion of Ackroyd's novels, pursuing connections attempts to pin down the text (Peck 1994, 447; he alerts us to this in his critique of Claude Rawson's review of *First Light*, where Rawson sets out to establish the intertextual connections between Hardy's *Two on a Tower* and Ackroyd's own novel). Ackroyd's resistance to the inclusion of any 'stabilising perspective' (Peck 1994, 447) in his writing leads Peck to suggest that 'it would be hard to think of anything more unhelpful than showing off one's familiarity [with other texts] ... as a way of establishing critical control ...' (Peck 1994, 447–8). Many of the allusions are well known anyway, and play happily in full view, on the numerous surfaces of Ackroyd's writings; others are less obvious, but all require various degrees of literary and cultural knowledge. This in itself is a game which Ackroyd's text is involved in, even at the most banal level, which some reviewers assume, mistakenly, to be the only game in town.

Cross-, intra-, and intertextual allusion and reference all serve to construct structures consisting of a number of apparently intercommunicating passages, to borrow from the *OED*'s definition of a labyrinth. There is, to draw on this definition once more, an entangled or inextricable condition of things, events, and ideas, to be found in all Ackroyd's writing. Ackroyd even plagiarizes himself (Finney 1992, 254). As John Peck suggests, '[w]e are teased with the possibility of meaning, but then everything dissolves' (Peck 1994, 449). Hence, the idea of the text as labyrinthine signalled in the subtitle of the book. (Not that labyrinths dissolve exactly; unless, that is, they manage to dissolve one's sense of certainty concerning direction, orientation, fixed and geometric points.) The idea of the maze is, in itself, the idea of play, of a certain game, at once intriguing and frustrating. Language is itself a labyrinth, containing, concealing, confusing and unveiling numerous cultural and historical layers. A labyrinthine writing performs its own movement: ideas are kept on the go, on the move; and so, too, are readers. Historical paths appear to emerge, only to run into some anachronistic dead-end. Ackroyd, writes Brian Finney with reference to *Chatterton*, 'appears set on overwhelming his readers in a plethora of unending literary borrowing or plagiarism', and the game is that 'he freely admits his own involvement' (Finney 1992, 254). Acknowledging the labyrinthine potential discernible in Ackroyd's writing with regard to literary intertextual referentiality, we can say right now: we're not going down that path. This is not an allusion hunt, even though it may be necessary to respond to certain allusions in passing.

In part, Ackroyd achieves his maze-like effects not only through intertextual reference and plagiarism, but also through constantly reintroducing figures, tropes and motifs which dance on the surfaces of his writing, seemingly daring the reader to interpret the writing to which they belong thematically, and so to domesticate Ackroyd.[12] Acknowledging the play in Ackroyd's text, a play which affects and touches on all textual structures while affirming the structurality of structure, it is necessary to resist the temptation of proposing any kind of thematic reading of that text. At the risk of sketchiness, but also so as to avoid prescribing a programme for reading in advance of the various analyses here, we must proceed hastily for the moment, running the risk of distorting the text. Figures which recur often in Ackroyd's writing are: fathers, time, the self or subjectivity, text (or writing, or trace), the house, architecture, the city, children, light. The temptation to see any or all of these figures thematically is due to the frequency of their appearances, some having persisted since Ackroyd's earliest publications in the form of poetry. The few listed are only the most obvious. All are employed in their so-called proper or immediate senses, and yet all are employed 'figuratively' or 'metaphorically', to make, for the moment, a conventional distinction. Yet, because Ackroyd mixes the uses, the figures are revealed as being tropes, properly speaking; there is no conventionally 'literal' use of any of these figures which is not also, simultaneously, a *tropic* play. Such figures also assume their tropic quality in the ludic text of Peter Ackroyd in that their frequency assumes the character of choral embellishments, musical or painterly motifs. They appear to take on a structural regularity, even while that regularity is itself irregular, and are recurrent enough to suggest a pattern of re-iteration across the textual surface. It is precisely this recurrence, this frequency and reiteration, which the critic conventionally wrestles into a pattern of similarity, declaring it a theme, erasing and marginalizing the differences of context, the differences of use, the difference from one example to another, and the difference between texts. Ackroyd plays with the critical reception of his work ahead of that reception by tracing through his texts, in a manner which is simultaneously continuous and discontinuous, figures that provide the possibility for reading conventionally.

Even as the texts in question play and perform constantly, and even as that play unfolds the complexity of a labyrinth which can operate merely for the sake of play, so Ackroyd's writing should be read without giving in to the wholly understandable and conventional temptation of trying to discern a route out of the maze so as to come away from the act of reading with certain general 'meanings' for Ackroyd's work. To propose themes and the reading of such would be to imply the possibility of discerning a deliberate organization, a plan or model worked out in advance by Peter Ackroyd for all his work. The parent–child motif that occurs so often in Ackroyd's work could be handled with little effort in such a way as to provide a central focus for a study of Ackroyd. This, no doubt, could then, in predictable ways, steer itself in the direction of a wholly conventional study: of the 'life and works' or psychobiographical variety, whereby the failing or absent fathers of Ackroyd's writings become versions of Ackroyd's own absentee parent. Such suggestions and readings serve only to domesticate what is strange in any text. No doubt they comfort the fears of some critics and readers who go to work in the same way as they have done with regard to the meanings of words: thematization homogenizes, it explains the foreign, the strange. Reducing Ackroyd to a limited number of themes makes him safe and manageable; all his singular texts become knowable through an understanding of his not having had a father present through his 'formative' years, so called. A reading such as this allows for that gesture of domestication, which is simultaneously a gesture of institutionalization.

We may gesture towards a reading of the recurrent figures in a different manner; we may respect their seriality and strangeness, and the numerous singular examples which can be read. If the figures named above are the most obvious there are others also discernible: specifically, continuity and connection. It is not that Ackroyd necessarily makes his texts continuous, even though he has occasion to reiterate in part surface patterns and forms. Rather the concepts of continuity and connection surface repeatedly as textual traces, announced by various characters and in a variety of narrative contexts, only to be dropped. How are we to read this? The 'function of continuation', writes Gérard Genette, 'is not always to complete a work ... one can always decide that a work which is finished and published as such by its author is nevertheless in need of a prolongation or a completion' (Genette 1997, 175). Connection and continuation are but two parodic textual gestures, which affirm the text's resistance to closure by suggesting a future reiteration outside of the current context in which they are found. Figures, tropes, motifs: all become reinvented. They are in a constant process of *becoming-reinvented*, where reinvention is another name for the act of becoming. Dressed in borrowed clothes, they 'pass' as an *other*, as other than that other which they always already appear to have become. Figures of play, these tropes play with the possibility of the text's reformation, its reshaping, not only through future possible acts of reading and rereading, but also through the appearance of other texts which appear to 'take up' such concerns, and yet which do so in the singular example of a 'work of literature' which must be respected in all its singularity, and which cannot be controlled according to some thematic horizon of expectation. The figures of continuation and connection suggest the hypothetical endlessness of the textual weave, where context, intertext, hyper- and hypotext are all stitched together in a maze the identity of which is not yet determined, and not determinable.

This articulation of dis/continuity is what thematic reading strives to suppress; its gesture is definable as the critical movement or passage from thinking *the text of Peter Ackroyd* in all its complexity and singularity to thinking *the thought or life of Peter Ackroyd*, a few concepts, ideas, theories which stabilize and encapsulate an identity. Ackroyd's texts play with questions of identity by putting questions to the question of identity when thought as a general concept. Each text does so in a singular and idiomatic manner (in part through the pantomimickry of styles and voices) which playfully assigns the *ludic* possibility of deluding or deceiving the reader into believing s/he can abstract a theme or concept equally applicable and equally discernible in all the texts in question.

There is in this one more textual effect which resists and laughs at the efforts of attempted thematization, which is already implicit and in play here: the comic. The comic is everywhere in Ackroyd. It is that which resists all possible thematization (not only in Ackroyd's writing but also in all writing), while challenging the solemn boundaries with which genre is demarcated.[13] It breaks down boundaries between forms, it plays with the identities for which it has no respect, its playful laughter is not produced in the same manner each and every time, and yet it produces its effects constantly. It refuses to take its subject seriously or to be taken seriously itself. Laughter and the comic suggest that within identity which is not proper, which is always available to be made *ludicrous*. If any non-definable, non-stable trace can be said to resurface continuously throughout the text of Peter Ackroyd, it is the comic. The comic and ludic disassemble identity, often bringing out the other within, and often with a political resonance, as the author shows in his study of transvestism.

There is, then, always some discomforting *other* identity within the normal, so-called. Whether the discussion is of transvestism, or engaging in tropic disorientation, Ackroyd calls into question the stability and sufficiency of the idea of a full and unambiguous selfhood or subjectivity. It is perhaps this aspect of Ackroyd's play that seems repeatedly to disconcert his reviewers over the years. These reactions to Ackroyd's publications should be considered, if only as a means by which to gain a further understanding of the complexity of play in the novels, poems, criticism and biographies.

Playing with the reviewers

Reviewing, especially of the journalistic variety, is an unenviable and, often, an unhappy task; as Peter Ackroyd in his reviewer's guise has said, the waters of journalism are frequently, if not always, 'turbid' (27 March 1988). As often as not, the reviewer is constrained by an aesthetic straitjacket of post-Aristotelian design, where issues of harmony, organic wholeness, proportion, properness and taste dominate, whether the reviewer wishes them to or otherwise. Frequently, reviewing begins by holding up a template of the ideal form of the novel, the biography, or whichever genre is under consideration, working dutifully to see how well the single example under immediate consideration matches up to the perfect template which is nearly always implicit, though resolutely *there*. When the writer under consideration deviates from an implied pattern, the reviewer attempts to recover the deviation as a variation, explaining departure and distortion, where possible, as a way of reinventing the form in the domesticating guise of the thematic. This explanation on the part of the review both allows for anomalies and keeps the organic unity of the ideal form in place, unquestioned by that which gets put into play by the writer. Furthermore, reviewing is pursued, whether it knows it or not, from within the paradigm of a Kantian or quasi-Kantian aesthetics, operating according to a 'subjective rather than an objective universality' (Kearns 1997, 54). Reviewing is thus a game; and those who play often behave as though they were the referees rather than the players, looking out constantly for the offside, the double dribble, or some other transgression. If reviewing is itself a game, that which is being reviewed is supposed, ahead of the game itself, to play by the rules, even when it cheats. There is little room for reinventing the rules because it cannot be admitted that the game can change. For, if it does change, the question has to arise, is it even, any longer, the same game?

Playfulness, therefore, must be within the guidelines for playfulness, it cannot be wholly ludic, that is to say of a seemingly spontaneous and unorganized nature. What is perhaps more disconcerting than the absolutely ludic, though, is strategic and radical ludic-rousness, whereby game- and role-playing deliberately flaunt their apparent knowledge or ignorance of the rules and, in doing so, question implicitly the need for those constraints and acts of definition by which the game is given meaning.

Play is spoken of frequently in reviews of Peter Ackroyd's writing, especially the novels. It gets mentioned a lot, along with games, tricks, conundra, problems, puzzles, mazes, playfulness, deception, illusion, staging, acting, performance, masks, parody, pastiche, campery and exaggeration. All such qualities and definitions are so much a part of the various styles of Peter Ackroyd that, when he writes in *Dickens* that '[t]he things closest to Dickens's heart are those he most readily turns to laughter' (*D* 151), we get the sense – do we not? – that, if Peter Ackroyd is not writing of his own writing exactly, then the critic may at least turn this seemingly performative statement (from the chapter of *Dickens* which deals with Dickens's love of everything theatrical) into a commentary on Ackroyd's text. Play is everywhere then. Performed by Ackroyd, observed by him in others, and observed by others in him.

For example, we read of 'agreeably comic effects' in the poetry (Anon. 1974), while one novel is described as 'brilliantly quirky' (Lurie 1992); Ackroyd's 'cast of mind is defensively playful' and he 'has a lot of fun at the expense of his material' (Nye 1987); there is Ackroyd's penchant for 'modern literary games of intertextuality' and his 'toying with tropes' (Hislop 1983); 'fact and fiction ... [are] playfully intertwined' (Keating 1994); Ackroyd 'makes great play' of particular figures, playing 'a clever but precarious game', which game, the 'reader is required' to understand as being underway (Hislop 1983); but, as we are informed elsewhere, we as readers are 'well aware that we are being hoaxed' (Fenton 1985), and no doubt Ackroyd's fiction 'will please readers who enjoy literary theory and literary puzzles' (Lurie 1992); Ackroyd's fiction contains 'dreamlike conundra' and 'tricky, even tricksy, problems about the epistemological status of his text' (Hollinghurst 1984), while, elsewhere we are asked to acknowledge a 'tissue of allusion ... [a] network of coincidences' and 'structural self-consciousness' (Strawson, 1982), all of which leads to the suggestion of 'an intellectual puzzle' (Fenton 1985). 'Teasing narrative and bizarre cast allow Ackroyd the freedom to play', to toy 'with fact and fiction', and to engage in 'ludic narrative' (Keating 1994); the novels are filled with 'camp stylization' (Dodsworth 1987), 'camped-up eccentrics' (Glendinning 1987), 'camp excesses' (Kaveney 1994), exaggeration, subversion and reinterpretation (Hollinghurst 1984); *Hawksmoor*, we are told, is a 'witty and macabre work' (Oates 1986) and presents '"a game that had got out of hand"' and there is 'something ... unnerving about the game Mr Ackroyd plays with in this book' (Fenton 1985); 'Mr. Ackroyd mingles historical fact and fiction', we are told, in order 'to play witty erudite games involving ideas, coincidences, and interconnections' which is nothing other than '... a blending not only of fact and fiction but of the theatrical and the real' in a 'study in illusion' (Bernstein 1995). *Chatterton*, compared with *Hawksmoor*, is

> best thought of as a game played between the author and his reader ... or, to come a little closer to the point, as a game played by words themselves in the field of meaning.
>
> (Dodsworth 1987)

The last remark of Martin Dodsworth's sounds almost promising, until he goes on to ask, somewhat irritably in a tone reminiscent of a minor public-school headmaster, '[i]f this is Ackroyd's idea of being amusing, just what is the game?' (Dodsworth 1987). Still, we should have expected this, because '[i]t is easy to become impatient with this novel' (Dodsworth 1987; doubtless we're glad to be told this, just in case we'd read it – several times – and were not yet impatient with it).

Dodsworth's review of *Chatterton* (which will be given greater attention shortly) is the most extreme case of critical dyspepsia; curmudgeonly and pompous in its commonsensicality, it reveals most clearly the reviewer's adherence to a form or game-plan by which the reviewed work is to be judged. There are, of course, other reviews of Ackroyd's writing which have negative criticisms to make, but Dodsworth's is almost parodic in the expression of its dislike. While the majority of reviews of Ackroyd's publications are largely favourable, there is occasionally the sense that Ackroyd's ludic sensibility is aggravating. David Lodge, for example, dislikes the use of 'glib paradox' and 'meaningless metaphor' (Lodge 1976), which he assumes is a stylistic adoption from French structuralism. Yet such gestures, aesthetically pleasing or not (depending on your critical and ideological stance), are part of a larger play, strategy or gambit, which Ackroyd employs in a number of ways and for various purposes. The text most given over to the direct exploration of such 'dressing-up' concerns not language but behaviour – Ackroyd's *Dressing Up –* *Transvestism and Drag*, a history of 'an obsession' as the subtitle tells us, and a book which, according to David Sexton, provides the 'key to all Peter Ackroyd's work' (Sexton 1994). In this history, Ackroyd examines the 'coolly self-celebrating artist' and 'takes it for granted that our identity is the product of the clothes we wear' (Conrad 1979). Identity is a constant concern for Ackroyd and, in retrospect, it seems as if this early essay, where 'visionary African dancers turn into Cyril Fletcher's leering panto dame or Craig Russell's simulations of Streisand and Garland', all of whom are 'amateur exorcists' with a 'magical purpose' (Conrad 1979), substitutes language for clothing as that which dresses up identity, that which makes possible the play of masquerade, theatricality, campery and burlesque. Understanding this, we can come to see how playing with identity is the most serious game in the world for Ackroyd.

This points not only to Ackroyd's own interest in those who 'dress up', who put on masks or other staged identities, such as Dickens, Wilde, the transvestite, Dan Leno, and, indeed, all who take theatricality into the everyday. Some reviewers have suggested that in rewriting the identity of others, it is ultimately Ackroyd who adopts masks; impersonating others, he hides himself: '...because Ackroyd has chosen a medium in which it is difficult to find him, the discovery of his presence destroys his subject – much more so than if he were an actor obviously playing' a particular character (Hislop 1983). This 'charade' of writing involves the 'technique of disarming by caricature' (Cosh 1983) and proves to be precisely that which most troubles Ackroyd's reviewers. As Francis King points out, while critics have 'praised the power of Ackroyd's imagination' the 'brilliance' of his 'styles' relating to the impersonation of identity is less readily acknowledged (King 1993).

It is not because Ackroyd does perform the charade so well that he can irritate reviewers – he does, and is acknowledged, often favourably, for this capability. Instead, mild annoyance to outright irritability occur for two principal reasons: he can be seen to be doing it, even as he apparently hides, and he has fun with this game. What could cause more effrontery than that one could be seen not taking one's own game seriously, and yet playing it so well? Toying constantly with preconceptions about the stability of any identity, Ackroyd does not even allow the reader the comfort of assuming that the game stops somewhere and that, sooner or later, even the author, Peter Ackroyd, will step out from behind the mask, stepping away from the performance. Even

> [d]inner with him is like an audience with some latter-day Lord of Misrule. He begins quietly enough: with evasive anecdotes and camp banter. But he ends in a grand, slurred, interrogation of the idea of Creation and the place

of the imagination in the universe ... . He goes through the motions of self-parodying flirtation ... [saying] 'take me home, Timmy, and tuck me up' – then, absolutely alert, will set in train some elaborate and unanswerable argument ... construct[ing] a series of animated, frequently contradictory aphorisms.

(Adams 1998)

This is the closest this book will come to making a connection between 'life' and 'work'; it is done only so as to suggest the futility of any such critical attempt. Even the title of this present book – *Peter Ackroyd: the Ludic and Labyrinthine Text* – implies the name as a primarily textual focus, a shorthand for that which is published in his name. As we see from this one incident in an interview, Ackroyd, a 'writer of some agility' (Dyer 1985), is as much the actor, the performer, the player, as he is performed and constructed in writing. There is no more a central truth here to the image of Ackroyd than there is the sense that a true Ackroyd lurks behind the personae adopted, the caricatures and characters performed in his writing. The self has no centre, no stability, no essence, unless it appears in the guise of some estranging momentary manifestation which plays against the grain and toys with the illusion of essentialism; reviewing comes unstuck when confronted by the performativity of the subject if it cannot calm down the play into the stable identity of the author. Even when spoken of as a 'theatrical spirit-medium' (Hollinghurst 1985), Ackroyd is understood as a performer who empathizes with other performers; he likes nothing better, as we've already implied, than a bit of 'literary ... transvestism', he 'likes nothing better than to get some kit on and cut a caper' the purpose of which is to produce 'laughter' (Sexton 1994). Ackroyd is an accomplished impersonator, doing all his characters 'as turns – and to a turn' (Kaveney 1994). Even in his 'straightest' piece of writing, the highly praised biography of T. S. Eliot, Ackroyd is acknowledged as comprehending 'the heterogeneity of Eliot's character', as well as the poet's 'playing of poetic roles'. Ackroyd successfully dramatizes the 'various aspects' of Eliot's character (Montrose 1984).

It is precisely the extent to which role-playing and game-playing are apprehended as being in process without end which is troublesome for some, even when reviews are favourable. That such games are involved – often ludicrously (in the most positive sense) as in *The Great Fire of London* or *Dan Leno and the Limehouse Golem* – in the dismantling of a stable identity makes the problem for some even greater. For the ludic mutability of the subject is not only part of the discernible pattern of the maze in Ackroyd's text: it is the fluid architecture of the labyrinth itself, which serves to destabilize the very idea of fixable, constant form. Were this to end with the question of content, reviewers and critics might well find that their game at least could resolve itself by proclaiming that Ackroyd is a 'postmodernist' (as a couple have done). But with his 'endlessly revenant style, [and] his love of pastiche' (Sexton 1994), Ackroyd has the capability of disturbing even the understanding of conventional forms of the novel. *Hawksmoor* is 'less a novel in the conventional sense of the word (in which, for instance, human relationships and their development are of central importance) than a highly idiosyncratic treatise, or testament, on the subject of evil' (Oates 1986). It is notable here that in her largely positive review, Joyce Carol Oates is stuck for precisely the right word to describe what *Hawksmoor* is or seems. Disturbance in the field of meaning or the field of identity brings to the fore the question asked by Victoria Glendinning (in her appreciative review of *Chatterton*, 'Who's to say what is fate [sic.] and what is real when you can't tell the difference?' (Glendinning 1987).

While Glendinning puts her question in a more or less neutral manner, Peter Keating is not so sure about Ackroyd's games. In his review of *Dan Leno*, Keating highlights what he takes to be Ackroyd's 'apparent belief that there is *no longer any point in even trying to distinguish* between fact and fiction, and the whole elaborate structure is held in place, *in theory at least*, by a Dickensian philosophy of a sort of all-embracing interconnectedness' (Keating 1994; emphases added). There is a degree of wariness on the reviewer's part which, again, has to do with a resistance to the games of illusion and destabilization which are prevalent in the text of Peter Ackroyd. Certainly, Ackroyd does make much of connectedness and coincidence, though whether it is an 'outrageous use' as Keating proposes is debatable (Keating 1994). The desire to connect goes back to Ackroyd's poetry, as we shall see in the first chapter. To call this Dickensian is to provide momentarily a stable identity for what Ackroyd does in a moment of filiation. The reviewer desires – no, *needs* – the family resemblance, and so sketches the portrait himself. Inadvertently, the historicality of the connection counters any notion of Ackroyd as a playful, though nihilistic, postmodernist, if only because implausible though playful interconnections are prevalent throughout the history of the novel, whether one speaks of Dickens or Lawrence Sterne.

History – the history of the novel, history as a source of narrative – and temporal arrangement are also played with by Ackroyd. 'Real' figures such as John Dee are moved from their historically verifiable locations to invented ones. Ackroyd plays fast and loose with dates also. As Francis King generously suggests of *Hawksmoor*, *Chatterton* and *The House of Doctor Dee*, 'it would be foolish and futile to look here for historical accuracy' (King 1993). Eric Korn asserts that 'time can be deconstructed by any magician or novelist' (Korn 1993). In *Dan Leno*, Dan's birth is given 'incorrectly' as 1850 (he was born in 1860). The Golem murders are based on those of Jack the Ripper, 'but they are dated eight years earlier, and no mention of the Ripper murders is ever made. Why, in a novel of interconnections, set up this kind of connection at all? Most readers will recognize the similarities. Are they intended to? Does it matter?'[14] asks the frustrated Peter Keating (Keating 1994). In *Hawksmoor* architect Nicholas Hawksmoor is simultaneously reinvented as twentieth-century policeman, Nicholas Hawksmoor, and eighteenth-century architect, Nicholas Dyer, while the Commission for Building Fifty New Churches of 1711 is moved to 1708. A church is 'invented' for the purpose of the narrative, while Dyer's other churches all exist, buildings designed by the 'real' Nicholas Hawksmoor. The fact that no fact is sacrosanct suggests that, like the play with identity, history is there to be used. Peter Keating's frustration misses the point, which is that connections are made because they can be made, and for no other purpose than the ludic possibility presented in teasing the identity of historical moments. From conventional perspectives the reviewer may well criticize Ackroyd for having 'conceived' his narratives 'as a series of brilliant scenes rather than as an organic whole' (King 1985), but this is still to insist on a supposed or assumed primacy of organic wholes as grounding definitions in aesthetic considerations. We would do well to bear in mind the following statement, from the review of *Chatterton* in the *New York Times Book Review*: 'Plausibility is not an issue; by disconnecting the orthodoxy of sequence and causation, Mr. Ackroyd makes it seem natural that any event should summon its kin' (Donoghue 1988).

Dodsworthiana

Not that this is enough to satisfy Martin Dodsworth in his review of *Chatterton*, already mentioned briefly (Dodsworth 1987). While Dodsworth does acknowledge the game-playing in the novel, it is not a game for which he cares greatly, primarily, it seems, because he cannot tell what Ackroyd is up to and because the spirit behind such games is unidentifiable. Once more, the real effrontery for the critic lies in the absence of a locatable identity, even that of a stage manager or puppet master. In a moment sounding like F. R. Leavis on Thomas Hardy, he compares Ackroyd's literary playfulness with that of Henry James, but thinks James the better writer because he kept his stories short at least. Dodsworth points out the elaborate patterning of *Chatterton*, gesturing to its paradoxes, coincidences and connections, which lay between the 'layers of fakery'. All of this means nothing, says Dodsworth. Meaning nothing is precisely what Ackroyd aims to mean, it's 'precisely what he is after'.

It is this 'signifying nothing', to return to an earlier phrase, that troubles Dodsworth, or, to come a little closer to the point (to use the reviewer's own words), it is that *Chatterton* seems to mean or signify nothing, when *in fact*, to adopt a favoured phrase of Ackroyd's, we find that Dodsworth thinks he has discerned what the game is: it's '[s]omething fearfully semiotic'. Of course, Martin Dodsworth has already done his duty at the conclusion of the first paragraph by warning us about what we are up against with Ackroyd. The reader is informed that she or he would 'do well to remember' that Ackroyd is not only a prize-winning biographer and chief book-reviewer for the *Sunday Times*; he is also an 'avant-garde poet in the line of John Ashbery' and 'the author of *Notes for a New Culture*, a blast against English empiricism in favour of writers who take their Nietzsche, Sartre or Barthes without too much salt'. There is a kind of Wordsworthian – or should that be Dodsworthian? – xenophobic ludicrousness here, this time of the most pejorative kind, where Ackroyd, seemingly benign in his identity as the most English of writers – the critic, the biographer – is really a Wyndham Lewis-like infiltrator of English letters, and a champion of 'Johnny Foreigner' to boot. Americans, Nihilists, Communists, Gays, Structuralists, Existentialists. It's all about identities, the proper identity, identifying the self, opposed to the other. (Dodsworth's review is nothing so much as a disguised *cri de coeur* to Ackroyd to 'play up and play the game'.) Let's not forget this, Dodsworth warns us. (And we haven't Martin, we haven't.) All other identities are dangerous, especially when they implicitly challenge English empiricism and epistemological certainty. They're all being put in a line (we're back to the border patrol, once more, this time in the guise of a shooting gallery where ducks and windmills find themselves confused).

Of course, there is one name missing from the usual suspects here. Your suspicions are almost certain to be on the money. Follow the argument through this passage. Misunderstandings occur between characters talking on the phone; these

> ... exemplify that slippage of meaning which is Derrida's subject-matter; Charles's friend Philip has a vision of the Derridean universe in the basement of the library where he works, 'a world where there was no beginning and no end, no story, no meaning', the very world which, as a novelist, he wants to celebrate.
>
> Ackroyd, too wants to celebrate it, and in order to do so he must somehow forego the element of story which suggests that there are beginnings and endings. In *Hawksmoor* the very banality of the plot was to make it dispensable; in *Chatterton* the object is to make it clear that whatever the plot does it cannot represent events in a real world. The camp stylization of much of the dialogue, the clash of styles within the book, both undermine the status of the plot as an ordered, Aristotelian representation of reality.
>
> (Dodsworth 1987)

In a plot which reads as if David Lodge sketched it out and then thought better of it, Derrida kills Aristotle, getting away with the crime because of the lack of anything other than circumstantial evidence. It is as if Martin Dodsworth is using Ackroyd's novel as merely the excuse for misrepresenting Derrida. (Wait a minute. Doesn't that sound like a character, if not from a David Lodge novel, then from a novel by a certain Peter Ackroyd, the one Dodsworth imagines?) Dodsworth travels so rapidly here that he allows himself to move from one point to the other, from Charles's confused telephone conversation to Philip's subterranean biblio-vision without any sense that the scenes might serve different functions, and, in the process, confusing matters himself in a Dodsworthian fog. Apart from the obvious misunderstanding of Derrida here, Dodsworth's equation of 'no beginning' and 'no end' with a Derridean discourse ignores Ackroyd's frequent use of this and related formulae as an expression of his – Ackroyd's – comprehension of the interanimation and contamination of multiple temporal moments, and what the author describes in the final interview in this book as his spiral concept of time. Dodsworth then goes on to assume that what both Philip and Ackroyd want is to celebrate the same vision. This is akin to assuming that there is no ironic distance between Stephen Dedalus in the final episode of *A Portrait of the Artist as a Young Man* and James Joyce. All of which finally leads us to Ackroyd's abandonment of Aristotle, that well-known Englishman and muse of reviewers (nearly) everywhere. Clearly, playing with one's identities is not allowed; at least in public. If we're going to do that sort of thing we'd be better off climbing back into some (presumably foreign) closet. There's a wholly predictable, and, for that, all the more depressing, *Englishness* about Dodsworth's review: stuffy and tendentious in a carping, bullying manner, which manages to wheedle and whine simultaneously as it attempts to browbeat. Martin Dodsworth sounds like no one so much as Trollope's Mrs Bunce.

None of this is to suggest of course that Ackroyd's novels might not be flawed, structurally or aesthetically. Whether they are is not an issue. We're not concerned with aesthetic considerations of the more conventional kind. Reviewers have to be, to an extent. (That, as Oscar Wilde might have said, is their tragedy.) As we have tried to show however, playing with the conventions raises all manner of issues, which, through an acknowledgement of the reviewers' responses allows an insight into the ludic and labyrinthine formalities of Ackroyd's text.

The reviews cited so far have dealt with Peter Ackroyd's novels for the most part, with a couple of references to the poetry and its reception. Little has been said about the biographies or their reviews. The following section of the introduction offers a brief consideration of one of these, as it concerns questions of identity, of language, and the play in, and between, these.

Play, performance, and undecidability: the example of *Dickens*

With the exception of *Dickens*, Ackroyd's biographies are, on the whole, ostensibly less playful than his novels. The critical reception of the biographies of Pound, Eliot, Blake, and More is, for the most part, critically and uniformly favourable. Ackroyd's tone and respect for his subject are frequently noted, as is his dispassionate distance from and fairness to that same subject. He is 'a sympathetic, kind, uncondemning biographer' (Levi 1984), a 'very temperate writer' (Davie 1984); he 'exercises judgements without being censorious', writing with 'imaginative sympathy' (Julius 1998); Ackroyd is also 'remarkably fair and sensitive' about T. S. Eliot (Litz 1984); with Blake he is 'careful and kind' (Moore 1995), the 'gentlest of biographers' (*Economist* cit. Anon. 1996).

Yet it was the *Dickens* biography which gave some reviewers trouble,[15] largely because of its attempts to do Dickens in a number of voices, pantomimickly in places, using the voices not least of the subject himself, but also those of his own characters (as well as a supporting cast of thousands, real and fictional, including, at one point, Wilde, Chatterton and T. S. Eliot [*B* 450–5[16]]). For one critic, *Dickens* was a 'dramatic success in reanimating' its subject (Behrendt 1997, 447). The role-playing of the biography was dictated to Ackroyd, at least in part, by the challenge of finding something new to say, in a new way, about an author of whom there have been over thirty biographies published in slightly more than a century. As Ackroyd puts it in an interview from 1987, at the time of writing the biography, '[w]ith Dickens, there have been so many biographies that it's an equal challenge to do something different ... it's just as difficult simply because there *is* so much material, and because it has been interpreted and reinterpreted so many times' (Ross 1989, 4). Of Ackroyd's attempts, Verlyn Klinkenborg comments that the purpose is not to write a life; instead, it is to 'rescue the character' through pantomimickry and pastiche, by crossing 'the boundary between Dickens' fiction and his life' (Klinkenborg 1993). This is not to everyone's taste of course, and John Sutherland quotes Anthony Trollope's remark that no '"young novelist should ever dare to imitate the style of Dickens"' (Sutherland 1990).

By far the most engaged and interesting, if perplexed, review of *Dickens*, however, is that by James R. Kincaid, from the *New York Times Book Review* (1991). Kincaid's highly witty, not to say at times 'Dickensian', review, finds as many positive aspects as it does negative qualities to Ackroyd's biography, beginning with the line '[t]his new biography of Dickens waddles along like a maudlin elephant that has attached itself to us against our will'. This in itself seems a pastiche, if not a parody, of the image of that 'elephantine lizard', the muddy Megalosaurus, wandering up Holborn Hill at the opening of *Bleak House* (Dickens 1996, 13). Let's continue with the negative first. In a

Dodgsonesque moment – as opposed, say, to a Dodsworthian one – the elephant transmogrifies into the biographer, who 'lumbers along with no concern at all for twentieth-century modes of understanding ... recalling the boozy-familiar tones of G. K. Chesterton at the turn of the century and the sturdy unsubtlety of John Forster' (Kincaid 1991). The biography is smug, 'relentlessly self-absorbed', 'couched in a prose that often slithers and simpers', while still managing to 'insinuate its importance'. This camp performance aside,[17] there are times, we read, when Ackroyd 'is a bore and a nag. Worst of all is that he won't go away, droning on for so long that the reader may start to root for death to come to Dickens just to get it over with.'

These and other criticisms are telling in a very peculiar way, which may just have to do with what Ackroyd can be read as attempting to enact in this mammoth performance. (Another digression: whether or not he achieves it is, I feel, ultimately up to each reader. This is what the reviews reveal [see n.15, below]. Once again, it comes down to exercising aesthetic judgements by which the reviewer is curiously constrained. It has to be said that there is no sense of the malicious in Kincaid's review as there is in Dodsworth's review of *Chatterton*. Frustration, yes. Bemusement, yes. Exhaustion, also; but then, at the risk of sounding like Peter Ackroyd at times in this biography – or a parody of Peter Ackroyd in rhetorical questioning mode – which of us has not found Dickens, in *The Old Curiosity Shop* for example, a bore and a nag? In a novel of over 600 pages, haven't some of us at least longed for the death of Little Nell?) Perhaps what troubles James Kincaid is that the biography reads like 'bad' Dickens, or, perhaps more to the point, G. K. Chesterton and John Forster as he acknowledges, and whose own literary 'voices' and 'styles' may be said to be indebted to the overarching influence of The Inimitable himself. Perhaps it is, precisely, a question of the anxiety of influence, though not consciously for Ackroyd who has disowned such a notion in an interview with Susana Onega (1996, 212). This is a complicated performance, where mimicry can be read determining the anxiety of influence in others if not in the novelist, whose own mode is marked by anxiety and yet who disavows such a sense. The performative affect can have it both ways, neither being any more or less valid than the other. Certainly one recalls John Sutherland echoing Anthony Trollope at this juncture.

There is more to it than this, however, more to the question than merely the aesthetic consideration of whether Ackroyd 'gets it right'. We can read Kincaid's criticisms generously as a means of understanding to what extent Ackroyd's language in the biography is *performative*; that is to say, it seeks to enact not only the influence Dickens exerted on the imagination of writers who were the next generation or near contemporaries (J. B. Priestly, Arnold Bennett, H. G. Wells, even George Gissing, all have their moments of homage to Dickens in their writing); it also attempts through its mediumistic act to perform in a language not of our time but of another, recognizable enough but oddly discomforting nonetheless. Phrases like 'jot and tittle' (*D* 288) and '... in the year of Our Lord 1847, ...' (*D* 546) are so sorely anachronistic in a biography – or any form of writing for that matter – at the end of the twentieth century that we might sense something is 'afoot', so to speak. To risk mixing figures of speech, expressions such as these 'stick out like a sore thumb', small performative spectres of another, older mode of articulation embedded in their culture like fossils, recognizable, yet not our own. There is a sense also that the performative in Ackroyd's prose is part of an effort to express both Dickens's own emotional responses to various situations (as far as this is ever recoverable or knowable, which, in itself, is highly debatable as the author does allow) as well as to perform in character, as numerous Dickensian characters, particularly those who are in some way strange, warped, twisted, marked indelibly, to greater or lesser degrees, with the trace of evil or malevolence, or downright foolishness. If we recall Kincaid's identification of smug, slithering, simpering and insinuating prose in the context of Dickens's writing, Uriah Heep, Bradley Headstone, Wackford Squeers, Quilp, Pecksniff, Podsnap, Arthur Gride, all spring to mind, as do countless others.

Then, as if to affirm further this sense of the performative as a way of reading *Dickens* and, through that, comprehending the ways in which Ackroyd attempts to play his material, there is the sense of uncertainty which Kincaid also alerts us to in the biographer's expression. This is both positive *and* negative simultaneously for the reviewer. It is positive in that it opens up Dickens in all his strangeness to the reader; negative, in that Ackroyd's 'work seems unsure of its audience'. Undecidability, that with which Ackroyd is so constantly concerned in his novels with regard to the question of the problematic representation of an unmediated reality in discourse, is everywhere in the biography. Not only is it Ackroyd's (he admits frequently that he does not know and cannot tell something about Dickens because that kind of knowledge is not recoverable), it is also, we read, Dickens's and is allied to doubt and anxiety. A few examples should suffice:

> [of *Dombey and Son*] ... no book had caused him so much endless concentration and trouble ...
>
> (*D* 550)

> ... he [was] anxiously uncertain about his son's health ...
>
> (*D* 550)

> ... Dickens's financial anxieties ...
>
> (*D* 556)

… he told his sister, dying of consumption, that at times of great anxiety or exhaustion he was sometimes gripped by 'dreadful' ideas and oppressive mental 'sufferings'. The 'nervous seizure in the throat' may be another clue to his suffering; a few years later he was again affected by nervous exhaustion …. [he was a] man of immense nervous and imaginative susceptibility …

(*D* 557)

'My anxiety to know that secret reason of Sarah's', he wrote …

(*D* 564)

Dickens was the entire professional whose own class status was insecure enough to make him grandiloquent …

(*D* 569)

[Dickens felt] Private anxiety [which fuelled] public denunciation.

(*D* 605)

He had a horror of being wrong about anything …

(*D* 623)

and a few others,

… he became invaded by nervous anxiety at the same time as his characters …

(*D* 695–6)

For the first Reading, in the Town Hall, he rose a little nervously before the seventeen hundred people who had endured a snow-storm in order to hear him.

(*D* 719)

The fame and fortune of his years as a novelist had effectively repressed all the symptoms of his old panic and disorder but now, as he entered middle-age, they were reasserting themselves once more.

(*D* 747–8)

… the recuperation in France had not materially affected his anxious state.
(*D* 749)

His son, Charley, was to say of *Little Dorrit* that '… my father started [it] in a panic lest his powers of imagination should fail him' …

(*D* 784)

> In early October ... he read in a carpenter's shop and was, according to
> Mark Lemon's daughter, 'very nervous'.
>
> (*D* 786)

These few are extracted from hundreds, if not thousand of examples. Their
relative proximity might give us to read the frequency of a pulse or rhythm,
which generates a field of nervous energy across the text. The performance of
this tic is suggestive of an attempted interanimation on the part of the writer
between his own activity and his subject's compulsive and repetitive concerns. A nervous writer, then, or rather two of them, and a nervous text. This
goes beyond pastiche or the simple imitation of a style; it extends also beyond
the writer's attempt to convey a sense of what his subject's personality is like.
It is a strenuous, even nervous, effort to play out through writing the subject's
sense of self in all aspects of his life: personal, public, professional, and
financial. Dickens is the nervous text. *Dickens* is the nervous text. Ackroyd's
performative gesture foregrounds through the perceived anxiety and uncertainty of the Victorian subject the epistemological doubt concerning the
writing of a life after the death of the author. At least we may read it in this
manner (may we not?). Uncertainty and anxiety are embedded everywhere.

Most interestingly, this gambit of Ackroyd's is given voice in an interview
with himself (it is not made clear who is doing the interviewing) or, at least,
one performed, performing version of the author's self, in the sixth of seven
fictional acts[18] (which the *Dictionary of Literary Biography* describes as being
like 'interludes in a stage show' [Johnson 1996, 8]). In an interview where
confidence tricks, performances, magic tricks and other forms of illusion and
cheating are spoken of quite openly, and the possibility that the author
imposes a pattern where none exists (*D* 943), uncertainty on the part of the
writer plays a large role. In reference to his act of writing *Dickens* this Ackroyd
– who is as much a performance as any other figure, and not necessarily the
true Peter Ackroyd – states:

> Is it a fault or a virtue, that I often imply more certainty ... than in fact I
> possess? ... I might be quite wrong. I might be half-wrong and half-right. I
> suppose you might call it the uncertainty principle, but it is a principle
> quite impossible to build into biography; of all forms, the biographical one
> seems to demand certainty and clarity. Once you introduce ambiguities
> and doubts, the whole enterprise starts to collapse.
>
> (*D* 942)

Yet uncertainty is everywhere (is it not?), even at the banal level of the endless
rhetorical questions, of which there are 'thousands' as Kincaid points out
(Kincaid 1991). This is identity in ruins, the monument of identity in the

form of a biography, a 'life' so-called, undone and reformed as a playful labyrinth. Uncertainty and anxiety fuel the desire to know, which is confronted endlessly and everywhere with one more blind alley, one more doubt. As the interviewee admits: 'I suppose, in the end, I'm worried about everything' (*D* 944).

This double sense of anxiety and uncertainty, equally Ackroyd's and Dickens's, is not always a problem for the reviewer because it leads into the reading of the positive aspects of the biography. Having thus far emphasized those elements of James Kincaid's review which are somewhat negative, it is only fair to point out that, despite the fact that so much seems to worry him with this biography, the reviewer generously gives at least half the review to searching out the good in *Dickens*. Indeed, it is possible to read this review as either indulging in, or being caught up in, the same shell game in which Ackroyd is involved. Having pointed out that 'they say in "The Rocky Horror Picture Show," "Let's do the time warp again!"' Kincaid's next remark is that '[s]ane people do not attend "Rocky Horror"'. Yet, the critic has just quoted the film. Is he casting the certainty of the review into doubt by seeming to suggest that (a) he's seen the film and that (b) he's not sane and therefore not a reliable critic of this biography? Admittedly, that's a huge leap of logic, if not one of faith. But there is a kind of epistemological undermining under way which is part of a greater performance. The critic toys with the role assigned, doing an impersonation of a reviewer, rather than being a reviewer. Perhaps. He gets into the game and, dividing his review into two opposed, opposing identities – one of annoyance, one of admiration – baffles the reader who desires to have a particular identity confirmed, as does Ackroyd, as does *Dickens*/Dickens.

Either way, this performance does ask us as readers to give Ackroyd centrestage for a time 'precisely (and only) because it is so open to the strange ... to the peculiarity' of Dickens (Kincaid 1991). With telling acuity in so brief a space as a review, Kincaid points to the ways in which Ackroyd opens for the reader a view of a strange, undomesticated Dickens, estranging all familiar Dickens's in the process. There is the Dickens for instance who takes cold showers, combs his hair at public dinners, dresses in outrageously showy colours in the age of obligatory masculine black, and who reads, fresh from the pen, the brutal death of Nancy to his near-bed-ridden wife who is suffering one of her numerous and extremely debilitating bouts of post-natal depression. This is hardly Mr Popular Sentiment. What makes this estranged Dickens so palatable is, for Kincaid, precisely the uncertainty with which Ackroyd tells his tale: 'By refusing to shoo away the strangeness in his subject or his project, he provides for us a variety of possibilities for understanding that they are engaging just because they remain uncontrolled, even unexplained ... not knowing, paradoxically, keeps us from closing off the issue with easy judgments .... Ackroyd's great achievement is that he reinvests Dickens, that familiar figure of hearth and home, with an alien, slightly repellent mystery' (Kincaid 1991).

What emerges from this embattled review, a review the identity of which is deeply divided in itself and from itself, is, precisely, the ambiguity with which Ackroyd invests his writing in *Dickens*. It is also the ambiguity with which Dickens is invested, and that which Dickens, as performed by Ackroyd, appears to have invested in himself. As Kincaid's review shows through its own performance, Ackroyd produces a doubled and paradoxical Dickens who refuses to become a settled identity; the biography performs a double figure whose strangeness has slipped away from us since Una Pope-Henessey said of Dickens, that he was someone who 'could sit immobile in his study in front of Mary [Hogarth's] picture mourning as if he could not be comforted [yet] who would in a few hours preside over a book-banquet or dance delightedly at a party .... His temperament cannot be accounted for; it is only possible to state how it operated' (Pope-Hennessy cit. Morton 1952, 385). The purpose of spending so much time on this review is to show how, if we can disregard the biography *as* biography, we can see how it is possible to become caught up in role– and game-playing and how Ackroyd is involved in a project which seeks to challenge through play our conventional reading habits. Even the identity of a genre is not stable; the ludic gambit infects the critical process. We find ourselves involved in ludic structures which do not give themselves away but, instead, involve one in forms of play in which the self becomes lost. The question of play, that question which play puts to us, is a question concerning whether we are prepared to give up our identities, to lose ourselves in the uncertainty attendant on any performance.

Conclusion (an end and a beginning)

We should be wary then of how we approach so playful, deceptive and illusory a text. What emerges from the very different reviews by Martin Dodsworth and James Kincaid (and that of *Notes for a New Culture* by David Lodge, discussed below in Chapter 2, n. 1) is that, for a number of reasons, each reviewer is caught up in or attempts to play the game with Ackroyd, rather than making Ackroyd's text conform to the rules of the post-Aristotelian game. To his credit, Kincaid, unlike his British counterparts, strives generously to work with the play; if there is a discernible difference here, it is that Kincaid seeks to engage the play at some conscious level, while Dodsworth and Lodge read as if they are caught unawares, becoming parodies of themselves, the public-school master and the pedant respectively. The difference between Kincaid and his English opposite numbers may well have to do with their own constructedness within the differing national identities of their respective cultures. There is a meanspirited bourgeois Englishness in the English academic reviewers that is so completely absent from the American voice (and after the polemic of *Notes for a New Culture* it may be suggested that reviewers – some of them at least – are like maudlin elephants; they never forget). This is of course no more than a speculative supposition, which we can do little more than gesture towards in an introduction of this sort. Yet if we consider one more review briefly alongside Ackroyd's history of trans-vestitic practice, it may help to clear the ground from which, in concluding this introduction, we can view the text of Peter Ackroyd.

This is not a review of one of Ackroyd's publications. Instead, this is a review by Ackroyd of Neil Jordan's film, *The Company of Wolves* (Ackroyd 1984b). Ackroyd finds this a 'mysterious, rather horrifying, but consistently fascinating film … [with] an inner coherence and purpose'. He likens the film's strange and disturbing qualities to the 'strongest elements' in British writing in the mid-1980s. He approves of its qualities of spectacle, its disturbing, dream-like land-scapes and its escape from 'pallid realism', all of which, he argues, presents the possibility in Britain of a very real 'alternative form of cinema'. The elements of the fairy-story format are not only enumerated through the critical praise given to the formal and technical elements of Jordan's early work. Such elements are also crucial, for Ackroyd, in the critique which he feels the film provides of 'respectable middle-class family' life. At the heart of such family life, lived out in a 'conventional English countryside' are 'secret passages and desires'. Thus, for the reviewer, the film opens out the strangeness at the centre of normality, its heart of darkness if you will. In unveiling this dark heart the film not only reveals the strangeness but also, importantly, estranges our perception of so-called normality in the form of conservative middle-class Englishness. National identity is given over to Northern European modes of narrative and analysis (the Freudian elements of the story-telling are also approved of), and, in the process, deconstructed, revealed to be as much a myth as the fairy story, based as it is on the repression of identity and the coercion of selfhood. Sexuality, the werewolf, violence 'mediated in the relationships between men and women', all displace and estrange the idea of the normal family. It is these very political ges-tures of which Ackroyd's review is so approving.

What we can see in this review is Ackroyd's sense of the ways in which 'unreal' and 'playful' narrative structures can often be more powerful ideolog-ically than realist and social realist narratives in the revelation of the struc-tures of conventional identities, whether these are sexual or national. The playful narrative, the ludic structure, cannot be domesticated; it cannot be recuperated into dominant narrative forms. Instead, endlessly, playfully, annoyingly, it shows up conventional forms and identities as just that: con-vention – constructions for the purpose of incorporating and domesticating the other, for stifling the secret passages and desires which are within us all.[19]

This strangeness within our most cherished constructions of normality is also addressed in Peter Ackroyd's *Dressing Up*. In this small essay, Ackroyd once again addresses identity politics, albeit in a highly different context than that of film reviewing. Ackroyd stresses the pervasiveness of transvestism throughout history and in many, otherwise distinct, cultures. At the heart of transvestism is the need to confuse gender identities through cross-dressing. It is so pervasive, argues Ackroyd, that 'it exists wherever sexual behaviour exists, perhaps lying dormant in most human beings' (*DU* 10). Transvestism is an 'expression of social or political dissent', the sign of a 'repeated need for inversion and disorder' (*DU* 10). These notions are commonplace enough. However, Ackroyd estranges cherished conventional notions concerning transvestism, by arguing that most transvestites are heterosexual, not gay (*DU* 14). Also, and perhaps most importantly in the light of the other challenges in his writing to the straitjacket of Anglo-Saxon bourgeois culture, Ackroyd pursues two telling arguments: that, for all the 'dressing up', the man is still there, still visible, behind the costume (*DU* 18, 20), while transvestism is not confined to one class, but can be found among 'lawyers, post-office workers, policemen, farmers, engineers, clergymen and labourers ... [all of whom] spend their evenings in women's clothes' (*DU* 18). Transvestism is not the simple mimetic assumption of another's identity; it is deliberate play, which is traced throughout culture and which leaves its marks in all walks of life. What is wonderfully telling in Ackroyd's list is that the power structures which supposedly formulate the 'most normal' aspects of Englishness are themselves traced by the signs of dissent, inversion and disorder.

This is highly disturbing to some. But, for the purposes of 'reading' Peter Ackroyd, the importance of play cannot be stressed too strongly or too often. Awareness of play should make the critic hesitate to seek out themes, as we have already suggested, and which we wish to stress once more, in conclusion. Ackroyd himself offers a *caveat* against reading thematically, in *Dickens* of all places. The 'search for themes, or symbols, or meanings', writes Ackroyd, 'is the late twentieth-century equivalent of those earlier attempts to attach localities, or inns, or real people, to Dickens's narratives; it is part of the attempt to domesticate, to explain, and therefore to control'.

> Whether Dickens was conscious or not of such matters is quite another question ... when we talk of Dickens's themes and purposes, we must always be aware that they are likely to be diverted or ignored or overturned at any time. Which is another way of saying his 'meanings' and 'values' change from book to book, and even within the same book.
>
> (*D* 1019–20)

To domesticate, to explain, and therefore to control. This is the conventional critical impulse, most obviously at work in New Criticism but also there in other critical models, however ostensibly radical. Ackroyd, correctly, signals the idiomatic and the singular in writing which domestication, explanation and control seek to erase, to downplay, when, instead, it is the singular, the idiomatic, which must be respected from text to text and within particular texts.

This is not only Ackroyd's idea, of course; nor does he develop it as fully or rigorously as he might, even though, in the context of understanding the author's constant games of up-ending versions of national identity through critiques of middle-class life, aspects of normative sexuality and Anglo-Saxon empiricism, we might suggest that he is constantly engaged in a playful guerrilla-gambit of exploding English national identity's most carefully preserved Bunburys. It is useful to observe how his own sense of the strange, the singular, and all those textual features which resist thematization becomes reinvented time and again in his own writing, whether this occurs, in different ways in his polemic against English empiricism, *Notes for a New Culture*, in his review of Jordan's *The Company of Wolves*, in the various narrative games of the novels, or in the essay on transvestism. Understanding Ackroyd's resistance to thematization, we must also understand the singular in his work. As John Peck says in his summary of Ackroyd's novels, while the novelist appears to have much in common with other writers, what has to be acknowledged is its 'eccentric quality' which, in turn, serves to produce novels which have in them the combination of 'the incongruous and the commonplace' (Peck 1994, 442), the profound and the crass, the serious and the comic. None of these binarisms stays in place. For Ackroyd shows their mutual interdependence on each other for the possibility of their definition in the first place, while also performing the collapse into and cross-contamination of any binary pair.

What we read therefore in the ludic and labyrinthine text of Peter Ackroyd is that structures of identity will just not stay in place. Their architectures refuse to stay still. In doing so, they disturb any overarching system, any perceived or perceivable architectonic form, whether that system is one which becomes available for critique through the possibility of play, or whether it is a system which the critic seeks out in Ackroyd's text. Ackroyd constantly gives us to think the 'what if?', that question which articulates all ludism and disarticulates the monumentality of the system and the assertion of being in any given identity. This is especially the case at those moments when there seems to be the possibility that we might 'only connect'. His play, his comedy, his 'dressing up' and 'doing a turn', allows us the possibility of departing, in John Rajchman's words, from the 'fixed geometries of our being, [while] opening out onto virtual' identities (Rajchman 1998, 2). Ackroyd's play involves the exploration of identity politics, but this does not occur in the same fashion every time; nor does it employ the same devices every time. Ackroyd's play respects the identity of the other to the extent that what we engage in, in reading Ackroyd, is the other's play, the play of the other. The ludic in Ackroyd's text relies for its mobility on difference, which disarticulates a stable identity even as it slides between (in the words of Catherine Bernard) plagiarism (so-called) and elegy (Bernard 1994, 15). Difference for Ackroyd is always difference from *and within* normative identity constructs and effects. In Ackroyd's text each difference is different from all other difference, and so is the singular and exemplary. Difference is not an identity; difference is different from *and within* itself. Yet, to go further, it is important that we recognize that this exploration of identity politics and the play of difference which sustains it is the also a performance on Ackroyd's part: for each narrative, each novel, each consideration, whether 'critical' or 'creative' is itself written as the play of difference within any given identity.

The ludic and labyrinthine text opens the possibility of affirming otherness within any construct through the exploration of the unseen, the virtual, the immanent. Whether through the dismantling of rigid time frames, the pastiche of a 'past style' or the parody of a perceived cultural heritage or system, Ackroyd's text seeks to assert the play of language, writing and thought. Ackroyd's play performs that most necessary ludic gesture: in the words of James R. Kincaid, like comedy (of which the critic is writing), the ludic moves beyond the positive/negative aesthetic binarism, it 'allows us a new way of looking at the stories we get told and a new way to devise stories ... we can, with comedy, stop looking for endings, for continuity, for linearity, for the causal, for power, for authority, for the decorous ... we have not regularity but movement ...' (Kincaid 1996, 11). The ludic loosens structures and systems, it affirms difference and resists sameness. In the words of Peter Ackroyd (and to return to our earlier commentary on comedy), ludic humour 'dissolves ordinary categories, ... [it] explodes or defuses the most serious attempts at meaning' (D 1020).[20] This is Ackroyd's game, where restrictive aesthetic, narrative and genre-based paradigms are questioned anew. His textual play foregrounds the singularity of what is always already singular – literature or, the literary – even as it toys with, and so tampers with and tickles what amounts to the architectonic system that is Literature. To borrow once more from John Rajchman, this time on seeing the possibility for new forms of construction, Ackroyd '... deviates from things known, inserting the chance for indetermination ...' (Rajchman 1998, 9). In doing so, time and again, his writing keeps the game going.

1

'A tiny light/seen in the mind's eye as a phoneme': the Poetry of Peter Ackroyd

It is so hard to tell parody from pathos

Geoffrey Hartman

I have long had a taste for discontinuous writing

Roland Barthes

I do not know any other way of associating with great tasks than play

Friedrich Nietzsche

Allusion and/as archive

The three volumes of poetry written by Peter Ackroyd – *Ouch* (1971), *London Lickpenny* (1973), *Country Life* (1978) – appeared over a seven-year period. Subsequently, they resurfaced in 1987, albeit partially, like the erased phrases of writing found on stone walls in Ackroyd's *The House of Doctor Dee,* as a selection entitled *The Diversions of Purley and Other Poems*, a slim volume of fifty-three poems, some in prose. The poems of these hard-to-find publications appear densely allusive. A first, or even a second encounter will not, however, yield the meaning behind such use of allusion or reference, supposing that some ulterior meaning is at work in the frequency of allusion. We find ourselves in a textual archive without a key to the ordering or purpose of that structure. The archive of apparent reference obtrudes itself everywhere across the already fragmentary texts, seeming to demand or command: 'read me'. Yet they remain not-read, even when the source is known, recognized or identified. Thus, the purpose of allusion, reference, parody and, in short, all playful troping, all the while on the surface of the text, if not in fact constitutive of the very texture of the text itself, remains undecidable, demanding in this undecidability that we continue to try to read. Yet it is precisely because the archive is not so easily resolvable into a purposeful unity that its play demands it be taken seriously. It is as if Ackroyd's poetry, rather than awaiting passively the scholarly attention of a careful reader, searches for another kind of reader altogether, whose interest is in the act of masquerade, and not in what might lie beneath or behind the performance. That which Ackroyd places in the archive seems to seek a correspondent, someone who will receive these wayward transmissions; the identity of the addressee remains to be known, however. And if we rely on reading, nothing, we will find, is less reliable.

Thus, we find that we seek to orient ourselves according to a textual archive, the archival memory that is Ackroyd's poetry, where phrases from poems and novels, references to authors canonical and minor, central and marginal in western literary culture, allusions to both high and low culture (as well as all points in between), all are to be found. In Ackroyd's poems we find, for example, possible references to 'David Watts' ('Foolish Tears' *DP* 51; either from the song of the same name by the Kinks or the name of a journalist writing for *The Times*), and 'stairway to heaven' ('A love poem' *DP* 63). These allusions are possible rather than certain only because we cannot tell for sure that they *are* allusions or references (especially in the case of the second of the two citations, a common enough phrase, seeming to suggest a song by Led Zeppelin). It may even be possible to speculate that, if these are allusions, then there is some undisclosed function to their inclusion. It may be the case that such allusive populism is in itself an acknowledgement of sorts to the poetry of the so-called Mersey poets. This is no more than speculation though. More certainly allusions are the mentions of 'Captain Scarlet' and 'Tinker Bell' ('Only Connect ...' *DP* ii 22, iv 24), though if they have a function in the sense of referring to something, some meaning 'beyond' the surface of the text, that remains undecidable. Indeed, in the installation of such apparently wayward, differing and, seemingly purposeless allusions and references – in this case to a 1970s puppet show and *Peter Pan* – in the same poem, the undecidable is instituted. The assumed connection being children's entertainment, the examples being separated by over seventy years (and, presumably, the possibility of conventional aesthetic arguments over cultural 'value'), this knowledge still will not suggest anything more about the poem 'Only connect ...'. The reader has 'connected', responding to that Forsterian imperative which supplies the poem's title, but this still does not calm the referential play of the text, unless, once again, we acknowledge the text's archival function. Thus, like many of Ackroyd's poems, the text-as-archive is composed in part of cuttings, excerpts, extracts, fragments. A poetry in ruins, *anarchival poiesis*, the anarchic displacement and movement, making as unmaking;[1] textual assemblage without the semblance of meaningful assembly, other than the acknowledgement that *the archive is*.

Then there are the still more obvious forms of acknowledgement and allusion such as the use of proper names of poets and novelists, which Ackroyd's poetry seems to wear like badges, daring the reader to indulge further in defining possible relationships, surmising about a particular literary or poetic indebtedness or heritage. There are Ronald Firbank and Grahame Greene in 'the novel' (*DP* 28), T. S. Eliot, in 'the day...' (*DP* 32; there are also other more or less hidden allusions to Eliot's poems in numerous other places, for example the line 'we read novels late into the night' from 'the novel' [*DP* 28], with its nod to *The Waste Land*), H. G. Wells and *The Time Machine* ('you do the best ...' *DP* 50), Marcel Proust ('A prose poem' *DP* 57). There are the references to E. M. Forster, W. B. Yeats and Andrew Marvell ('Only connect ...', 'Among school children', 'a wounded / fawn'; *DP* 21, 9). There is a reference to Angel Clare, also in 'the novel' (*DP* 28). There are snatches of popular song – 'goodnight Eileen' ('Out of the ...' i 36); 'Jeannie with the light brown hair' ('The secret is ...' *DP* 48) – alongside indirect allusions to Joyce, citations of W. H. Davies, more T. S. Eliot, Gerard Manley Hopkins and so on, as Susana Onega spells out in her detailed discussion of intertextual reference (1998, 8–23).

The question of allusion is seemingly central to Ackroyd's poetry, as shall be seen in the critical commentaries. The question is not one of reading the allusions, or, for that matter, the parodies or other stylistic acknowledgements, so as to produce a meaningful, though latent content for the poems (as though these texts were somehow inadequate as poems, or otherwise dissembling and deceitful). Allusion and other apparently referential devices do not operate in Ackroyd's writing as manifest details implying latent content. Allusions and related techniques are present everywhere. In being everywhere, they are so placed by Ackroyd as to challenge and subvert the ways in which we are taught to read conventionally. Indeed, in a number of poems – 'country life' (*CL* 1–2; *DP* 7–8), 'among school children' (*LL* 2; *DP* 9), 'and the children ...' (*O* np; *DP* 11–12) 'there are so many ...' (*CL* 4; *DP* 14) – the very idea of interpretation is actively engaged, challenged and subverted through parodic performance, as will be discussed below. The allusion and its kin are deployed in order to disable conventional literary and poetic engagement. In short, these effects are there not to confirm some identity, whether that of the author as 'postmodernist' poet or that of the text through its supposed indebtedness either to modernism or the poetry of John Ashbery, to take two examples. Instead, they call into question the very idea of identities, literary or otherwise, challenging the sufficiency of such acts of reading. Everywhere in these texts is readable not the act of connection or communication, but the playful articulation of the frustrated desire for communication on which many acts of reading are founded.

The question of allusion and its purpose in the poetry of Peter Ackroyd is raised then if only so as to dismiss acts of allusion hunting ultimately. It is enough to acknowledge, along with Ackroyd's reviewers (to whom we shall turn shortly), that allusion and allegiance are markedly observable, even if

they resist being read in a manner conventionally consistent with the normative function of allusion in the poetic text. Knowing the allusions, and searching out others will not help the reader determine the meaning of these poems.
This is not mere intertextuality typical of what might otherwise be termed a
'postmodern' style. Ackroyd's references and allusions, his stylistic and strategic allegiances, serve in what J. Hillis Miller describes as the programming of
the destined receiver (1990, 171–80), even though that addressee is shaped
differently according to the extent to which the archive is recognized (this
will be discussed further, below). The reader-as-receiver does not read the allusions and references, thereby making sense of the text. Instead, in responding
to the textual fragments and extracts, the traces of other texts, the reader's
identity is shaped in unpredictable and differing ways, according to the degree
to which reference is identified. The reader who recognizes the reference to
Yeats or Eliot might not comprehend the allusions to popular songs, or to
obscure Elizabethan poems, and vice versa. There may well be the reader who
recognizes all of these, yet is unaware of some other reference. There is in this
'shoring up' of fragments and ruins the question of the archive, of poetry as
an act of 'archiving', to which we have already alluded. To reiterate: the
archive is there as the text itself, but it is not just – even – a question of
encryption and the obscurity of the signature. Much seems to be on the
surface of the text, if not *as* the text itself. This is an archive without purpose,
except to be an archive. The poetic text of Peter Ackroyd takes on the form of
a gathering of cultural memory, misunderstood when simply seen as intertextuality. The installation of memory as archive is, perhaps and arguably, the
very work of poetry itself, or, rather, the poetic as the archival textualisation
of the intimate, turned outwards in a gesture of always frustrated communication, doomed to be transmitted and received as ruins, fragments, excerpts.

Reading, against reading, or, reading's not reading

As mentioned above, certain of Ackroyd's poems, 'country life', 'among school
children', 'and the children ...', and 'there are so many ...', parodically mimic
the act of interpretive analysis, where the text is treated as though it were the
manifest content of a subject's dream, and stripped of its traces, images,
layers, in order to unveil latent truth, in an act of textual striptease which proposes ultimately to lay bare the meaning. Such a gesture, comic in its defiance
of the appropriation of poetry for the purposes of education, denies the much
sought-after depth, and the kind of depth model on which much close
reading in the humanist critical tradition is based. Also, it works, with the
constant display of fragments to resist any sense of, or search for, the unity of
the text. The texts frustrate through communicating their ruined state, parodying and mimicking, and masquerading all the while as those very acts of

reading against which they so self-consciously parade. Thus, these poems, in their comic approximation of reading, may be read as being positioned against reading, locating themselves in the process as aporetic configurations of 'not reading' between reading and the unreadable. In being so situated, these – and, by extension, Ackroyd's other poems – bring the reader face to face with the undecidable, and forcing the reader, in Nicholas Royle's words, 'to acknowledge the demand that reading cannot stop, that reading begin again, that reading always and necessarily belongs to another time' (1995, 161). It is not that the texts cannot or should not be read, rather, they perform through their pantomimickry, the inadequacy of a particular assumption concerning reading's ability to assert meaning.

'Country life' is a prose poem, and the text most intimately and farcically related to the question of analytical practice, specifically psychoanalytical practice in certain forms. The poem is presented as a dream narrative in its first paragraph, while the subsequent paragraphs assume the voice of the therapist, in their confident probing of 'the manifest elements' and 'manifest text' of the dream. The analytical commentary provides the reader with a number of details not in the dream narrative, which are either contextual or interpretive, seeking some coherence from the imagined latent level. Comic effect is achieved when the reader reads the reading closely enough to realize that the analytical intervention is inaccurate, that it conflates and displaces elements of the dream text in its own reading. This is apparent in the enumeration of 'three childhood memories', which have 'come to light' through 'the analytic technique of free association around the manifest elements'. The first 'memory' gained by free association will suffice here. It supposedly recalls that the 'sun is a noise'. Re-reading the dream narrative, this is not seen to be the case:

> The streets of a great city when they are empty. I have a pain
> in my finger although everything is happening at once although
> it cannot be seen. The light is making a vague noise and so I
> move closer to myself.
> ...
> ... The colours of the advertisement get brighter
> as the sun rises above the buildings and I know the noise will
> increase.

The analysis is seen to get it wrong about this narrative if we rationalize the elements which are mis– or not read. The subject appears to be thinking of the city at night. We can tell or read this because the streets are 'empty' and the sun subsequently 'rises'. In this narrative logic the noise is being made, in the first instance, not by the sun, but by artificial street lighting. The second reference to 'noise' should not be inferred as being the same as the first, but, perhaps, the noise of city streets in the daytime. This is the most prosaic, bland reading of the passage imaginable. It won't do to take it any further, if only because, like the poem's analytical passages, it too relies on the very kinds of inferential logic through which the writing of the mock analysis achieves its comedy. Importantly however, what this brief excursus into the pedantic exercise of a certain reading technique shows us is the flawed analytic process as an act of reading which conflates and confuses the different lights, the different noises, in order to make the text meaningful, as though the narrative were somehow unintelligible or inadequate without being subjected to this process.

There are other interpretive errors. The analytic retelling insists twice on the detail of a 'red building', which the dream does not mention. 'Country life' thus can be read as cautioning us against acts of reading which are over-hasty, and which fail to comprehend the text at all. However, at least the imitation of a psychoanalytic reading does not reach the pedantic extent of the interpretive approach parodied in 'among school children':

> And everyone heard the wrong story
>   my terrific love-cries
>   are probably for sale
> the technician said, 'these poems are a wounded
>   fawn':
> oh the strange story of the quantum!
>
>   if I smile will she smile
>   no one smiles, your eyes
>   are like broken glass are
>   you unemployed?
>
> What do these words mean? (a) love-cries
> (b) quantum (c) unemployed.
> Have you ever met anyone with eyes
> like broken glass? If you have, write about it.
> if not, would you like to? Why?
> read the poem again, and think about
> the last lines. Why was nobody smiling?
> Try to explain in your own words how
> the writer felt when he saw the girl
> with eyes like broken glass.

The obvious allusion is in the title, to W. B. Yeats' own poem, 'Among School Children'.[2] As Susana Onega suggests in her reading of the poem, not only are there echoes of Yeats and Wordsworth in this poem, but also Eliot's 'The Hollow Men', in the line 'your eyes are like broken glass' (1998, 9). From this, Onega argues that the poem is not a 'parodic transformation' of previous texts but is, instead, 'simply a self-conscious and imitative linguistic palimpsest, whose only meaning is to suggest the free play of language and meaning' (10). This, however, cannot be the sole function of the poem, if only because of its self-conscious division into two parts, like 'country life', between the text to be read, and the directions for reading. Taking that part of the poem which is ostensibly the poem (ll. 1–10) and not the commentary on how to read the poem first (ll. 11–20), the 'wounded faun' can clearly be read as alluding to Andrew Marvell's 'The Nymph Complaining for the Death of her Fawn'. This allusion is itself an utterance, a metacommentary within the so-called poem towards details of which the children are directed. This complication renders the split between text and commentary somewhat confused, and it might even be suggested that the image of the technician might be taken as a some-what arch vision of the role of the teacher and critic.

However, whether this is the case is undecidable. What we can read is the role of pedantry and analysis in the directions concerning reading. In a parody of what Ackroyd sees throughout *Notes for a New Culture* as the humanist Anglo-Saxon critical method of reading indebted to Quiller-Couch, Leavis, the Cambridge School and *Scrutiny* and pursued from secondary to higher education (*NNC* 80ff., 117ff.), the teacher begins by asking questions concerning specific meaning, to expand breathlessly to questions of personal experience by which the student can 'relate to', that is to say 'understand', the poem. Thus the poem is not of worth in its own right but only as a conduit to self-expression given final valorization in the edict to 'explain in your own words'. The poem serves a purpose and is in itself shown to be inadequate through the recourse to paraphrase.

As with 'country life', 'among school children' subverts the analytical process by masquerading in part as that self-same process, performing in a knowing manner for the reader a bald approximation of the worst of critical approaches. Yet we don't need to work our way through 'among school chil-dren' to reach this point, for it is hinted at in the first line, where 'everyone heard the wrong story'. Even as the first ten lines confuse the supposedly dis-tinct positions between text and commentary through the inclusion of the technician's words (which, of course, is yet one more figure for the movement of the entire text, where commentary becomes the text itself, instead of stand-ing simply outside the text), so the opening line of the poem – of the poem in the poem – has already commented on the failures of critical appreciation.

While 'country life' and 'among school children' subvert institutionally approved and practiced interpretive procedures, 'there are so many ...' and 'and the children ...' issue their caveats against critical practice less directly. In 'there are so many ...' an unidentified speaker seeks connections 'with human love, as if it were a story in which the ending /has never been understood'. From this analogy comes the second stanza, and particularly the first eight lines, the first four of which enumerate the narrative of the story, page by page, until we're told: 'and this is the part that no one understands'. From this, it is suggested that 'It might be better to begin at the beginning/and read the story for examples of bad grammar, /sloppy characterization, literals and so forth ...'. The crass certainties of the psychoanalyst and school teacher give way to a sense of uncertainty here in the face of the text. Reading subsequently resorts to the most technical of exercises as a response to the subject's lack of comprehension. Connection gives way to an act of joining the dots, and the text remains unread, decided on as unreadable, rather than not read. In this, reading which is too hasty, too general, not rigorous enough and not responsive to the contours of the text can be seen as an activity which aims 'to recreate what was not created, /making the figure still', to take a line from 'and the children ...'. This last image, of 'stilling the figure' can be read as what criticism often seeks to effect.

Critical reading all too often attempts to calm the movement and rhythm, the constant making of *poiesis*, to reduce and reproduce the play to a still life, an ordered whole. Such a gesture is challenged as facile in the second part of 'and the children ...':

> it would be easy to get lost
> in a prosaic description of this light
> on water, clause upon clause
> opening out into a definition of light
> praised for its subtlety and distance

Here, critique involves parody as the two enfold one another in a gesture that addresses the poetic's resistance to critical appropriation indirectly, by anticipating the gestures of that attempted approximation. There is in 'and the children ...' no description, no poetic rendering of light on water. The poetic remains ineffable, as the poem resists the very im/possibility with which it toys in its ludic strategy of showing up critical definition (even as it also anticipates and mocks my own attempted definition of its performance). What is also troublesome, and, yet, simultaneously playful here in this stanza is the undecidability concerning that which is addressed in the last three lines. Even as the third line is divided between clauses by that comma, so the verse begins to address the layering of 'clause upon clause'. The verse opens itself onto its own movement, its own concerns, so that it is impossible to decide strictly speaking on whether it is the absent poetic 'definition of light' or the equally absent 'prosaic description of this light' which is 'praised for its subtlety and distance'.

Are we reading here an approximation of the anticipated critical interpretation, not yet written ('it would be easy'), yet so easily paraphrasable ('it would be easy') in its own imagined paraphrase? Is it imagined that the criticism will be praised for qualities of 'subtlety and distance', while the poem is abandoned, the critical text assuming arrogantly a greater significance than the poetic text? Or does the verse, 'clause upon clause', open out, and is subsequently praised by that 'prosaic description'? Or, to force this reading a little more, and thereby become the anticipated object of Ackroyd's poetic parody (though without necessarily either the subtlety or the distance), is there not figured in this verse what Ackroyd calls 'the abyss of language' (*NNC* 15), as imagined verse and imagined criticism retrace each other in acts of mutual palimpsest?

The play refuses to be calmed down. It activates and reiterates itself. The persistent dalliance with domesticating methodologies, prosaic paraphrase, and the relation between narrative and human experience undermines all such approaches in poems which do not talk about themselves exactly, so much as they talk about themselves being discussed. Such gestures speak of the poetic indirectly by considering what happens to poetic language in any act of translation, such as critical transformation. Ackroyd's poetic language aspires, in his own discussion of J. H. Prynne, 'toward completeness and self-sufficiency .... The formal and written attributes ... give it its status' (*NNC* 132). Completeness is not suggestive of unity, however. Like Prynne, Ackroyd can 'retain varieties of contemporary language', as well as the extracts and fragments of other 'literary' and poetic texts, 'within a written paradigm which changes their function' (*NNC* 132). In this wayward appropriation of the critical function, Ackroyd's poetry can be read as addressing the condition of writing itself. Furthermore, if, as Jacques Derrida suggests, that which we name 'poem' names 'a certain passion of the singular mark' (1995, 297), Ackroyd's poetic texts enact that singular mark and that passion, confronting in the four poems considered above the futile attempt to have done with the singular. In such a confrontation there is traced that which cannot be reappropriated, singularity itself.

Reviews and other critical stances

Yet still the desire for appropriation goes under different guises, often enough in acts of attempted orientation through the reading of filiation. The reviews and critical assessments of the three volumes and the subsequent anthology, *The Diversions of Purley,* are few and far between. Those which do exist provide possible means of orientation, affiliation. The reviews and criticism seek to locate Ackroyd within a tradition and discuss his uses of parody, of pastiche, literary allusion and self-knowing intertextual reference, in efforts which seek to trace family lineage, family resemblances.

Robert Nye describes the poems as 'defensively playful ... preoccupied with the subjectivity of the creative act'. The ludic strategy is already observed and the poems are read as being not about anything so much as themselves. The 'flat, hallucinated style' is 'reminiscent of early Auden and recent Ashbery' (1987).[3] The review of *London Lickpenny* in the *Times Literary Supplement* describes Ackroyd's poetry as 'entertaining', yielding 'many rather beautiful effects as well as some agreeably comic ones'. Ackroyd, we are told 'is a delicate and insistent stylist, based very firmly on American models' (1974). Once again, there is that sense of the critic seeking to locate Ackroyd in a tradition, understanding his poetry through reference to a larger body of works. J. D. McClatchy also observes this in *Poetry* (1989), but finds it ultimately unconvincing. The poems, we are told, 'may be witty, curious, fey, but rarely pay attention to their own purposes or possibilities' (36). Perhaps the lack of paying attention may well be part of the purpose, as might be the 'drift' of 'cultural flotsam and jetsam' (36). McClatchy's assessment is a more temperate variation of the question put by Martin Dodsworth when it is asked what Ackroyd's game might be. The assumption behind the question and behind the assessment of the poetry as aesthetic failure is that assembly should result in a finished model or organic whole, rather than the conscious display of fragments and ruins. This is, however, a poetry already in ruins, the fragments not even shored against the ruin of the self. Or, to borrow from Nicholas Royle, to whom I have already alluded in the previous line, 'nothing can be determined out of context but every context is in a state of ruin' (1995, 127). (Recalling the issue of filiation and betrayal, of fathers who fail their sons, it might be argued that the ruins of poetry which Ackroyd's text performs is the most sustained, if elliptical, acknowledgement of parental, paternal breakdown *as* the only condition of inheritance.[4])

Again, McClatchy notes, there is the comparison between Ackroyd and John Ashbery (37), a comparison which appears again in the two principal critical commentaries on Ackroyd's poetry, by Susana Onega and Ian Gregson (Onega 1998, 6–23; Gregson 1996, 219–22). However, McClatchy finds the comparison between the two writers as being akin to the difference between 'a list of ingredients' and 'the finished dish' (37). The preference here on McClatchy's part is exactly that: a preference, which prefers the illusion of an organic whole, and longs to cling to Ashbery's Whitmanesque post-romanticism, rather than that poet's own 'elliptical, fragmented' poetry, with which Ackroyd is more favourably compared by Ian Gregson (1996, 222). Yet the 'sweet daffiness' McClatchy finds unpalatable across an entire book of poetry may indeed be the sign of a certain masquerade or performance. If this is not an identity for Ackroyd's poetry, however provisional and fragmentary, then it is at least an identity that is already in ruins and is always being reformed. These 'fey' and 'daffy' traces may be the signs of a certain Englishness, the marks of a camp self-awareness which find themselves given more forceful shape in some of Ackroyd's novels. The list of ingredients can only be given meaning as a dish in being assembled. Indeed the figure of the list suggests its own logical tyranny which the separate fragments effectively resist, despite the reader's desire for assembly.

Ian Gregson describes allusion in Ackroyd's poetry as a 'red herring' (1996, 216). So too does Susana Onega, who also discusses the 'accumulation of inter-textual echoes' and 'allusions that lead nowhere' (1998, 10, 12). All of these games, the critics correctly conclude, mark the text's resistance to critical appro-priation. In Onega's assessment, Ackroyd 'builds his poems on allusion, parody, pastiche and the ironic rewriting of earlier texts' (1998, 17). This irony is itself constitutive of a certain knowing performance, which disturbs the serenity not only of an assured identity for a particular poem, but also for the reader. For Gregson, this strategy is itself a sign of Ackroyd's indebtedness to John Ashbery, or at least that Ashbery who is elliptical and fragmentary, rather than Whitmanesque (1996, 219). Ackroyd, like Ashbery, begins with a sense that meaning or understanding is possible and then progresses to undo comprehen-sion (1996, 219). However, unlike McClatchy, Gregson finds Ackroyd's approach more convincing than Ashbery's for, while Ackroyd is 'playful at times', the English poet 'rarely seems gratuitous' in his play, 'and his poems have few of the camp mannerisms which can be irritating in Ashbery' (1996, 220).

Importantly for Gregson, Ackroyd is able to raise questions 'about the way even the self gets fictionalized' through the poems (1996, 220). The question of subjectivity and the articulation of the self in the poetic text is also noted by Onega with regard to Ackroyd's poetry. In addition to the, by now, stan-dard acknowledgement of Ashbery's influence on Ackroyd, Onega also points to Prynne and O'Hara (following Ackroyd's own commentary in *Notes for a New Culture*), who, she argues, create 'a unique space for the experience of subjectivity by shifting the emphasis from the fixed or central perspective of the lyrical "I" to the procedure of the poem itself' (1998, 6). As we shall see with the operation of 'I' in Ackroyd's poetry, this procedure effects a radical evisceration of any subject in his poems. As Onega suggests, there is 'the refusal to acknowledge the existence of any consistent or identifiable notion of subject' and this is produced by means of 'baffling slips and shifts of view-point, [as well as by] the change in direction in mid-sentence and the resist-ance to giving a poem any identifiable perspective' (1998, 6). Or to quote Ackroyd, on the poetry of Prynne and Roche, and in reply to J. D. McClatchy's vision of Ackroyd's poetry as an uncooked omelet (rather than as two eggs, a few chives and a dash of tabasco):

his poetry excises completely the role of the poetic 'voice', whether as a personal or as a synthetic medium of expression, and so it moves beyond the range of purely aesthetic effects ... we are not asked to participate in the lucidity and harmony of the poetry, we can only recognize its exterior signs .... Ambiguity is caused by a language coming into itself against the power of that aesthetic context which had given it meaning and strength for so long .... we read a language that constitutes itself beyond an authorial 'I' and outside the aesthetic contexts of 'meaning' and 'experience'. The language seems arbitrary in a purely radical way. (*NNC* 132–33)

Not so much a reading on Ackroyd's part, this statement, written concomitantly with much of Ackroyd's poetry, is the articulation of, on the one hand, a desire to write poetry in a particular way, and, on the other, a manifesto concerning the writing of such poetry. Ackroyd stages this manifesto even as it seems to describe the poetic text of another. This doubleness is typical of much of Ackroyd's writing, whether poetry or fiction (and, in some cases, biography also). Ackroyd's comprehension of the radical movement of language beyond 'an authorial "I"' directs us to his own poetry, which functions, to borrow from Samuel Weber, as 'a structure of articulation in which direct identification no longer functions' (Weber 1991, 134). This commentary of desire and intent outlines the resistance which is always implicit in the parody of explication to be found in certain of Ackroyd's poems.

Carry on camping

Edward Larissey mentions Ackroyd briefly in his *Reading Twentieth-Century Poetry: The Language of Gender and Object* (1990). He speaks of Ackroyd's 'discordant registers' and 'camp, dead-pan parody' (172, 173), while also acknowledging the similarity between Ackroyd's 'surreal scenes' and those of the 'early Auden' (1990, 173). Clearly, between Ian Gregson and Larissey, one person's camp is another person's straight. Camp, it seems, is only camp if you can read it as such; it's as much a question of identifying the subject's performance as it is of the subject's performance itself. Certainly, as Jonathan Dollimore has observed, there is little consensus on what camp is, or might be (1991, 310), for the 'definition of camp is as elusive as the sensibility itself'.

Dollimore goes on to suggest that 'camp undermines the depth model of identity from inside, being a kind of parody and mimicry which hollows out from within, making depth recede into its surfaces' (1991, 310). The 'masquerade of camp', writes Dollimore, 'becomes less a self-concealment than a kind of attack'; such 'hollowing-out of the deep self is pure pleasure, a release from the subjective correlatives of dominant morality (normality, authenticity, etc.)' (Dollimore 1991, 311). While camp, strictly speaking, is concerned with codes determining or resisting the reading and performance of gender- and sexually-orientated identities,[5] the problematic of camp in relation to

Ackroyd's poetry is important, not least because, like so many other identities, the camp masquerade is a form of dis-identification which refuses both to allow itself to be taken seriously and to be pinned down. Camp, in Alan Sinfield's words, disturbs 'any idea of fixity' (1994, 199). If Gregson does not allow for camp in Ackroyd's poetry to the extent that Larissey does, then perhaps this is because Ackroyd's camp self-referential poetics have done such a good job of dressing themselves up in another's (modernist) clothes, the Englishness of it all being so hard to read, to register as any *single* identity.

Part of Ackroyd's camp sensibility is expressed through moments of exclamation or exaggeration. An otherwise straightforward line is given an exclamation mark, as in the apostrophe from 'the small girl ...' (*O*; *DP* 46), 'what disasters of the night!' Elsewhere, for no apparent reason, 'Marcel Proust!' is exclaimed ('Prose Poem' *LL*, 16; 'A prose poem' *DP* 57). Frivolity is cast in mock-tragic terms: 'Underwear or toilet accessories: this was an age-long dilemma, worrying Arthur almost to extinction' ('Prose Poem' *LL*, 16; 'A prose poem' *DP* 57). While, I would suggest, the stress is to be placed on that 'almost', the use of 'extinction' is itself hyperbolic, exaggerated and knowingly poised. Then there are exclamatory phrases such as 'ah' and 'alas' ('the hermaphrodite', *DP* 60); the passing parenthesis 'dear god' ('the secret is ...', *DP* 48), or the wistful 'and oh so many jokes / were silent and Joe dear / Joe pretended to sleep' ('the small girl', *O*; *DP* 46). Another aspect of camp textuality already apparent in the mischievous use of exclamation and exaggeration could be described as the sheer *irresponsibility* manifested in appearing to throw around allusion, parody, pastiche, irony, without due care and attention (apparently), either for the question of textual meaning or for the reader's assumed comprehension of the author's identity. What is it that Ackroyd is playing at, mixing high and low, farce and pathos? Take, for example, 'country life' yet again. In the dream narrative, an advertising slogan, 'Have another before you', is recalled. This is then reiterated in the analytic interpretation, which the analyst assumes is addressed to the subject, Jeremy. In the midst of this 'straight' analysis a parenthesis intrudes in a camp exaggeration of Jeremy's name, phonetically amplified: '(Jay-ray-mee)'. Completing the slogan – have another before you go – recalls, however indirectly, Eliot's barmaid ('HURRY UP PLEASE ITS TIME'). Arguably, the incompletion of the slogan adds a slight touch of innuendo to it, a little potential moment of vulgar *double entendre* so difficult, like camp itself, to pin down.

This is, admittedly, entirely in the reading of the line. The fragment itself says nothing. But it can call to mind a range of camp comedic voices of demotic utterance, for the British reader particularly. There is discernible in this 'off the cuff' throwaway remark a number of spectral utterances, if not camp identities, and not only that transvestitic moment of mimicry in *The Waste Land*.[6] There is a certain cultural currency, an oscillation of a particular aspect of national identity in the phrase. The words of the fragment may be completely straight, but haunting them are the echoes of voices of comedians such as Frankie Howerd, Kenneth Williams, Eddie Izzard, and drag queen Danny La Rue, all of whom manifest a particular vocal trait. Each is able to modulate their voice, and with it the identity perceived by their audiences. Each performer is capable of shifting in an instant from a certain plummy, perhaps effeminate, possibly public school tone, swooping into a coarse working-class London voice.[7] In the context in which this occurs, the vocal modulation is at once disturbing – which, after all, is the real voice, the authentic identity? – and, given the contexts of the monologue in which it occurs, highly suggestive without being absolutely, definably smutty. (This is not a question of Eric Idle's 'nudge nudge, wink wink' routine from Monty Python's Flying Circus, which doesn't have an element of camp in it, merely forced crudity.) The effect is, perhaps, most strikingly comic *and* unsettling when engaged by Danny La Rue, the voice of a London worker suddenly emerging from the image of a Mae West impersonator. The examples given are merely that, of course. The point is that the voice belongs to a tradition of camp music hall entertainment, the cultural history of which is particularly strong in working-class areas of London. The camp and the common seem to be inseparable. Everything is in the interpretation, but the interpretation is unsettled ahead of itself; it cannot be calmed down. It is this dissonance within the utterance that can be read at work in Ackroyd's 'have another before you'. It is a dissonance which makes every identity tremble. Moreover, as has been intimated, the effect being so transient, it becomes hard to tell whether it was in fact camp.

It is precisely impossible to read Ackroyd on either side permanently or simply of the camp/not-camp definition, not only because camp is so hard to define, the moment so fleeting, and the identification so dependent on the willingness to read, but also because of what Dollimore calls the hollowing-out of 'deep self'. As other critics such as Onega have observed, the stable, central self is evacuated from the text absolutely, and this in itself is the performative work of the ludic, playful text. (This might, in itself, return us to the undecidable question of camp.) To borrow from James McCorkle's discussion of American postmodern poetry, the world of Ackroyd's texts is 'seen as an arena of representational possibilities, where each sign, each word, each assumed voice is an act of role-playing' (1989, 48–9). As the novels will make explicit, this is not a postmodern aesthetic. Role-playing belongs to the articulation – at least in part – of Ackroyd's abiding interest in the dissident, disruptive elements of London's working-class music hall tradition, to which the camp comedians mentioned above belong. Particularly, Ackroyd's interest is in those aspects of camp and transvestitic performance which assault normative gender identities.[8]

For Ackroyd, projection of contingent identity is always performative, subject to alteration. There is no stability of truth and, equally, no 'deep self' as Dollimore puts it. Identity and meaning are both strategic moments of performance, and the elements of camp belong to a range of poetic strategies. Such strategies not only disturb our ability to read the content of the text, they also operate at the formal level. Defining one particular formal feature of postmodern poetry, Edward Larissey describes 'the erosion of the difference between "inside" and "outside"' (1990, 177). The erasure in Ackroyd's poetry is not so much the absolute erosion of this difference as it is the destabilizing of identities such as 'inside' or 'outside'. We can still read the 'inside' and 'outside', in Ackroyd's poetry, but we read them as being precariously staged. At the most fundamental level Ackroyd's titles, with their triple dot ellipses, seem ready to slip into the 'inside' that we take to be the text.[9] At the same time, recalling Ackroyd's own comment on Prynne and Roche, we read the partial erasure of the inside that is the poetic text through its gathering of the fragments of numerous different discourses, cultural references and textual allusions. The poetry never settles into the poem. Instead, it disrupts that in a constant drifting, like the modulation of the camp comedian's voice, at one moment refined, insinuating and feminized, often helpless and seemingly under threat, at another coarse, insinuating, and masculine, threatening and conspiratorial. We read what Ian Maclachlan describes as 'a rhythmic scansion, a movement of *poiesis* which is irreducible to any propositional content' (1999, 81). The effects of erasure and movement, along with the performance of difference and the creation of 'self-conscious linguistic palimpsests of the accumulated echoes' (Onega 1998, 17) of modernist and other poets, is readable as part of the ludic affirmation of the pleasure of the text, for no other reason than the articulation of that pleasure as a gesture of resistance to the location of an identity. As the authenticity of 'voice' is abandoned, the ambiguity of language comes into its own, in radical and subversive ways. And what is perhaps most subversive, most threatening, is the sense of exhilaration and pleasure, even – especially – in those little 'ahs' and 'ohs'.

(Dis)orientations

Without giving into the impulse to find a meaning for these texts then, putting them into the cuisineart of critical tradition, what might be said about the small body of hard to find, hardly read poems? Approaching from another angle, we can observe that, along with the frequency of literary allusion, there is the frequency of certain images, tropes or figures, which is however in no way suggestive of interpretative possibilities. We can observe through the briefest glances – not yet amounting to, and resisting all temptation of, a reading – the recurrence of:

- *darkness and night* ('country life', *DP* 7–8; 'and the children ...', *DP* 11–12; 'This beautiful fruit ...', *DP* 13; 'There are so many ...', *DP* 14; 'the rooks (after Andrew Lanyon)' *DP* 20; 'Only connect ...', *DP* 21; 'the novel', *DP* 28; 'how did it ...', *DP* 34; 'out of the ...', *DP* 36–39)
- *sleep* ('a dialogue', *DP* 19; 'Only connect ...', *DP* 21; 'the cut in ...' *DP* 27; 'on the third ...', *DP* 35; 'love falls ...', *DP* 72; 'the empty telephone ...', *DP* 74)
- *dreams* ('country life', *DP* 7–8; 'on the third ...', *DP* 35; 'I took ...', *DP* 62; 'A love poem', *DP* 63; 'There are so ...', *DP* 73)
- *the construction of selfhood or subjectivity* ('the cut in ...', *DP* 27; 'the novel', *DP* 28; 'the poem', *DP* 29; 'In the middle ...', *DP* 30; 'there was no rain ...', *DP* 31; 'how did it ...', *DP* 34; 'madness ...', *DP* 41; 'the room is ...', *DP* 43–44' 'the empty telephone ...', *DP* 74; 'there are so ...', *DP* 73; 'It was no longer ...', *DP* 70)
- *landscapes* ('Only connect ...', *DP* 21; 'the novel', *DP* 28; 'the poem', *DP* 29; 'there was no rain ...', *DP* 31; 'madness ...', *DP* 41; 'the room is ...', *DP* 43–44)
- *connections and the desire to connect* ('Only connect ...', *DP* 21; 'how did it ...', *DP* 34; 'out of the ...', *DP* 36–39)
- *reading and writing* ('Only connect ...', *DP* 21; 'the poem', *DP* 29; 'the day ...', *DP* 32; 'the room is ...', *DP* 43–44; 'The secret is ...', *DP* 47–48)
- *traces* ('Only connect ...', *DP* 21; 'the poem', *DP* 29; 'the room is ...', *DP* 43–44; 'The secret is ...', *DP* 47–48)
- *colour* ('Only connect ...', *DP* 21; 'the novel', *DP* 28; 'In the middle ...', *DP* 30; 'how did it ...', *DP* 34; 'out of the ...', *DP* 36–39; 'the room is ...', *DP* 43–44)
- *parody of poetry* ('Only connect ...', *DP* 21; 'the cut in ...', *DP* 27; 'In the middle ...', *DP* 30; 'the day ...', *DP* 32; 'The secret is ...', *DP* 47–48; 'you do the best ...', *DP* 50)
- *synesthesia and/or the parody of synesthesic effects* ('Only connect ...', *DP* 21; 'there was no rain ...', *DP* 31; 'out of the ...', *DP* 36–39; 'The secret is ...', *DP* 47–48; 'you do the best ...', *DP* 50)
- *signs and the signs of signs* ('a dialogue', *DP* 19; 'Only connect ...', *DP* 21; 'the poem', *DP* 29; 'on the third ...', *DP* 35; 'out of the ...', *DP* 36–39; 'the room is ...', *DP* 43–44)
- *snow* ('I took ...', *DP* 62; 'It was no longer ...', *DP* 70; 'love falls ...', *DP* 72)
- *children and childhood* ('Only connect ...', *DP* 21; 'the day ...', *DP* 32; 'Lovers But Still Strangers', *DP* 33; 'out of the ...', *DP* 36–39; 'the room is ...', *DP* 43–44; 'you do the best ...', *DP* 50; 'It was no longer ...', *DP* 70).

This list is not of course the only possible list. Equally one could add to the list 'pastoral', 'elegiac', 'sight' or 'reflections'. Also, a number of other poems not mentioned from the four volumes could also be added to any – or in some instances, all – of the above. Frequency of these and other images does not imply either order or unity, an organic whole, however. It only gestures in the direction of a more or less rhythmic pulse, even as the sense of fragmentation is reasserted. Such a pulse or rhythm serves only to impress upon the reader the fragmentary, ruined, and dressed-up, masquerading, unfinished nature of these texts.

One of the troping figures in Ackroyd's poems, which recurs throughout his writing, is that of light. Or rather, lights, for there are several, not all the same, even if we ignore images of brightness, of the sun, of sunshine, illumination, reflection, the moon. There is the completeness of the light radiated by snow, which in itself is double suggestion of both a possibly blinding illumination and a lack of weight ('love falls', *DP* 72). There is the light of the sun ('country life', *DP* 7–8; 'The great Sun ...', *DP* 64). There is the light of torches and the unspecified lights reflected on a face ('the little tune ...', *DP* 65). There is a 'moving light' photographed on a body ('the room is ...', *DP* 43–4) and a 'silvery light/outside its cage' ('opening ...', *DP* 45). Light 'steps backward/becoming grey' and a 'light hand' in opposition to a 'dark hand' 'in the same field' ('out of the ...', *DP* 36–9). Of the fifty-four poems in *The Diversions of Purley*, twenty-two mention light.[10] If, as J. D. McClatchy implies, there is a certain 'lightness', a lack of organic weight appropriate to poetry but apparently lacking in Ackroyd's poems, then this lightness has to do with light, though not enlightenment necessarily. Light may shed light but it can also blind. Throwing momentarily an object into relief, it can leave the surroundings in darkness. Enlightenment or illumination may allow us, metaphorically or literally, to see 'where we are', though not necessarily where we may be going. Paradoxically, illumination can reveal to us that we are in the dark. None of the lights mentioned above are necessarily the same light, emanating from the same source. Nothing suggests they are. We get no illumination from them. Indeed, looking into the light only ever serves to remind us, either through making us squint or blinding us, that darkness remains exactly that. In the light of the day, or by artificial light, it is possible to orientate ourselves, but light can also disorientate. The flashes of light in Ackroyd's poetry are not unambiguously sources of illumination however. Neither the subject of the poetry nor an object, a thing, as such, the light of Ackroyd's poetry is never the same as itself. An unstable metaphor, it offers to blind and confuse, even as it seems to suggest the possibility of a field of vision. The various lights pulse intermittently.

We have already encountered indirectly the question of light, and of lights, in both 'country life' and 'and the children ...'. The former distinguishes artificial from natural light, challenging the attentiveness, the sufficiency of illumination in the second-hand analytical perception, which seeks to 'bring to light' that which is unilluminated, yet which itself is in the dark as to its own unconscious connection between sun/son. 'And the children ...'

addresses directly the impossibility of addressing the poetic play of light, except through the indirection of, once again, second-hand commentary. In 'country life', ignoring the distinction between the representation of artificial and natural light, two direct references to light make plain the distinction between literal and metaphorical light: 'The light is making a vague noise'; 'three childhood memories come to light'. The play of lights in 'country life' between 'artificial' and 'natural', between 'literal' and 'metaphoric', serves as a commentary on the ludic movement in the poetic itself, as the possibility or otherwise for coming to comprehension, of perception and illumination. 'Light' or, rather, the different and differing manifestations of light erode the distinctions between stable positions such as literal or metaphorical, artificial and natural, because the work of light in the poetic text is fundamentally metaphorical, always at a remove from that which it casts light on, and yet promising to make a connection, creating the illusion of connection through illumination. Yet light does not bring with it the truth, it does not reveal some presence or meaning, even if it blinds us with this promise. For, as the example of 'country life' shows, the movement between the different lights is the rhythmic movement of the poetic itself.

Ackroyd's play with light appears to play against a certain history of the use of light as metaphor. In the history of western thought, particularly in the history of metaphysics, light has been if not a founding, then, at least, a dominant metaphor, as Cathryn Vasseleu argues in her significant study, *Textures of Light: Vision and Touch in Irigaray, Levinas, and Merleau-Ponty*. Drawing on Derrida and Luce Irigaray in her introduction, Vasseleu traces the history of light as metaphor in the text of philosophy (1998, 3–18).[11] 'Seeing light', she suggests, 'is a metaphor for seeing the invisible in the visible' (1998, 3). Summarizing Irigaray's development of Derrida's arguments Vasseleu states that metaphor is, of course, 'both a means of passage to, and an inevitable detour or provisional loss of meaning in the arrival at, a proper meaning' (1998, 7–8). For Derrida, 'light is the concept-metaphor by means of which truth can be made to appear or become present to consciousness' (1998, 5–6), while, for Irigaray, light as metaphor in the text of Plato serves to enact 'the drama of concealment and unconcealment' (1998, 7). Light as metaphor or trope therefore engages in little acts, perhaps pretenses, of *apocalypse*, of revelation, and of *aletheia*, unveiling. Light brings truth to light supposedly, yet it does so indirectly. Light promises to be a figure of *anastomosis*, providing a connective thread *between*: between reader and text, between subject and object, between the conscious perception and the reality. As Vasseleu puts it, 'light is a medium which sustains and bridges the difference between a subject of perception and perceivable things...light... fills and maintains the interval of separation' (1998, 78, 79).

Ackroyd's use of the figures of light acknowledges in a somewhat ironic manner the desire to connect and, simultaneously, the maintenance of intervallic difference as that which moves *poiesis*. It plays with issues of representation, with the question of metaphor, and the issue of reading in a manner which comments on the very question of the poetic itself. It promises all the while to illuminate while ultimately never doing so. It intimates revelation and unconcealment, but only reveals itself and the desire for meaning. To borrow from a discussion of light and poetry by Derrida, 'playing with the apocalyptic tone it none the less refuses to assign or otherwise settle on, as a possible meaning for poetry, for the poetic, light draws the subject's desire to read, to fix on a meaning, into the light, illuminating nothing other than this desire' (1993c, 148). The numerous flashes or pulses of light connect with nothing so much as themselves. This connection does not provide a flow of unbroken illumination. The numerous lights, such as those cited above, pulse irregularly and with different intensities. They draw our attention as readers, the attention and focus Derrida describes as the subject's desire to read, but resolutely resist all acts of reading which seek to control the periodic illumination. Their meaning undecidable, their relationship being only ever a relationship marked by difference, the numerous lights of Ackroyd's poetry do nothing so much as illuminate the dazzling play of image and the desire engendered by such play. The images of 'the pale blue light' ('how did it ...', *DP* 34), the concealed light brought by the 'image of hurt' ('the cut in ...', *DP* 27) and the 'pinpoints of light' which 'reflect/ the dry, enormous plain' ('my own ...', *DP* 15) draw the reader to them, but can be understood as nothing so much as their own performative instances, illuminating the poetic structure constituted by what Samuel Weber describes (in speaking of the subject's construction) as 'an irreducible movement of repetition' (1991, 135).

The title of this chapter, a line from 'Only connect ...' (*DP* 21–6), is exemplary in its destablizing play of, and with, light. The poem does, however, mention a number of other lights also, worth giving passing attention. The title of the poem not only cites E. M. Forster, it also names the desire to find figures promising *anastomosis*, even as it simultaneously speaks that desire. Illumination as connection is promised but never comes, even though it recurs throughout the poem, driving the desire of which it speaks. Thus the poem performs wistfully and knowingly the very desire with which it toys. At least it can be read in this fashion, seeing in such play once again the erosion between inside and outside. In this poem light 'which I have created' 'withers' minor characters. The reader is told, 'look down and see your own face blurred among all this / suffering / as if you were changed by it'. Illumination thus effects transformation internally and externally. In the fourth of the poem's six stanzas, light in the form of a secret ray 'holds your face in a fixed position'. As we shall see below, light and identity are related in Ackroyd's poetry, the former having the power to fix or change the latter, as the two lines just cited show. Light thus operates in contradictory, not to say paradoxical ways.

In the fifth stanza, the light of days holds 'our gaze wasting our lives' and 'the lights grow smaller and smaller /.../until they appear in a fixed pattern'. If light as concept-metaphor traditionally conveys the promise of truth or presence, here, as elsewhere in Ackroyd's poetry, it does no such thing, for it is impossible to say that light operates as a single metaphor, as a metaphor for a single source of light. Light, conventionally put to work in texts – if it is a concept-metaphor it is also in some senses a tool metaphor operated by the philosopher or writer – has a utilitarian function. In Ackroyd's poetry, light is remarkable for its apparent inutility, its modernist *foundness* if you will, except that, unlike the chance collision of found objects, light's illumination in Ackroyd's text still tempts us on toward a flood of connection and interpretation. The figure of light in blinding us seduces us to tip over the cliff's edge in an overflow of too-hasty reading. Like that apocalyptic tone, light plays – as do so many of Ackroyd's figures, images, tropes – with the meanings it refuses to assign. Finally, the play with light and the play whereby light plays with the reader is given one last playful twist. In the last stanza come the lines taken as the title of this chapter: 'this song .../... rose in a straight line with a tiny light/seen in the mind's eye as a phoneme'. There is a certain gesture of synesthesic effect here, as the line moves between two instances of auditory signification to the moment of metaphorical visual perception. It is not, after all, a representation, the eye does not perceive the tiny light, but, rather, the line conveys this perception at a double distance. Between song and phoneme, the latter already a 'translation' in sound – the reading of poetry? – of the invisible tiny light, the light is not a light at all. It is imagined as such, or at least so we are told. For here, poetic language wrestles with the inadequacy of its own imagination, its own lack of illumination if you will. Relying on conventional if confused metaphors, Ackroyd's poetic text plays with the impoverishment of poetic language through overworked stock images, which speak of desired poetic effects as well as the desire for meaning. All the while, what is described, what we read and are asked to imagine, is the banality of a screened, projected 'sing-along', where wholly artificial light projects the words of a song, broken into syllables onto a screen, and a small bouncing ball, the 'tiny light', plays along the top of the fragmented words, inviting us to join in. The poem thus plays its readers, as the song is reported erasing difference, making faces 'all alike' in the 'great urban centre', 'in factories, / offices and homes'. This is hardly the light of truth. Forster's humanist imperative becomes a ludicrous technological game of mass acquiescence. Significantly, however, Ackroyd's text can be read as being markedly polyvalent, drawing as it does simultaneously on 'high' poetic devices and the suggestion of the technology of mass culture. Light motivates the text, but it does so in a manner which resists the conventional appropriation of light as a founding metaphor or guarantor of truth or meaning.

We find everywhere then, and given exemplary expression through the play of light(s), what Geoffrey Hartman refers to as remnants or stubborn surpluses, 'capable of motivating a text or being motivated by it' (1981, 15). This might well be one more way of defining the effect of the multiplicity of wayward allusions, their seemingly anarchic play refusing to settle into anything except the unreadable archive. In addition to allusion however, a momentary skimming of the list of other recurring figures above suggests how remnants and surpluses can operate. They serve in the erasure of simple static positions of outside and inside, They spill from one text to another, being transformed and translated both within and beyond themselves in the endless process, and intimating in this that there is always the surplus, always the excess beyond the ability of reading to accommodate and incorporate. Light is merely one such trace. Such traces serve to articulate the text, while dis-articulating the possibility of locatable referent and final meaning. They belong, as already suggested, in part to the erosion of the stable identities of 'inside' and 'outside', 'original/authentic' or 'pastiche/inauthentic'. As seen in the example of light from 'Only connect …' or the function of light in 'country life', all such meanings are invalidated, to say the least.

To take another example, this movement is observable in the following lines:

> suzanne by camouflaging her language has run
> into the sunshine with a key to these structures
> as green as grass …

Originally published as an untitled poem in *London Lickpenny*, this comes from 'The secret is …' (*DP* 47). The title is tantalizing, for it promises, or appears to promise, the revelation of a meaning. It 'motivates' both the text and the possibility of reading it. Suzanne, the subject with whom the stanza begins, and discernible as a possible reference or allusion to Leonard Cohen's 'Suzanne' (the poem *and* the subject for whom the poem is named) is given movement within the poem which is capable of narrative paraphrase, through the encryption of her language. The act of encoding and disguising is what makes possible running into the sunshine. This at least is what a reading of the logic of the line tells us. The movement of the line, across the poem's surface, teases the reader with the suggestion of imitation, of language imitating a reality or sorts. Yet the logic by which this is possible is purely that of grammatical consistency, not of some correlation between language and reality. It does not take an act of camouflaging my language to make it possible for me to run, either into the sun or anywhere else. The semantic movement returns upon itself in the image of suzanne running, motivated by the transvestism of language. Furthermore, the subject appears to possess 'a key to these structures' which is – seems to be – as green as grass. If suzanne holds the means for making plain the meaning of the poetic text, she doesn't give the key up, yet, once again, the logic of the lines appears to insist by force of the simile, that the key is obvious, 'as green as grass'. One might just as well say 'as plain as day'. The cliché prohibits reading: in being a cliché (and therefore, for some, not poetic) the phrase has a cultural verisimilitude which is so understood as to be *not read*, and to arrest the possibility of reading. In the sunshine, in the light once again, the play of language is in full view; illuminated by the sunlight language is itself the key, as well as being the structure. What 'the secret is...' is simultaneously revealed and not revealed, for the secret is in full view, as the poem on the page, as the structures of language, and yet it is nowhere precisely, because it is not implied that the secret might be somewhere else. The poem is 'the secret is ...'. The secret is the poem (is the secret). There is in effect here a doubling of the surface structures, suggested in Hartman's formula, as well as a doubling of the play which articulates and makes possible meaning through language, even though the meaning is itself, and not some extra-textual referent.

Typical of Ackroyd's poetry, the gesture in this example is one that emphasizes textual surface and form, while displacing the possibility of 'depth-as-value' or 'depth-as-meaning'. Certainly this is akin to the displacement or hollowing-out of any 'deep self' or meaning, as referred to by Jonathan Dollimore in his discussion of the difficulties of defining camp. The pleasure of and in this text is its ludic surfacing. Form, texture, structure and writerly movement and making (*poiesis*) play across these surfaces – and *as* the surfaces themselves – confronting the reader everywhere on the page, in each successive poem, as the arrangement *on* and *of* the page. They amount to what Roland Barthes in *The Pleasure of the Text* describes as *drifting*, that movement which resists and does not respect the whole (Barthes 1975, 18). Such constant surf(ac)ing on the part of the poetry, denies access to a locatable subject or originating, original voice. Indeed, to cite Barthes again, there can be no voice behind the text (1975, 30). Furthermore, such play 'liquidates all metalanguage', to borrow Barthes' words once more (1975, 30), whether this be the metalanguage reading seeks in the text to calm its play (what does Ackroyd mean) or the metalanguage the critic brings to the text in order to put it in its place (Ackroyd is a postmodernist poet). Instead, and to quote Hartman again, what we mistake as 'voice' (as the name we give to the indiscernible in order to orientate not the text but ourselves) 'reverberates in the labyrinth of writing and in dying, lights it up. Even the labyrinth, of course, is not to be put on the side of permanence' (1981, 5–6). Hartman's identification of 'voice' is merely the naming of a produced effect, a modulation or rhythm, of course, and not the location of some stable subject behind the text.

Comprehending Ackroyd's poetry in this manner can allow for a provisional definition of the text as an 'open', rather than as a 'closed' text.

(Certainly, the reiteration at work and alluded to in the list above, is indicative of a constant opening and folding gesture.) This definition, which resists the identification of Ackroyd's poetry with a particular school, movement, or tradition, is drawn from an essay on contemporary poetry and poetics by Lyn Hejinian, 'The Rejection of Closure' (1996, 27–40). Her definition is a useful model for explaining Ackroyd's poetry, not in terms of what it might mean, or indeed 'how' it means. Instead, we can begin to see how the poetry resists the act of reading that limits the play of the poetry, and dislocates the reader from herself. Even as the text drifts, so too does the reader. A 'closed text' is

> … one in which all the elements of the work are directed towards a single reading of it …. In an 'open text' meanwhile, all the elements of the work are maximally excited; here it is because ideas and things exceed (without deserting) the argument that they have been taken into the dimension of the work …. The 'open text' … invites participation, rejects the authority of the writer over the reader. (278)

Developing this argument one stage further, we would suggest that the authority of the reader is also rejected. However, it is precisely this rejection of the writer's authority, which is played with and played out in Ackroyd's poetry. Although the poems have been described as fragmentary already, even this is not a stable identity for Ackroyd's text. The very idea of the poetic ruin, as a modernist gesture of reinventing tradition otherwise, is also played with as another prevalent ludic gambit. Ackroyd's text is neither wholly conventionally fragmentary (as is a more recognizably 'modernist' text from the Anglo-American tradition, say the early Auden or the recent Ashbery); nor is it completely unreadable for we can read, after a fashion, certain narrative possibilities, for example, as in the line already quoted from 'The secret is …'. 'Language is thus never in a state of rest', as Hejeinian puts it (34). This recalls both Maclachlan's discussion of the scansion of *poiesis* and also Barthes' idea of *drifting*. However, drifting, and what Derrida calls disinterrance, is now understood as textual play or movement as much as it is comprehended as the Barthesian abandonment of the reading self to a state of drifting. Such double movement will not allow for any sense of stable subjectivity, whether for the 'I' in the text or the 'I' who reads.

Identities

I am nothing but the spoken word.

Edmond Jabès

Given the difficulties Peter Ackroyd's poems present the act of reading, they might best be defined, albeit provisionally, as 'events'. They are events in that one cannot determine their meaning 'ahead' of one's encounter with them, either through attempting to read the title of the collections or each poem's title, where it has one. For that matter, the meaning cannot be determined in the act of attempted act of reading the poems themselves. The reader must encounter each poetic text completely unprepared. The reader, giving up the idea of reading, must prepare herself to be unprepared, and, in the encounter between self and poem remain open to the unpredictable changes likely to be effected by the playful, wayward arrival of the text. In this encounter, the reader is dislocated from herself, becoming the 'destined receiver' of the poems, who is, in the words of J. Hillis Miller, 'programmed ever after to be, a part of him or her at least, the self' called into being by the text (Miller 1990, 180).

Miller expands on this unforeseen dislocation of the reading subject and its transformation, in an essay which, in drawing on 'Télépathie' by Jacques Derrida, discusses a similar effect to that just described (Miller, 1990, 171–80; Derrida 1991b, 5–41). His essay, 'Thomas Hardy, Jacques Derrida, and the "Dislocation of Souls"', concerns the possible effects of transmission and communication. In presenting a reading of 'The Torn Letter', Miller considers the performative effects of a letter in the form of Hardy's poem on the addressee as this is given exemplary expression through Hardy's text. For Miller (as for Derrida), writing, even as it seeks to communicate and to connect, only serves in its very movement to displace by the very rhythm and spacing of its transport and transference. Indeed, displacement and dislocation are always already the movement *of* and *in* writing, ahead of any transference or communication. This displacement is often most economically and most violently read in the 'I' effect, where the articulated subject is already dislocated within any articulation of identity. Moreover, as Miller puts it, the letter is also capable, unintentionally, of creating the identity of the addressee. The performative power of the letter and its address to 'you' is in its ability to 'produce its recipient'. Miller thus shows how, in a certain way, writing operates upon the reading self, who becomes not the 'I' who speaks in the text, but the self who becomes instead that 'you' to whom the poem addresses itself. Writing dislocates. It spaces addresser and addressee, not only from one another, but also from themselves, within themselves, graphically. The self is translated in the event of writing into 'multiple simultaneous selves'. Writing thus marks a differentiation, a spacing, as well as always having the power to transform 'you' into the 'you' which it addresses, ahead of its reception.

Ackroyd's poetry takes this act of unexpected address further, for 'you' are rebuked in another poem precisely for seeking a determined identity. In the poem, 'In the middle ...' (*CL* 15; *DP* 30) the reader is apparently chastised for desiring to give meaning, for attempting repeatedly to read in a particular manner. We read the following: 'In the middle of nowhere / you adopt this uncertain expression / as though you had lived for "significant form" / and then forgot your own name'. Here the text appears to address the reader directly, chiding the reader for a certain loss of identity (his or her own). Then, in the final line the text defiantly demands that it be spoken to by the reader in 'your certainty'. The text reads as though it calls the activity of reading and its shortcomings into question in the face of the poetic. In doing so, it challenges the reader's identity as reader. The poem itself never settles into an identity even as it mocks the reader for seeking the very same, and for clinging perpetually to the mastery and solace that 'significant form' supposedly provides. Becoming the 'you' to whom the 'I' of the text addresses itself, the reader is shaken, translated by the unexpected arrival of the text. Accused of searching for meaning and seeking to impose this on the text, the reader is confronted with the destabilization of his or her identity. The desired stasis of an 'I-you' relationship subservient to some imposed narrative or logical rationale brought to the poem by the reader is violently displaced as that relationship is transformed in the encounter between reader and text.

Performances of such encounters, the poems erode both the stability of the reading subject and the narrating self, even as that subject utters 'I' in a number of locations. This articulation of the self in Ackroyd's text operates only as the trace which marks its absence, its already having left, its always having left its mark on the textual field, and being constituted only as that mark within the textual field. Indeed even to talk of this moving self as an 'it', as singular, is to assign it an identity which might have been present, which might be continuous even though mobile. Rather, subjectivity in Ackroyd's poetry is dispersed, displaced and deferred, differing from and in it-selves, so that it is made impossible to construct a single speaking 'I' which is not already an assumed fictive effect, a performance of textuality.

Take, for example, the following line from the poem 'the cut in...' (*CL* 11; *DP* 27):

> and then, seeing you,
> I am a rhyme for 'weep'

Here, 'I' is affected by the visual response to the other. The subject – 'I' – is transformed, translated by what the 'eye' sees. There is a moment here of the dissolution of stable identities and, with that, a certain effect of border crossing, of liminal transcription. Returning momentarily to the question of light, this relationship between visual perception and the self can be said to be connected with the transmission of a certain light or enlightenment, the projection of which makes the perception possible. 'I' may be read not as the subject but as the sign of a sign, reflecting on itself, enlightened. The trace of a re-marking, a projective play or performance in writing of the transformed subject, 'I' is written into the structure of the text, and acknowledged as such in its own enlightened or illuminated commentary on the function and role of 'I' as an inscribed pulse in the poetic structure. What that rhyme, what 'I' becomes, remains unspoken, perhaps even unspeakable. There is no rhyme with which to stabilize the identity of the 'I'. Yet this absent rhyme is, on the one hand, totally in the open, acknowledged as a rhyme and, on the other hand, and simultaneously, secret. Neither the secret itself, nor the rhyme which remains elsewhere beyond this trace, 'I' is not, simply, a subject.

We may wish to stabilize this poem, as well as others by Ackroyd, by reading the 'I' and its articulations as constant. We may desire to read the articulation of 'I' as the voice of a present author or narrator, behind the enunciation of the 'I', whether within one poem or across the poems. We may even orientate ourselves by identifying, however passively, with that 'I', assuming the role in reading the first-person utterance. But, to paraphrase J. Hillis Miller, the reader is not allowed by these poems to assume the position of the 'I' who speaks, invisibly, in some anterior location, 'behind' the poem, so to speak, or even 'in' the text (1990, 180). The 'I' is not constant, either in its self-referential gestures or when it speaks to 'you'. Who the self is, is multiple. Allusion, pastiche, parody, palimpsest and reference do not constitute the unified voice of the poet or the identity of some hidden subject. Rather, they chatter incessantly, their final organization impossible.

In that displaced, unarticulated rhyme from 'the cut in...', then, in which place stands this 'I' as the sign of displacement, 'I' is the economical trace, the re-marking of the function of the poetic text. 'I' signs the cut, 'the cut in ...', which is the poem. 'I' is the poetic figure, a performative projection of the poetic 'subject', that movement spoken of in the poem as the 'slow rhyme' which 'begins in the forehead'. Which is nothing other than to suggest that the poem is itself its subject, always remarking (on) itself, transforming itselves, otherwise, and always displaced, other than itself in any encounter with the reader. Not an identifiable subject as such, not a stable identity, but the cut, the rhythmic trace and remark of its projective, textual play, signed and assigned in the iterative 'I'.

This rhythmic trace is again read in the poem named appropriately 'the poem' (*CL* 13; *DP* 29). In this poem of fragments, of seemingly incomplete lines scattered across the page, I is to be read on several occasions:

so   the way

                              to be described

        landscapes   or   portraits
    which seem
        only

                                        true feelings

                are singing
                    singing it

<pre>
                I wish I
                                              well
      they are
                        traced
          today and gone
                              self fades
                              into
                                        each other
              and   finally
              spreads across
        has been written
          I don't know how to
              how
                        against the wind
      thinking about
                        will I be
          the beginning
</pre>

One of the most immediately performative poems by Ackroyd, 'the poem' affirms its resistance to reading neither through direct parody, nor pastiche of critical commentary, nor indeed through any overt statement concerning poetry. Instead, it stages itself knowingly and playfully as 'the poem', spreading itself in tantalizing 'cuts', which invite wreckless acts of reading. There is something very witty in this poem, because it clearly 'lifts' all its phrases, turning them into 'found' expressions in an act of willful *bricolage*. The words and expressions are taken directly from their places in the lines of the prose poem on the facing page in both *Country Life* and *The Diversions of Purley*, 'the novel'. They are even oriented on the page in the same places as they are to be found in 'the novel'. Thus, the reader is placed in the position of having to decide on what possibilities of reading this might encourage. Indeed, it may well be possible to construct a reading which suggests that the reading is already put in place by the selections Ackroyd makes concerning which excerpts are repeated. This gets us nowhere, of course. The transformation of 'the novel' into 'the poem' demands that any reading take into account the difference between the identities of the two texts. The erasure between stable identities is marked in and by that partial reiteration between texts, where even the titles speak of difference and address at least on an implicit level the very question of how a particular genre or form is read. Seeking to impose any narrative on 'the poem' is to desire its transformation or translation into a novel 'the novel', a form where everything is 'there just to be described ... which seem most real when they are not so' ('the novel' *CL*12; *DP* 28).

Against the descriptive impulse, that expression of desire to impose verisimilitude and mimesis on the artificial to which 'the novel' speaks ('I wish I could immortalize them / like Ronald Firbank or even Graham Greene'; 'the novel', *CL* 12; *DP* 28), there is the stress on 'I' in 'the poem. The fragmentary composition of 'the poem' forestalls narrative description, emphasizing instead those brief, fragile articulations of identity: 'I wish I', 'self fades', 'I don't know how to', 'will I be / the beginning'. In each of these remarks, the articulation of 'I' seems hardly certain of its 'self'. 'I' is displaced from itself, barely readable, fading 'into/each other/ and finally/ [spreading] across/ [what] has been written'. The subject is no more than an effect of writing, the movement of difference. Wherever there is 'I', 'I' am not, though 'I am' is, in effect, the admission that 'I am written'. This, in its turn (and return), is constantly remarked each time the text is read, for this inscription of 'I' marks that 'rhythmic scansion, a movement of *poiesis*' commented on by Ian Maclachlan. This irreducible rhythm is multiplied and fragmented further every time the poem is encountered, every time the reader reads those 'I's that address the reader. In reading the pulsing disinterrance of the 'I' from any stable self, the identity of the reader is dislocated. If, as Maclachlan correctly suggests, 'I' marks a double temporalization: that of writing and reading (1999, 81), then, in the poetry of Peter Ackroyd, this temporalization is effectively more than merely double, more than simply a binary instance between the text and its audience. For, every time the text is read, 'I' becomes other than the 'I' written in every place, or in the moments of all previous readings. Yet even this is written into the text, in its performative 'spread' of the self across the written; 'the poem' in its ruined state performs this condition and anticipates its own attempted communication. As if in some recognition of this impossible position – the very impossibility of the stable position for the articulation of 'self' – the poem, 'the poem', ends without ending, in a moment of undecidability, where 'I' seems to be put into the position of asking whether 'I' will be the beginning. What 'I' will be is unpredictable except to say that the text articulates multiple selves even as it addresses, thereby calling into being, the reader in ways the reader can never anticipate.

Any articulation or reading of 'I', of identity or subjectivity is fraught with problems wherever 'I' is encountered, therefore. The movement of 'I', a textual figure within and belonging to a 'structure of articulation' (recalling Samuel Weber's words), allows for no direct identification. As if to acknowledge that the self is nothing that can be identified directly, at one moment Ackroyd writes of the precarious self: 'So winter is coming in, and the self fades / and flickers' ('the novel', *DP* 28). Ackroyd makes a provisional connection here between identity and light, as he does elsewhere ('madness ...', *DP* 41; 'there was no rain ...', *DP* 31). The self is constructed as a narrative possibility brought into being by the light. The self is caused to perform through illumination, as 'The great Sun' intimates: 'The great Sun wastes its energy upon small objects/and catches me in the art of being myself' (*DP* 64). Here, self-consciously the subject admits to the performative nature of a 'true' subjectivity. This self-awareness of the 'I's' address to the reader in Ackroyd's poems forestalls the possibility of a reading which calms the movement of any stable identity. The 'self' is instead the locus of undecidability. The self is always aware of its being an effect, a trace supposedly given meaning only by its location within the larger text. And yet, because of this very condition, it is always different from itself every time it comes to be remarked, from each desired utterance of 'I' as the possible expression of the 'in-itself'.

Reading the movement of 'I' in Ackroyd's texts, we may suggest that 'I' affirms itself only as its own lack ('the self fades / and flickers', *DP* 28; 'the dusty light / in which I lose myself', *DP* 41). Yet this lack is deliberately staged, as much so as is 'I'. The masquerade of self and lack is a double performance: of the desire for self-meaning and self-presence, and in the awareness of the impossibility of this, the acknowledgement of the lack and the perpetual frustration of that desire. That is to say, every time that 'I' says 'I' in one of Ackroyd's poems, it acknowledges both its iterability and its function as rem(a)inder or signifier of lack, to borrow momentarily a somewhat Lacanian formulation.[12] 'I' is identified by Lacan as the *point de capiton*, the 'quilting' or 'anchoring point', 'by which the signifier stops the otherwise endless movement (*glissement*) of the signification' (Lacan 1977, 303). It provides what Dylan Evans describes as 'the necessary illusion of a fixed meaning' for the subject who speaks (1996, 149).

Where matters become confused further is in the shift to the attempted interpretation of the literary or poetic text. In the act of reading, 'I' is assumed to represent someone, a fictive narrator or the author for example, where meaning appears to be fixed in some other who says 'I'. 'I' provides the momentary utterance which is conventionally read as arresting the movement that *poiesis* describes, where the reader alights upon the promise of a stable presence or meaning. Such a promise acts as the guarantor of this stable location for the purpose of the orientation of the reader. Recognizing the 'I' of the text as some supposedly full identity, the reader should be able to say, here 'I' am, to reflect and arrest the textual performance. 'I' is thus read as being the location as well as the locution of the subject. However, Ackroyd's performative 'I' has inscribed in its self-conscious mo(ve)ments its own challenge to the sufficiency of that reading. The performative 'I' or 'I-effect' subverts the reader's attempt to locate it, thereby displacing the reader's sense of identity on which the act of reading 'I' is implicitly grounded. Ackroyd's 'I' knowingly plays with the authority which 'I' is assumed as having and, in doing so, doubts its own stability.[13]

It even, on occasions, expresses concern that it will become fixed, that its identity will become stable, losing the ability to become other or to play. Once again, this is related to the projection of light, in 'there was no rain ...': 'this light might go on for ever / and then my personality would never change' (*DP* 31). The anxiety of performance is that performance will give way and the masquerade will be transfixed in unchanging light, transformed into some permanent identity. This is not likely to be the case though, for as 'I' acknowledges in 'a dialogue', 'as a reflection upon glass I / but a solid object cannot last' (*DP* 19), while in 'the room is ...', 'I wake up as a different person' (*DP* 43). The 'simple idea of myself' ('The great Sun', *DP* 64) never lasts long, and as the reader is informed, 'your identity ceases to matter' ('the room is ...', *DP* 43). Identity is then a construct glued together by a range of more or less acknowledged and readable allusions. (Even pastiche and parody are comic or farcical versions of some supposedly true identity; terms of transgression, they are employed in critical discourse as markers which orient, however obliquely towards the normative and unified.) Turning the light on, we see the identity on the stage and mistake it as a reference to the human subject beyond the masquerade. However, as Ackroyd's use of 'I' intimates, there is no 'beyond' the performative 'I', the subject who is only and ever a subject for others, self-reflexive, knowing, and playfully specular in its own strategic acknowledgements. 'I' addresses itself to its potential addressees, its future readers, anticipating both the 'I' it will become and the 'I' 'I' will have been changed to, in my attempted reading of these other 'I's.

'in the fold of a quotation'

In the light of all we have said so far, it would be foolhardy to pretend we can approach anything resembling a conclusion, having the 'last word' on the poetry of Peter Ackroyd. Nothing would be more problematic, especially if we accept the critical-aesthetic judgement of Ackroyd's poetry as being somewhat slight, perhaps even 'underdone', in comparison with, say, the early, surrealist Auden, or the more recent, fragmentary Ashbery. If as J. D. McClatchy suggests, that Ackroyd's poetry seems not so much a completed dish as the list of ingredients, then it might be argued that the ingredients can make any number of dishes, with a little ingenuity. McClatchy's metaphor accidentally speaks to the very condition of Ackroyd's poetic texts. Their identities remain in suspension awaiting any number of audiences. Allusion, reference, pastiche, parody, the performative 'I'; all hinge on future possibilities of reading, and on the constant play with identification. All such effects fold themselves onto one another, even as they remark a certain fold in the text. Even the poet's use of the first person pronoun behaves not as if it were the constant voice, the quilting point or *point de capiton* with which it apparently plays, and which we read as being plied throughout the poetic text/ure. For, every time 'I' is uttered, there is the apparent reference, the playful allusion to, the parodic acknowledgement of that very stability which is resisted.

What the various ludic gambits of Ackroyd's poems effect is to create suspens/ion. That slash in the word(s) suspens/ion suspends a meaning, a single value for the inscription. Suspension we should also remember is that medium in which fragments float without necessarily coming together. Moreover suspension relies on tension, while also creating that feeling. There is thus implicitly suspense in suspension. Ackroyd destabilizes meanings, values, identities through suspending the very possibilities which he seems on the verge of as/signing, which possibilities so tantalizingly play in the light, in the suspension of the text. This playfulness in turn effects the suspension of reading as the determination of the text's identity. Acknowledging the undecidability which suspension puts into play and calls to light, such suspension in turn creates both tension in the reader-text transaction, and also suspense. Ackroyd's poems are like Poe's purloined letter; everywhere the text is in full view even as the mystery seems to be perpetuated. What the secret is, is on display, unable to be brought to light because it is already in the light.

But perhaps another literary analogy is more telling. Perhaps Ackroyd is not so much indebted or related to Poe, as he is to Lewis Carroll, if not the Mad Hatter. Recall the Mad Hatter's tea party, at which the following riddle is asked: 'Why is a raven like a writing desk?' (1970, 95). Leaving aside all temptation to see in this a possible allusion, once again, to Edgar Allan Poe, we know that the riddle remains unanswered, and Alice decides that what she knows about either ravens or writing desks is 'not much'. This concludes the well-known amusing, and playful, semantic debate between the various members of the tea party concerning the eventual outcome when the phrases of various sentences are inverted. (doubtless Martin Dodsworth would see this as something 'fearfully semiotic', seeking to say *J'accuse* to M. Derrida.) However this 'not much', which anticipates the assumption of a number of Ackroyd's critics (as has been seen in the introduction) is, like that riddle, quite telling: for, even as Ackroyd's poems seem to toy with questions concerning the possible connection of such heterogeneous objects as ravens and writing desks, even though these are mentioned nowhere in the poetry as such, yet that 'not much' might well signal the undecidability with which we are confronted, time and again. For, if we are forced to conclude that these poems are about 'not much', we might perhaps modify this to say that they are not about much except the very nature, or play, of writing, of *poiesis* itself. Yet this is not an in-itself. Ackroyd's texts, through the devices and effects tending toward the affirmation of *différance*, acknowledge that the movement of writing is like that of the Lacanian unconscious, described here by Jean-Luc

Nancy: 'the inexhaustible, interminable swarming of significations that ... proceed from a significance or signifyingness [*signifiance*] that whirls with a quasi-Brownian motion around a void point of dispersion, circulating in a condition of simultaneous, concurrent, and contradictory affirmation, and having no point of perspective other than the void of truth at their core ...' (1997, 46–7). Not much, indeed.

2

'A bit of a game ...': the Styles of Peter Ackroyd I

> ... a bit of a game *en travesti* ...
>
> *Dan Leno and the Limehouse Golem*

> On the one hand Ackroyd may have intended ... trivialization as an
> indication of the fact that mystery has been reduced to an innocent
> game. On the other hand, the conceivable frustration of the reader
> must not be underestimated ... . Ackroyd undoubtedly encourages
> the puzzling ...
>
> Luc Herman

Introduction

Having looked at the poems, it might seem that a long space has to be travelled before one connects the poetry with the carefully constructed relationships and apparent clarity of Peter Ackroyd's later prose. However, that
distance might not be quite so far. In Ackroyd's poetry and prose there is an
abiding interest: not in the distance between this collection of words and that,
but in the distance between words and what we call 'reality'. For Ackroyd that
vaster space, between words and reality, reveals a condition of undecidability
which he continuously traces and retraces in a play between representations
of the physical world and its past, and wry meditations on the values of such
representations. This play of traces is to be read reciprocally entwining itself. It
promises connections as figures, characters, images, phrases are unfolded and
reiterated throughout Ackroyd's writing. One novel may be read as possibly
alluding to, or being ghosted by, the mark of the poetry, or otherwise, and in
retrospect, anticipating any other text. This is seen, for example, in the possible overflow between the poem 'Across the street ...' (*DP* 42) which features
the amusement arcade, Fun City, and *The Great Fire of London*, in which Fun
City also appears. If the poetry and criticism do not share ostensibly in the

reiterative and open-ended seriality of Ackroyd's narrative labyrinth (though it is the case that the poetry is marked and re-marked by its own reiterations), then they may be said to reconfigure it in some manner and in other words.

Already there is a problem here, raised by such ludic and labyrinthine gestures: of how we come to terms with Peter Ackroyd and the texts this signature underwites. This has to do with the very terms – specifically 'reality', 'representation', 'mimesis' – in which it is possible or otherwise to speak of Ackroyd's writing, given the language games and the labyrinthine intertext which Ackroyd's writing establishes according to models which are primarily textual and literary. Ackroyd's textual ludics, his serious games of pantomimesis, challenge any simple idea that words mimetically or faithfully 'reproduce' or 'represent' any simple or simply understood 'reality' or the so-called 'real world'.

Given Ackroyd's interest in prior texts, in pre-texts and intertexts, and given also his interest in performativity, theatricality and play, even supposedly straightforward notions of representation are troubled. The problematization which play, which textual give and take, engenders puts the very idea of reality into doubt, if by that term we mean that which is simply, empirically knowable, verifiable, quantifiable, unmediated in any fashion. This problematization is all the more complex when one considers Ackroyd's spiralling temporal games, which at their most obviously artificial can affront critics, as was the case with *English Music* which, structurally, may be described as a conical spiral with Timothy Harcombe's subjectivity and lack of awareness as its dual focal point. For a visionary, Tim is comically blind about himself, about his role in the narrative of his life.

Even as the earlier writings may be read as anticipating in some way the expression of later texts, so there are occasions when Ackroyd rewrites various pasts speculatively. Doing so, he incorporates possible visions of a parallax future/past/present horizon of comprehension. For example, there is the lunatic's vision of men on the moon in Bedlam in *Hawksmoor* (*H* 130), the life of John Milton in America, the fictive removal of John Dee from Sheen to Clerkenwell, and the image of Charles Babbage's Analytical Engine in *Dan Leno and the Limehouse Golem*, for which the nineteenth century is not yet prepared (*DLLG* 109). For, in Ackroyd's textual and intertextual labyrinth, there is never a simple correspondence between word and world, term and object. Ackroyd alerts us to the undecidability which is the condition of all possible transmission of the written word.

If this seems more visible in the poetry than in the prose, this is not to suggest that undecidability is less a concern of the fictions than of the earlier publications. The concern is still there though performed in other ways, as Ackroyd develops different performative strategies, utilising not only multiple narrative voices but, specifically, multiple *written*, that is to say textual forms, such as diaries, journals, court and newspaper reports. For it is important to understand that Ackroyd conceives the world and being as profoundly textual; as written, in short. Writing is both productive and performative of the self. The two are intricately and intimately connected, across space and through time, as he makes clear in *Notes for a New Culture*. Here, the author, in a reading of Eliot's *The Waste Land*, suggests that the self 'is constituted by the past of written literature' (*NNC* 54), while the poem as a whole is to be understood as a writing exercise 'that implicitly denies the realm of orthodox meaning' (*NNC* 56). Such ludic performativity creates undecidability and, with it, the possibility of the text's regenerative affirmation. Resistant to being pinned down by the location of a single meaning, writing is the chance of continuation, of inheritance and survival.

However, for readers brought up in the Anglo-Saxon tradition described and criticised by Ackroyd in *Notes for a New Culture* (and much to David Lodge's chagrin in his review of that book [1976][1]), the weave of writing in its play with what we take for 'reality' can cause uncertainty. Historical 'truth', a definable past, and 'the real' are names we give to discourses so as to deny their discursivity, and the purpose of such naming is to domesticate, to explain, and therefore to control. However, the text can be always be read as articulating the opposite: it can be read as encouraging us to think at least twice about the ways in which we see and interpret the world. For the most part, for instance, we trust that the words we use to communicate with one another are reliably meaningful. Yet in reading the words of a fiction we imaginatively interpret what we have learned conventionally to comprehend as what Roland Barthes has called the 'reality effects' of language (Barthes 1982, 11–18), so as to maintain the referential illusion while creating possible worlds, different ways of seeing. To this end, the act of writing is one that highlights the unreliability of words, making them speak of the unreal, while mimicking that same voice by which we trust them to speak of a supposedly knowable reality.

Literal or fictional languages both conjure up uncertain realities: they articulate the space between the real and the words we use to interpret, translate, represent or stage the 'real', so called. What language comprehended as writing, rather than language understood as voice, does, is to challenge any simply received or conventionally understood notion of a correspondence between what we call words and what we choose to call 'reality', or the simple representation of the latter by the former. Writing foregrounded *as* writing, as both textual and textile, inserts itself between the word and the world; unfolding this binary economy which is at the heart of all such logic, writing unfolds a space in which to write, even as it enfolds prior traces, partially obscuring them. Ackroyd's writing inhabits this uncertain space with relish. His writing confronts issues of reality, of mimesis and representation in favour of performance, play and texture. Erasing the authorial voice and all post-romantic conceits that accompany this notion, Ackroyd opens onto the weft of all writing as a discontinuous chain of being. In doing so, he plays in the chiasmus between writing and reading, rewriting *as* rereading, and vice versa – and all of this as part of the ludic gesture which, through its various gambits seeks, in the words of Linda Hutcheon, to 'de-naturalize representation' (Hutcheon 1989, 95).

For Ackroyd the denaturalizing of representation involves continual performance; it involves in part the foregrounding of stylistic gestures which are culturally and historically specific and yet altered through being reinvented by the game of modern writing. It is this very gesture which, for Ackroyd, demonstrates an understanding of what it means to be English. Whether by pastiche, parody or some other knowing turn, Ackroyd creates an ironic distance in the moment of most intimate proximity to his subject, which through such sleight of hand, shows him to be the most English of writers, even though his Englishness is of an other kind to that of critics such as Christopher Ricks, Martin Dodsworth and David Lodge. Ackroyd's Englishness belongs to the alternative tradition of camp performativity; one performed in one instance through 'elegant Italian suits' and permed hair, as Ackroyd explains in describing his difference from mainstream English literati (Appleyard 1989).

Ackroyd makes us aware of his Englishness by showing us precisely to what extent his writing is not so much an unaware expression or representation of Englishness as it is a pantomimic impersonation of it. Like Max Miller's asides and confidences, Ackroyd's knowing nods to the literary are never quite real, yet we comprehend the truth of them. In the words of Miller, he 'has a go'. In his as yet unpublished 'London Lecture' for London Weekend Television (LWT), in December 1993, Ackroyd describes what he considers to be a characteristic of English art, that is, a self-conscious exploitation of stylistic mannerisms from various historical periods which is to be found everywhere in his publications:

> Some thirty-eight years ago Nicholas Pevsner gave a very interesting series of lectures on the Englishness of English art, and he located one of the enduring features of English style as what he called 'historicism', by which he meant the interest in English artists and architects in the self-conscious use of past styles, and in experimenting in the details of various historical periods.

Clearly this remark is self-referential, easily applicable to the techniques of construction and performance the author employs in writing novels. The remark also relates closely to the function of transvestism as seen by Ackroyd and discussed in the Introduction.

Through his biographical subjects and the major historical figures of his fiction, self-conscious performative Englishness emerges from Ackroyd's works as, principally, an alternative tradition (one of subversion and laughter) and a theatrical gambit: from Catholicism and ceremonial, to music hall and pantomime, history and the present become stages on which performances can be enacted. And the material for Ackroyd's performances is the history of English literature. Becoming more specific, Ackroyd goes on to add, in the LWT lecture, that he feels that there exists a peculiar 'London genius' for the eclectic assimilation of artistic styles, and indeed for London itself as the generous host of the different, multiple realities for which these styles might speak:

> But when we talk about stylistic variety, when we talk about display or heterogeneity, we are discussing something very close to what I have outlined tonight as the characteristic London genius.

Ackroyd's writing then has, arguably, consistently been concerned with a response to, if not a notion of, a self-conscious, often camp, frequently theatrical Englishness, of which his own writing is a part and which statements such as those from the LWT lecture self-reflexively perform, as we have already suggested. But it is very much a stylized Englishness that has been established through the imaginations of the artists of England's capital, London, and through the imaginative re-inventions of London itself, as will be discussed at length below in the final chapter.

Such knowing stylization, especially with regard to the depiction of London, has become one of the distinguishing characteristics of Ackroyd's prose, as he adopts the imagined voices of the past and interpolates them with a highly mannered, *written or textualized* version of the present, fabricating alternative pasts in the process. However, while the image of London recurs, the image alters and changes with its recurrence, so that we could not elevate the frequency of London's representation to a thematic level. The author's use of past styles of writing suggests his interest in the ability of fiction and narrative play to speak of different realities in different times, and the continual spectral trace of the past in the present moment. By performing through the language of past styles – whether from architecture, literature, music – Ackroyd argues that the ways of seeing that such stylization created can be re-created in the present, bringing the past into the present in a way that can transform our perceptions of both, and the relations between them.

Effectively, Ackroyd suggestively undermines any discrete and stable notion of the present, whether this is what we call our present, some past-present, or some supposed future-present.[2] The ironic adherence to the styles of English writing, recuperated and reinvented, makes plain the fact that the present is neither a present, nor a presence as such. It is instead a textual weave, both an affect and effect of writing, as in the example of the constant interpolation of writing styles, of 'voices', as the manifestation of events which ghost one another, as in both *Hawksmoor* and *The House of Doctor Dee*. In the words of Jacques Derrida, 'the text overruns the limits assigned to it' (1991, 257). This is nowhere more apparent in either novel than in the overlay, in different 'styles' or registers where similar events are narrated at the endings and beginnings of chapters, so that the present destabilizes as one moment bleeds into and contaminates the other reciprocally. The example of London in Ackroyd's writing may be said to be that figure which performs the co-existence of multiple writings, multiple narratives, multiple and heterogeneous weaves and moments, all of which overdetermine the act of story-telling.

Ackroyd explains in the London Lecture that the display of stylistic mannerism is as much a matter of what is written, what is textual, *today* – a series of 'todays', not simply today, the here and now, as though this were fixed and present – as that which has been written in the past. The past is no more fixed than is the present or, indeed, the future. Frequently, Ackroyd writes out these movements in a specific set of contexts, all of which pertain to London. The city may be understood to have helped shape and continues to shape narrative form and the representation of the self. (Even in *Wilde* and *Milton*, the two novels which rely least on London for setting, the city determines or mediates in some part, some aspect of fictive subjectivity.) As he explains here:

> this variety, this heterogeneity, is of more than just historical interest. It means that it can include and empower anything which strays within its bounds. That is why London writing is always open to new themes and new concerns. In our time this has included black writing, gay writing, feminist writing: I could mention here Michael Phillips, or Neil Bartlett, or Jeanette Winterson, whose identities as strikingly individual writers are strengthened by their association with London. I'm not talking about one, exclusive, inheritance, in other words, or in some form of private property. I'm describing an open sensibility which is continually being regenerated.

It is in terms of this notion of regeneration that Ackroyd's stylizations and readings of English history and literature can best be understood. There are two aspects to this.

First, that Ackroyd holds a belief in the endurance in English culture of a Catholicism which explains much of the character of English history and literature, while being a supposedly marginal influence with the establishment in England of Anglicism and Protestantism.[3] Ackroyd's writing engages with what he perceives to be this Catholic inheritance and in the more visionary aspects of his writing suggests that it is some kind of true home or mode of being that can regenerate and be regenerated by the transcendental identity of those who seek it. Secondly, this regeneration is manifest, more technically, as less of a continuous tradition, and more of a radical re-imagining of the past and of figures from the past. Ackroyd literally regenerates the past as he reinvents and performs it through his own creations. The 'present' and 'reality' give way before the differential play of English writing and London narratives. All of which serves to destabilise and make uncertain supposedly fixable meanings as indicators of some so-called truth in literary discourse.

Ackroyd can be distinguished from among the greater number of his contemporaries, then, through his adherence to what one might call the imaginative or performative and self-conscious, as opposed to the realist, literary traditions. In this, he marks himself as both eccentric and anachronistic. His work may well resemble certain strands of what is called postmodernism or magical realism, if by the use of those terms, we unproblematically situate Ackroyd's texts within purely formalist concerns, which take no account of literature's history. Seeing Ackroyd as a writer indebted to pre-romantic anti-realist and, even, 'nonaristotelian'[4] modes of narrative, we come to understand how Ackroyd is not a postmodernist or magic realist *per se* but, instead, belongs to an alternative tradition, alive in both English and European writing from the early modern period onwards. Ackroyd at least shares concerns with self-conscious form, with Cervantes, Sterne, Hogg, Carlyle, Proust, Joyce, Borges, to name only the most obvious.[5] If we return to the London Lecture, we find that, in terms of this so-called English style,[6] there is a question at stake of authenticity and the performative resistance on the part of self-conscious stylization to organic form:

Perhaps that's why Pevsner chose so many examples of London architecture in order to make his point. He describes a gentlemen's club in Pall Mall that is made to look like a Renaissance Italian palace, he talks about Holloway Prison conceived as a Gothic castle, and of Wren's Church of St. Mary Aldermary in Queen Victoria Street, which is an amalgam of fourteenth and seventeenth century styles. I'd like to mention one of my own favourite architects here, Nicholas Hawksmoor, who could create two sets of designs, one in Baroque the other in Gothic, and allow the appropriate authorities to choose according to their taste. If you go into some of the older London churches you will find, as Pevsner notes, Elizabethan funereal monuments designed to look medieval. It's reminiscent of the work of Thomas Chatterton, who committed suicide in a street near the Grays Inn Road: in the middle of the eighteenth century that doomed young man was writing *authentic* medieval ballads.

(emphasis added)

'Authentic' as used here by Ackroyd does not signify that Chatterton's poems are written in the thirteenth or fourteenth centuries, obviously. Instead, by this use of the word, Ackroyd intends to convey a sense of authenticity of sensibility, rather than one of mimetic fidelity.

The author is thus effectively engaged in unveiling the deconstructive poss-ibilities of what we call literary language, through techniques of parasitism, grafting, pastiche, contamination and parody – all of which are exemplary ludic structures and strategies. The infinite variety and invention of different languages and styles of language used is the clearest testimony to the funda-mental uncertainties language necessarily contains: that there is no finally authentic, or non-fictional, mode of representing the world.

Yet, at the risk of repetition, and to amplify on an earlier point, in order to avoid offering a facile reading of Ackroyd's texts as 'postmodernist' – where the principal concern is supposedly with language games and that, ultimately, Ackroyd's work only ever refers to prior works of fiction – we need to under-stand that writing is not merely a device for representation.[7] It is necessary to comprehend how, in the words of Susan M. Griffin, 'character *is* fictional structure' (Griffin 1991, 4). Talking of visual perception in the late texts of Henry James, Griffin's understanding is pertinent to our approach to Peter Ackroyd who, like James, is clearly to be understood as a stylist concerned with the possibilities of narrative form. Unlike James, however, Ackroyd is removed enough from the drag of realism, so that his artifice is more fre-quently foregrounded. Ackroyd interests himself with the ways in which we structure narratives and the outcomes this can have. Ackroyd perceives history 'not as a body of determined and determining facts, but [as] a text ...' (Griffin 1991, 4); writing is, in the texts of Ackroyd (as Griffin points out it is for James, albeit in a very different manner), 'the *experience* [in writing] of identity over time' (Griffin 1991, 5). Identity – the self, the subject – is *written* and this is both a temporal as well as a spatial act, as Ackroyd makes us aware.

Language is, then, a means by which we may speak of our experiences of our worlds and ourselves, not a true rendition of the world. The performance of an identity *takes time*; it is constructed across a space, the space which writing reveals in being traced across, as well as being involved with, the double time of writing and re-telling. And, as we read in *Chatterton*:

> There is nothing more real than words. They are reality ... The poet does not merely recreate or describe the world. He actually creates it. And that is why he is feared.
>
> (*C* 210)

This is the fear of the world and its values being turned upside down by radi-cally different ways of seeing, so inimical to those complacent Anglo-Saxon habits of reading identified by the novelist. Indeed it is precisely this disruptively creative potential in language that fires Ackroyd's scepticism about purportedly natural realities and his faith in invented realities, first explored explicitly in *Notes for a New Culture*.

Notes for a New Culture

Notes for a New Culture: An Essay on Modernism (1976) offers a forcefully argued, if flawed, critique of English cultural and philosophical traditions. It provides, in the words of Susana Onega, 'a comprehensive critical assessment of the parallel yet divergent evolutions of English and European cultures from the late seventeenth century to the present era' (1998, 5). In this essay, one can discern an early consideration of certain of Peter Ackroyd's recurring preoccupations with written language and the concomitant construction of identity. Equally, if not more importantly, in this book we have a polemical, if not a theoretical, model by which to measure the subsequent writing. It is not going too far to suggest that Ackroyd's later disdain for conventional narrative form is given first airing in this early volume of critical thinking. *Notes* is both a critique of literary *mores* of the time and also a critique of what Ackroyd considers to be an enduring subjective humanism in English modernism, a culture of literary stagnation in contrast to a more radical continental modernism. Brian Finney's summary expresses astutely those elements which, we feel (do we not?) are the real reasons for the furious responses of David Lodge and Christopher Ricks in their reviews:

> ... seen in a British context, his assertion that form and language constitute the true subject of contemporary modernism ... was inflammatory material. In the book he ridicules F. R. Leavis's belief in the moral force of literature. He also deplores the English subscription to a great tradition of literature (as defined by Leavis) built on a conventional aesthetic which rests on key notions of 'subjectivity' and 'experience'.
>
> (Finney 1992, 241)

Ackroyd's criticisms of Anglo-Saxon modernism and British critical practice point explicitly to its recuperations in empiricist and positivist epistemologies, while, historically, he seeks to resituate the rise of modernism by aligning its first birth pangs in the Age of Enlightenment. Moreover, in positioning such contentious, though not unfounded, arguments, Ackroyd discounts literary realism through arguments that emphasize the self-referentiality of language. Furthermore, Ackroyd, quoting Derrida, suggests that language, specifically literary language, is the express play of (or in) structure; it is 'ce jeu, pensé comme l'absence du signifié transcendental' [that play, thought as the absence of the transcendental signified] (*NNC* 144).[8] Through his arguments we can begin to see ways in which his own writing fits into, or responds to this assessment: to go, in his words, 'beyond humanism'; to develop his interest in the 'creative discovery of theory' he identifies in continental culture. In this there is a certain element, yet again, of performative pastiche inasmuch as his oblique and very English relationship to continental philosophy may be taken as analogous to the earlier relationships of Coleridge and Arnold to German idealist philosophy, discussed by Ackroyd in *Notes* (*NNC* 30–6).

Written in the early 1970s while the author was at Yale University, completed in 1973, and first published in 1976, *Notes* was a prescient reading, if not an informed and somewhat arch staging of radical continental theory and philosophy in relation to literature. The book engages with a number of theoretical positions, especially those of Jacques Lacan and Jacques Derrida. Ackroyd is in self-assertively polemical style mapping and drawing on continental thought to trace his own path away from an implicitly moralistic humanism in English literature and academic culture:

> The 'humanism' which the universities sustain, and which our realistic literature embodies, is the product of historical blindness.
>
> (*NN* 147)

> The humanism which we take to be our inheritance and our foundation – apparently unaware of its origin in the late seventeenth-century – has turned out to be an empty strategy, without philosophical content or definitive form.
>
> (*NN* 148)

Universities, or, more specifically, English Departments, in Great Britain have since been developing the kinds of theoretical commitments Ackroyd then saw them lacking (though not all of them equally or, in some cases with anything like unalloyed enthusiasm). Certainly they were in the processes of exploring continental thought at the time of the publication of *Notes*. As a result, literature is now considered less in terms of reflecting the human condition, and more as a means by which we realize the mediations of the realities we imagine we should see. In other words, that 'reality' is an interpretation of the way humans imagine it ought to be, whether by art or science, rather than the arts and sciences apparently reflecting the 'true' conditions of 'reality', so called.

Ackroyd may well have changed positions somewhat since writing *Notes for a New Culture* – at first glance it is difficult to reconcile the position of this early text with the implicit concerns with English tradition readable in *English*

Music – but Ackroyd's interest in language, as much a result of the influence of John Ashbery as it is Jacques Lacan, as much an inheritance from Frank O'Hara or Ronald Firbank as it is from Stéphane Mallarmé or Jacques Derrida, is still in evidence. As Brian Finney puts it, summarizing Ackroyd's position stated in an interview, '[r]eading literature may make you a better writer ... but not a better person' (Finney 1992, 243).[9]

The Great Fire of London

To discuss Ackroyd's writing it is important to question just what one might be referring to when using the label 'text'. Part of what a text 'is' is contingent upon what it becomes when it is read. This engagement is sophisticated in that part of the process of reading involves acknowledging the conventions by which stories exist to be experienced. Stories cannot mirror the endless chaos and multiplicity of actual experiences, but rather orchestrate selected mediations of such experiences over a teleological foundation. In structuring sequences of events, those events, in their structured form, are apparently dislocated from the never-beginning and never-ending historical flow of actual experience, and the unquantifiable space of all events. How this structured representation of events is ordered raises questions about the functioning of narrative.

The Great Fire of London is Ackroyd's first foray into novel form. In this first novel, Ackroyd explicitly links his novel writing debut to Charles Dickens's *Little Dorrit*, as is well known. It also demonstrates Ackroyd's interest in what Susana Onega terms 'transhistorical connectedness' (1998, 28). This connectedness is, however, specifically a textual or written structure which, because of its interweaving of Dickensian and modern elements suggests (again in Onega's words) that 'the boundaries between fiction and reality are nonexistent, that the difference between "fictional" characters and "real" people, and between "real" and "fictional" worlds, simply does not hold' (1998, 30). At its beginning, *The Great Fire of London* purports to be a twentieth-century continuation from where Book One of Dickens's novel ends. It is a novel which shows, amongst other things, that the 'past is unrepeatable' (Finney 1992, 243). We see this from the example of the preface.

The narrative is prefaced with a brief summary of Dickens's story, headed by Ackroyd 'the story so far' (*GFOL* 3). Even this phrase is 'unoriginal' and yet playfully mocking of the conventions of nineteenth-century serial fiction. Outside the novel proper, serving as a connective fibre between texts, this novel begins before it begins, presenting itself as no beginning at all but stitching itself to that prior work with the performative phrase which exists out of time. With this, readers are immediately encouraged to consider the ambiguity between reality and illusion in a world of fiction as they consider two texts separated in time by over 100 years – but both of which might be considered to offer some kind of contemporary mediation of their respective 'realities'. In suspending one's disbelief imaginatively to accept the internal reality of Ackroyd's story, one also has to accommodate the ghostly apparition of a character from a different fictional paradigm.

Ackroyd's textual model is no more (or less) 'actual' than Dickens's, and that both novels are narrative constructions is conventionally a consideration the reader is allowed to ignore. However, Ackroyd confronts passive acceptance of this illusion by inviting the spirit of the world of *Little Dorrit*, and the spirit of the character Amy Dorrit, the child of the Marshalsea, into his text, as he will later do in his biography of Charles Dickens. As the preface concludes:

> This is the first part of the novel which Charles Dickens wrote between 1855 and 1857. Although it could not be described as a true story, certain events have certain consequences ...
>
> (*GFOL* 3)

Ackroyd's placing of *The Great Fire of London* within a literary frame of reference, by citing its precedent in Dickens's *Little Dorrit*, demands of the reader that the former's context partly be constructed in relation to the latter: a communion of fictional reference.

At the same time, Ackroyd calls into question our prior knowledge of narratives before we have even begun the novel, specifically through the device of 'the story so far'. However, this device is 'inaccurate' with regard to the details given of the narrative of *Little Dorrit*. Ackroyd states in his preface that, together, Arthur Clennam and Pancks discover the 'truth' about Little Dorrit's family inheritance (*GFOL* 3); this is not the case, Pancks alone discovers this. Also, the preface states that Amy Dorrit's friend, Maggy, is known as Little Mother, when, in fact, this is also not the case, Little Mother being Maggy's name for Little Dorrit. This second 'error' occurs throughout the novel, as Galen Strawson points out in his review. As he also points out, with a generosity lacking in some reviewers, 'most fiction is made from altered fact, and can be made from altered fiction too' (1982). The past, whether the historical or literary past, is truly unrepeatable. The epistemological uncertainty which Ackroyd establishes makes it difficult to 'neutralize the game he is playing', as Luc Herman puts it with reference to *Hawksmoor* (1990, 122).

We see this elsewhere. To move back before the moment of the preface before the beginning: the title itself narrates and recalls a historical fact which, while providing the title, never takes place as a narrative of that historical fact in the novel as such. The Great Fire of 1666 is merely, here, a narrative occasion for a fictive dislocation between history as fact and history as writing. Where the Great Fire of 1666 does occur is as a 'preface' of sorts to *Hawksmoor*.

Outside the novel, it provides the reason for the rebuilding of the churches of the City of London. This would not be worth mentioning at this point, were it not for the fact (an overworked word in the context of writing about a novelist whose play with facts teaches us to distrust their supposed truths), that, in *The Great Fire of London*, Spenser Spender, the film-maker intent on filming *Little Dorrit*, points out to his wife that if lines were drawn between the churches of Nicholas Hawksmoor this would form a pentangle (*GFOL* 16).

If the past is unrepeatable, the future is all too easily iterable, as historical and textual detail interweave.[10] The 'real' fire of London of Ackroyd's first novel begins as a conflagration on a film set, a place for the performance and technological re-invention of narrative illusion and illusory narrative.[11] The place of this fire, and the historical moment signalled through it by the title, is one of the first of many examples in the text of Peter Ackroyd of the interaction between the traces of the past and technology, another being the comic 'connection' between Audrey's mediumistic powers and her job as a telephone exchange operative.

These examples of epistemological confusion caused by the play of textual details and historical facts, where narrative and historical pasts are all available as part of the textual weave, suggest Ackroyd's confrontation with the idea of a stable identity. Details of other texts are performed and reinvented within Ackroyd's writing, seeming to locate, contextualize, and identify it both historically and fictionally, while simultaneously dislocating any single location or identity. It is appropriate in any discussion of Ackroyd's writing, therefore, to think of the distinction between history and fiction, or between one narrative and another, one textual trace and another, as always blurred. Also, Ackroyd is careful to construct his texts with an organizational intricacy similar to Dickens's, intertwining plot strands which gradually converge. In *The Great Fire of London* we find Spenser Spender musing over similar concerns:

> For once, Spenser Spender had a sense of other peoples' lives – of a different set of constrictions, of other and more difficult circumstances than his own. And yet his life was linked with theirs, and all who had preceded or would follow them.
>
> (*GFOL* 36–7)

The desire for and sense of connections recur from the poetry through the novels to the most recent of the biographies. Because connection is, in every example, a different type of connection – historical, personal, literary, national – it cannot be said to be a consistent theme in Ackroyd's writing. However, precisely because we cannot talk of connections in relation to some literary-critical discussion of thematics, connection disconnects, even as it is profoundly, idiomatically, textual in every case. The sense of connection felt by Spender connects text and self, weaving self into a textured sense of being.

There are many other references to the idea of what Derrida has termed 'a fabric of traces referring endlessly … to other differential traces' in the narrative, conspicuously foregrounded. For example, We read of the interpolation of the past as fiction into a present fictional reality, thereby transforming past and present:

> … *Little Dorrit* was no longer his fantasy. It was, now, a reality …
>
> (*GFOL* 54)

or, in a more complex moment,

> The music from a juke-box collided with that from the television set, making an awkward counterpoint between the fake Victorian tune and the real contemporary one.
>
> (*GFOL* 10)

This of course is a direct parallel for the novel itself. Once again, the act of writing takes on a self-knowing performative air, as technology is used to invoke a disjointing spirit, a spectral trace through different times, where the *faux*-Victorian melody comments indirectly on the impossibility of recovering the truth of the past as anything other than a textual simulacrum or palimpsest. It also speaks to the nostalgia for an imagined past which is so typical in western culture at the end of the twentieth century. As a motif for Ackroyd's practice, the mock musical hall tune works nicely. It suggests that Ackroyd never lets us forget that his 'historical' voices are always pantomimic and playful impersonations. They are no more real than Audrey's possession by Amy Dorrit. The tune, already a fake or imitation, is dressed up in knowing reference to a particularly artificial form of entertainment. As the confusion which issues from the technologies suggests, Ackroyd's writing, in the immediate example of *The Great Fire of London* and in the more general example of all his texts, engages in what Gérard Genette describes in defining parody as 'playful distortion' (Genette 1997, 24). While parody is but one gambit employed by Ackroyd, and while every text is absolutely singular and must be respected as such, nonetheless, Ackroyd's engagement with literary stylization is transformative rather than imitative.

Once more, in terms of constructing a fabrication, resulting in a dislocation from any simple or simply knowable reality or identity, the transformative and performative gambit is seen here:

> The black canvas was hoisted up even higher above the set, and several smaller canvas awnings were placed in position beside it, *in order to create*

darkness where there had been none before. Black felt was tacked into place along the narrow alley between the warehouses, and the sides of the vast and empty buildings had been coated in grey paint. Spenser Spender supervised the work, alternately looking through the camera which was now pointed away from the river and towards the warehouses. They rose in front of him like houses of darkness, oppressive yet *unreal. They had been transformed into replicas of warehouses. Reality itself had been suspended.*

(*GFOL* 108; emphases added)

The passage is exemplary in its attention to surfaces, to the forms of artifice and the artifice of forms. Darkness, so conventionally considered as the natural and inevitable absence of light, is, here, created by the director. The canvas, connected to the grey paint which overlays the buildings, is suggestive of the possibility of a landscape painting, which is given further intimation, through the first name of the director which, were we intent on seeking national-artistic inheritance, speaks possibly of two other Spensers, Edmund and Stanley, both of whom, like Ackroyd himself, involve themselves and their texts in the landscape of artifice and allegory, and both of whom have a stake, each in his own singular fashion, in the textual construction of a version of Englishness.[12] As the scene becomes a scene, that is to say, framed through the lens and made to assume an artificiality through directorial intervention, the real is absorbed into and erased by its own simulacra. Given the setting, even the adjectival choice – unreal – is not so much simply descriptive as it is evocative of T. S. Eliot's definition of London in *The Waste Land* as the 'Unreal City'.[13] Spenser Spender is, of course, attempting to direct his film version of *Little Dorrit* on location in those parts of London where Dickens set his novel. He becomes so wrapped up in his work that his wife, Laetitia, leaves him for a shallow socialite, Andrew, a liaison she subsequently regrets. Spender seeks advice on the screenplay from Rowan Phillips, a tutor at Cambridge University who is researching Dickens in order eventually to produce an academic textbook.

The other two plot strands follow the Dickens connection in more intricate, intertextual, ways. First, Rowan has a brief affair with Tim Coleman, who is having a relationship with Audrey Skelton. Audrey becomes 'possessed' by the spirit of Amy Dorrit, as already noted (and as, perhaps, does Peter Ackroyd in his later biography of Charles Dickens[14]) at a seance (a medium and excuse which Ackroyd dispenses with after this novel). Amy infiltrates the text as a 'clear, small voice':

'Where do I come from and where do I go to? London is so large, so barren and so wild.'
'Yes, I know, dear. Tell us a bit more about yourself.'

'Why, sir, I am the child of this place.'
'A little bit more, love. We're interested. We want to help.'
'Little Dorrit. I am the child of the Marshalsea.'

(*GFOL* 40)

We already know by this time that Audrey is liable to role-playing ('she became, as it were, possessed' [*GFOL* 8]), and through this Ackroyd renders more legitimate Audrey's adoption of Amy Dorrit's spirit. Audrey begins to act strangely, becoming obsessed with the novel *Little Dorrit* and beginning to resemble the character of Amy:

It was after this that things started to go wrong ... . She had bought a shawl, second-hand, and would work with it wrapped around her.

(*GFOL* 61)

She eventually burns down Spender's Thames-side film set as if to destroy the modern impostor of Amy's genuine spirit which exists not in film but in narrative, in text. Because Amy exists only as a written or textual identity, Ackroyd's own inclusion of her character in his fiction ought not to be read as being inconsistent with the implied outrage of a filmic appropriation of her. Ackroyd's novel presumes in some way to inhabit the legitimate realm of intertextual authenticity.

The second plot strand concerns Little Arthur, a midget who had stopped growing at age eight (*GFOL* 5), and runs an amusement arcade in Borough High Street.[15] Whenever the reader encounters Little Arthur the present tense is used for the narrative. This tends to displace Arthur and his excursions from the rest of the narrative somewhat, while reading something like a film treatment. This exclusive temporal displacement sits oddly against the rest of the novel, more conventionally related. His name clearly echoes and conflates that of both Little Dorrit and Arthur Clennam from Dickens's novel. The association with Arthur Clennam is strengthened when the narrative enters Little Arthur's thoughts and we are told,

He will make a point of saving her – make a point of it. All that innocence cannot go to pot.

(*GFOL* 42)

That repeated phrase in the first sentence suggests a verbal 'tic' on Arthur's part and, indeed, his speech patterns appear to have a tendency to reproduce, albeit in parodic form, certain mannerisms of various characters from Dickens's novels. There is something of Quilp, but also of Jenny Wren, the dolls' dressmaker from *Our Mutual Friend,* about Little Arthur. The concern of

Little Arthur's for a small girl also echoes Clennam's paternalistic concern for Amy Dorrit, especially when recalling Dickens's description of Amy as very childlike in appearance: '... Arthur found that her diminutive figure, small features, and slight spare dress, gave her the appearance of being much younger than she was ... . she had all the manner and much of the appearance of a subdued child' (Dickens 1988, 93). The irony is that Arthur Clennam comes to desire Dorrit because she seems so much like a subdued child, while Little Arthur, looking little more than a parody of childhood, desires female children.

Clennam's concern with, and for, Amy Dorrit, ultimately leads to Pancks's discovery that the Dorrit family, although incarcerated in the Marshalsea, are in fact heirs to a great fortune. But the relationship is transformed and played with in Ackroyd's text: Little Arthur harbours a dangerous obsession for young girls. He takes up a bread knife, goes out and, coaxing a girl, kills her in the delusion of possessing her as his 'love' on the site of the Marshalsea prison (*GFOL* 30). He is locked away in the modern prison where, in a disused wing, Spenser Spender is filming his version of *Little Dorrit*.

But coming back to an earlier point that Ackroyd deliberately makes clear the constructed nature of his narrative and foregrounds intertextual allusions, narrative tricks and other textual signposts, it must be observed that the climax of this book could only operate successfully under such conditions. In it a significant portion of London is supposed to burn down, but Ackroyd's description of the fire is cursory:

> Tim turned towards the river, as if for relief. But it had become brilliant and fiery, taking on the shape and quickness of the flame. The city's skyline was hidden by smoke, and the surrounding neighbourhood was fully ablaze. A strong wind was blowing, pushing the flames forward. They burnt for a day and a night. It seemed to Tim that they would burn for ever, taking the whole of London with them.
>
> (*GFOL* 165)

That is Ackroyd's great fire of London – otherwise the descriptions of the fire are relegated to its origin in the film set. The real is almost ineffable, while it is the question of staging which takes precedence. It is nearly impossible to talk of the fire as such, and so the performance of the fire is considered. Even in the description above the emphasis is on the reflection, the representation of the flames in the Thames and the wind. The Great Fire of London cannot be repeated, any more than *Little Dorrit*, except as staged, and sometimes stagy, devices.

This play is not a frivolous game, however. Ackroyd's re-invention of the spirit of Little Dorrit through the activation of textual traces in which it once existed – its characters, its settings – opens his own text as a response to the trace of the other text. Ackroyd's narrative structure takes its cue from Dickens, but Ackroyd upsets the referential illusion from within the narrative itself, turning a self-conscious disclaimer on the whole illusion:

> This is not a true story, but certain things follow from other things. And so it was that, on that Sunday afternoon, that same Sunday when Spenser Spender had died in the Great Fire caused by Audrey, Little Arthur set the prisoners free.
>
> (*GFOL* 169)

Ackroyd's flirtation with Dickens and Little Dorrit is less a matter of style, than a comparison of different versions of a similar faith in the imaginative world. The unrepeatability of the past is even caught in the opening line of the quotation above, which is itself a reinvention of the last words of 'the story so far', in which it is stated that '[a]lthough it could not be described as a true story, certain events have certain consequences' (*GFOL* 3). In *The Great Fire of London* we find not a real world but one composed of mannerisms, performances. This indeed anticipates the 'world' of *Dan Leno and the Limehouse Golem*, in which, as one reviewer puts it, 'Ackroyd has Dickensian ambitions and tries to show a city full of interlocking coincidences leading inexorably to tragedy .... The intricacies of his plot seem ultimately to trace vectors rather than lives' (Gray 1995). Such a criticism of course is rooted in the aesthetic comparison which is set up in the use of the pronominal adjective, 'Dickensian'. Ackroyd respects the otherness of previous texts too much to aim at a simple reproduction, unaware of its own cultural location. Given Ackroyd's dislike for realism as an aesthetic mode of representation (expressed frequently but, perhaps most forcefully in that review of *The Company of Wolves*), the criticism of Ackroyd's characters as merely 'vectors' need not be a criticism at all. Instead, we can comprehend such figures and the curt ending of *Great Fire* as an initial 'working-out' of a particular dynamic in Ackroyd's fiction, which will become reiterated in different and differing ways in the novels which come after this.

While *The Great Fire of London* seems to flounder at its conclusion for a purpose for its own existence, Ackroyd can be said to discover other ways of seeing and playing, upon which his novel writing has developed, in particular the technique of literary ventriloquism, first attempted in the next novel, *The Last Testament of Oscar Wilde*, the start of his fascination in his writing with London visionaries, in *Hawksmoor*, and the ability of artifice to challenge notions of authenticity in *Chatterton*. It is almost as if *The Great Fire of London* ultimately gives way in its collapsing ending. Eaten up in the flames which consume narrative convention, Ackroyd clears the stage in order to play with other, more compelling ideas, and to explore other styles.

The Last Testament of Oscar Wilde

With *The Last Testament of Oscar Wilde* Ackroyd explores for the first time a territory that has in many ways been his subject ever since, that is, the common ground between biographer and novelist. Where that common ground exists, so also does the disruption and cross-contamination of conventional divisions between fact and fiction, between biography and fictional narrative, versions, visions and re-visions of the past and present. It is, as Laura Giovannelli suggests, the first of Ackroyd's novels which works out the opposition between fact and fiction through the paradigm of *travestimento*: disguise and costume (1996, 77).[16] Initially and ultimately these are questions concerned with the performance of identity and the resistance to a single identity.

Written in the first person as a journal, a form which, as Ruth Robbins reminds us, is 'always a double form of writing' (1996, 103), Ackroyd employs in this novel the ventriloquism or pantomimickry that has become characteristic of many of his novels. He adopts the stylistic 'personae' of Wilde, performing the discursive and rhetorical gestures of the other writer, in the prosopopaeic play which opens the space for a rendition of his imagined reality of Wilde through the artistry of its articulation: the reader is conjured – albeit only ever partially – into the illusion that this is an autobiographical journal of Wilde's last days.

Here Ackroyd is experimentally adopting or impersonating a well-known 'style', hauling it away from its historical context, and supposed owner. Moreover, Ackroyd has his Wilde perform in yet another style belonging to literary tradition, as Susana Onega points out: the 'literary tradition of the "confession" of a repenting sinner' (1998, 31). This undoes the specific historical legitimacy of both the style of Wilde and that of a specific genre, since these styles must now operate in a twentieth-century context. In this way Ackroyd inserts his interpretation, or vision, of the past, and uses *that* interpretation reciprocally to colour our understanding of our present-day inheritance. In rethinking the past, we rethink the path that has led to the present. What this technique also does, in a more conventionally literary critical manner, is encourage the reader to rethink the figure of Wilde, and how we have variously interpreted this figure and his history through his writing. Furthermore, we understand this Wilde as only ever an interpretation. At the same time, however, if Wilde's identity is a question of textual play, then the reader is also being put in the position of considering the identity of Ackroyd and the impossibility of gaining access to that identity.

The reviewers of *The Last Testament* register the play with identities, which is Ackroyd's ludic *métier*. Mary Cosh points to the ways in which Ackroyd draws out the paradoxes of Wilde's own sense of identity, paradoxes which were, for Wilde as they are for Ackroyd, performative and strategic rather than accidental and unconscious (1983). Even as Wilde relied on masks, 'disarming by caricature', and the role of the 'clown-dandy' to make his most serious points, so too does Ackroyd. Yet, Roger Lewis argues in his review for *The American Spectator*, while the author is a 'master of disguise ... it is not he who dresses up. His talent is to divine the masquerades of other people' (1984, 39). Furthermore, Lewis suggests, underpinning this performance of Ackroyd's is the figure of the androgyne. This is most immediately apparent when the Wilde of Ackroyd's imagination compares himself with both Miranda and Prospero (*LTOW* 8). Whether it is the androgyne – who is merely mythical – or the transvestite – who is merely anxious (*DU* 18) – who informs Ackroyd's performance of Wilde, the important thing is that the identity of Wilde is never single, though it is singular. When Wilde, or Ackroyd posing as Wilde, says 'I am an "effect" merely: the meaning of my life exists in the minds of others and no longer in my own' (*LTOW* 2) this is as much as to admit that one's identity is never one's own simply. Rather it is a projection, at least in part. It is the manifest desire of others seeking to define the contours of some dimly perceived subject. This is all the more complex when the subject acknowledges not only its own writtenness but also its own multiplicity:

> 'I feel like Andrea del Sarto in Browning's exquisite poem,
> Had I been two, another and myself,
> Our work would have o'erlooked the world'.

(LTOW 66)

Ackroyd's Wilde is not only self-conscious and self-aware, he is also, by his own admission, defined by the traces of the textual.

This is of course 'not exactly Wilde but pseudo-Wilde or just plain Ackroyd', as Andrew Hislop puts it, someone who 'rewrites Wilde – employs, mutates, promotes, even mutilates his writings' as he adopts a mask in a 'clever but precarious game' (1983). Certainly the game is precarious for it involves playing on the very edges of definable identity, and letting the reader know that the stability of identity is being played with all the time. If the game is precarious it is because the play is vertiginous, the reader bedazzled. There is a doubleness here, and not merely surrounding Wilde, or a certain version of Wilde. Ackroyd's playfulness has a serious purpose beyond this novel. The novelist can be read as engaging in acts of radical prosopopoeia, whereby the play of character and the 'dressing up' in the form of others speaks to the very sense of identity, of what it means 'to be'. Identity is displaced from itself and within itself through Ackroyd's acts of writing the self. These resist, in the words of Ruth Robbins, 'stable interpretations and definitions of the self', which, even as they are written, are 'also haunted by a fear that the multiplicity of significance which [many of Ackroyd's characters] always [embrace] might simply collapse into meaninglessness' (Robbins 1996, 103). This is the case, though never addressed in the same manner twice, whether one considers Ackroyd's performance of Wilde, Chatterton, Dickens, Eliot, Dee, Milton or any of the other performative and playful characters who inhabit the author's texts. If language is the 'house of being' to borrow Martin Heidegger's famous dictum, then Ackroyd's principal players frequently feel homeless, never at home with themselves. It is this feeling of the uncanny which disturbs so often Ackroyd's readers.

The roles of the biographer and novelist, far from calming things down, work to open up the reader and the subject to new forces. They are equally reliant on the mediation of interpretation, translation, invention or pseudo-invention and, in Ackroyd's case, plagiarism. This play of forces involves and relies on the 'pseudo-speculative character' (Picard 1986, 192) of the 'what if', whereby the life of someone who has existed and is not merely a fictional character (in this case, Oscar Wilde) is partially re-written and retraced, so that the figure's supposed familiarity for the reader is at once foregrounded *and* estranged. The identity of Wilde is disturbed through a performance that is discernibly Wildean, or quasi-Wildean – there is enough that is familiar to make us feel (do we not?) that this both is and isn't Wilde. As Ackroyd's Wilde states: 'I am positively Whitmanesque. I contain multitudes' (*LTOW* 8). As with the self-referential quotation drawn from Browning already mentioned, the allusion to Whitman does, of course, give the game away, so to speak; inasmuch as this Oscar Wilde admits to his being a subject of discourse as well as being subject to his construction by others. He is nothing other than a performance dependent on the play within a field of textual forces. Such play opens the historical or biographical ground onto the textual *mise en abyme* and is a typically ludic effect (Picard 1986, 192), where the multiplicity of signification can all too easily be mistaken for meaninglessness, to recall Ruth Robbins' discussion of the novel.

The ontological certainties of the conventional historical or biographical narrative fall away before – and *in* – the play between narrative modes, genres, and identities. This ludic gambit is all the more pronounced when the subject is not one, so to speak. 'Oscar Wilde', the ironic, performative, playful discourses that are signed by that name, is always already engaged to a certain extent in the ludic, prior to Ackroyd's rewritings. We already recognise what Michel Picard has called 'l'ambguïté excessive des «signaux d'ironie»' (1986, 191). The excessive ambiguity of the 'signals of irony' installs a powerful undecidability, as Picard goes on to suggest (191) which makes it all but impossible, once again, to stabilize any identity. These ludic effects are redoubled at least and, as is more likely, exponentially increased in Peter Ackroyd's adoption and adaptation of various pseudo-, quasi-, or, occasionally, wholly Wildean personae. Far from asserting an historically knowable Oscar Wilde,

Ackroyd plays implicitly with historical knowledge not for the purpose of pinning Wilde down but, ultimately, in order to make us question what we think we can know about both Wilde and, by implication, any historical figure.

As far as the interaction of historical and biographical text is concerned within what is supposedly a purely fictive context, we can see that the function is not to *explain* the facts of a particular life such as Wilde's, or even to present them as representations of a particular, verifiable reality. Instead the reader encounters a particular translation, interpretation or imaginative understanding of, and response to, what we call 'the facts'. This response is responsible to the spirit of Wilde, even if the performance brings out tensions in the space between the texts of Ackroyd and Wilde. In this way, we come to understand how neither the present nor the past have a stable identity. They are themselves subject to a process of difference within a field of forces which we are unable fully to comprehend, and which is itself open to reinvention.

The journal form is particularly effective as a device where the past can always resurface in and as the present or, at least, a version of the present. Not only is it a double writing as Ruth Robbins suggests (1996, 103), in the sense that a journal is both private and public. It is also double in that, written in the past, as a trace of the past it is only ever readable and re-readable in any given moment which is not the moment of its inscription. The double act of writing and reading is always already separated by the movement of difference. The performance of the journal displaces the self-same from within. The journal is also a series of days or dates, past moments, which are endlessly iterable. Such iteration, we know, serves to disturb any fixed notion of the present as such. The supposedly stable identity of the temporal moment is subsumed in the iterable process, which is already installed in the very idea of the journal, in its structure. Each journal entry, written after the event it places before us, is already a performance of that event and not the event itself. Yet the memory of that event, already a narration, relies on and is 'rooted in the singularity of the event' which the date of the journal assigns (Derrida 1992, 381). In *The Last Testament of Oscar Wilde* various events of different pasts are brought together, as the fictive Wilde performs various versions of his 'selves' at different moments in his life. Ackroyd's text thereby resists definitions based on discrete 'identities' such as biography, history, novel, both for his own writing and that of Oscar Wilde.

It is on this blurred ground, between biography, history and novel, that one must place ludic gestures of *The Last Testament of Oscar Wilde*. Ackroyd's artificial Wildean journal is part construct, part historical or biographical and all performance. He has adopted the mask of Oscar Wilde, the historical figure, but, of course, this textual manifestation cannot be Wilde; the reader can believe, but does not assume, that it really is. In the text itself one is confronted with statements such as 'that is the truth behind the terrible process I was forced to undergo in the courts' (*LTOW* 135). Obviously it is not the *truth*, but this statement in its context becomes credible and we believe it. We feel its poetic veracity rather than distinguishing it as an approximation of an historically verifiable statement. Again, it is a matter not so much of *what* is said here, so much as the *way* in which it has been said. Particularly, the way in which Ackroyd puts words in Wilde's mouth – his tongue firmly in the other's cheek – is, once more, a prosopopaeic act, unveiling this 'truth' through the constant comparison, in this instance, between the court and the stage, between the Old Bailey and the Comédie Française (*LTOW* 136): 'I entered the courtroom of the Old Bailey ... as if I were going upon a stage.... an audience ... had come to watch me perform and I suspect, to forget my lines' (*LTOW* 137). Further on, Wilde will talk of delivery and state that 'I created a drama in which I figured prominently as a benevolent relation' (*LTOW* 138). Directing us through this aesthetic response to the situation of trial – and, in Wilde's case, we feel (do we not?) error – Ackroyd brings us to Wilde's highly self-conscious closing argument with regard to the trial:

> I, who had constructed a philosophy out of the denial of conventional reality, found myself impaled upon it. I had always asserted that an interpretation is more interesting than a fact: I was proved unfortunately to be right. I was destroyed by the sordid interpretations which others gave to my affairs: it is amusing, is it not?
>
> (*LTOW* 138)

From this remark, we may suggest that Ackroyd's play, the scene which he restages, is constructed out of a desire to shift the possibility of interpretation away from the sordidness of that imposed by the High Court and the banality of melodrama which it dictates to Wilde. The closing rhetorical question is part of a performance, which stands self-consciously in between reader and subject, disrupting any illusion of simple mimetic verisimilitude. It leaves it open for the reader to judge matters, and to understand the irony of Wilde's remarks as part of Ackroyd's ludic strategy. Interpretation *is* more interesting than fact; it is also more sympathetic for it allows both novelist and reader to rescue the transgressive identity from being placed in the straitjacket of the *pièce bien fait* of English courtroom drama.

Under the heading '6 October 1900' Ackroyd's Wilde decides to reveal to Bosie and Frank Harris the existence of this journal, which had hitherto been kept in secret, as he is flushed with pride at his account of life in prison, describing it as 'the pearl I had created out of two years' suffering' (*LTOW* 160). Here Ackroyd is allowing the fictional character of Wilde to boast about Ackroyd's own artistic creation or interpretation of Wilde's life. However, in response to this, when Wilde shows the extract to his friends the following exchange is reported:

> 'You cannot publish this Oscar. It is nonsense – and most of it is quite untrue.'
> 'What on earth do you mean?'
> 'It is invented.'
> 'It is my life.'
> 'But you have quite obviously changed the facts to suit your own purpose.'
> 'I have no purpose, and the facts came quite naturally to me.'
>
> (*LTOW* 160)

Harris goes on to point out many errors and plagiarisms. Ackroyd indulges the opportunity to flex his Wildean wit:

> 'And you have stolen lines from other writers. Listen to this one –' 'I did not steal them. I rescued them.'
>
> (*LTOW* 161)

Wilde demands a reaction from Bosie, who in response makes clear the implicit point of this episode, and, by extension, the whole novel:

> 'It's full of lies, but of course you are. It is absurd and mean and foolish. But then you are. Of course you must publish it.'
>
> (*LTOW* 161)

This exchange highlights the fact that even if one were reading a journal by the historical Wilde, one would not have access thereby to some 'genuine reality of its author'; one would still be reading a characterized performance. When Ackroyd's Wilde says of his childhood self that he 'fancifully blurred the distinction between what was true and what was false' (*LTOW* 24), as part of a game of story-telling at school, the reader is made to recognize Ackroyd's own gambit. Ackroyd deliberately isolates the text from any possible corruption from the alternative fiction of factual truth, by pre-empting and disabling any potential claims to greater validity on the part of history or biography. The ludic text disables such claims. Wilde might perhaps be interpreted in a different style through a reading of a journal entry, but not with any certainty. Ackroyd, we can say, albeit in somewhat labyrinthine form, writes Wilde writing, writing himself as a performative figure in writing – and thereby acknowledging the playfulness of Ackroyd's writing – in playful mode, and as nothing other than that: as the text aware of its own status and the constitution of its own identity, resisting all the while the temptation to suggest the possibility of moving beyond or behind the surface. The truth is that there is no truth except as an acknowledgement of the performative inscription.

Ackroyd engages the historical Wilde's interests through his own Wilde to elaborate this idea. The performative nature of writing which affirms itself also resists analysis of the kind which seeks to draw the textual veil aside and so reveal the author, free from all dressing up, transvestitic or otherwise. Ackroyd can be read as drawing on the author's own texts in order to work up the performance of his writing, as an extract from *The Portrait of Mr W. H.* indicates:

> I insisted that [Chatterton's] so-called forgeries were merely the result of an artistic desire for perfect representation; that we had no right to quarrel with an artist for the conditions under which he chooses to present his work; and that all Art being to a certain degree a mode of acting, an attempt to realise one's own personality on some imaginative plane out of reach of the trammelling accidents and limitations of real life, to censure an artist for a forgery was to confuse an ethical with an aesthetical problem.
>
> (Wilde 1994, 302)

The passage from Wilde's text addresses the issues of ludic dissembling and artifice, which is raised not only in *The Last Testament of Oscar Wilde* but throughout Ackroyd's texts. Concerning *The Portrait of Mr W. H.* Ackroyd's Wilde makes the telling comment on this 'extraordinary essay' that it 'was of no concern to me if the facts were accurate or inaccurate: I had discovered a truth which was larger than that of biography or history' (*LTOW* 121).[17] The truth is in the words, in the inscription that speaks of and to itself, not an apparent reality towards which those words gesture. The lesson of Ackroyd's performance of Wilde is that Wilde was and is unknowable, undecidable, always already a series of performances of Wilde, a personality formed and re-formed through acting and the playful adoption of masks.

However, since the reader exposed to the artifice has only an expression of the artist to be interpreted and reiterated at every reading, ultimately the reader will inevitably be put into play also, appreciating and engaging in a performance of his/her own imagination and forms of comprehension. It is in this manner that one begins to comprehend the subtlety of Ackroyd's pastiche. Less a copy, more a carefully orchestrated 'turn', it is a performance, a play on the possibility of constructing from a perceived style a particular identity. Perhaps this seems obvious on an immediate level – of course, Ackroyd wrote it – but it is important to stress the distinction if only so as to apprehend that this 'pure Ackroyd' is nothing other than a question of 'style' as performative play. It no more gives us access to 'Peter Ackroyd' than do the nervous, energetic stylistic rhythms of *Dickens*.

The focus is on the artistic creation *itself*, in Ackroyd's case the artistic ordering of imaginative events in stylized narrative, seeing art as a construct before its character as a representation, or concentrating on the *way* in which it represents, its identity as form and not as meaning. So, in the present case, we return to Ackroyd *via* the artistic construct – the expressive, and seemingly animated mask. The novel is not a portrait of an historical figure, but a performance based upon a reading of an historical figure. Blurring the line between what is true and what is false, Ackroyd offers a figure in the form of a certain Wilde, which has as much – or as little – 'reality' for the reader, as any other textual reconstruction.

In *The Last Testament of Oscar Wilde* Ackroyd creates events of both 1900 and the years recalled in this invented journal. Ackroyd's performance is such that he appears to achieve a level of empathy with the character of Wilde which is convincing in its emotional power, and presents the tragedy of Wilde as a figure whose fear of not meaning sits alongside his delight in his own multiplicity, as Ruth Robbins reminds us (Robbins 1996, 103). As Robbins argues, Ackroyd achieves this through miming Wilde's own reinscription of himself as a 'characterological palimpsest' (103).

Despite this, there is still that sense that this Wilde is somehow real. Yet Ackroyd's interest is not in realism *per se*: The reality-effect in *The Last Testament of Oscar Wilde* ought properly to be read as another textual *style*, a ludic device by which other concerns can resonate with an historical as well as a contemporary credibility. Ackroyd's invention of Wilde is one owing allegiance to both the present and the past as we imagine ourselves to inherit it. Yet we only imagine this, for, as his Wilde lets us know, constantly, through the act of writing a journal about his previous selves, and through the playful device of telling stories to oneself about the games of identity one has played, the subject is only ever a textual effect, whether for others or for the self. Ackroyd's concerns then focus upon language as the medium by which all of this is made possible: language as construct, as iterative movement; language as the spectral trace of past in the present, language as ludic communication, where meaning and identity are always displaced, and ever open to negotiation and misunderstanding.

Hawksmoor

I have liv'd long enough for others, like the Dog in the Wheel, and it is now the Season to begin for myself: I cannot change that Thing call'd Time, but I can alter its Posture and, as Boys do turn a looking-glass against the Sunne, so I will dazzle you all.

(*H* 11)

Thus Nicholas Dyer, Satanist and architect under Sir Christopher Wren, fictional architect of the churches designed by Nicholas Hawksmoor.[18] Dyer has been transposed for the historical figure of Hawksmoor, whose namesake appears as a detective in a contemporary setting in *Hawksmoor*. Each converges mysteriously upon the other, for the detective is seeking the murderer Dyer, even though he never understands that his search is for the architect, separated as they are by over two centuries. In *Hawksmoor* Ackroyd takes ideas concerning possession and the narrative possibilities of 'history' which had informed his previous novels further. The narrative operates in two time periods where events in the past and present are intimately connected. We come to understand that 'the connections between Dyer and Hawksmoor are undeniable, but the nature of those connections is always elusive' (Janik 1995, 172). Thus the play between centuries never settles into some comfortable, discernible pattern awaiting the reader's acumen to decipher the code. To quote Del Ivan Janik once more, '[t]he connections are not clear-cut; the determinism of the historicist has no place in this novel's world' (1995, 173).

Moreover, the 'styles' of the novel are not simply those of the eighteenth- and the twentieth-century narrative solely; they are not merely the styles of the intimate autobiographical journal or the detective novel. Stylistically, the novel cannot be read as being stable even within a particular time-frame or narrative. Mysticism and mystery proliferate in the narrative of the twentieth century, rather than diminishing as they are supposed to in most detective stories. The earlier narrative is plagued by the same disturbance. Ackroyd has himself described Nicholas Dyer as a 'patchwork', echoing with hundreds of voices – including those of Sir Christopher Wren – and texts of the eighteenth century (McGrath 1988–9, 44). The textile image employed by Ackroyd is wholly appropriate. It acknowledges the discontinuous connectedness, spoken of by Adriaan de Lange (1993, 153), which is central to Derrida's use of the figure of the sheaf in his explication of *différance*, the provisional term chosen to explore the graphic, iterable and textual nature of being (Derrida 1982, 3). Ackroyd's exploration of history plays with the epistemological comprehension of history conventionally comprehended as a linear progression or grand narrative. The play in language unfolds, through the oscillation and resonance between moments in time, which Derrida has termed 'this graphic disorder' or the '*general system of this economy*' (1982, 3). Dyer disorders time, not as fictional human who has access to satanic powers (even though he believes this to be the case), but as a patchwork or network of textual traces which disorder graphically both narrative and time. Ludic dissonance forbids the very identities with which it toys.

Yet *Hawksmoor*, winner of the Whitbread Prize, is, arguably, Peter Ackroyd's most successful novel, at least commercially. Its own identity is unstable, transporting itself between the most arcane intellectual concerns and the most obvious of fictional forms. Certainly it is the novel which has, so far, encouraged most academic criticism. In the broader context of Ackroyd's work, it is instructive then to understand the reviewers' responses – and perceptions – of this particular text, if only so as to begin to come to terms with the playful disturbances with which the novelist invests his writing.

Seen as a dark and cold novel generally by the reviewers, it was, nonetheless, generally well received, although some commentators did find the twentieth-century plot not as convincing as that told in the first person in the eighteenth century (the odd numbered chapters). The appropriately named novelist, Geoff Dyer, found the novel to be steeped in darkness (1985), as did Joyce Carol Oates, who found the novel 'witty and macabre' (although she did think Hawksmoor a weak character) (1986). Francis King's review in *The Spectator* again found the modern-day narrative lacking, describing the detective as a 'dispiritingly lifeless and shabby character' (1986). Walter Kendrick in *The Village Voice* called *Hawksmoor* the 'darkest' of Ackroyd's fictions, though his personal favourite (1989). Ackroyd, he concluded, offers 'rare, strange ... educated [and therefore] ... dangerous' pleasures. The question of whether Hawksmoor is convincing is of course an aesthetic concern, having to do with the expectations of the reader conditioned by the genre and tradition of mystery or detective fiction, yet overlooking the formal qualities of such fictions when reviewing a novel which is not simply a murder mystery. We will come back to the question of the detective in a moment, but first some other reviewers' comments.

The reviewer for *The Times*, James Fenton (26 September, 1985), while enjoying the novel, compared it with a game of Cluedo in which Miss Peacock is not only murdered but also tortured and raped beforehand. He goes on to describe the overall effect of Ackroyd's writing as being akin to a rather unnerving 'game that had got out of hand'. The game metaphor is clearly important, even though Fenton might not be quite aware to what extent Ackroyd's game is one which plays with the genre of the murder mystery itself. Yet that this is some kind of game is clear to the reviewer. He has qualms over this 'intellectual puzzle' as he calls it, in which we find ourselves enthralled, perhaps against our better natures, even as 'we are well aware that we are being hoaxed'. The question of the ludic paradigm is one which operates at a number of levels therefore, and is all the more unsettling for that, playing as it does not only with genre but also with readerly expectations, even as it seduces the reader and makes the reader complicit in his or her own seduction: we know we're being toyed with, yet with an emotional or intellectual response akin to masochistic voyeurism (where we cover our eyes at a particularly nasty scene in a movie, all the while peering through our fingers), we carry on reading. Fenton's more general concern is that a book such as *Hawksmoor* which interests itself so intimately with evil, might, in fact, be an evil book. However, he is not completely certain about this, and his ambiguity strikes the right note, in a narrative which refuses to solve anything and, ultimately, leaves the reader to decide, as Susana Onega points out (1991, 138).

Novelist Allan Hollinghurst doesn't share James Fenton's equivocal doubts. He reads the text as being too stage managed, 'theatrical' and marked by 'trumpery' (27 September, 1985).[19] With this review there is a decided move away from playfulness to a sense of – perhaps camp? – performance which somehow sits uneasily with its subject matter. While admiring the 'eccentric pastiche of the Dyer chapters', Hollinghurst finds the novel unambiguously dark and cold; characters in the twentieth-century narrative are sketchy, he suggests, and the dialogue implausible. All the concerns here are typical of an aesthetic criticism which holds mimetic realism as its yardstick. Yet to look at this from another angle, and to return to the question of the detective who gives a number of the reviewers such a problem, are not sketchiness, implausibility, and even banality, all characteristics of the most generic of detective fictions? What is being described here sounds like a third-division impersonation of Agatha Christie. What we seem to be confronted with is a parody of a genre which all too readily falls into its own parodic gestures, albeit inadvertently.[20] Richard Swope describes Hawksmoor as 'the classic detective' (1998, 222), while Jean-Pierre Audigier, without criticizing the novel negatively, suggests somewhat wittily that, in finally denouncing the absent presence of the author, *Hawksmoor* with reference to the 'texte policier-source' and its narrator who is (always) beyond suspicion, might well be given the subtitle, *The Murder of Peter Ackroyd* (1994, 148).

Following this line of enquiry, we are led by the trail of clues to acknowledge fully that Ackroyd's game is being played with the 'policier', the detective novel (as already briefly noted), as much as it plays between genres, between styles, and between historical periods. Nicholas Hawksmoor is a wholly predictable detective, who, as James Fenton suggests, is 'the latest in a well-known tradition' (1985; the question of how well-known the tradition is seems to be in doubt at least with regard to the conventional forms and styles of that tradition). Hawksmoor is the most obvious of English detectives, a humourless walking parody, not of policemen but of fictional detectives, who themselves are often nothing more than barely sketched cardboard cut-outs (and there's nothing wrong with that). Nothing more than a virtual trope himself, he succumbs to a lack of form and internal, hermeneutic logic because the narrative in which he finds himself will not behave according to the rules of the game. Out of his depth, or, more precisely, out of the novel in which he should be found, Hawksmoor finds himself quite literally ill-placed in Ackroyd's text. John Peck is therefore incorrect when he compares Hawksmoor to Dickens's Inspector Bucket, from *Bleak House* (Peck 1994, 444–5). Bucket is eccentric as far as the typology of fictional detectives go, because he is written, if not before, then certainly at the moment of the historical inception of detective fiction, when the delineation of character has not yet become reduced to a mould. Hawksmoor, on the other hand, is written when the detective genre seems almost exhausted. He appears to us in the semblance of a P. D. James knock-off, a shadow of what we expect him to be, in much the same way that James's Adam Dalgleish becomes an imitation of his earlier selves.

This is still not to consider the genre fully, however. To write a murder in the tradition or fashion of Agatha Christie may well be a 'sordid trivialization' of murder, as Fenton puts it (but then aren't most murder mysteries?). The problem for Fenton is one of duration and detail. Ackroyd appears to insist that the reader loiter 'too long in the environs of murder' (Fenton 1985). But surely the question is: shouldn't we? If we choose to read about murder, should the writer let us off the hook with just the merest soupçon of blood, the briefest of glimpses of the body sticking out from behind the sofa? The problem is, at least for Fenton, both an ethical and an aesthetic question. The reviewer tries to reconcile these concerns even as he discusses the double plotting of Hawksmoor. What is being forced on us, at least by the twentieth-century detective story, is this very troubling estrangement and disjunction between the violence of the subject matter and the extent to which it forces the reader into discomfort in the face of the mystery genre, paradoxically a form which is sought after in the final analysis for the comforts it brings, through the reassurances it offers traditionally concerning the re-establishment of hegemonic and epistemological order. What is so troubling in *Hawksmoor* is the extent to which it estranges the identities which the reader seeks to bring to the text.

To return to the question of past and present as identities then: in *Hawksmoor*, Ackroyd plays with past and present. In doing so he unveils the present to itself as a textual form, interanimated by a past textuality. Indeed, the haunting movement of the past in present language disturbs the identity of language as the novel oscillates between contemporary and early eighteenth-century written styles. Ackroyd explores conventional historical and narrative boundaries in this novel, eventually effecting the dissolution not only of the boundaries but, also, the idea of the boundary as anything other than a narrative or fictional device, erasable by the difference of writing's trace, along with the possibility of the text being iterated outside the locus of its generation and production. In Adriaan de Lange's words, Ackroyd effects the 'obliteration of the boundaries between fiction and reality' (de Lange 1993, 148). Of course such 'obliteration' is not total. For otherwise, how could we discern the mark of the boundaries in the first place? But the partial erasure of such boundaries also takes its effect on the comprehension of temporal moments, which can be read as palimpsests of other temporal events haunted by and articulated through writing.

Arguing that Ackroyd's novel is not so much a detective novel as it is a missing person's novel in the tradition of Hawthorne's 'Wakefield', Richard Swope suggests that *Hawksmoor* explores 'disappearance beyond the three dimensional realm' (1998, 222). This is not to imply, however, some banal mysticism or occult explanation as the rationale for the narrative. Rather, the ludic temporal play is concerned with the intimate relationship between being and time and the 'mystery' or the undecidability that is always immanent within narratives of history.[21] Of course, this necessarily forces upon one an acknowledgement that the past is only available through textual media, as already suggested. As Linda Hutcheon puts it, the past is 'always already interpreted' (Hutcheon 1988, 143). Or, to put this another way, 'Ackroyd's historical fictions never pretend that they are anything else but fictional constructions, subjective versions, reinventions and rearrangements of a cultural past that can only be made accessible through a *staging of various textual voices*' (Schnakertz 1994, 495). In recreating the past the author also performs it otherwise, while also having to rely on those interpretations of past realities which have survived, and which are themselves always already performances. Any interpretation of events – including fictional events – relies upon previously existing texts which become patterns by which the interpretation becomes defined and understood. All such patterns, such texts, including the present interpretation overlap. They inform and are informed by each other. All are part of an open-ended seriality of texts opening onto each other, and translating, transforming the identities of the others, even as the other of the each text, within each text, and every other of all other texts returns to haunt all future textual form/ulations, as the condition of ludic spectrality.

Acknowledging the play of text across time, Ackroyd frees the reader from the comprehension of time as merely the consecutive non-iterable occasions – or illusions – of the present, of presence. The spatial and ludic architectonic of Ackroyd's 'historical' writing subordinates all conventional notions of time, by opening itself to its own irreducibly haunted, uncanny texuality. If we choose to read the historical part of the novel as having a greater sense of realism than the merely schematic presentation of the twentieth-century narrative, we miss the extent to which play affects both periods. Luc Herman points out that the novel's play with historical detail involves 'playing around' with ascertainable facts, and that this is part of a marked tendency towards falsification (1985, 114). So, to suggest that the eighteenth-century narrative is any more 'real' or 'realistic' (as reviewers such as Hollinghurst have done) is to misinterpret not only the novel but also the play of play itself. Both Dyer and Hawksmoor are literary characters, 'given' says Herman 'very schematic presentation'. Dyer will only be seen as more real paradoxically because the modern reader has no immediate experience of the past. Thus the effect of play is make us believe in that about which we have less knowledge. As Susana Onega puts it, *Hawksmoor* 'attempts to recreate the intellectual atmosphere of the period of the Enlightenment from the double perspective of both its emergent empiricism and its submerged and repressed occultist practices' (1991, 125). [22]

Yet what is significant in one period loses significance in another, if we search for continuity and connection. Parallels may not be parallels at all, but only seem to be as the act of reading attempts to restrict the ludic oscillation. Recalling a remark of Adriaan de Lange's cited earlier, '[d]espite the symmetrical and parallel patterns which create a strong sense of continuity, Ackroyd paradoxically also succeeds in subtly creating a sense of discontinuity ... by means of the dialectic between changing and yet similar relations between his characters and through fictional asides' (1993, 153). As an example of such playful disjunction, consider Ackroyd's use of the figure of the fly, both metaphorical and real. Onega notes how Dyer's metaphor for humanity's existence – 'the Flies on this Dunghil Earth' (*H* 17) – is repeated when Hawksmoor accidentally squashes a fly on the edge of a report (*H* 195). What holds cultural significance at one moment becomes reduced to an accidental and marginal textual mark at another. What is a metaphor in the earlier period is a hapless organism in the latter (or is it?) Connecting the metaphor to the chance mark on the page leads us – where, exactly? The reader is played once more, and (with a cynical laugh and a nod in the direction of the author) perhaps nothing can be recalled here so much as King Lear's comment concerning wanton sport.

Another aspect of this play is that characters in the past can be given the capacity to read the future. An episode of this nature occurs when Christopher Wren and Nicholas Dyer visit Bedlam:

> We went back into the Mens Apartments where there were others raving of Ships that may fly and silvered Creatures upon the Moon: Their Stories seem to have neither Head nor Tayl to them, *Sir Chris. told me*, but there is a Grammar in them if I could but Puzzle it out.

> (*H* 99)

Nothing further is made of this because, obviously, it *does* seem like nonsense from the perspective of the novel's characters in the eighteenth-century narrative. Ackroyd thus plays with the potential for the ways in which utterances can both simultaneously seem to signify and yet not signify.

This gambit is developed when the architects visit a new 'Demoniack' in an isolated cell (*H* 99–100). This madman prophesies also, this time with devastating effect on Dyer, referring to Dyer's secret crimes and the detective who, in another time, is on his trail. Dyer appears to recognize something in this. The episode is not without a touch of humour also:

... the Madman turned to me crying: what more Death still Nick, Nick, Nick, you are my own! At this I was terribly astounded, for he could in no wise have known my name. And in his Madness he called out to me again: Hark ye, you boy! I'll tell you somewhat, one Hawksmoor will this day terribly shake you! ....

Who is this Hawksmoor, *Sir Chris. asked me* as we left the Madhouse and entered the fields.

No one, *I answered*, no Man I know. Then leaving him I went quick into a Tavern, and swallow'd pot after pot of Ale till I became drunken.

(*H* 100)

The madman's narrative ability offers a connection with Dyer's view of the world, in which he claims that 'the Lunaticks speak Prophesies while the Wise men fall into the Pitte' (*H* 100). This is not the only reading available to us, however. The joke with the play on possible meaning is, of course, that the madman's ludicrous word-play may well become, at another time, the novelist's narrative propulsion. The scene in Bedlam is open to various narrative possibilities, various connections or interpretations, none of which excludes any other. the 'Wise men' can be, equally, Dyer or Hawksmoor; the 'Pitte', all too easily, can come to figure the *mise en abyme* which is opened in the interpretative act struggling to come to rest on a single meaning. Simultaneous possibilities overlay one another, displacing and distorting a single identity.

The past and present most immediately displace each other as discrete and knowable identities through the anachronistic play of language. If time cannot be changed, then, its 'posture' can be altered, as Dyer says. Language is itself open to appropriation and performance, the author 'dressing up' in the language of the other time, yet speaking of the double time of writing and reading. Bearing this in mind, consider the very first sentence of *Hawksmoor*:

And so let us beginne; and, as the Fabrick takes its Shape in front of you, alwaies keep the Structure intirely in Mind as you inscribe it.

(*H* 5)

That the words are artificial is of course emphasized by the display of an apparently anachronistic 'style' and spelling. The words invite the reader to construct some meaningful form from the 'fabric' of the text; it appeals to an abstract structure by which the meaning of the book will become apparent. Perhaps we will be able to understand why a book by Peter Ackroyd, a writer of the late twentieth century, begins in this fashion.

At the same time, this expression on Dyer's part is one of the 'self', of identity coming to terms with itself; the act of writing is an act of self-inscription of the self inscribing the self with an eye to what is to come. Consider this utterance momentarily in the light of Heidegger's understanding of human being's temporality and the question of *ecstasis*. The utterance is traced by an awareness of 'time future' and 'time past', from the subjective position of 'time present'. On the one hand, it articulates a sense of being's 'always already inhabiting the possibilities and projects that come toward it as its own *future*'. On the other, implicitly inscribed within the acknowledgement of the arbitrary beginning, there is acknowledged also being's 'being already in the world'. Finally, that communal utterance, 'Let us beginne', expresses the self's awareness of its being in the world, 'alongside beings in the world' (Krell 1997, 74–6).

Broadening our understanding of the performative nature of the opening sentence of the novel in this fashion, we move away from reading it merely as some supposedly 'postmodern' 'joke' relating to fiction's self-commentary. We see how writing is intimately enfolded in the consideration of identity and time. In the book, of course, this opening sentence is Dyer instructing his pupil, Walter Pyne. Yet, the immediate doubleness of the remark is itself significant. Or, to put it another way, the uncertainty of address, and, by extension, the uncertainty inscribed in all literary language, is significant. The significance of uncertainty is that it obviously does not give way to meaning or stable identity in the form of a knowable addressee. Locution dislocates, articulation disarticulates, as the text is read apparently invoking the necessity of maintaining the fictive 'make-believe' of a beginning. Yet this is all it is: appearance. Simulation. A 'style' from the past speaking to narrative concerns in the present, and collapsing all time in a statement concerned with all narrative moments. (Apparently.)

The dis/continuity of written, performative language, which plays between narratives and across centuries, deconstructs any simple notion of time. It is evoked in other ways in *Hawksmoor*, not least through many quotations from children's rhymes, which originated in the eighteenth century and earlier, but are still a part of common culture today. Fragments of poetry are also remembered by various characters. Dyer's landlady recites an interesting poem of her own on the nature of language haunting supposedly discrete temporal moments:

> O Blessed letters, that combine in one
> All ages past; and make one live with all!
> Make us confer with those who now are gone,
> And the dead living unto counsel call!

There is a want of Sense in that line, *she mutters* before continuing quickly:

> By you th'unborn shall have communion
> Of what we feel, and what does us befall.

(*H* 46–7)

Here we have a poetic rendition of Ackroyd's comprehension of language containing its own historicity like 'fossil strata' beneath the surface features of any specific cultural moment. At the same time, or, rather, a different time, a time other than the assumed 'time' of the utterance, the comment speaks, in other words, to Ackroyd's comprehension of the passage of language, its play throughout human time. The text hints at the spectral which this might imply. Dyer has no response to this portentous poem; he does not recognize any strange relevance to himself or his existence as he did with the madman; it is of interest mainly to the reader, regarding the survival of written communication into the future. As with the madman, Dyer's landlady relates what might be considered 'truths' from the margins of the narrative. It is as though, while the main elements of the narrative are contained within their particular temporal moment, there occurs seepage across time in the form of oblique commentary concerning the transference, the transportation, the translation of writing.

By such means, Ackroyd highlights the processes of story-telling, emphasizing the particular stylization or definition that differing formal approaches can lend to the material. For example, elsewhere Dyer engages fellow architect and playwright Thomas Vanbrugghe in a discussion concerning, amongst other things, the nature of time. Given Dyer's interlocutor, Ackroyd provides the debate in play-form, complete with a title (*Hospital for Fools*), dramatis personae, and stage directions (*H* 174–81). For Ackroyd such matters of construction are of equal importance to the narrative events. Everything about the play reminds us of the text's performative, playful nature, while serving to acknowledge specific popular cultural textual forms of the period in which Dyer's narrative takes place. Modern artifice and period artefact meet in a manner which unsettles reciprocally the identity of either time and, along with this, our act of reading. Such an effect speaks indirectly of a certain 'untimeliness' of the literary. Time and the text are disorganized by the play between different moments, and between form and content.

We do not meet Nicholas Hawksmoor, the detective, until the second part of the novel, at which point three murders have already been committed. This late arrival seems almost an afterthought. Yet it dictates – for a number of reviewers and critics certainly – that the book be read as a novel belonging to a particular genre. In the first part, in the twentieth-century narrative, the boy Thomas is murdered in a labyrinthine tunnel under Christ Church Spitalfields in Chapter 2. The other murders are those of the tramp, Ned (who has his own parallel character in the eighteenth-century narrative),[23] who arrives in London from Bristol and upon whom 'the shadow fell' by the steps to the crypt of St Anne's Church, Limehouse (Ch. 4), and that of another boy, Dan, this time by St-George's-in-the-East (Ch. 6). Other parallels with the eighteenth century abound in overt or implicit mirroring of phrases or situations. For example, the eighteenth-century first chapter closes with the church mason's son falling from the steeple, during a ritual of placing the last stone: 'he fell away from the main Fabrick and was like to have dropped ripe at my own Feet' (*H* 25). Chapter 2 opens with a group of tourists being led on a sightseeing tour, and as the narrative joins them they are at the church:

> 'What was that falling there?' One of the group asked, shielding his eyes with his right hand so that he might look more closely at the sky around the church tower, but his voice was lost in the traffic noise ...
>
> (*H* 26)

For the sightseers this is merely a chance trick of the light. At most, it might be described as an ocular echo, a resonance – dissonance might be the better word – of eighteenth-century events, a ghostly moment of return to disturb time.

All the chapters are then either directly or indirectly linked in similar ways, as other critics of *Hawksmoor* have noted. The parallels between Hawksmoor and Dyer are especially acute.[24] There are the many incidental details: for example, Dyer and Pyne abstractedly gaze over the Thames to see 'a Wherry in which there was a common man laughing and making antic Postures like an Ape' (88). Later, Hawksmoor abstractedly looks along the Thames after visiting one of the murder sites, as 'two men passed on a small boat – one of them was laughing and grimacing, and seemed to be pointing at Hawksmoor' (115). Also, Hawksmoor lives in lodgings on the same site as did Dyer, both suffering the attentions of flirtatious landladies, whose names are Mrs Best and Mrs West. They share the same Christian name. They both have assistants whose names are similar (Walter Payne, Walter Pyne). They drink at the same pub. These are suggestive connections, and remain exactly that, tempting the reader into a search for particular meanings, yet denying that these might be anything other than coincidences.

Laura Giovannelli in particular goes to great lengths in pointing out the interwoven connections between the eighteenth and twentieth centuries. To paraphrase her argument, the archaic syntax and spelling notwithstanding, the conjunction between the two periods results in a series of innumerable parallels, including reiterated phrases and the distribution of roles and characters. Phrases, vocabulary and dialogue resonate across the two narratives and centuries with strange resemblances. All the while, this is accompanied by the perennially intoned refrains, occasionally background music, proverbs and children's rhymes.[25] These rhymes travel not only across time, between periods, but also throughout the city of London to become as much a part of its fabric as the stones of Dyer's churches (Giovannelli 1996, 107ff.).[26] Like the image of the boy falling from the steeple, the city and the novel are threaded with numerous traces, all of which attest to or signify, however obliquely, what Levinas calls 'the condition of time [which] lies in the relationship between humans, or in history' (1987, 79). Earlier, it was suggested that the connections and parallels might be nothing other than coincidence; coincidence, we would contend, might be readable as another name for this 'condition of time'.

One trace remains to be read however: dust.[27] One interesting passage in Chapter 2, a debate between Thomas and his mother concerning dust, appears innocuous enough, initially. But this becomes a recurrent figure, for the passage of time, and as the undecidable trace across time. Barely discernible, dust is the unreadable trace, the mute sign of Being's historicity (much like the residue, we might speculate, of 'older' language within our own articulation). 'Look at the dust in here,' complains the mother, 'Just look at it!' and Thomas asks,

> 'Where does dust come from?'
> 'Oh I don't know, Tommy, from the ground probably ... I don't know where it comes from, but I do know where it's going to,' and she blew the dust from the table into the air.
>
> (H 34)

This does not in itself appear to be of any great importance, yet, when other references to dust appear throughout the novel, it appears to take on a significance. Dyer, complaining to Walter Pyne about the dust in his office asks, 'Is Dust immortal then ... so that we may see it blowing through the Centuries?' (17); Ned, the tramp, settles into a disused house for the night, inhabited also by other vagrants, and a woman says 'Dust, just look at the dust ... and you know where it comes from don't you? Yes, you know' (69); when Hawksmoor and his assistant, Walter Payne, examine some excavations beside one of Dyer's churches Walter remarks, 'It looks like a rubbish tip to me,' to which Hawksmoor responds 'Yes, but where did it come from? You know, Walter, from dust to dust' (160). As one of Dyer's victims is buried, Vanbrugghe remarks 'in a jovial Tone the words of the Service: From dust to dust, (says he), From dust to dust' (172). Dyer, musing over the nature of time, writes 'All this shall pass, and all these Things shall fall and crumple into the Dust, but my Churches shall survive' (208). Dust remains, then; or perhaps dust as remains, that which remains and yet remains unreadable.

The question of the dust is at once trivial and profoundly disturbing, haunting even, we might suggest. For it is there – and there, and there. Never in the same place or same time twice, it remains as the remains of the past at the very limits of readability and unreadability. It cannot be recuperated in any normative interpretative sense, yet is found everywhere, throughout the text and throughout time. An unreadable trace, it remains to be read, and we can only read its unreadability; we can only decide on its undecidability as signifying trace. We cannot decide on a meaning for dust in terms of the narrative, as it figures otherwise the aporetic in the hermeneutic project. At the same time, however, we are forced to acknowledge it as the trace of the absolutely other. The merest sign of our being and the mark of being's temporal horizon, this trace, plays with readerly expectations. A labyrinthine clew, it leads us nowhere, except to itself as evidence of undecidability, the movement of alterity in the field of meaning.

The novel is, therefore, not organized towards resolution or closure in any conventional realist sense, even as the narrative seems to tease us with this possibility. Rather, the question with which we are plagued concerns the limits of reading, the play between the limits of reading and not-reading as these pertain to being's consciousness of itself. As Hawksmoor explains to Walter in a pub:

> 'And where does that interpretation come from? It comes from you and me ... Don't you think I worry when everything falls apart in my hands – but it's not the facts I worry about. It's me.'

(*H* 200)

Uncertainty concerning epistemology, genre, and identity leaves everything in play, everything to play for, and the growing suspicion that there's some kind of game, if we could only determine the rules. To quote Martin Dodsworth, though this time against the grain, we comprehend *Hawksmoor* 'as a game played between the author and his reader ... or, to come a little closer to the point, as a game played by words themselves in the field of meaning'. Certainly there is discernible the game, both games identified by Dodsworth. The field of meaning is not solely semantic as the critic suggests however. It is not merely a question of the abilities of the reader. The field of meaning has to do with the coming to (self-)consciousness of being. Language and writing are the places where reading, we believe, begins. But language, text, serves to disturb any notion of unity, such as is suggested in the goal of producing meaning. Articulated by difference, it breaks, in the words of Emmanuel Levinas, the 'continuity of being or of history' (1969, 195). Beginning with the act of reading, as Hawksmoor does in the quotation above, we are forced, in the end (which is only another form of beginning) to question the sufficiency of 'me' in the face of that which is undecidable, in the face of the Other.

– here we are again!

– Art is the only serious thing in the world. And the artist is the only person who is never serious.

– … have another before you …

– How true. The critics can never see this. There is a deep resemblance always between a writer and his work, but it has nothing to do with his expressed opinions or sentiments; it is rather that the form of his work embodies the form of his personality.

HURRY UP PLEASE ITS TIME

– … have another before you …

– However, this is not the only consideration. In an utilitarian age, of all other times, it is a matter of grave importance that Fairy tales should be respected …

– God forbid that Ackroyd should pastiche this one…

HURRY UP PLEASE ITS TIME

HURRY UP PLEASE ITS TIME[1]

… however it is considered, the question of time is neither simple nor simply defined. Yoking the problem of time to that of narrative further complicates the issue. Any discussion of *Hawksmoor* alone should direct the reader towards the complex issue of temporality, the time of telling, and the time of re-telling. Before speaking of narrative and temporality, however, a brief detour and return.

The Great Fire of London disturbs through undermining the stability of fictive levels: within the novel the world of its characters is supposedly real, while that of *Little Dorrit* is not. Historical time – in this case, the recent past – is caught up with narrative time and the fictional past. This relationship and the notion of 'identities of fiction' on which the relationship is based find themselves troubled internally, which in turn presents epistemological problems for the reader. This reaches a moment of uncertainty in the fire on the film location. A real building dressed up to appear to be a fictional structure is the starting point for the fire. The 'great fire of London' becomes a performance, thereby foregrounding issues of in/authenticity. Performance and in/authenticity are also among the principal interests of *The Last Testament of Oscar Wilde*. Here, historical knowledge is challenged through the performative reinvention of the historical subject, who self-consciously acknowledges his own role in the constructedness of his identity. Epistemological certainty – founded implicitly on notions of knowing of the 'real' Oscar Wilde and being confronted by a fictional variation – is unsettled through the act of writing in markedly literary styles, which connect only to disjoint. Conflated, confused, and played out, are the connections and tensions between the places of the so-called 'literary' and the 'real', the Wilde we presume to apprehend through his publications and the Wilde who we read, knowing all the while that he is an invention of Peter Ackroyd. In addition to the dualism of the literary and the real, and the attendant aporetic experience opened between the Wildes and brought about by the act of reading, there are also questions of the disjunctions effected by the presentation of a recognised literary genre (the 'confession') and the most intimate form of writing (the journal). The latter form is always a form caught up in the subject's representation of him- or herself to him- or herself through the performative inscription that is inescapably temporal. The history of the journal is one which stretches from the Early Modern Period to the present day. It is a form always involved with the self-conscious performance and dressing up of the self, of what Francis Barker calls the 'tremulous private body' (1984).

If nothing else, therefore, *The Last Testament of Oscar Wilde* should be read, not as a postmodernist novel at all (any more than any of Ackroyd's other works). Rather, as a provisional definition of what kind of animal this text is, it would be more accurate to state that *The Last Testament* (which title for some reason seems to suggest last wills, last suppers, last orders [HURRY UP PLEASE ITS TIME], testaments old and new, and all things eschatological) is the most traditional and typical of literary texts, acknowledging the time, the history, of subjective self-reflection, which is as old (approximately) as the consideration of the self, whether 'literary' or 'philosophical', public (published) or private. I write (myself) therefore I am (reading myself [as other than myself]). It is the very act of writing the self which connects private and public, the act of journal writing being the performance of one's public actions and private thoughts, written in a private space. This is, in Francis Barker's words, '[t]he I surrounded first by discourse, then by the *domus*, the chamber, and finally by the public world...' (1984, 10). Like Samuel Pepys's diary, of which Barker is writing, *The Last Testament of Oscar Wilde*, 'despite being so richly populated with others and with the furniture of gossip and events, is [also]... the record of a terrible isolation' (1984, 10). The apparent 'connection' between private and public is, in fact, the acknowledgement of, simultaneously, the artifice of the self's performance and the deferral and displacement of any supposedly true self.

This is peculiar neither to Pepys at one point in the history of which we are speaking, nor Wilde, at the other. Ackroyd's text speaks intimately and also playfully of the condition of being, of being one who writes. Writing to connect oneself to the world only distances one further. As Barker points out, the subject turns inward, becomes private and intimate as it considers itself in and through self-textualisation. Peter Ackroyd thus offers the reader a view of one moment in the history of the modern self. It is one moment, yet it acknowledges the remembered past and anticipated moments in the untotalisable totality of modern identity. The reader encounters through Wilde the modern subject as intensely narcissistic. This is a performance of the self in lieu of any supposedly true or essential self. Such narcissism is not peculiar to Wilde. It is, instead, the inescapable effect of writing the self. (Ackroyd's) Wilde at least has the advantage of being 'true' to himself, so to speak, in acknowledging to himself his own performativity. At the same time, the writing subject, in order to maintain its interest in itself and for itself – in being *inter-est*ed in itself, locating its subjectivity as a *between-being* or *being-between* for the writing and reading selves – dresses itself up, or dresses up for itself. Paradoxically, the self who supposedly writes only for the self becomes all the more playful and performative, as subjectivity undergoes ever more complex and labyrinthine detours in the act of self-writing-self. The cultural, temporal and historical project of textualized subjectivity is also, we can speculate, the *projection* of the self's performances. Anticipating film, journal writing and other forms of self-projection (such as Nicholas Dyer's autobiographical narration in *Hawksmoor*) constitute what D. N. Rodowick calls 'movement-image' which, it is argued, 'provides one way of apprehending or understanding duration as an image or a spatialization of time' (1997, 79). The writer projects onto the page an image which moves through the space of the journal and across the time of journal-keeping, which is then re-presented through the act of reading, when the movement-image appears to 'come alive'. The modern subject is therefore involved in a process of (self-) narration, which act Fredric Jameson sees as 'the central function ... of the human mind', and which is, in turn, 'the essentially narrative and rhetorical movement of language and writing *through time*' (1981, 13; emphasis added). Journal keeping as one example of auto-narration is an act of teleological retrospect in which the movement into the past so as to bring the self up to the present also involves a contrapuntal movement into the self's future moment. Timothy Harcombe and Nicholas Dyer, each in their own fashion, return to their past selves even as they narrate themselves towards their own future moments. Movement names play, and Jameson's final phrase does double service, economically. It speaks to the act of the self's narration, as in the example of journal keeping. It also, importantly for understanding Ackroyd's play, signifies a cultural and historical process at work, from, say, Pepys to Wilde, or from Dyer to Hawksmoor.

We read such movement in *Hawksmoor* of course, as just noted. However, if the rhythms of temporality were merely implicit in both *The Great Fire of London* and *The Last Testament of Oscar Wilde*, in *Hawksmoor* time is figured explicitly as a component of being, chiefly through the consciousness of Nicholas Dyer. Time serves to define being in the novel. Similarly, time is that on which the subject reflects and which his consciousness mediates. The literary and subjective histories which are implied in the form and concerns of *The Last Testament of Oscar Wilde* are mapped more explicitly in the vectors of *Hawksmoor*'s two narrative historical mo(ve)ments and its two principal characters, Dyer and Hawksmoor. If, to return to a point made in the discussion of *Hawksmoor*, the twentieth-century, third-person narrative of the detective's fruitless quest and the murders which drive that search seem less 'real', less historically 'vivid', than the words and world of Nicholas Dyer, perhaps this is not only a question of formal literary consideration, already considered. It is also a matter of our having forgotten the consideration of being, of our having lost the sense of self-consciousness of the self, except as that is considered to be the domain of philosophical expertise, or otherwise discerned as the alleged formal and aesthetic interest of literary postmodernist practice, so-called. Given Hawksmoor's belief in rationality and the method of scientific deduction, we may even venture the suggestion that his separation from self-consciousness, made formally manifest in the shift from Dyer's first-person narrative to the impersonality of the third-person, is a symptom of a larger condition. This condition is best described as a certain fall from philosophical consideration on the condition of being in general into the empirically orientated study of technology and science within the discursive and practical parameters of given disciplines, defined by Martin Heidegger. Heidegger describes this movement as happening 'everywhere on the basis and according to the criterion of the scientific discovery of the individual areas of beings .... This ... corresponds to the determination of man as an acting social being' (Heidegger 1993, 434). If Hawksmoor is so obviously schematic as a character, recognizable as a literary type, then he is also, from the Heideggerian perspective, and in relation to the almost excessive self-awareness of Nicholas Dyer, typical of human forgetting in the late twentieth century. Governed by the discipline of scientifically based forensic deduction, he suffers a crisis when reacquainted with the question of being and the inextricable link to the temporal. Hence the temporal shift from the I of the eighteenth century (if one recalls, for the moment, Francis Barker's comments on Samuel Pepys), to the lifeless third-person narrative of the twentieth century. The movement of time in this case suggests the loss of self. (Not that there was ever a plenitude of 'self'; rather, its playful self-awareness obscures the hollowness at the heart of identity through the traceries of allusive acknowledgements.)

Nevertheless, time, to recall the opening remarks above, is never simply time. It is not an 'it'. It is not a simple or single identity. Even to write a sentence, which begins 'it is' or 'it is not', as a means to define time, is to misunderstand temporality. There are a number of times to be acknowledged.[2] There are numbers of times. There is universal time, the totality of time which exists supposedly outside and independently of individual perception, consciousness or existence. Arguably, time, not a thing as such, might be defined provisionally as a concept defined by human perception, when considered as a linear movement from the past through the present and into the future. However, time is not simply linear, the past can be conceived or recalled via narrative, and subjected to movements backward and forward, at different speeds. This leads to the next understanding of time: personal or phenomenological time. This is understood by the subject who considers herself in a present, as a presence within the present (although the present is never present, never stable or fixed). From the ever-moving moment of the present, from the rhythm of *différance* which hides within the idea of the present and forestalls its absolute possibility, the subject considers and comprehends her being in relation to 'time past' and 'time future'. The subject considers personal or phenomenological time as part of the comprehension of being, and, in so doing, reflects on the time of the self within the perceived totality of the temporal. This is not necessarily to consider phenomenological time and universal time (or 'cosmological time', to use Paul Ricoeur's term [Osbourne 1995, 47]) as separate. As Peter Osbourne puts it, 'the phenomenological present contains the totality of the temporal spectrum within itself' (1995, 53).

Ricoeur, distinguishing between historical and fictional time, describes the phenomenological subject's comprehension of time in such a manner that past and future are not absences of time or moments of non-time. Instead, they are perceived as the times of memory and expectation, while the present moment is defined as attention (Ricoeur v.1, 8; Osbourne 1995, 49). In following Augustine's consideration of the subject's relationship to temporality, Ricoeur provides a model of the subject's time which incorporates the temporal totality. Jean Hyppolite offers a still more fluid model in his discussion of Hegel's *Phenomenology of Spirit*. The consideration of the totality or 'eternality' of the temporal is described by Hyppolite as 'philosophy's element'. In his reformulation of the Hegelian *Erscheinung* (appearance), the 'eternal' is, for Hyppolite, 'the perpetual movement of appearance [*manifestation*] which implies the exchange of the future and the past, of sense and being, and exists as the present permanence of this exchange which is internal reflection' (Hyppolite 1997, 5). Hyppolite's formula, which seamlessly connects the self-awareness of being and the subjective temporal instance of that awareness to the totality of the temporal, is valuable to the comprehension of the nature of narrated time and the times of reading. First, however, we must briefly consider a particular remark of Paul Ricoeur's.

In Volume 2 (1985) of *Time and Narrative*, Paul Ricoeur begins Chapter 3, 'Games with Time', by positing, in the distinction between historical and fictional time, a greater flexibility in fictional time's play. In speaking of fictional narration, he demonstrates the temporal doubleness implicit in the narration of a story: 'to narrate a story is already to "reflect upon" the event narrated. For this reason, narrative "grasping together" carries with it the capacity for distancing itself from its production and in this way dividing itself in two' (1985, 61). While Ricoeur would see this division as a capacity, a potentiality, we would argue, drawing on Hyppolite, that the doubling is already more than this. Narrative doubling is always already at work in its self-division, even – or especially – when that narration is told in the first-person and in the present tense. Narrative carries within it its own possible iteration outside the supposedly 'proper' context of its articulation. This is figured by the instance, or to use Hyppolite's phrase, the 'perpetual movement of appearance' of I, of the mo(ve)ment of being's narration, its trace or writing, of itself as a temporal rhythm or pulse within the totality of time which returns, and, in doing so, disrupts linearity. The iterable re-mark of 'I' 'implies', as Hyppolite states, the 'exchange of the future and the past'. The constant exchange between future and past effected by and in the movement of 'I's appearance in writing signals both internal reflection and the doubling of narrative indicated by Ricoeur.

Moreover, such movement, such doubling and appearance, is further complicated in the act(s) of reading. The times of the reader and the times of the narrator (and narration) interact and mutually overlay one another. As we read, we move forward with the rhythm of the narrative and the appearances of the narrating and narrated narrators. At the same time, or, more precisely, at several times, we return to various past moments of the narrative 'I', as we comprehend the narrating 'I's appearances in relation to one another, as a series or seriality of appearances within the perpetual temporal exchange, and as the negotiation between self-reflection and the self's reflections on its external world and the time of that world. The narrator reflects back on him- or herself, recalling the movement towards the numerous moments of narration, from which s/he is moving forward. Similarly, the reader moves forward in the time of reading while recalling and thereby re-marking previous moments in the past of the narrative, which may either have been the 'present' moment of narration or the re-marked memory of the 'past' moment of that which has been narrated. As readers, therefore, we come to find ourselves inextricably involved in the tempi of the narrator's self-reflective exchanges of future and past, even as that exchange is reiterated outside of its supposedly 'original' moments or movements in, and approximated by, reading's times.

We may then propose that, through the act(s) of reading, the times of reader and narrator in tracing temporal movements which approximate reciprocal palimpsests connect, only to displace, the distinction made between historical and fictional time in a manner markedly similar to the displacement and deferral of being which is effected through the temporal double-act of writing the self. Ackroyd works in *Hawksmoor*, in *First Light* and *The House of Doctor Dee*, and in *Chatterton* also, each time in a singular fashion, through this displacement. In each novel, Nicholas Hawksmoor, Damian Fall, Matthew Palmer, and Charles Wychwood are presented with the temporal traces of past moments and driven to attempt to read them. Their own narratives come to resemble the past narrations of Dyer and Dee, the origins of light in the universe and, to a lesser extent, Chatterton. (In *Chatterton* the temporal trace and its reiteration is less 'localised', the novel given up to a more general play of voices and texts.)

Formally, the end of *The House of Doctor Dee* and the beginning and end of *First Light* perform the temporal displacement quite economically, as form and content, structure and narrative, time and being, fold, each over and under the other, reciprocally. In *Doctor Dee*, Matthew Palmer describes a visit with his mother to a disused garage in Wapping, which had been owned by his father (*HDD* 261–8). In visiting the garage, Matthew sees a tramp, and so appears to recall the vagrants from *Hawksmoor*, stepping as it were into 'someone else's plot or words ... relying upon the themes or images of other novelists' (*HDD* 223). This is merely an incident in passing, however, for the visit appears to take place at least twice and, possibly, three times. The first time ends in Palmer's return to his father's house and a visionary encounter with Dr Dee, which leads to Matthew discovering himself to be Dee's homunculus (*HDD* 266–7). Whether this is merely part of the vision or the reality is left undecided, for Daniel Moore, Matthew Palmer's friend and his father's lover, vanishes upon imparting the revelation to Matthew concerning his origins (*HDD* 267). At this point the narrative is fragmented, the paragraphs divided by asterisks. Immediately following the scene just described, we find ourselves back with Matthew and his mother at the garage, as though they had never left (*HDD* 267). Once more, Palmer encounters Dee, who this time speaks directly to him. Then the passage is broken once more, and the chapter concludes with what appears to be a third visit to the garage, or the same visit with different outcomes, Matthew Palmer's mother asking what certain signs marked on the brickwork might mean, which she had first noticed in the previous scene (*HDD* 267). Of course, if we accept that magic exists at least in the novel, then Matthew's visions can be explained away within the logic of the narrative. He is given three visions within the same narrative moment, the visit to the garage. However, the three moments can also be read as displacements in time – in the time of the narrative and in the structure of the text. Furthermore, they are also displacements, disjointings of time(s) in relation to the unveiling of self-awareness. Conventional linear narrative form is displaced in the event of self-comprehension, while Palmer's subjectivity is subject to moments of being, displaced from each other. Temporally, the narrative folds upon itself, making the moment undecidable in the movement or event of the narrative, in the same movement of temporal dislocation when Palmer is brought face to face with a crisis concerning his identity. Ackroyd thereby plays with the temporal structure and the possibility of meaning presented by the apparent partial structural reiteration, the narrative and the narrating self, dividing itself in seeking to make connections about itself. Matthew Palmer's 'epiphany' implies the 'exchange of future and past' in the 'perpetual movement of appearance', to recall Hyppolite. This movement of appearance or manifestation is not simply the revelation of Dee to Palmer, but the process of internal reflection on the relation between being and time described by Jean Hyppolite, and given performative expression in the fragmented, tripartite structure of the narrative at this moment of crisis.

We read another 'manifestation' of movement, deferral and displacement in *First Light*. Here are the relevant passages, taken from the first and last pages of the novel, and quoted in full:

Let me be drawn up into the immensity. Into the darkness, where nothing can be known. Once there were creatures of light leaping across the firmament, and the pattern of their movement filled the heavens. But the creatures soon fled and in their place appeared great spheres of crystal which turned within each other, their song vibrating through all the strings of the world. These harmonies were too lovely to last. A clock was ticking in the pale hands of God, and already it was too late. Yes. The wheels of the mechanism began to turn. What was the painting by Joseph Wright of Derby? I saw it once. Was it called 'The Experiment'? I remember how the light, glancing through a bell-jar, swerved upwards and covered the whole sky. But this too went out: the candle flame was blown away by the wind from vast furnaces, when the electrical powers swept across the firmament.

But there were always fields, fields of even time beyond the fires. Empty space reaching into the everlasting. At least I thought that as a child. Then there came a tremor of uncertainty. There was no time left.

Let me be drawn up into the immensity. Into the darkness, where nothing can be known. Once there were creatures of light leaping across the firmament, and the pattern of their movement filled the heavens. But the creatures soon fled and in their place appeared great spheres of crystal which turned within each other, their song vibrating through all the strings of the world. These harmonies were too lovely to last. A clock was ticking in the pale hands of God, and already it was too late. Yes. The wheels of the mechanism began to turn. What was the painting by Joseph Wright of Derby? I saw it once. Was it called 'The Experiment'? I remember how the light, glancing through a bell-jar, swerved upwards and covered the whole sky. But this too went out: the candle flame was blown away by the wind from vast furnaces, when the electrical powers swept across the firmament.

But there were always fields, fields of even time beyond the fires. Empty space reaching into the everlasting. At least I thought that as a child. Then there came a tremor of uncertainty.

No space to float in. And everything began moving away. Nothing but waves now, their furrows tracking the path of objects which do not exist. Here is a star called Strange. Here is a star called Charmed. And after this, after this dream has passed, what then? What shape will the darkness take then? I ... Damian Fall turned to observe his companion. "Of course you know what we will be observing?"

"Aldebaran."

"Yes. There." Damian pointed towards the horizon and both men looked out at the great star. "One hundred and twenty times brighter than the sun," he said. And he put his hand above his eyes, as if shielding them from the heat. Burning star. Seeming to be red, but the colours shifting like an hallucination. In the same area of the sky they saw small cones of light, called the Hyades and believed to at a greater distance from the earth – cool red stars glowing within the clouds of gas which swirled about them. And close to them the lights known as the Pleiades, involved in a blue nebulosity which seemed to stick against each star, the strands and filaments of its blue light smeared across the endless darkness. Behind these clusters they could see the vast Crab Nebula, so far from the earth that from this distance it was no more than a mist or a cloud, a haziness in the eye like the after–image of an explosion. And yet Damian could see further. He looked up and could see. Galaxies. Nebulae. Wandering planets. Rotating discs.

There was no time left. No space to float in. And everything began moving away. Nothing but waves now, their furrows tracking the path of objects which do not exist. Here is a star called Strange. Here is a star called Charmed. And after this, after this dream has passed, what then? What shape will the darkness take then? I ... Damian Fall turned to his shadow. Of course you know what we will be observing? Yes, Aldebaran. One hundred and twenty times brighter than the sun.

Burning star. Seeming to be red, but the colours shifting like an hallucination. In the same area of the sky they saw small cones of light, *known as* the Hyades and believed to at a greater distance from the earth – cool red stars glowing within the clouds of gas which swirled about them. And close to them the lights known as the Pleiades, involved in a blue nebulosity which seemed to stick against each star, the strands and filaments of its blue light smeared across the endless darkness. Behind these clusters he could see the vast Crab Nebula, so far from the earth that from this distance it was no more than a mist or a cloud, a haziness in the eye like the after–image of an explosion. And yet Damian could see further *still*. He looked up and could see. Galaxies. Nebulae. Wandering planets. Rotating discs. Glowing interstellar debris. Spirals. Strands of brightness that contained millions of suns. Darkness like thick brush–strokes across a painted surface. Pale moons.

Glowing interstellar debris. Spirals. Strands of brightness that contained millions of suns. Darkness like thick brush–strokes across a painted surface. Pale moons. Pulses of light. All these coming from the past, ghost images wreathed in mist which confounded Damian. I am on a storm–tossed boat out at sea, the dark waves around me. This was what the earliest men saw in the skies above them – an unfathomable sea upon which they were drifting. Now we, too, talk of a universe filled with waves. We have returned to the first myth. And what if the stars are really torches, held up to light me on my way? I see what they saw in the beginning, even before the creatures of light appeared across the heavens. I can see the first human sky.

"Yes," he said. "Aldebaran. Once this region was thought to form the outline of a face in the constellation of Taurus – " He looked at the face of his companion, but he could see only a silhouette in the darkness. "But the Pleiades contains three hundred stars in no real pattern. Just burning, being destroyed, rushing outward." The last vestiges of cloud had now drifted away and the entire night sky had reappeared, so bright and so clear that Damian Fall put out his hand to it; then he turned his wrist, as if somehow he could turn the sky on a great wheel. And for a moment, as he moved his head, it did seem that the stars moved with him. "Why is it," he went on, "that we think of a circular motion as the most perfect? Is it because it has no beginning and no end?" (FL 3–4)

Pulses of light. All these coming from the past, ghost images wreathed in mist which confounded Damian. I am on a storm–tossed boat out at sea, the dark waves around me. This was what the earliest men saw in the skies above them – an unfathomable sea upon which they were drifting. Now we, too, talk of a universe filled with waves. We have returned to the first myth. And what if the stars are really torches, held up to light me on my way? I see what they saw in the beginning, even before the creatures of light appeared across the heavens. I can see the first human sky.

Yes, Aldebaran. Once this region was thought to form the outline of a face in the constellation of Taurus. He smiled at his shadow. But the Pleiades contains three hundred stars in no real pattern. Just burning, being destroyed, rushing outward. The last vestiges of cloud had now drifted away and the entire night sky had reappeared, so bright and so clear that Damian Fall put out his hand to it; then he turned his wrist, as if somehow he could turn the sky on a great wheel. And for a moment, as he moved his head, it did seem that the stars moved with him. Why is it that we think of a circular motion as the most perfect? Is it because it has no beginning and no end?

Time. Another time. He looks out of the window, from the confines of his bed. But he can see nothing now. Only the sky filled with light. (FL 327–8; emphases added)

The passages which open and close the novel are almost the same and would, on a hasty assessment, lead to the assumption of a kind of narrative circularity, of an act of closure on Ackroyd's part. Even the more obvious variant in the form of Damian's narration having now become entirely an interior monologue rather than a partial conversation is explainable by the occasion by his breakdown. As with *The House of Doctor Dee* there is a certain 'logic' at work internally. Or, to put this another way, this is the 'logic', a logic of continuity, connection and closure, with which Ackroyd toys. It is perhaps tempting from a wholly conventional standpoint to suggest in a retrospective moment that Damian's breakdown is 'foreshadowed' by the opening pages, thereby explaining away the narrative repetition through giving that repetition a significance or meaning confined within the text. However, with Ackroyd it is always important to read against the grain of narrative convention even – especially – at those moments which appear to invite the most conventional of analyses.

There is a superficial intertextuality at work in the two passages quoted above. The interest in light and dark, the focus of the subject upon time and immensity, the surrender of the self to temporal and spatial infinity; all might be said, by rough analogy, to correspond somewhat with the closing of *Hawksmoor*.[3] But if there is a connection, that which might be defined according to a seemingly sublime if not apocalyptic tone, there is also displacement, between the texts and between the passages. Certainly, there can be read the apprehension of an imminent moment of revelation, but what that revelation might be is ineffable, suspended forever beyond the end of the subject's utterance, and beyond the novels' narratives. The passages from *First Light* neither reveal directly any 'truth', nor do they create an unbroken and perfect circle.

The first paragraph of each passage is precisely the same. Reading the two side by side, or at a distance of over 300 pages, the reader might easily be seduced into hurrying to conclusions. However, the more obvious differences of dialogue and monologue aside, there are two minor changes in the last chapter's paragraphs, highlighted above. These are not necessarily significant in themselves – to decide on their significance or lack thereof is to decide on a meaning ahead of acknowledging that the purpose of the play in these changes is undecidable and to recognize the passage's acknowledgement that reiteration is not repetition, that the identity of the passage is displaced.[4] These slight changes, in a passage which mediates against the imposition of giving meaning or imposing patterns (the stars do not, after all, form a pattern or tell a story; only human consciousness imposes this upon them), suggest that there is no circularity, and that there is no beginning and end as such. Variants in themselves, the small changes bear a synecdochic relationship to the passages from which they come, implying that the passages are themselves variants, without there being necessarily a 'first' or 'original' passage.

(How many times has Damian thought these thoughts? How many times, according to the implications of Damian's thoughts, have others thought similar thoughts, reflecting on their being in the consciousness of temporality?) There is only the possible reiteration, marked by the perception of that 'human sky', as Damian puts it.

Formally, the passages are displacements of displacements, two moments of internal reflection from a potentially infinite series. They belong to a temporal movement between past and future moments of being. The passages are iterable instances of that 'perpetual movement of manifestation', of the exchange between sense and being, to recall Hyppolite once more. Moreover such displacement and movement enacts in writing the condition of writing reflexively while enacting also the inescapably *written* condition of being. The understanding on Damian Fall's part of the temporal nature of one's being, an awareness which through the doubling of the passages is an awareness of the displacement in writing of the self, is given slight, subtle formal performance through the insistent use of sentence fragments and the seven sentences beginning 'and'. 'And' promises connection, passage and continuation. Together, these enact an irregular rhythmic pulse which is also the double inscription of displacement and deferral. There appears a constant 'saying' of being, as the expression of the subject's self-awareness, but not limited by this. Particularly, in this passage, the fold and intimation of circularity, of return, is, as suggested, not a neat gathering, a structural moment of completion. It is, rather, and as part of the ludic gesture, an act of mimicry of such completion or closure. There is readable a deliberately misleading act tempting us to an act of misreading, whereby we read for the purpose of control through the stabilization of meaning (Damian's identity, Damian's breakdown).

Yet, even as the horizon of Damian's perception remains unfixable – there is the recognition despite desire that the first light, the first sky, remain unknowable – so the passage cannot be mastered. The passages do not enact what Marion Hobson describes, in reading Derrida's reading of Mallarmé as a subversion of phenomenological criticism, as the 'mirroring of mirroring through tidy embedding' (1998, 75).[5] Rather, and to borrow from Hobson's astute commentary on this act of subversion, Ackroyd's writing grafts itself onto itself as its own imperfect and fragmented palimpsest. Thus, if the passage can be read as exemplifying the constant exchange, as described in Hyppolite's phenomenological consideration of being and temporality, then this reciprocity of folding exists in Ackroyd's writing as both a performance already having occurred and, simultaneously, a mimicked parody of itself. It tends not towards continuity and connection, seamless, faultless filiation or delineation. Instead, it opens out the text as an acknowledgement of that very writtenness of being already mentioned, even as writing seems to 'sew things up' or 'stitch things together'. There is here a playful and parodic gesture of *mise en abyme* where the determination of the self and 'self-reference' operates through what Hobson describes as 'textual operations of quotation: ... grafts, borrowings, incisions' and 'asymmetric repetition' (1998, 75, 78).[6] Ackroyd is not so much closing the circle as he is, in citing himself, grafting his text onto itself in an altered form which in turn alters the identity of the text.

Such self-grafting is then both an act of self-mimicry, a doubling and displacement of identity, which acknowledges the performative and playful in language, and a promise of continued performance. In this self-conscious grafting and reiteration, in the knowing and parodic use of flawed semblance there is a ludic irony which is wholly serious in its playfulness. We may suggest that such destabilization characterizes all of Ackroyd's writing, ahead of any effort to assign to that writing a finite or knowable identity. The question of temporal transference, between reading (the first chapter) and re-reading (the final chapter) opens *First Light* to the instability which is already implied in that 'first' passage which, while opening the text is not necessarily 'first' at all. Reaching the end, we have the feeling (do we not?) that, in appearing to return to the beginning, we have in fact been forced into a recognition that the beginning is lost to sight, and the so-called beginning cannot be assigned as such. Or, in other words, first light can never be encountered or known.

Ackroyd plies this strategy in a number of different ways, a few of which are signalled throughout the chapters of this book. One more will suffice for now, from *Dan Leno and the Limehouse Golem*. In the first chapter, Elizabeth Cree, a music-hall performer famed for her transvestite performances, about to be hanged for the murders which are detailed in the novel, utters the words 'Here we are again!' (*DLLG* 2). The phrase, immediately suggesting a return of sorts, unsettles the notion of a simple beginning. Indeed, as the hanging itself suggests, this novel begins with a violent end, and any comprehension of that end will require an act of turning back. We are already placed in relation to an implied act of re-reading, while not yet having read.

In the final chapter, Lizzie having already been hanged, a play is staged, based on the life of Elizabeth Cree and her husband. The play is itself not 'original', being an altered version of a play begun by John Cree, and completed by Elizabeth. This serial variation, and the narrative of the play, are themselves palimpsests or parodies of aspects of *Dan Leno and the Limehouse Golem*, a novel which is already composed of diverse documents, including court transcripts which themselves resemble nothing so much as acts from a play. Historical order and temporal linearity is disjointed, dismantled through the play of texts. The new version of the play includes the hanging of Elizabeth Cree, already witnessed in the first chapter and based allegedly on newspaper accounts of the hanging (*DLLG* 279). The actress playing Cree, Aveline Mortimer, walks to the scaffold, refuses a blindfold, looks at the audience (which includes both Karl Marx and Oscar Wilde) and says 'Here we are again!' (*DLLG* 279). Unfortunately, an accident occurs with the machinery and Aveline hangs as she disappears through the trap door. Before the audience realize what has happened, Dan Leno quickly assumes female dress and appears on the stage as 'Elizabeth Cree in another guise', uttering the words in response to the audience's laughter, 'here we are *again!*' (*DLLG* 280). With these words the novel closes. It is not, however, simply the moment when Leno takes the stage, but the memory of the moment. The performance, performed in the eternal present tense of Leno's utterance, is also, simultaneously, remembered and therefore narrated *and* recalled, returning, in the collective memory of the audience who spread out across London. Once again, here we are, – are we not? – caught in the memory, the movement and moment of performance, of transvestism, of the self as other. Once again, there is the promise of connection through the reiteration of the words of the dead, the horror of the double hanging transformed into the grotesque comedy of the cross-dressed performer, a spectral enunciation in which the eschatological gives way, and is opened up, in a promise of endless revenance.

This phrase, with its insistence on return, forms a series in the text, therefore. Each time projected from another's mouth, the utterance economically announces both a staged performance and an unspecified number of past and future moments. Indeed it is the act of 'staging' which gives the reader to comprehend the iterability of the statement outside of any apparently 'original' context. 'Here we are again' is a performative statement, enacting its own utterance with every occurrence. As much as that 'again' announces the serial reiteration, 'here' at once gives the illusion of stable location, the place from which identity speaks, and yet marks also a number of 'heres', as the trace of the fractured structure of the movement of displacement and deferral. There is implied the possible totality of perception and also the constant division of that totality. The phrase economically attests to the disruptive return of a performative language. The words, 'here we are again', mark a certain overflow within language, a certain act of destabilizing citation which cannot be reduced to a single presence, an authoritative voice, but which announces, once more, that movement of opening. We read and re-read – we never do anything else but reread, even as we have not yet read, once and for all – a structural doubling and serial refraction as the text appears to recite itself. The words of Dan Leno, of Elizabeth Cree, form the iterative trace, the memory of which returns as other than itself, becoming the constant moment of utterance, and always promising that shared recognition of the temporality of being, even as every reader of *Dan Leno* reads, time and again,

— here we are, *again* ...

3

'A bit of a game …': the Styles of Peter Ackroyd II

Chatterton

"There is nothing more real than words. They are reality … I said that the words were real, Henry, I did not say that what they depicted was real. Our dear dead poet created the monk Rowley out of thin air, and yet he has more life in him than any medieval priest who actually existed. The invention is always more real. … Chatterton did not create an individual simply. He invented an entire period and made its imagination his own: no one had properly understood the medieval world until Chatterton summoned it into existence. The poet does not merely recreate or describe the world. He actually creates it. And that is why he is feared." (*C* 157)

Chatterton invents entire moments of time. In this novel, fiction is scrutinized in terms of authenticity and authorship, in three time periods and through a plot concerned with fakery, as critics and reviewers have acknowledged.

Essentially Part One questions the authenticity … of both painting and manuscript. Part Two confirms the

"Oh yes," he said, "it's a question of language. Realism is just as artificial as surrealism, after all." He remembered these phrases perfectly. "The real world is just a succession of interpretations. Everything which is written down immediately becomes a kind of fiction."

Harriet leaned forward eagerly, not bothering to understand what he thought he was saying, but looking for another opening. "That's it, Charles," she said triumphantly. "That is precisely why I need you. I need you to *interpret* me!" She stressed the verb, as if it had come as a revelation to her. (*C* 40)

You hear it don't you? That constant babble through, and across, time, different times? At various speeds and rhythms, voices, styles, merge in ludic polyvalence, in acts of 'monopolylinguism', converging and pulling apart at different times, in different ways. Charles Wychwood, Thomas Chatterton authenticity of Chatterton's continued forgeries of poets like Blake. Part Two is an extended meditation on the authenticity of artistic forgery, using Wallis's faked death scene of Chatterton as its principal extended ... metaphor. Part Three .... Celebrates the dissolution of the distinctions between authenticity and forgery, reality and its representation in art. (Finney 256)

We are told in a brief preface that Thomas Chatterton was born in Bristol in 1752 and died in London in 1770 (*C* 1).[1]

... a few facts ...

As a starting point, the dates are historically accurate. This far at least, Ackroyd's Chatterton is less a fabrication than Nicholas Dyer. However, after the 'historical' preface, a device used by Ackroyd for both *The Great Fire of London* and *Hawksmoor*, ascertainable historical fact, and, along with it, time, give way rapidly in a narrative of ludic realities. Ackroyd's preface offers a brief summary of Chatterton's short career, and how its image has been 'fixed for posterity' (*C* 1) in Henry Wallis's painting of Chatterton's death scene.

"And that is why," he added quietly, "this will always be remembered as the true death of Chatterton."

(*C* 157)

However, as the reader learns, not only is nothing 'fixed', everything remains in process, especially the fragmentary identity of Chatterton, as that comes to be performed by a number of textual variants.

(which one?), Henry Wallis, George Meredith, Peter Ackroyd (the last one being the one about whom we remain the most uncertain). A ceaseless *chatter*ing, in the name of the poet.

Voices argue across the centuries like overlapping tracks of a gramophone record ... this is ... a set of propositions about forgery, imitation, and plagiarism. Who's to say what is fate [sic.] and what is real when you can't tell the difference ... recurring images ... [get] stuck in specially resonant grooves. (Glendinning 1987)

Plausibility is not an issue. (Donoghue 1988)

Whereas Wilde in *The Last Testament* had articulated his own games of performativity, along with his awareness of the extent to which the self is a multiple construct, Chatteron addresses, and is used to address, questions of in/authentic identities more overtly conceived through textual forms.

"Well, you know these writers. They'll steal any ..."

(*C* 100)

This is also the case with *Chatterton*. As the Romantic poet and forger/ventriloquist is employed by the author to foreground questions concerning largely Romantic notions of origins, artistry, creativity, and

In *Chatterton* the illusion of a living past is woven with the contemporary scene, to include, again, that past within the text, but the technique is problematised, through Ackroyd's movement between historical fact and historical fiction, between questions of authenticity and questions of forgery. Here, a first person manuscript, allegedly by Chatterton, turns out to be a fake, although a (fictional) historical fake – for what it's worth, and as opposed to a *trew historie* – and not produced in the twentieth century. The painting of a middle-aged Chatterton, discovered by Charles Wychwood, is also found to be a fake. In fact, so too is half of the initially established plot of the novel. Ackroyd thus focuses upon questions of form, style, and historical veracity all the more emphatically to draw their very authority into question. In so doing, he plays with the reader's epistemological certainties about questions concerning artistry and originality.

> "How goes the poet Rowley in your Bookshop?"
> "The Monk is too prolific," he said ... "I cannot sell him as much as I did before. There are some Voices raised against him ...There are some who say that he is an Imposture."
> I turned around quickly. "He is as real as I am!"
>
> (*C* 90)

Like *Hawksmoor* before it, *Chatterton* is an intricately structured text. *Chatterton* is riddled with possible – as well as impossible – connections and plagued by plagiarism. Such forgery and fakery, along with the ludic possibilities which these present originality, so, too, is the novel put to work, to tease out the reader's assumptions behind these supposedly stable notions.

> [Chatterton and Wychwood] ... **conduct an unwitting conversation: they echo each other, speaking in fragments that yield a coherent dialogue only when the walls of time dissolve (as they do at the arsenic-clouded, visionary close of the novel) ... characters grow fragmentary – become beings whose missing portions quest through another era.** (Leithauser 1988)

> [Ackroyd] ... tells us, repeatedly, that fiction is deceit. That all art is forgery ... Then he tells us a few facts and allows us to mark them as true or false. Within the fiction, we put them down as true because – we try to play this game as best we can – they are false in a historical sense, and therefore fiction ... Ackroyd has always been interested in the play between the reader's and the writer's fictions (and their realities) ... (Manguel, 1988)

Indirectly, through the figure of Chatterton, Ackroyd asks the reader to consider on the one hand the nature of artistic production, and, on the other, the extent to which Chatterton's invention of Thomas Rowley and his texts may legitimately be considered 'true' or 'false', in relation to normative assumptions concerning acts of plagiarism or pastiche, solicit the equally normative comprehension of realist narrative concerns. Issues of style and play are not only devices for playing with the narrative, however: for they are shown to be immanent within narrative and fictional form, neither deviations nor aberrations but central to all fictive and novelistic enterprise.

Chatterton is reflected by and reflects Charles Wychwood, also a poor poet, married to an art gallery assistant, Vivien, and with a son, Edward.[2] Charles is 'haunted' by images of Chatterton's ghost and becomes obsessed with Chatterton after acquiring a portrait and manuscripts he believes to be of and by Chatterton. Chatterton's alleged manuscript takes the form of a confessional memoir:

> These are circumstances that concern my conscience only but I, Thomas Chatterton, known as Tom Goose-Quill, Tom-all-alone, or Poor Tom, do give them here in place of wills, Depositions, Deeds of Gift and Sundry other legal devices.
>
> (C 81)

At first one reads this pastiche as the words of Chatterton. Ackroyd appears to allow that the document is from Chatterton's own time, not some later act of impersonation.

However, while the document is authentic inasmuch as it is old, it is still a fake, written not by Chatterton, but by his Bristol publisher, Samuel Joynson, a number of years after Chatterton's death. That narrative and autobiography are

'real' or 'fake', when the alleged author never existed in the first place. In causing this to happen, a particular 'style', supposedly historically grounded, is taken out of time, and replayed, so that authenticity becomes questioned through the displacement of temporal stability; it comes to *chatter* anachronistically in another moment.

Chatterton is a Chinese-box sequence of deceits. (Manguel 1998)

… the contemporary story also illustrates the increasing complexity of the relationship between fiction and reality. In an age of highly sophisticated techniques of reproducing reality and of multimedia simulation, the problems of imitation, plagiarism, copy and originality can only be experienced by means of multi-layered fictions that signal an informed awareness of their own fictionality. (Schnackertz 1994, 498)

Chatterton is a multilevel construction. (Firchow 1989, 681)

The time of a text is, then, never simply that of its production; its times are multiple, and all of equal importance or unimportance. Chatterton, for example, does not 'invent' medieval poetry so much as he ventriloquizes or otherwise acts as a medium for the textual revenant.

Chatterton is, however, merely a privileged agent for the temporal already falsified in the past leaves the reader with no possible certainty, and the uncertainty is further complicated, the textual *mise en abyme* opened ever wider as we acknowledge the references in this so-called 'authentic-fake' to *King Lear, Bleak House*, and, in that unnerving temporal displacement where anticipation or foreshadowing can only be read retrospectively, to Ackroyd's own later novel, *Milton in America* in the figure of Goose-Quill (Milton's secretary).[3] Writing, pseudonymity, literary relations and disguise are all invoked, gathered in the figure of the faker *par excellence* Chatterton.

> ... the painting contained the residue of several different images, painted at random times.
>
> (C205)

Paintings can also be 'faked', of course. The art gallery 'Cumberland and Maitland', at which Vivien works, has separately and inadvertently been lured into trafficking fake paintings, and it is here that Vivien meets Charles' old employer and acquaintance, Harriet Scrope. Scrope is an ageing novelist who plagiarises her plots from the neglected nineteenth-century author Harrison Bentley (who, interestingly, is the author of a novel titled *The Last Testament*).[4]

> When Philip accidentally comes across Harrison Bentley's novels in the library, the first title he reads is *The Last Testament* (a flagrant piece of self-plagiarism) ... Another of Bentley's novels is called *Stage Fire* [which is] ...

conjuring which Ackroyd effects. He is as much a prey to the *chatter* of voices, styles, texts, as he is their imitator. Not only is he disturbed by the spectral traces of the past, he also, in turn, assumes the same role, as stylized projection. In this novel, the poet is no more 'real' than, George Meredith or the poet Charles Wychwood. Moreover, Ackroyd accords none of the so-called principal characters either a central role or an authoritative voice,

> [Ackroyd's text] ...**refuses to put forth a central, reliable narrative voice that stands up and delivers judgments about life, that is firmly anchored in a particular historical time** (Pritchard 1989, 39)

all are left to echo, to *chatter* free of any moorings. They have no more authority, finally, than the constant misdirected and playful, desultory utterances of Harriet Scrope, which at least have the appearance of either seeming to miss the point altogether (and therefore being meaningless) or, otherwise, always being on the verge of meaning something terribly significant.

> "... Who's to say what is real and what is unreal?"
>
> (C 30)

Chatterton ... highlights questions of artistic originality, of truth and invention, of imitation a sly reference to Ackroyd's own *The Great Fire of London* ... Ackroyd appears set on overwhelming his readers in a plethora of unending literary borrowing or plagiarism in which he freely admits his own involvement. (Finney 1992, 254)

Oltre ad imbattersi nel libro di reminiscenze, Philip riporta alla luce il compromettente passato di Harriet, individuando precise analogie fra i romanzi di quest'ultima e le opere di un misconsciuto scrittore vittoriano, Harrison Bentley. L'episodio fornisce un tipico esempio della struttura speculare di *Chatterton*, che que adotta pure la forma della *mise en abyme*. (Giovannelli 1996, 156)

She tries to gain possession of the fake manuscripts and portrait also believing them to be authentic. Scrope's friend and foil, Sarah Tilt is writing a book on the subject of death as represented in painting, thereby simultaneously reiterating the trace of death once more and keeping the subject alive, as it were. This, of course, brings her into acquaintance with Wallis's 'Chatterton'. Also, in the nineteenth-century narrative which mixes fact and supposition, certainty and speculation, Wallis himself appears, along with the poet George Meredith who models as Chatterton for Wallis and whose wife leaves him for Wallis at the same time as the picture is completed. Meredith masquerades as the figure of Chatterton,[5] and his childless, failed marriage stands in contrast to Charles's loving, if strained, marriage. Also appearing, of course, is Chatterton towards the end of the novel,

and plagiarism as well as of forgery and literary make-believe ... By combining several narrative levels with a pastiche of various styles, Ackroyd succeeds in producing a text that in many respects resembles Chatterton's fabrications. (Schnackertz 1994, 495)

"Are you in the realm of fiction? Or merely the imagination?"
(*C* 10)

Chatterton is a novel about plagiarism and forgery and the ways they necessarily complicate traditional notions of truth ... Ackroyd interrogates the idea of plagiarism by suggesting that there is not much difference between Chatterton's inventing his Trew Histories from fragments of old bills and the accounts of earlier historians, and his "forging" the verse of actual dead poets under his own name ... Rowley is Chatterton, and Chatterton's gift is not for forgery but ventriloquism, the ability to refract his own voice through a variety of personae. (Shiller 1997, 552–3)

"He's all written down, *he* is ..."
(*C* 55)

By recreating the life and legend of Chatterton in passages that never deny their status as fictional reinventions, Ackroyd seems to on the last day of his life. This brings us back to Charles, whose resemblance to the poet is part of the larger ludic structure of possible resemblances:

> [Ackroyd] links events, real or imagined, by likeness and not by chronology. He sets aside the official privilege of sequence, cause and effect, and produces a simultaneous concatenation of likeness and differences, regardless of temporal impediments. (Donoghue 1988)

Ackroyd's manipulative temporal and narrative play summons elements from the various pasts. Furthermore, he acknowledges the primacy of texts as mediations of history over any knowable or verifiable past. Historical documents, as we come to understand from Chatterton, are

> ... texts that supplement and rework 'reality' and not mere sources that divulge facts about 'reality'. (La Capra 1983, 18)

All three principal figures, Meredith, Charles and Chatterton, are intimately related within an explicit context of 'false representations'. The reader is confronted by epistemological uncertainty concerning the status of historical figures, literary characters and the nature of the novel itself. Here one finds the 'real' Chatterton, the Chatterton invented by his publisher, the Chatterton of a fake portrait, the Chatterton of Wallis's painting, a modern variation of Chatterton in Charles.

> "There are so many different layers".
> (C 205)

have put into practice critical insights expressed by his fictional characters. (Schnackertz 1994, 497)

We have knowingly alluded above to the occasion of *chatter* in *Chatterton*, for much of the text is comprised of gossip, doxa, informal conversation, hearsay, and, generally that kind of speech or text which appears marked by what Peter Fenves has termed 'the phenomenon of meaninglessness' (1993, 1).

> "Is that what they say?"
>
> *But the whole discourse totters on the verge of saying nothing in a way that is perilous for Ackroyd's enterprise, or ought to be, were it not for the fact that saying nothing is precisely what he is after...* (Dodsworth 1987)
>
> "Yes, that's what they say!"
> (C 38)

As Fenves makes us aware, chatter is disruptive, especially of teleological conceptions of the function of language (1993, 6). Chatter chatters on (and on). It never ends, and, in its disruptiveness, it continues, effecting alteration and rupture. Through time, chatter echoes and resounds, as hearsay and dubious evidence suggesting several different narratives and fates (or fakes) for Chatterton (though no 'authentic' or 'original' Chatterton is ever available,

Ultimately, such multiple figuring turns upon the understanding that 'Chatterton' is only knowable as an invention of literary and cultural history; he is as 'invented' as any so-called historical character, a product of various official, institutional, aesthetic, and historical discourses, commentaries and narratives, but also, equally the product of two hundred years of hearsay, gossip, and *chatter*. Furthermore, a production and performance of discursive techniques and devices which seek to 'make him real', Chatterton – all of him/them – is neither more or less 'authentic' than is *Chatterton*. As Philip, a librarian and Charles's friend, says of the 'Chatterton' manuscripts:

> None of it seemed very real, but I suppose that's the trouble with history, it's the one thing we have to make up for ourselves.
>
> (*C* 226)

'And where does that interpretation come from? It comes from you and me ... Don't you think I worry when everything falls apart in my hands – but it's not the facts I worry about. It's me.' (*H* 200)

The subject of authenticity is not only addressed by Ackroyd with regard to works of art, manuscripts or paintings. Death comes under scrutiny also. Chatterton's death, which Ackroyd imputes to an accidental overdose of arsenic intended to cure venereal disease, inculcates the initial plot idea of the book: that Chatterton, from the appearance of the fake first-person manuscript,

any more than had been Oscar Wilde).

> The Lenos ... are two living palimpsests of accumulated echoes ... (Onega 1998, 35)

This is effective in the text because assumptions are made according to what is one possible visual equivalent of 'chatter', similarity or resemblance, rather than logic. As Denis Donoghue puts it, Ackroyd 'links events, real or imagined, by likeness and not by chronology'.

He sets aside the official privilege of sequence, cause and effect, and produces a simultaneous concatenation of likeness and difference, regardless of temporal impediment. (Donoghue 1988)

In *Chatterton* events have consequences, even if they violate our usual assumptions about cause and effect. There *are* coincidences and merely thematic connections: Chatterton's forgeries are recalled by Harriet Scrope's acts of plagiarism, for example, and just after his wife announces her intention to leave him (for Wallis), Meredith sees in a shop the portrait that Wychwood acquires more than a century later (173). But coincidence does not in itself account for the interweavings of the novel's events. (Janik 1995, 173–4) actually faked his own death at the suggestion of his publisher, Joynson, in order to write pastiche fakes of the popular poets who had recently died:

> And so it was (to look forward a little) that after my untimely Departure from this Life I first began upon the newly discovered Works of Mr Gray, Mr Akenside, Mr Churchill, Mr Collins and sundry others: I even coppied Mr Blake, for my own love of his Gothick style, but this was for the Foolery only.
>
> (C 92)

This faked manuscript and the portrait, seemingly of a middle-aged Chatterton, are picked up by Charles from an antiques dealer, a certain Mr Leno.[6] Charles is convinced the manuscript and painting are 'real', that is to say by and of Thomas Chatterton.

> The Lenos ... are two living palimpsests of accumulated echoes ... Harriet Scrope ... has the striking inborn capacity of the ... 'monopolylinguist' to assume different roles and voices and to mimic other characters ... (Onega 1998, 35)

He becomes obsessed with this, but his enthusiasm is marred by the symptoms of a brain tumour from which he will die.

> "*Pasticcio.* It is *all pasticcio.*"
>
> (C 160)

We may wish to make the distinction that, in the temporal play of the novel, while Chatterton is consigned to die repeatedly,

Coincidence, chance, both are meaningless in themselves unless we seek to order them, to give or enforce upon them the meaning we believe they lack. The relationships between the various narratives and the comments of various characters tantalizingly nudge up against the possibility of significance, if only we could work out what the significance is. Yet, even as they do this, so the possible logical connection falls prey to the 'chatter'. Indeed, it is often the case that it is in the act of seeking to decode the chatter, that we believe we have found a connection, lured as we are by a certain promise. The promise of organisation is, to borrow from Peter Fenves once more, 'prone to fall into the hands of "chatter" once its immanent telos – answering a question posed and imposed in turns – no longer finds its security in incontrovertible *seriousness, authenticity, and reality* – or, inversely, in mere irony, playfulness, and humor' (Fenves 1993, 26; emphasis added).

> ... our expectations as readers are ... baffled. (Peck 1994, 496)

The 'tone' or 'style' never stays in place. Were it in fact to do so, then critics and reviewers could, with great confidence organise the ludic text according to some definition, such as 'pastiche' or 'comedy'. Yet it is this play, between the possibility of meaning and the meaninglessness of events which just happen to be drawn back into the nineteenth and twentieth centuries, only to die all over again, Charles Wychwood dies only once. Imitating Oscar Wilde again, it seems perfectly reasonable that Chatterton dies repeatedly, this is his tragedy; Wychwood, on the other hand, dies once, that is his. Or is it? As John Peck acknowledges, Wychwood's death is comic and Ackroyd signals the estrangement of the 'tragic death scene' by repeating the phrase 'the last time' five times (and not, as Peck states, four) (1994, 446).

"He didn't die ....

At that instant of recognition he smiled: nothing was really lost and yet this was the last time he would ever see them, the last time, the last time, the last time, the last time.

(*C* 169)

... Thomas Chatterton didn't die"

(*C* 97)

The novel therefore reads as though it were an articulation of the dictum that history is destined to repeat itself, the first time as tragedy, the second – and the third, and the fourth, *and* the fifth – as comedy or farce.

"You only live once, don't you?"

(*C* 107)

Flippancy aside, however, the multiple deaths or, to put that another way, the continual dying – Chatterton, it seems, just can't help himself, he will continue to do it – acknowledges the problematization of any simple notion of temporality. The

similar, with which Ackroyd disturbs the reader.

Harriet Scrope's chatter is the most obvious, though by no means the only, example, of the way in which relentless chattering always seems on the verge of seriousness, while resisting all the while that meaningful recuperation through seemingly constant dalliance. This ambiguity is particularly pointed in two conversations: the first with Charles Wychwood over his 'discovery' of the Chatterton papers and the questions of authority, authenticity, plagiaristic license (*C* 97–9); the second with Sarah, in making comparisons between themselves and two women, sitting on a park bench (*C* 107).

"Why not?" Sarah seemed mollified. "You only live once, don't you?"

"Well in your case, let's hope so."

(*C* 107)

In being neither simply serious nor simply playful, Ackroyd effectively suspends seriousness, which is not, as Fenves points out, the same as simply playing (*pace* Dodsworth). In doing so, He 'opens up the magical circle of "chatter"' (Fenves 1993, 26), and thereby makes possible the numerous resonances within characters dialogues, and across time, which might mean everything or nothing, in spite of the reader who seeks coherence, unity and closure.

novel is not working out the dialectic between historical and fictional time so much as it is collapsing all distinctions between the claims of differing temporal models. I am not able to experience 'my death' properly speaking, as Derrida argues,[7] but the death of another is endlessly transmissible, not as an experience, but as a textual trace, which, of course, is not death as such even if it bears within it as the guarantee of its iterability the possibility of the death of someone. Death is figured in the novel as that which cannot be experienced as such – not only can I not experience 'my death' but, also, I cannot experience the death of another – except as that which can be 'faked' so to speak through textual transmission. Death in the text is never authentic.

"But is it Meredith or is it Chatterton?"
(*C* 161)

... usually when someone ... dies, you read it in the newspaper 'So and So Died'. Now, if the next day, you read 'He or she died', and, then, on the third, and the fourth, days, you read this yet again, after a year you would start asking the question, 'What's happening with this dead person'? Because s/he goes on dying for years and years and years! (Derrida 1996, 224–5)

"He is always *pasticcio*."
(*C* 160)

It is this idea which is given comic textual form in the insistent reiteration of last times, as a form of textual joke at the expense of the eschatological (and the unpublished poet). There is then,

This law collapses at the slightest challenge to a strict boundary between the original and the version, indeed to the identity or to the integrity of the original. (Derrida 1985, 196)

Chatter intrudes everywhere, of course. Even in the act of novel writing. Philip Slack, Charles's friend and a librarian, abandons his efforts to write because his novel 'had become a patchwork of other voices and other styles, and it was the overwhelming difficulty of recognising his own voice among them that led him to abandon the project' (*C* 70)

... a patchwork of other voices and other styles ...
... to fake the world of a faker
...
(*C* 221)

Philip abandons his project for two reasons at least, both having to do with chatter's temporal, textual contamination. First, the patchwork of voices and styles, coming from numerous and disparate 'sources' and times (all of which are 'lost' as far as the novel is concerned), reveal for Philip the impossibility of being 'original' or of inventing anything. Chatter drowns the single voice speaking of its own myth. Second, the form of the novel, described by Bakhtin as 'the sole genre that continues to develop, that is as yet uncompleted' (1981, 3), is always already chatter. Heterogeneous and protean, again, no 'authentic' death in the text – in any text for that matter; there is only the 'inauthentic' textual simulation. This is guaranteed by the very title of the text, by its 'improper' use of a proper name, used to name a fiction.

> He would always be here, in the painting. He would never wholly die.
>
> (C 230)

A question of signatures and styles then, always iterable outside of some proper context, always living on, in some form, in another time, as a textual trace.

> **There is no proper name ... that does not begin to insinuate itself into the language system: what will be called literature ... the proper name bears the death of its bearer in securing his life and insuring his life.** (Bennington 1993, 107)

it resists having imposed on it the solemnity and propriety of an authorized definition, where, in the guise of an institutional authority, with the full weight of authorization, some voice, some critic, comes to speak, authentically as it were, of a genre, as if it were dead. In the face of that unaccountable 'monopolylingual' patchwork, this authentic voice is recognisable, all too inevitably we feel, as what Peter Fenves terms 'the customary discipline of last resort', aesthetics (1993, 254). Last resorts, last things, last times. In the face of these, there is *Chatterton* as exemplary carry-on, escaping 'the dialectic of meaningfulness and meaninglessness, as it likewise escapes the distinction of past and present...' (Fenves 1993, 226), a text where no writer ever seems to finish a project, and every one just chatters on, and on, and ....

English Music

> ' ... it's a looking-glass book. You're only meant to hold it and *look* as if you've read it. That is the meaning of criticism.'
>
> (EM 31)

> 'One view is quite enough for one book.'
>
> (EM 33)

Published in 1992, *English Music* presents the first-person narrative of Timothy Harcombe. The novel begins in 1992, when Timothy returns to the East End of London, where he was raised by his father, Clement Harcombe. Timothy is talking to someone, and his opening words, addressed directly to the unknown companion, evoke the relationship between being and time: 'Yes. I have returned to the past. I have made that journey. "You can't go back," you said when I told you of my intention. "Those days are long gone." But, as I explained at the time, that is not necessarily true. One day is changed into another, yet nothing is lost'

(*EM* 1). From the first word, we are aware that this is a response, an act of responsibility. A number of times are indicated in this passage: the unending present tense of Timothy Harcombe's response suggests that this response will always continue, that nothing will be lost, at least to memory or in a textual form. Timothy and his father used to perform a mediumistic faith-healing act during the 1920s in a local working-class theatre, known as the Chemical Theatre. Of course, the theatre is no longer there, replaced by a car-rental showroom and a Superdrug store (*EM* 1). However, Timothy believes he can discern the outline, the ghostly trace of the lost building. Thus, *English Music* opens ambiguously, moving between times, between the memory of the distant past, the moment of response to the invisible interlocutor, and the visit in the more recent past to the place where the theatre had been. Ambiguity and response remain determining figures throughout the unfolding of the text. When Timothy Harcombe says 'Yes' once more, towards the end of the novel, we should doubt the certainty of the affirmation: 'Yes, I have inherited the past because I have acknowledged it at last' (*EM* 399). Acknowledgement may be acceptance, but this is not to say it is comprehension.

The visit prompts Timothy into a teleological retrospect of his life, which will culminate, in the final pages, in the providential 'fall of a sparrow' (*EM* 400), which he helps to bury with his friend, Edward's, daughter, Cecilia. She shares the name with Timothy Harcombe's mother. In the context of the novel's ostensible concerns with the spirit of English culture, there appears to be something of an allegorical resonance to the name, as well as the suggestion that everything returns, 'nothing is lost'. However, we shall return to the end, if only to call it into question.

Tim's narrative involves a period of time spent with his grandparents, who live in the Wiltshire countryside, near the village of Upper Harford, where he attends school and meets Edward. Following his time at school, Tim drifts into a job as a guard at an art gallery in London, eventually to become a circus entertainer, passing from being a clown, to becoming a 'thought-reader' and a 'ventriloquist' (*EM* 396 cit. Onega 1998, 41). This pairing is itself ambiguous, in that Tim's powers are open to interpretation as being equally genuine or merely an act.

Periodically, throughout his life Tim comes back into contact with his father, who appears increasingly, to the reader if not to Tim, shabby, pathetic and helpless. At the same time, Tim gradually, slowly comes to be aware that he has certain spiritual powers, when at first, in the Chemical Theatre, he had believed his father to be the medium. Perhaps the greatest comic conceit of *English Music* is that, for a medium, Tim is stunningly short on insight or foresight. As Chris Goodrich puts it, 'we understand which Harcombe is truly special long before the son himself does' (1992). The conceit is further played by the fact that this 'autobiographical memoir' *is* a teleological retrospect, a carefully constructed and playful narrative reinvention of the life on the part of a somewhat unreliable – because obtuse – narrating narrator, the elderly Timothy Harcombe, who ventriloquizes the narrated narrator, his younger, other self. Acts of ventriloquism and possession, of mediumistic revenance cross-fertilize one another, so that the reader is hard-pressed to tell whether everything is a staged, and stagey performance, or, within the terms of narrative possibility, a 'genuine' act of possession.

The epistemological uncertainties of Timothy's narrative, and how, exactly, to define the paradigm within which to place this fictional autobiography, are further confused by a series of mediumistic 'scenes' or 'seances', appearing as the even-numbered chapters of *English Music*. At particular crises in Timothy's life, the narrator escapes, literally and psychically, into visions and dreams constructed from his favourite reading matter as replayed, distorted versions of the canon of English culture – narratives from Dickens, Conan Doyle, Lewis Carroll, Bunyan, Defoe. Yet the dreams are not explained through Timothy's alleged spiritual powers. They emerge, in the words of Hermann Schnackertz, not from this so-called power, but from 'critical notions such as pastiche and palimpsest' (1993, 499–500). The dreams are then, in themselves, ambiguous, not clearly dreams, but formulaic imitations of literary forms of imitation, so to speak. All intrude in the alternating chapters, as do scenes which draw on Blake, Mallory, Hogarth, William Byrd, with, seemingly, touches of Edward Upward and Ronald Firbank, as well as a supporting cast of many more. This cultural heritage, in which Tim finds himself involved, amounts to the 'English Music' of the title, or so we are led to understand. There appears to be little particular order to the vision-narratives, no progression in terms of Timothy Harcombe's story, other than as contrapuntal moments. In musical fashion, these scenes suggest fantasias and interludes, rather than having any construction of thematic importance (except as they are texts which are personally important for the narrator, their significance for him being purely personal and untransmissible, untranslatable). This 'English music' is, it seems, 'taffelmusik', or the entertainments during a Jonsonian masque, rather than the elaboration of some grand narrative. There is not even the suggestion that the narrator of the dream chapters is necessarily Tim (who is, in each narrative, as much its subject as any of the other fictional characters), or indeed, the same narrator from one chapter to the next.

This 'extremely playful novel', involving 'chronological gaming' and 'accomplished mimicry' (Dieckmann 1992), which transforms 'the story of English literature … [into] a parlor game' (Klinkenborg 1992), received largely negative reviews, even from critics who professed themselves erstwhile admirers of Ackroyd's ventriloquial acts of historical pantomimesis. However, the negative criticisms are in themselves instructive, not so much because they fall into the annoyance or wrong-headedness of a few of Ackroyd's reviewers – they don't – but, instead, as a critical tendency, the reviewers all stop just short of a point from which a reading can be sketched, or, at least, proposed. If anything, there appears to be a consensus of critical expectation as to what is expected of Ackroyd. *English Music* throws the reviewers for a loop. It does so seemingly through being, in a particular light, playfully gaming with the very expectations of what Peter Ackroyd will do next, based on the *a priori* evidence of what he has already done in the previous novels. If we expect one, or perhaps two, pastiched voices, here we get several, and some of those play with one another. At least Chatterton, Wilde, Dyer, all stayed were they were meant to be, more or less (allowing for the transferential ghostly temporal drift). *English Music*, on the other hand, confounds expectations and anticipation by seeming to perform a pastiche of the pasticheur, parodying the ventriloquist. It does it in so bald a ludic manner that all 'purpose' or 'meaning' is unknowable, making it difficult, if not impossible to 'read' this novel at all. At best, all we can perhaps hope for is to explain it. If a novel is all too quickly surrounded by that 'filter of commentary' described by Derek Attridge, mentioned earlier in the book, then the established novelist, we would speculate, can never arrive without such a network of complicating traces which enmesh and distort the reception of 'Peter Ackroyd'. What therefore remains to be done, if only in order to forestall the transformation of the proper name into a constricting adjective of supposedly self-explanatory definition? (Kafkaesque, Borgesian, Shakespearean, Beckettian, Dickensian ...)

Chris Goodrich of the *Los Angeles Times* (already quoted) admires a number of the novel's features. Finally, however, he is forced – or, at least, forces himself – to ask 'what does "English Music" add up to?' Not to worry though, in case you thought this was a merely rhetorical question. The critic answers himself, albeit hesitantly: 'It's tempting to say "not much"' (1992). If no one forces the critic into a response at least, it's good to see he's capable of putting words into his own mouth, pursuing his own act of ventriloquism. Goodrich does have some ready reasons why the novel does not add up to much.[8] These are, we are informed, 'the book's unrelenting Englishness' and the fact that '"English Music", as written, feels insular and constricted' (1992). Wondering momentarily about that 'as written' – opposed to what? 'not written' in this manner? 'not written' at all? Transmitted in some non-graphic, non-inscribed fashion? –, we move on to the two accusations, wondering if there might not be some connection here of which Goodrich is not aware.

D. J. Taylor also suspects something is going on in *English Music*. There is a certain familiarity for the reviewer between Ackroyd's latest and other, unspecified predecessors:

Labouring beneath the weight of ulterior motives, *English Music* ends up oddly similar to one of those Victorian novels that are not really novels but philosophical juggernauts.

(Taylor 1992)

Well, we've caught Peter Ackroyd dressing up in public again, looking for all the world, and oddly too, like his grandparents and great-grandparents ('for my next impersonation – the great panjandrum wheel!'). But 'Victorian' hardly feels like the appropriate description. Like Susana Onega's assertion that *English Music* is Ackroyd at his most 'Dickensian' (1998, 40), Taylor's comparison with the Victorian novel of heft doesn't quite fit properly. If we're going to play Peeping Tom with the novelist, we had better be certain our knowledge of historical costume is fairly accurate. Arguably, and for reasons I will come back to, we should consider *English Music* not as some pseudo-Victorian text, but as equally Edwardian and, if not exactly Thatcherite in its attitudes and responses to, and manipulations of, English literature and culture, then certainly marked by or manipulating its historicity, showing the signs of its cultural moment of production, to indicate in shorthand fashion particular discursive, ideological and epochal resonances of this novel. (Which is not to suggest that Ackroyd identifies with either the Edwardian or the Thatcherite strain.) For, as Verlyn Klinkenborg puts it, 'it's hard to tell whether [Timothy's] visions are meant to be some sort of curriculum or a sign of spiritual election' (1992). Perhaps it is not quite as difficult to decide as the *New Yorker*'s reviewer thinks. As one possible answer to Klinkenborg's doubt, we cite James Buchan's assessment of Ackroyd's mix of major and minor canonical authors, which he describes as offering an Englit anthology, of which 'even Sir Arthur Quiller-Couch would have approved' (Buchan 1992).

Buchan's *Spectator* review acknowledges Ackroyd's 'distorted or even partly demolished' versions of Englit, while also indicating the importance of fathers and 'father surrogates', who find themselves combined in the 'person of the Maim'd King and of Albion itself' (1992). Instead of reading these as signs of a certain perspective on Englishness, he decides, negatively, that the novel somehow 'fails'. Instead of being in the land of hope and glory, we're in the last resort of aesthetic judgement once more. Hermann Schnackertz finds the novel 'especially irritating' because of the 'exclusively English character of its ancestry and the repeated emphasis on the Englishness of English art and literature' (1993, 500). The novel 'fails' because Ackroyd's 'national platonism [is] ... sentimental, incoherent, and selective' (Buchan 1992). 'The view of culture *English Music* implies', writes Schnackertz, 'is that of a closed entity which reproduces itself by continually repeating and varying some eternal quality of Englishness' (1993, 501). Alison Lurie, in the *New York Times Book Review*, comments similarly that the '"English Music" of [the novel's] title is not only insular but conservative, even reactionary' (1992). Lurie's review, generally positive, finds *English Music*'s insular paternalism hard to take because of its political incorrectness. These sentiments are echoed in Verlyn Klinkenborg's discussion of paternal inheritance: ' ... the real issue in this novel, as in all matters of cultural transmission, isn't inheritance. That may be the means, but authority is the end, and the two are inseparable ...'

> The anxiety of influence is one familiar model of inheritance – a model full of pompous poetic fathers and upstart poetic sons fighting over the literary estate.
>
> (Klinkenborg 1992)

If authority is the issue at stake, then it's dead-end authority, for its own sake (isn't much authority just this?). This is, as John Bemrose asserts, in Eliotic vein, 'the self-conscious shoring of tradition against ruin [which] ... has the effect ... of an unwitting obituary for [English] culture' (1992). Quibbling over the accuracy of that 'unwitting', we feel – don't we? – that Bemrose is onto something, as are all the others in their own way, when he says that the 'novel founders in its depiction of Timothy's dreams'. Although Bemrose means this as an aesthetic criticism of the novel's composition, taken as a deliberate gambit on Ackroyd's part, such floundering becomes readable as a performative critique of crisis, not in English culture *per se* – that is to say not in novels, plays, poetry, music and art – so much as in its reception, transmission, and dissemination. This critique is precisely that which engages a number of the critics already cited above, directing them in their negative commentary.

As the 'unwittingness' of Ackroyd's project is questionable, so too is the defining moment in Christopher Lehmann-Haupt's review. He points out that '... the dreams don't really develop the narrative's point, but instead keep repeating it' (1992). Yes, they do, and if these dreams are, in fact, Timothy's dreams, then surely, as dreams they should be a form of repetition of Timothy's crises, rather than some form of surreal development of the narrative. The insistence on and inevitability of a cycle of repetition-compulsion born out of both the anxiety of influence and the cultural myopia of limited perception, which leads to misinterpretation, is wholly typical of a certain historical and cultural impulse in the narrative of Englishness. We find, for example, such a response in Wordsworth's appropriation of Shakespeare, Milton, Sidney and others in his 1807 sonnets as a cultural nationalistic defence against the perceived 'threat' of the French to 'British freedom' (Wordsworth 1987, 63–64). We find it equally in the mistaken belief of every public-school boy who assumes that Blake's poem, which becomes the hymn 'Jerusalem', is a paean to English national identity, and not a critique of industrial capitalism from a radical Christian perspective.[9] But, to return to Lehmann-Haupt, who continues:

> ... This suggests that the sound ... [not the meaning] ... matters, ... which
> in turn implies an unfortunate sentimentality toward English music, an
> attitude that if it's traditional, it must be good.
>
> (Lehmann-Haupt 1992)

The defining moment, spoken of above, is in that choice of 'unfortunate'. The
sentimentality might not be unfortunate if it is included for a particular
purpose, or if it can be read against the grain. The reviewer, in common with a
number of the other critics of *English Music*, begins to understand what
Ackroyd is doing, but not why he is doing it.

Recall briefly particular phrases and expressions in the reviews so far quoted:
unrelenting Englishness; insular and constricted; some sort of curriculum; sentimental, incoherent and selective; not only insular but conservative, even
reactionary; sentimentality; national platonism; Sir Arthur Quiller-Couch
would have approved. Let me add one more, from T. A. Shippey's review in
the *Times Literary Supplement*. Shippey discerns in Timothy Harcombe's narrative of failures and nostalgic longings a narrative form similar to that found in
particular works by William Golding and Julian Barnes. He describes this as
'all very recognisably English, but not the kind of national image that everyone would like to have' (1992). The novel, Shippey concludes, is 'Englishly
simple'. Shippey's is not a negative commentary, but helps lead the way.
There is discernible in the reviews a movement towards a reading of *English
Music*, towards which we have ourselves been heading, by tracing with a
degree of ironic distance *and* proximity that same movement. The question
here is one over a degree of separation: separating Ackroyd from the text, separating Ackroyd from Harcombe. What Shippey's comment suggests is somewhat obvious, yet it is the reading we would emphasize, over those readings
which merely see the novel as a wooden or somewhat mechanical acknowledgement of the power of 'English music'. This understanding of the novel
finds in it an indirect critique of all those very same qualities of Englishness,
which the reviewers apply to the novel without irony, and which find themselves given voice in the sentimental and limited figure of Timothy Harcombe.
It is not, as John Bemrose suggests, that the novel represents 'a militant assertion of an unfashionable conservatism in the trendiest format imaginable'
(Bemrose 1992). Instead, we would read in *English Music* the ironic mimicry of
cultural attitudes, especially towards the teaching of Englit, of the all too fash-
ionable conservatism of the 1980s and early 1990s.

However, this is not to suggest that Ackroyd's critical attack is solely a local
response to a particular cultural and political moment, for Thatcherism's cultural agendas are merely the most forceful and overt expression of a group of
impulses and attitudes, extending back through the history of Englishness,
and belonging to a more general anti-modernist trend. One expression of this

in an educational and cultural context is to be found in the effect of F. R. Leavis, the journal *Scrutiny*, and the legacy of Leavisism on 'the rapid expansion of higher education and teacher-training in the 1950s' (Sinfield 1989, 183). Leavis desired literature's centrality in any articulation of the Englishness of English culture and tradition. That desire came to serve in the definition of the teaching of literature from both liberal and conservative perspectives, as Alan Sinfield points out, so that, on the one hand, it 'claimed to define the "good culture" that most pupils were to enjoy under welfare-capitalism', while, on the other, 'it insisted that only "the best" would do and promoted a call for "standards"' (Sinfield 1989, 183). Ackroyd also points out the effects of Leavisism in *Notes for a New Culture*: 'Leavis's writings have redefined academic notions of "poetry" and "tradition", as they appear to us in a national guise. His critical works have exercised a pervasive influence in the teaching of literature in the universities and schools ...' (*NNC* 80). This is Ackroyd in the early 1970s. First published in 1973, Ackroyd's statement still held true in 1993, the year after *English Music* and the year of the republication of *Notes for a New Culture*. Tory culture of the 1980s and 1990s was only the latest manifestation of this identity. As we know at the close of the twentieth century, the Leavisite model still remains central to any reinvention of education, regardless of particular party politics. When Christopher Lehmann-Haupt criticizes Ackroyd's yoking together Lockean rationalism with the ratiocination of Sherlock Holmes in *English Music*, he sees this as something of a tired gesture, and 'a point that the critics like Hugh Kenner milked dry many decades ago' (1992). Yet the reviewer misses the point, we feel. For the versions of Englit which are generated through Timothy Harcombe in the 'national guise' of *English Music* are those which have persisted from Leavis to Kenner, down to the present moment. Talking of the Edwardian and Georgian periods, Ackroyd describes the legacy thus: '[i]n England [of the early part of the twentieth century] the dominant tone is still liberal, anti-theoretical and humane; the seventeenth-century values upon which this tone is based became more and more transparent until they left only a residue of familiar truths which survived by being decorative. This would be of simply historical interest were it not that one of the few major innovations of the period was the establishment of "English studies" in the universities. The tone of the age still leaves its imprint here, since it was precisely that humane and practical culture which was defined and indeed institutionalized within 'English studies' – and it is the one which persists into our own time' (*NNC* 37–8).

The ideological investment in the idea of a continuous tradition founded on literature, which in turn serves a hegemonic purpose is, partly, the focus of Ackroyd's critique of Anglo-Saxon culture in *Notes for a New Culture*. Timothy Harcombe who, the reader will notice, never connects in a visionary moment to any literary work produced after the end of the nineteenth century, is not

only the privileged agent of a particularly pervasive and often dominant manifestation of Englishness, he is also the embodiment, described by Ackroyd in
Notes, of the 'rationalist-romantic "I", which continued and still continues to
exert so powerful a spell within our culture' (*NNC* 22). Harcombe, who narrates with the '"I" of moral experience' (*NNC* 37), is the imaginative (and,
from a distance, comic) projection of Leavis's sense of the English 'tradition',
and his humanist belief in the ability of human experience to impart
significance to English literature (*NNC* 117–18).

We can read the struggle for the assertion of the dominant 'Leavisite'
version[10] of Englishness in at least two places in *English Music*. The first is in the
dialectic between the characters of Lewis Carroll and those of John Bunyan, into
the midst of whom Tim is placed in Chapter 2, where a debate concerning the
meaning of the text and the meaning of criticism is pursued (*EM* 27–47). Carroll
and Bunyan's texts serve as exemplary texts of two interrelated yet distinct traditions within English culture: the didactic and moral, and the subversive and
carnivalesque.[11] The second example of the contest for the tradition comes in
the pastiche of Dickens, in Chapter 4. An initially unidentified voice utters the
following statement: '"My father's name being Pirrip now, what I want is,
Facts"' (*EM* 73). The easily recognizable remarks, belonging to *Great Expectations*
and *Hard Times*, are brought together in a clash between the imaginative and
the rational, where, in this deformation of Dickens, the former appears subordi-
nated to the latter. The constitution of Englishness, we can speculate from
Ackroyd's reinventions, involves the constant struggle between alternative traditions, both of which are fully at work, until the twentieth century, when the
establishment of English studies marks the ascendancy of one tradition over the
other. For Ackroyd, a key moment in this ascendancy and its establishment is
the founding of the English School at Cambridge (*NNC* 48–50), under the guid-
ance of Sir Arthur Quiller-Couch in 1913, from which, as Ackroyd puts it, somewhat archly, it is 'only a short step' to the 'two jewels of the Cambridge English
School, F. R. Leavis and Raymond Williams' (*NNC* 49).

English Music thus enacts the experience of the institutionalization of
English studies within a 'national guise', through the figure of Timothy
Harcombe, its mapping of 'Leavisism' demonstrating the connectedness
between the cultural moments of the Edwardian and Georgian eras and that
of our own. If *English Music* is selective, insular, incoherent, sentimental, in its
tracing of tradition, then this is because Timothy is also the textual figuration
of these qualities of Englishness, as well as being the embodiment of the critical reception of literature for most of the twentieth century. The teleological
retrospect of his life demonstrates that being, while it has a temporality, also
is culturally embedded.

I am tempted to say at this point, in a particularly English idiom, that it goes
without saying that Timothy Harcombe is *not* Peter Ackroyd; except that, if it

does indeed go without being said, then the chances are that, in being left unsaid, the opposite will be assumed as being implicit on the part of certain readers. Certainly, this chance is at stake in many of the reviews which never quite divorce their comprehension of Englishness from the 'aesthetic failure' of the text. Put briefly, they mistake the playful performative critique of the text as an unironic constative statement concerning the nature of Englishness. The figure of Timothy Harcombe so effectively dominates the shape of the text – and why should he not, it being his narrative, after all? (as long as 'his' narrative names a certain narrative of English culture) – that 'his' visions or versions of English culture, English tradition, and the selection of texts which help construct these, must, perforce, be channelled and mediated through the conduit of his culturally, ideologically, philosophically, and historically generated identity. As Verlyn Klinkenborg proposes, 'the borrowed characters ... can be only be as big as Timothy ... and that is not big enough ... The story of English literature becomes a parlour game through which Timothy ... sullenly wanders' (Klinkenborg 1992). The figure of Timothy is written by that 'family of concepts' identified by Ackroyd in *Notes for a New Culture* – that which is 'continuous, familiar, simple, solid, sensible' – 'which initiated the modern movement in England' (*NNC* 15). If Timothy Harcombe's indirect, unreflective expression of national identity, given articulation through a selective tradition of texts of which Quiller-Couch would have approved, is a form of Platonic nationalism, then it is wholly coterminous with what Ackroyd defines as the 'neo-platonic colour' which confirms the 'pervasive orthodoxy of [for example] Coleridge's writing, a writing which stays "within the bounds of traditional opinions" – which are, in fact, the bounds of humanism and of that extension of humanism in subjectivity' (*NNC* 32–3).

The 'thick net of anglocentric allusion' (Dieckmann 1992) should not therefore be taken as simply, unequivocally celebratory. For, to do so, and to 'call Ackroyd's tea-and-crumpet cosmos retrograde' (1992), would be, as Katherine Dieckmann implies, to miss the point entirely. It would also be to fall into a simplism similar to that which is made manifest through Timothy's attitude towards English culture.[12] Of course, Timothy is not only shaped by the constrictions of an orthodox tradition, he is also, as a 'literary figure', determined by the unseen, silent contexts of his youth (unseen and silent that is, in this novel). For Timothy's voice is as careful a pastiche as any of Ackroyd's other pastiche voices – Wilde, Chatterton, Dyer – even if it is a pastiche of a cultural identity rather than being an impersonation of a particular person. If the reviewers were disappointed by *English Music* this may have been in part due to the fact that, behind their reviewing, there was the implicit assumption that Timothy Harcombe's voice was not a pastiche. The assumption is easy to make. Timothy is, after all, a character in the twentieth century, he is not some well-known historical figure or variation thereof (even though he is drawn in part from the Victorian medium,

Daniel Home, and Home's account of his son, as we learn from Ackroyd's 'Acknowledgements'). However, as with all Ackroyd's first-person narrators, Timothy's is a pastiche voice, a patchwork of texts. (As a rule from which he is otherwise yet to deviate, Ackroyd's twentieth-century characters are all generated through third-person narrations, frequently 'types', though not necessarily conscious pastiches of other writings, other figures.) Timothy's 'voice', and, with that, his cultural identity is generated, not only from the tradition of Bradley, Coleridge, Arnold, and, yes, Quiller-Couch, but also from the humane, sentimental voices of Edwardian and Georgian writers, such as Galsworthy, Wells, Priestley, and Bennett. The experimental modernism of Joyce and Woolf, of the Bloomsbury group, the Vorticists, and of Wyndham Lewis's *Blast*, passes Timothy by, as his voice lingers in the sensible tendencies of backward-looking, nostalgic-romantic writing, belonging to a predominantly male authorship.

Such influences, which mark Timothy Harcombe as undeniably English, attest to the ambiguity between the celebration of a culture and the anxiety which the tradition of that culture produces. There is, moreover, an irreducible gap between these and between the subjective experience or perception of a cultural spirit and the impossible narrative re-presentation of that spirit. (*English Music* cannot be said to 'fail' based on comparisons with other novels by Ackroyd; the pastiche in this novel is generated from another place.) When Tim, talking of his father, says:

> [a]nd in my imagination, as he talked, all these things comprised one world which I believed to be still living – ... it was a presence around both of us no less significant than the phantom images which I sometimes glimpsed in the old hall.
>
> (*EM* 21)

While we read that what Tim senses in his imagination might well be 'true' for him, – and we might also interpret Tim's perception of 'one world' as a partial recognition of personal time as part of the totality of the temporal structure – this is never available to us, any more than it is transmissible. Tim's father appears to convey to Tim what Tim cannot convey to us. On the other hand, it may just be that nothing is conveyed. Tim's narrative memory might be unreliable. In this image we read the 'dead-end' of paternal transference; The transmission from father to son comes to a halt. Despite the desire implicit in Tim's re-marking of the moment for the father-son regeneration, the myth of continuity – which is, after all, that on which all notions of tradition are built – comes to an end in the very act of narrative transmission.

It is for the unfolding of the paternal problematic and the revelation of the limits of transmission that Katherine Dieckmann praises *English Music*, which she describes appropriately as 'more necrofiction than metafiction':

The straight-up narrative portions of *English Music* deal with the simultane-ously joyous and stultifying legacy a father hands down to a son ... [in] a world where anxiety is exclusively paternal ... the dead weight of paternal tradition is too much to be anything more than mechanical ... Nothing happens in *English Music* without a permeating layer of loss and the recog-nition that while these authors and their works may be invoked and resus-citated ... mostly they're just dead.

(Dieckmann 1992)

Thus, Dieckmann concludes, *English Music* is a novel which 'explores the seemingly exclusive paternal anxiety of influence both culturally and person-ally' (1992). Dieckmann's review perceptively identifies the general tenor of the text. We would take this further only in suggesting that the 'permeating layer of loss' which shapes Timothy Harcombe's sensibility is not solely his. Once again, this sense of loss is peculiarly English, lending to 'the polyphony of English music', what Hermann Schnackertz defines as the quality of 'a strangely flawed nostalgic elegy' (1993, 500). Schnackertz intends this as a crit-icism of the novel's aesthetic design, but he is more accurate than he intends. For the elegaic sense of loss in Tim's narration amounts to a virtually invisible troping of one of the pervasive characteristics of national identity's narration to itself. We need only consider, in passing, the national ritual outpouring of sorrow over the death of Diana, Princess of Wales, given its crucial *English* voice in Elton John's transformation of 'Candle in the Wind', particularly the first line which synecdochically states 'Goodbye English Rose', to understand both the importance and the *Englishness* of this sense.

Timothy Harcombe is, then, inescapably, typically, English of a certain sort. He is English down to his family name, which is readable in a variety of playful ways. Combe – or coombe, or coomb – is a very old English word, the origins of which are obscure. It names a topographical feature, a deep valley or hollow, and occurs frequently throughout the South of England. It is thus sug-gestive of a linguistic continuity connected to a sense of place. At the same time, the first syllable of Timothy's surname echoes the name of the village in Wiltshire, near to which his grandparents live, *Har*ford. However, and unless we take this too seriously, there are also several partial homonyms to be heard in Harcombe, which, while being playful, are not merely puns but, seemingly, have a degree of possible significance for the reading of *English Music* we are advancing. Two words, then, ghosts or palimpsests, are heard or traced here: *hearken* and *hokum*. The former, of course, suggests the act of listening, of attending to the sound of 'English Music'. Tim is always listening, and responding also, from that very first 'Yes', which implies a response to some call, which the reader cannot hear, but which Tim can. The latter of the two words, *hokum*, signifies, appropriately enough, that which is sentimental,

popular, or that which involves sensational or unreal situations. If this resonance is extended momentarily, to catch other more distant aural similarities
or resemblances, we may hear *hokey-pokey*, a vernacular variant on *hocus-pocus*,
implying deception, conjuration or trickery. This is of course applicable to
both Tim's life and his narrative. Furthermore, there is also, ever more distant,
hoker, meaning to mock, or the figure of the *hokester* or *huckster*.

Admittedly, we have appeared to have travelled a great distance from
Harcombe. Tim is, however, only one in a line of visionaries and illusionists,
tricksters and conjurors, shamen and showmen, impersonators and ventrilo-
quists, not only as regards his genealogy in *English Music* but also to be found
throughout the texts of Peter Ackroyd: Joey Hanover, Thomas Chatterton, Dan
Leno, Charles Dickens, William Blake, John Dee, Oscar Wilde. The ambiguity at
the heart of Tim's 'performance' – his exercise of his 'powers' and his story – is
unresolvable. It is impossible to tell whether Timothy Harcombe is either a fakir
of a particularly English kind, or a faker, equally English. For, against the dead
weight of paternal authority, there is to be found in Tim, as the suggestion of
otherness within his identity, the circus tradition, the tradition of Dickens's
Sleary. For all his nostalgic seriousness, there is also in Tim the shadowy figure
of carnivalesque play at work. As Ackroyd makes us aware, not only in this
novel but elsewhere, the ludic counter-tradition will always resurface and return
at the very heart of Englishness, and as a necessity of that identity (as Sleary tells
Gradgrind 'you *mutht* have uth, Thquire' [Dickens 1989, 390]).

The playfulness confronts the paternal tradition in the very close of the novel,
when the elderly Timothy Harcombe walks into the garden – leading the reader
up the garden path, so to speak – to observe Cecilia burying 'a small dead bird'
(*EM* 400), as already mentioned. The merest possible allusion to *Hamlet* (or even
little Nell's death scene) aside, there is offered in this scene a double temptation
to make connections and suggest continuities: between this Cecilia and
Timothy's mother, Cecilia, as a means of completing a temporal circle of sorts,
while also gesturing allegorically towards St Cecilia; and between the dead bird
and the live bird, which fills 'the white lane with its song' (*EM* 400), and which,
as Laura Giovannelli says, may be connected to that other *Byrd* of English Music
(1996, 238).[13] Such meanings are no doubt possible. But, as the younger
Timothy asks the White Rabbit in the first of the dreams where *Alice's Adventures
in Wonderland* become mixed up with *Pilgrim's Progress*, 'how can you decide to
have a meaning in the first place? And who decides what meaning you should
have?' (*EM* 33) Deciding on a meaning is precisely what the final page of the
novel appears to tempt the reader into doing, in the name of continuous tradition.[14] But to be alarmingly naïve for the moment, disingenuously so in fact,
the fact remains that Timothy Harcombe is the last of the line. The anxiety of
influence is such that, ironically, despite his apparent reverence for the myth of
continuity, he is only, and will only ever be, a son, never a father. Paternal

authority is confronted by its own end, the only gesture of closure in an otherwise open-ended text. Cecilia, as we are told, is Edward Campion's granddaughter, no relation to Timothy. The desire to make a meaningful connection between her name and that of Timothy's mother is merely that, a desire engendered by Ackroyd's playful text. Similarly, there is no other connection between the live and dead birds, other than that which Timothy's narration would lead us into assuming as decidedly there. (Birds do happen to sing in trees in the Wiltshire countryside, after all, even when others drop dead.) Which is why, if nothing else, the reader should be wary of seeking out connections, especially those which are so teasingly obvious.

Like Edward Campion, we are wrong if we assume that the 'recurring cycles of history' (*EM* 399) trace a seamless, endless return, always returning to the same spot, in the same manner. Temporal moments never return as themselves to themselves, as we have seen in Ackroyd's conclusions to both *First Light* and *The House of Doctor Dee*. The past returns but only ever as other than itself. For, as Timothy Harcombe acknowledges, the so-called 'recurring cycles' 'disappear as soon as you recognize them for what they are' (*EM* 399). Narrating the cycle and tracing the connection effects a form of translation. The past moment is transcribed into something other than it might have been. So, there is reintroduced an irreducible gap, which desire for continuity seeks to close over, and, in so doing, to read the unreadable. What Timothy momentarily finds opened to him is an awareness of the aporetic between experience and re-presentation. No narrative or critical construction can ever do anything except reintroduce that aporia.

First Light

If *English Music* is, in part, a novel concerned wryly with the stultifying effects of a blind, unthinking adherence to literary tradition, *First Light* interests itself in the desire to create narratives, to construct a tradition from narratives and to perform a narrative of tradition, where all makes sense and is given meaning from the ever-present moment of self-consciousness within the temporality of being. Yet, it is also about the impossibility of achieving the full teleological closure of a narrative circle which might otherwise connect us as beings desirous of narrative completion and reflective wholeness. *First Light* parodies both narrative closure, and the narrative of closure even as it parodies those who seek to read such a narrative. It rejects not only adherence but also the desire for mastery against which *Milton in America* issues a caveat, even as *First Light* appears to tempt the reader with the promise of a mastery of sorts, through, once again, the obvious intertextuality of its construction.

Like *Chatterton*, *First Light* is a busy, occasionally feverish babble of voices, as John Peck suggests (1994, 447), which refuses to calm down or be ordered. One of Ackroyd's most densely populated novels, *First Light* takes place around Pilgrin Valley, in Dorset. It offers us Damian Fall, an astronomer, Mark Clare, an archaeologist, and his wife Kathleen, Joey and Floey Hanover, retired music hall comedians, Evangeline Tupper, a lesbian and civil servant responsible for liaison between the archaeological dig which takes place in the novel and Whitehall, The Mints, a farmer and his son who own the land on which there is an ancient burial mound in which the archaeologists are interested, and Augustine Fraicheur, a gay antiques dealer who specializes in time-pieces, and describes himself as being 'an old thespian at heart' (*FL* 70; 'I can't help it. Put me near a stage and I yearn for tights'). These are only the most prominent characters, and the polyvocal anarchy is not limited to them. As the example of Augustine Fraicheur demonstrates, many of the voices in this novel verge on the crass and excessive, to that extent that, from certain conventional critical perspectives, exemplified by the comments of some of the novel's reviewers, it might appear that Ackroyd is almost out of control, or that his material threatens to escape him. As Peck argues, the novel is 'an uneasy mixture' veering

> between seriousness, even attempted profundity, and the most crass effects ... The novel veers between comic and serious scenes, ... often shot through with literary echoes ... we are, consequently, thrust into genuine areas of uncertainty.
>
> (Peck 1994, 443, 447)

While Peck regards the dis-ease as a deliberate strategy which prevents the reader from obtaining any 'stabilising perspective' on the novel (1994, 447), this is described elsewhere, in a review of the novel from the *Daily Telegraph*, as 'ludicrous solemnity conspiring with grating frivolity', much to the reviewer's irritation (Cropper 1989).

Such destabilization is only part of the ludic play in which Ackroyd indulges in order to forestall and frustrate narrative mastery, along with the possible assumption of control and closure. Frequently, characters misunderstand one another's statements, while countless comments are ripe with ludicrous mala-propisms and blatant double entendres, which surface at those moments when the novel seems to be at its most serious. Again, like *Chatterton*, but to a greater extent, *First Light*, with its story involving 'London sophisticates, country rustics, modern technology, and ancient mythology' (Bovenizer 1989, 53), is a broadly comic, not to say farcical novel, which will insist on reinventing the high and tragic with broadside vulgarity. The most obvious examples of this are the novel's own play with Thomas Hardy's *Under the Greenwood Tree* and the amateur dramatic production in the novel of T. S. Eliot's *The Family Reunion*, which is played – the very idea! – for laughs. The comedy often arises not at the expense of Hardy, but at the expense of Hardy-ites and their faithful adherence to the 'seriousness' of Hardy's world view. Thus, while *First Light* does not overtly replay a particular historical and cultural moment through pastiche, it is somewhat reminiscent of *The Great Fire of London* in that it does play between narrative conventions concerning reality and fiction, while also resounding with the spectral oscillations of an earlier text, though not as obviously as Ackroyd's first novel had done.

Dealing once again – here we are, *again* – with a general sense of the past, with narratives we believe we can invent in order to reinvent and thereby control the past, *First Light* is nonetheless not one of Ackroyd's novels of possession. (Even though it might indirectly be said to parody a genre of pastiche fictions 'possessed' by the spirit of Victorian fiction, beginning with John Fowles's *The French Lieutenant's Woman*, which, like *First Light* takes place partly in Lyme Regis, known not only for being in 'Hardy Country' but also providing the literary landscape for Jane Austen's *Persuasion*.) As David Sexton puts it approvingly, *First Light* is a novel, which is 'not so much' an example of '"demonic possession", as Ackroyd getting togged up in the verbal equivalent of a white sheet and capering around going hoo-hoo' (Sexton 1989). We might follow this by recalling the words of Ebenezer Scrooge, saying of *First Light* that there is more of gravy than of grave about it. There is certainly plenty of sauce ladled on, much of it of the 'Carry-On' variety. It is as if it is Ackroyd, and not Fraicheur, who longs for tights, as well as a white sheet in this stagey, often melodramatic novel. Whatever the case may be, the critical agreement is that this is a 'deliberately mannered novel' (Glazebrook 1989) invoking, simultaneously, the horror and comic genres (Crowley 1989), amidst 'so thick a welter of allusion … [including] Kipling, Wilde, Blake, Thomas Hardy … Frazer … T. S. Eliot, James Joyce … [that] the plot is hard to delineate' (Abel 1989, 46). The novel combines both 'creepiness' and 'farce' (Prescott 1989), it grafts 'Wodehouse … onto *The Golden Bough*' (Gray 1989), and produces an effect that is both 'bewildering and sometimes beguiling' (Bradley 1989, 636).

There are numerous sites where the novel takes place, but the two which recur the most frequently are an observatory, run by Damian Fall, and an archaeological dig, organized by Mark Clare (Bradley 1989, 636; Massie 1990, 53). Clare's name is clearly meant to tempt us into making a connection with Hardy (specifically with *Tess*), yet we should be wary of this, as John Peck insists. 'Pursuing the connections between' *First Light* and *Two on a Tower* is, Peck argues, a 'mistake … it amounts to … an attempt at cultural possession of Ackroyd's novel … Indeed, it would be hard to think of anything more unhelpful than showing off one's familiarity with *Two on a Tower* as a way of establishing critical control over *First Light*.' (1994, 447–48). If the reader requires further warning against the desire to involve oneself in the literary equivalent of an archaeological dig, Mark and Kathleen Clare's dog, named Jude, should serve as another warning. The intimation is that the Clares have a fascination with Hardy which makes them vaguely ridiculous. This is double-edged, as is so much of Ackroyd's writing, for Kathleen, unable to have children and with a crippled leg, longs to retreat into literary worlds, away from the unbearable emotional pain she encounters in her reality. Such is the pain that she eventually throws herself off a tower. Like Damian Fall, Kathleen needs the reassurance which reconstructing narratives brings. Their demise is, however, only the most extreme effect in *First Light* of the desire for continuity and connection through narrative. Joey Hanover, the one-time music hall comedian, searches for his familial roots, and Mark Clare's work is a constant investigation of the past, a 'reconstruction of the abodes of the dead' (*FL* 78).

Specifically, the desired narrative of connection has to do with family, with the desire to locate one's identity within a general structure of family resemblances, traced back by narratives which are capable, through archaeology or astronomy for example, of reaching back into the past to lost and, ultimately, unrecoverable origins. This is alluded to through the comic production of Eliot's play. Ackroyd goes further by offering a punning connection between astronomy and the archaeological dig, in the name of the star, Aldebaran, and the title given by the Mints to the prehistoric figure buried in the archaeological site, the Old Barren One. The pun does serve a purpose, however. For, if the text is read as presenting the reader with the desire for the family narrative and with numerous searches for family resemblances and reunions, this is constantly thwarted. The suggestion in both the idea of 'first light' and the figure of the Old Barren One as the patriarch of successive generations is that origins and sources are lost, irretrievable, and that there is no unbroken line of generation. The myth of origin is merely that: one more narrative.

Everywhere in *First Light* is the implication that a pattern, a controlling or defining, meaningful structure can be found. Equally, everywhere, the text 'resists this desire', as John Peck puts it:

> We are denied the comfort of any one shape [even at the level of form, because of the text's 'ludicrous solemnity' and crude farce] ... We are teased with the possibility of meaning but then everything dissolves, [and] it is the same with the literary references ... But, as tempting as it is to use these references as keys, it seems far more likely that a game is being played around the very idea of interpretation.
>
> (Peck 1994, 449–50)

Peck is certainly right to make this assumption, for, as already suggested, there are numerous references to the act of, or desire for, story-telling. At every strata, the play with meaning and identity is in full force, whether through allusion and intertextual reference, or expressed on the part of the characters. Almost every character at one point or another makes mention of the importance of narrative. A few examples should suffice, beginning with Damian's interpretation of the stars:

This was the story written across the sky.

(FL 35)

Fall explains that there is no meaningful pattern, merely human desire:

We see what we want to see. In each generation the heavens become a kind of celestial map of human desires ... They reflect all our recent theories about the universe and although we no longer see the stars in the shape of the gods or animals our own theories are no less fabulous ... The stars take on the shapes we choose for them, you see. They become the images of our own selves ...

(FL 158–59)

Fall comes closest perhaps to explaining the only possible connection between humans: the need and ability to narrate as a means of giving meaning to identity. It is not that there is a connection between generations, other than in the connection in the desire for narrative, the desire to find the self mirrored outside the self and through time, even beyond the narratives of history.

The archaeological dig is equally the site of analysis and reading

[Mark Clare] 'Our goals include total recovery, objective interpretation and comprehensive explanation ...'

(FL 37)

Such goals are, of course, impossible, even though what Damian describes as 'fabulous' theories in the form of scientific and mathematical information pretend to objectivity and the totality of the reading act. Elsewhere, astronomers are described as 'interpreters' (FL 44), this being merely part of the text's constant dismantling of the separation between scientific 'fact' and narrative 'interpretation'. As a general principle of the novel, we may suggest that Ackroyd subverts the usual binary logic which insists that science and technology are in some way more pure, more objective, than narrative and interpretative, subjective forms, by showing constantly how scientific procedure is not only informed by narrative, but has developed the illusion of objectivity and technical precision as only the latest in a line of narratological acts. Historically, Ackroyd suggests, the narrative of science, that narrative which can be told of the ways in which science shapes its narratives over the centuries, involves the attempted erasure of narrative traces within scientific discourse, until scientific discourse and method, allied to the technological, hides its narratives even from its own cognition. (It is of course this recognition which dawns on Damian Fall.) Moreover, the impossibility of scientific reading's 'total recovery' is expressed in details of the dig. The archaeological site is 'read' through the use of Euclidean geometry to map its contours and through the measurement of trace elements and signals (*FL* 42, 43). The various traces and signals are read as there, faintly, but are so complex 'that they cannot yet be analysed' (*FL* 43).

There are a number of other references to reading, to interpretation and story telling:

'You're very good at telling stories.'

(*FL* 46)

'It sounds,' said Mark, 'like the beginning of an interesting story.'
…
'You're right,' she went on. 'It was like a story. It was like entering the plot of a novel. And when I was young, did I ever tell you, I always wanted to get inside a book and never come out again?'

(*FL* 50)

Here were the remnants of a culture … relics of that expanse of time which was a 'period' only in the sense that a story must have a beginning as well as a middle and an end. They [the archaeologists] might help refine the story, but it was a story being told in the dark…

(*FL* 93)

'Science is like fiction, you see. We make up stories, we sketch out narratives, we try to find some pattern beneath events … And we like to go on with the story, we like to advance, we like to make progress. Even though they are stories told in the dark …'

(*FL* 159)

And there were no stars, there were only words with which we choose to decorate the sky.

(*FL* 297)

Narrative and the desire for meaning are found everywhere in *First Light*, then. They form a constellation of remarks dotting the text, from comments which appear to strain after profundity, to the most everyday question, such as that asked by Augustine Fraicheur: 'Have you ever read Thomas Hardy?' (*FL* 274). At the same time, there are barely comprehensible signals, traces yet to be deciphered, 'spectral handwriting' (*FL* 295), and inviting inscriptions (*FL* 137, 268, 282, 288). However, there can be no definitive interpretation, no analysis which fixes the limits of meaning or identity. Mark Clare knows that some cryptic discoveries 'might never be deciphered' (*FL* 137). Even the notion of 'beginnings' and 'ends' is called into question, through Ackroyd's ludic gesture of serial repetition, as can be seen above in the quotation which describes the findings of the dig (*FL* 93).[15] The site is given a meaning, an identity by being assigned a period as a means of constructing a mastering historical narrative, but this, the passage reveals, is purely arbitrary. Of Mark's excavation, it is said that 'this was a beginning for him, but an ending for those other workmen who had preceded him' (*FL* 52). This description also assigns the beginning and end as both arbitrary and interchangeable, while this is expressed elsewhere as 'a succession of present moments' (*FL* 134), which itself recalls Hyppolite's discussion of the subject's comprehension of temporality. Mark will affirm the arbitrary assignment of limits and phenomenological perception of moments in time, when he says 'In the beginning there is an end. In the end there is a beginning' (*FL* 220). This is confirmed further when another character remarks 'to see the beginning is also to see the end' (*FL* 262). However, the insistence on the narrative nature of beginnings and ends, is pushed a little further, when it is remarked that 'there was no beginning and no end' (*FL* 289). Limits exist only as determined, interpreted narrative markers. Beginnings and ends are, themselves, narrated constructions, not absolute moments or framing devices outside narrative structure. Acknowledging this, we acknowledge that no narrative is ever fixed and can always be reinvented, against its supposedly 'original' meaning, its context or identity. Thus, to recall John Peck's argument, in *First Light* all meaning and identity constantly undergoes a process of formal and narrative destabilization. What is particularly precarious in this performance of Ackroyd's is that deconstruction in narrative is read in the very act of expressing the desire for narrative; narrative's end for the novelist is to frustrate the assumption of a final narrative form. Meaning is revealed as undecidable, precisely so that the play of narrative, and the concomitant desire to read, can survive.

The comic, the burlesque, farce and the carnivalesque are all identities which rely upon the destabilization of identities. This helps to explain why moments of apparent significance and profundity suddenly overflow their limits through comedic reinvention and displacement in *First Light*. Nothing is safe from the comedic, which is subversive in that it does not merely choose a target but, at its most effective, emerges from within the identity it destabilizes, displaces and reinvents. The comedic displacement is particularly noticeable in Floey Hanover's malapropisms, one of the most memorable of which is her allusion to the 'Hound of the D'Urbervilles' (*FL*164). Conflating Hardy's high tragedy with Conan Doyle's populist adventure, Floey's phrase alters the identity of both works and their canonical status irrevocably.

The most striking comedic transgression is the performance of Eliot's *The Family Reunion*, however. The play's 'quiet sad lines were delivered with a stridency that would have done credit to Gothic melodrama, and the somewhat boring characters ... took on a grotesque life quite different from anything the author could have envisaged .... It had acquired a higher reality ...' (*FL* 152). The description chooses its terms carefully, so that high art is, once again, lowered, the identity 'debased' in pursuit of the performative power. The acquisition of this higher reality has to do with comedy's performative power, its ability to be stagey, to show rather than tell, and to disrupt the constative condition of narrative through the performative revelation which reinvents reality, as Ackroyd puts it of Joey Hanover's performances (*FL* 152). Joey, who attends Fraicheur's production of Eliot's play, immediately recognizes the condition of the performance:

> The world had been transformed into a pantomimic creation, but that did not mean that it was any less effective or any the less moving. It had acquired a higher reality and, as soon as Joey Hanover heard the first lines with their refrain on clocks that stop in the dark, he was entranced by it. This was the kind of performance he had been giving all his life: strident, vivid, colourful, simplified beyond the range of 'character acting'. It had been part of his skill as a comic to understand that everything had its own form, an inner truth or consistency which was not revealed to those who insisted on some distinction between the real and the unreal. No one had asked Picasso to depict ordinary faces; no one asked a musician to transcribe the familiar sounds of the world; so why should not Joey Hanover himself create his own kind of truth by disciplining and reinventing reality? That was why in his own act he took on a character which was like no real Londoner but which still managed to capture the essence of London.
>
> (*FL* 152)

Because of the ludicrous nature of Fraicheur's production, a comic excess which is not accidental but desired by the camp antique dealer (*FL* 70; 'Frightfully highbrow, I suppose .... But I think it ought to be played as comedy, don't you? These tragedy queens aren't in my line at all'), there is that in the performance which Joey comprehends, to which he can connect and which makes sense in terms of his own performative stage persona. This has nothing to do with narrative or representation, but the ability of the comic and the grotesque to side-step conventional modes of representation which rely on stable identities and the illusion of mimetic verisimilitude. This carnivalesque production of *The Family Reunion* is disruptive *and* truthful because it is messy and uncoordinated. The costumes and make-up are badly done, the delivery of lines is poor, there is no suspension of disbelief, no assumption that the audience is watching anyone other than amateur actors caught in a pretence. The limit between 'reality' and the play is broken down because the abilities of the performers cannot enforce the rigid distinction between the two positions.

The first line of the quotation – 'The world had been transformed into a pantomimic creation' – is a fitting approximation of Ackroyd's novel, if not of his ludic strategy in a number of works. In this ludic gesture and in the recognition on Joey's part we may read Ackroyd nodding in the direction of his own 'ludicrous' text, with its frequently camp excesses, its overflow of crass humour. *First Light* effectively undermines itself repeatedly. It can be read as the powerful ludic articulation of the desire to narrate, to read, to structure connections through the attempt to trace meanings. Yet it must also be read as the equally cogent, equally playful enunciation of the impossibility within any act of narration or reading to complete itself. *First Light* explores this compelling double bind in a performative manner, from within the exigencies of the narrative compulsion itself, suggestively pointing to the impossibility of absolute beginnings or ends, and the possibility of other narratives to come.

Milton in America

His dark world has been turned upside down.

(MA 158)

He was turned upside down. His world upside down.

(EM 73)

One of the essential ways of describing carnival focuses upon the *ritual inversions* which it habitually involves .... Carnival inverts the everyday hierarchies, structures, rules and customs of its social formation .... Carnival gives symbolic and ritual play, and active display to the inmixing of the subject, to the heterodox, messy, excessive and unfinished informalities of the body and social life .... The carnivalesque ... denies with a laugh the ludicrous pose of autonomy adopted by the subject ...

(Stallybrass and White 1986, 183)

... what numbers of faithfull, and freeborn Englishmen, and good Christians have been constrain'd to forsake their dearest home, their friends, and kindred whom nothing but the wide Ocean, and the savage deserts of *America* could hide and shelter from the fury of the Bishops.

(Milton 1979, 95)

'World upside down' is the phrase employed throughout *The Politics and Poetics of Transgression* by Peter Stallybrass and Allon White to describe the nature of carnival and the carnivalesque. The words are also those employed of Milton in *Milton in America* when, wandering blindly in the woods of New England, he encounters the local Indians, and suffers a moment of epiphany. (As can be seen from the epigraphs, the words also inform the narrative of Timothy Harcombe in *English Music*.) At the same time, they also announce, comically, John Milton's literal upending, his having been caught in a bear trap. Milton's encounter or epiphany also stages his own recognition of a certain otherness within. It is this recognition which drives him to the brutality against others enacted in the climax of the novel.[16] This being the case, it is difficult to imagine a less carnivalesque figure than that of John Milton, especially the Milton of Peter Ackroyd's novel, that strange combination of self-appointed mythological hero and Puritan law-maker. How may *Milton in America* then be described as carnivalesque, even in part? How may the novel be measured against Stallybrass and White's description of the functions and expressions of carnival play and ludic inversion of commonly accepted social order?

As is well known, *Milton in America* suggestively alters historical narrative in order to posit the possibility that John Milton does not remain in England but travels to New England, to the New World, to become part of a Puritan community, over which he will eventually rule, after first surviving a shipwreck vaguely reminiscent of another wreck, that which opens *The Tempest*. This is only the most obvious of the numerous literary allusions which abound in the text and with which Ackroyd's readers will be familiar from his other novels. The play with history is summed up by Tony Tanner in his, ultimately, unfavourable review:

> While this Milton is historically grounded, he very unhistorically flees London, escaping to New England to establish a settlement called New Milton. There he becomes increasingly tyrannical and finally leads the Puritans in a bloody, exterminating war against a colony of Roman Catholics.
>
> This scenario is ... an instance of what E. H. Carr called 'parlor games with might-have-beens'

Leaving out a few narrative details on the way, Tanner continues:

> In his counterfactual fiction, Mr. Ackroyd swerves away from biographical fact and has Milton, instead of writing 'Paradise Lost,' becoming an almost insane, sadistic Puritan bigot in America. But to what end? Is the game worth the candle? Does it illuminate? Does it entertain?
>
> (Tanner 1997)

Twice, it will be noticed, Tanner resorts to the figure of the game, once in a cited authority. This has now become such a regular figure, along with other related images of play, trickery, performance, and so on, that this alone might give pause to resist taking the same route on which the reviewer is intent. Other reviewers, all more favourably disposed towards *Milton in America* than Tony Tanner, also pick up the same figure. Trev Broughton, for example, in the *Times Literary Supplement* describes Milton as the 'latest in a succession of Ackroyd heroes treading the fine line between prophet and performer, shaman and showman', although he also suggests that the novel's 'characteristic play with form', its mix of 'dream sequence with chronicle, epistle, journal, first- and third-person narrative, dialogue, and dialogue within dialogue', come to seem 'redundant in so densely allusive a work' (Broughton 1996).

Broughton adds to his catalogue of literary forms and styles to point out that Milton's speech is a 'choice medley of allegory and allusion, sermon, scripture, vituperation and song' (1996). Vituperation aside, which is not, as far as I am aware, yet raised to the level of a genre, Broughton's list-making directs our attention to the fact that, like so many of Ackroyd's other characters, this John Milton is not to be considered as a 'real' historical figure, so much as a 'patchwork', if not of voices, then of the movements and rhythms of writing and the text. Milton is, literally, literary. His self-presentation is the attempt to embody a figure of authority and truth. Yet, this is not his voice, but the textual record of that voice, kept by another, by Goosequill, Milton's secretary. As with all textual forms, it is open to the play of undecidability, to slippage and disinterrance from and within itself.

Added to this 'mono-polyvalent' weave, the reader has to contend with the 'reductive and schematic dichotomizing of Puritans and Catholics' (Tanner 1997), a cartoon Milton (Clute 1996), and a sometimes 'fractured, hallucinatory style, switching from one voice to another' (Bernstein 1997). None of this sounds promising, yet we may begin to get a sense of the ways in which this text – '[a]s a story it hardly exists' (Levi 1996) – can be read as wearing its carnivalesque heart firmly on its multicoloured sleeve, if not having its tongue planted firmly in its painted cheek. If this is a narrative which can be read as a tale of the world upside down, then it must also be a narrative which is to be read against the grain. For, despite – or perhaps because of – its ideological and characterological schematization and apparent reductiveness (categories which ring true only if we insist in the last resort on applying realist aesthetic criteria), Ackroyd's 'imagined version' (Jardine 1997) of an alternative Milton 'rings uncannily true' (Jardine 1997) in its depiction of the destruction of paradise. It is, as John Clute suggests, 'scary, deeply prophetic. *Milton in America* is a slingshot ideogram of our loss ... of all the world' (Clute 1996).

If Tony Tanner and other critics who found the novel less than pleasing or convincing have made a mistake then, as is implied above, it is in assuming that Milton is the primary focus of this novel. Milton in America may well name the subject of the narrative, but that is not the same as saying that Milton is the only concern or interest. To believe this is to render oneself, if not as blind as Milton, then certainly significantly myopic. Reading after

Milton instead of reading Milton as one performative figure, neither more nor less truthful than any other, is to be blind to various textual relations. This is certainly, obviously, a novel concerned with blindness and insight, darkness and illumination, even if only at the most banal level. Focusing on Milton, one runs the risk of blinding oneself. However, when Tony Tanner wonders about the price of a candle, and asks for illumination, we have to consider to what extent those remarks were made ironically. Beginning to shift our view of *Milton in America,* we can come to see, along with Peter Levi, that Goosequill is 'in a way ... the hero' (Levi 1996).

Goosequill serves to return us to the novel. Ackroyd's Milton is sententious, harsh in both morality and manner, and, as has just been implied, metaphorically as well as literally blind. He is, in Trev Broughton's words, 'a tyrant, a pedant, a grumpy old sod' (1996). Goosequill, by contrast, is a descendent of Lancelot Gobbo, and an 'unusual comic' for a modern novel (Levi 1996). He is full of 'Cockney repartee' (Broughton 1996), and in Tony Tanner's rather twee phrase, 'London cheeky' (1997; in all fairness, the phrase does have an unintentionally camp quality, it savours more of Barbara Windsor than Windsor Castle). Goosequill, who cheerfully and comically does his best to adapt to the exotic conditions of the New World away from his London soil, makes frequent comparisons between the old world and the new. Specifically, he seeks to orientate himself through peppering his speech with analogies and similes, by which New England is compared with London ('It might be Hackney Marshes on a wet morning' [*MA* 5]; 'Large enough, sir. Not of our London standard, of course ...' [*MA* 37]). There is even a touch of pathos in Goosequill, as he admits to his wife, 'Cowcross Street. Turnmill Lane. Saffron Hill. I could pity myself too, Kate, if I am never to see them again' (*MA* 23). But his comic nature soon surfaces once more, as he makes another of his seemingly endless comparisons: 'I know East Cheap from Golden Lane, but grass is grass' (*MA* 33). Milton's amanuensis is himself an Ackroydian patchwork. He is also that curiously insistent hybrid, the 'low' comic figure who disrupts seriousness through invention and laughter. A figure of aesthetic and epistemological resistance, he affirms his 'low' otherness, and his type is always to be found in 'high' literary forms soliciting laughter, cutting a caper, and leering from the sidelines of the text. At times in Goosequill there also surface echoes of other of Ackroyd's characters. He recalls imagining flying over the roofs of London (*MA* 44), as had Timothy Harcombe in *English Music,* and plays on the London place names which evoke natural features of the landscape (*MA* 75). Again, this is a feature of the conversation between Tim and his grandfather in *English Music* (*EM* 105–6), as well as echoing a conversation between Charles Wychwood and Philip Slack, in *Chatterton* (*C* 48). All of which may be read as mere intertextual play, yet more examples of the novelist plagiarising himself in games of 'postmodern' self-reflection. Yet this

misses the element here which is of vital importance, not only to the characters in question, but to Ackroyd's writing in general, and which will be discussed in the next chapter: the spirit of London, as that which always
intrudes, even in the least likely of narratives.

London is everywhere. So much so, in fact, that Milton himself cannot help
but cite the city, as in a somewhat Eliotic fragment on the first page, haunted by
the figure of Tiresias, perhaps: 'Lycidas. Wandering down East Cheap' (*MA* 5).
The poet's journal also contains reference and comparison with the city similar
to Goosequill, as in the passing reference to the plague (*MA* 38). Yet Milton is
determined to leave behind the old world, even though, ironically, his journal is
written for him by Goosequill, who will never leave London out of the picture.
Thus through the act of writing, the voice of the poet is compromised, cor-
rupted, contaminated, despite his desire for the autonomy and purity of his
voice. Knowing Goosequill to be the pen, it is impossible to read Milton as
simply, only Milton. There is always the implication that the journal is 'doc-
tored' in some manner, not simply because of Milton's metaphorical blindness
to the condition of the world, but also because the poet does not have charge of
the act of writing. Connecting the act of writing, of which blind Milton is no
longer capable, to the poet and ideologue's 'view' of the new world 'dangers' –
the Catholic and non-Christian other – there is to be read the 'anxiety of
influence' which connects and interanimates the personal and the political.

It is as a result of the 'anxiety of influence' felt by Milton that he undergoes an
intensification of his already peremptory character. The development is most
marked following his encounter with the Indians (*MA* 195–8, 216–22, 274–7), as
a possible sign of the desire to distance himself from that within himself which
he feels to be tainted, as though it were not *of* him but some alien contaminant.
Having momentarily regained his sight, a sexual encounter with an Indian
woman turns Milton's Manichean world view on its head. His blindness returns
and he is returned to the Puritans, only to begin a campaign of enmity towards
all those who are significantly different. His hatred of the Catholic community,
organised by the colourful, carnivalesque character of Ralph Kempis at Mary
Mount, grows ever greater, leading eventually to the war which destroys most of
the Catholic settlers and many Indians (*MA* 253 f.). In this war, Goosequill, who
now lives with his wife, Kate, in the Catholic settlement, is killed, as is Ralph
Kempis. *Milton in America* concludes with the image of a blind man wandering,
and weeping, through 'the dark wood' (*MA* 277).

The reader is left with the vision of the destruction of community in favour
of the solitary Dantesque figure, always at the beginning of a journey, rather
than at its end, and destined by blindness to repeat the same mistakes. It is
impossible to conclude that this Milton can ever be right, either in his judgements or his actions. His journey does not offer enlightenment but, instead,
the perpetuation and reassertion of blindness.

The final chapter ends, then, somewhat ambiguously. Blindness returns for Milton, and to him as the comforting reminder of the illusion of the unattached individual. If the final moment recalls Dante, it also suggests the idealist myth of the individual in the natural world, free of all social corruption. Milton longs for a blindness outside of history, as a condition of prelapsarian grace; yet he is blind to the fact that the fall is a fall into the history and time of the world and being. His knowledge of good and evil is within him, it is integral to his being-in-the-world. Forgetting what is within is that which blinds Milton. Blindness is, then, the necessary condition, on the one hand, for Milton's solitary self-absorption. On the other, it is also the necessary condition for Milton's attempted extermination of those not like himself. Blindness is not simply lacking sight, it is blindness to cultural and racial difference. Milton's blindness allows him the illusory vision of the ideal self he believes he embodies. (Ironically, the reader can see, as Milton cannot, that the world of Manichean dualism which Milton projects comes and returns to the poet; his vision already contains the evil which he so longs to extirpate.) Wilful blindness to difference – which is different from ignorance – is indispensable to all assumptions of bigotry and xenophobia. The refusal to see is not the same as the inability to see. As we understand from Ackroyd's formal arrangement of the chapters that tell of John Milton's encounter with the Indians, spread across the text, and the entire incident revealed to the reader's sight only gradually, the poet's response is unreasonable and selfish, born out of anxiety in the face of that which exceeds the self. Ackroyd's character is not eccentric to the point of tyranny; he is wholly self-centred. In being taken in by the Powpow, Milton is vouchsafed the vision of both his desire and his otherness, as it were, which decentres him, displacing him from the universe of his self-contemplation. As a result of this, and subject to seeing himself for the first time, in order to maintain his fragile belief in his autonomy, the poet must reject what Stallybrass and White describe above as the 'heterodox, messy, excessive, and unfinished informalities of the body and social life' (1986, 183).

Milton's blindness is, therefore, not simply his in its rejection of the communal, the other, and, as we shall see, the carnivalesque. If it can be understood in a broader context, if it can be seen from elsewhere as significant of something other than the individual's absence of sight, the reader may perceive a broader purpose. Milton's blindness has, in the context of *Milton in America*, a cultural and historical function in that it serves to define the driving force and condition for Ackroyd of a particular transitional moment in the history of English national identity. It is possible here to give only the barest sketch of the development of cultural blindness. The moment is somewhat sustained, lasting as it does from the Tudor break with the Catholic Church, at least, until the Restoration of the monarchy in the seventeenth century. The official rejection of Catholicism – many people still clung to their faith in secret, as is well known – marks the beginning of the modern separation of England culturally from much of the rest of Europe. As such, it also attests to a desire for national selfhood and self-governance, a desire for individual freedom which finds its obvious parallel in the flight from the old world to the new on the part of the Puritans. However, what is also involved in this act of turning away, of resistance against a dominant hegemony, is an act of turning towards oneself, turning inward, shutting one's eyes in the act of self-identification on that which is different, in order to construct the ideal image of oneself. Blindness acts as a form of parochial self-reflection in the formation of the national subject, leaving its lasting effect on the formation of early modern England. Milton's blindness is not unique. It is merely typical, from one perspective, of its historical and cultural moment, as we see, for example, when he expresses his poor opinion of the Indians, comparing them with the Irish (*MA* 133). The poet and his affliction signify the lengths to which identity formation will go in seeking to enact its narcissistic self-valorization.

As already hinted at, the question of blindness is not solely related to sight in *Milton in America*. There is also *anamnesis* and, within that, a deliberate *amnesiac* will not to remember the past, to be blind to what one cannot forget.[17] One of Ackroyd's achievements in this novel is to force the meaning of blindness in different directions, so as to encourage the reader to look blindness in the face from different perspectives. Blindness is estranged from its more usual sense of 'lack of sight' as it is employed to consider memory, forgetting, the 'remembrance of things past', and the narratives that are told with hindsight. Milton chooses not to see; that is, he wills himself not to remember the common cultural past he shares with others. In so doing, he blinds himself to memory, to that which is already blind.

One particular confrontation in the novel addresses the relationship between blindness, memory and forgetting. Ralph Kempis visits Milton, following the latter's punishment of Sarah Venn. (Venn had been accused of practising Catholicism. She was punished by being flogged with votive candles [*MA* 214].) On being upbraided by Kempis for the woman's punishment, the poet replies:

'It is a necessary thing. We want no Rome in this Western world ....'

'Be careful, Mr Milton, or you will throttle yourself with your own similes. *You forget* that there are many Catholics in our own old country.'

'You might as well tell me that there are some Londoners *addicted* to paganism .... Yet it serves only to prove what a miserable, credulous and deluded mind remains among the vulgar.'

'Do you hear that, Goosequill? Are you one of the vulgar Londoners?'

Where Milton connects the single mind to the unidentified group, Kempis retorts with the single example of Goosequill as a figure of a more general, indistinct form. The conversation continues:

> '*Do you see, then Mr Milton, how the vulgar are always with us*? But those whom you denounce as credulous and deluded are, for me, true worshippers of the pious and the sacred.'
>   'Oh, yes. Let them grovel in the dust with the Indians ....'
>   ...
>   '*You forget also*, Mr Milton, that our country was almost sixteen hundred years a Catholic nation.'
>   '*Do not try to blind me with the darkness of obscure times.*'
>
> (MA 227–8; emphases added)

This debate revolves around memory and forgetting, insight, hindsight, and the opposing claims of a monocular vision and a broader view of events, which rejects the personal and individual in favour of a collective and hetero-geneous social body, embodied in the common practice (as opposed to the institution) of Catholicism. Kempis accuses Milton of selective memory, in the face of the latter's desire for the supposed purity of a 'true' religion, guaranteed only by continental segregation. Milton's narration of religious 'truth' is the impossible invention of narrative deluded into thinking that *anamnesis* can be silenced. Milton's first remark concerning Rome (his use of the plural pronoun sits uneasily with his sense of selfhood, unless he sees himself as the body politic) signals, through the use of the preposition, the fear of the other within the Puritan body. Charged with wilful forgetting, Milton's response is shaped by the expression of sceptical disbelief – 'You might as well tell me ... ' – which harbours self-doubt and anxiety in the metaphor of addiction. This moves to the image of the masses (which, for the poet, is always connected to the practice of the Mass), in the somewhat Rabelaisian form of the 'vulgar', as a collective, undifferentiated noun, marked by repulsion and opprobrium.[18] Puritan Protestantism is clearly, though implicitly, figured here as a faith of the individual elevated above the common, whose worship is simple, private, not given to displays of ritual, and, therefore, hidden from sight. Milton's thought is, again, marked historically in its inward turn as the typical dis-cursive formation of what Francis Barker describes as the emergent 'private and judicious individual' located within the 'bourgeois discursivity' of the seventeenth century (1984, 55).[19]

However, Milton chooses not to see connections. Kempis employs the visual metaphor, in lieu of comprehension, to point to that very connectedness between old and new worlds. When Kempis asks Milton, 'Do you see ... how the vulgar are always with us?' he is employing the figure of Goosequill in an economically synecdochic fashion. The connection is triple: the thread worked by Kempis traces the connections between:

- Individual and group
- 'High' and 'low'
- 'Old World' and 'New World'

Milton would be blind to all these connective fibres, but, as Goosequill's own frequent allusions to London attest, identity can never be kept separate from those heterogeneous elements which inform its constitution. The mark of alterity always inhabits the self, whether that 'self', that identity is Milton's, the New World, or *Milton in America*.

Twice in the debate, Milton is accused of lapses of memory, once he is asked to open his eyes. It is a sign of the connection between memory and sight that the poet, finally, paradoxically, accuses Kempis of trying to blind him. This is paradoxical precisely because Kempis repeatedly attempts to force on Milton both vision and memory, which are related to the historical and cultural identities of a certain Englishness. It is indicative of the degree to which Milton chooses to (try to) forget, chooses to deny insight that, in his speech, he forms an undifferentiated and excessive – and therefore potentially threatening – mass, from Catholics, vulgar Londoners, and Indians (remember the earlier comparison between the Indians and the Irish). In his eyes, so to speak, there is no difference between these groups, as far as the perceived threat that they represent to the poet. The only difference for Milton is that which he invents as anathema, as a means of seeking to distance himself from his others.

Although Milton's distaste, anxiety and fear are directed at various times towards the vulgar, the Indians, the old world, frivolity, and improper humour, nonetheless it is principally Catholicism as cultural identity and practice to which he seeks to blind himself, to which he is in fact blind, and about which he desires to forget. He desires nothing less than the erasure of Catholicism's trace from Englishness. Specifically, it is the rem(a)inder of the cultural heritage within himself as other identity, which the poet would deny. Yet, as Kempis reminds him, Catholicism has had a hand in shaping national identity for approximately sixteen hundred years.

In returning to the question of *Milton in America*'s engagement with the discourse of the carnivalesque as a means of re-presenting the other within a specific identity, it is not suggested that Catholicism is necessarily, unproblematically carnivalesque in nature, even if, in comparison with Puritan Protestantism, its daily practices and public manifestations were certainly more ritualized, theatrical and performative. Catholicism, like the vulgar, is 'always with us', as Kempis asserts. In the dialogue between Kempis and Milton the carnivalesque challenge to the purity of identity is always at work in a certain fashion: the old and the new, self and other, past and present, the vulgar and Catholicism, are all intimately mixed in the constitution of identity. The implied connection between vulgarity and Catholicism is interesting inasmuch as, together, they figure a persistent, vital trace, an indelible contamination of identity. Or, to put that another way, the dialogue can be read as insisting that hybridity, hetero-geneity, otherness and contamination *are* identity. As Goosequill – another of the novel's carnivalesque figures – is always the ventriloquist, story teller and mimic behind the authority of Milton, so the 'low' is always there, within the 'high', vulgarity is always imminent within propriety, and Catholicism's trace is always imminent within post-Catholic Englishness.

In order to understand the carnivalesque function of Catholicism in *Milton in America* it is necessary to remind ourselves of the dual identity of carnival. 'On the one hand,' write Stallybrass and White:

> carnival was a specific calendrical ritual .... On the other hand carnival also refers to a mobile set of symbolic practices, images and discourses .... Symbolic polarities of high and low, official and popular, grotesque and classical are mutually constructed and deformed in carnival.
>
> (Stallybrass and White 1986, 15, 16)[20]

In this novel, Catholicism is not represented in its more obvious institutional, hierarchical and ideological aspects. Instead it serves as part of the carnivalesque play of the text. It functions symbolically as part of a ludic resistance to conform-ity. This is mapped by the text in the establishment of the Catholic-Indian set-tlement of Mary Mount. Here, Indians and English marry (*MA* 187), and camp city comedies are performed alongside Catholic observances (184–5). This is the place where the town's 'baptism' is also, simultaneously, 'a day of revel' (175), to use Ralph Kempis's own words, who says of himself, 'I am not their leader. I am only the master of ceremonies' (177). Catholicism and paganism are both intermixed and placed side by side, quite literally. The statue of one of the Powpows' gods is maintained next to a statue of the Virgin Mary (178).

The two figures are compared by Goosequill to the statues of Gog and Magog in London, and the constant reference back to London is important in this instance. In introducing the third element in the comparison, which directs the reader to a pagan English culture, older than either the Catholic or the Protestant elements, Ackroyd avoids the simplistic, reductive schematiza-tion (*pace* Tony Tanner) of old and new world inhabitants according to Christian and pagan beliefs. Indeed, as is typical of the carnivalesque play in *Milton in America*, several references are made which 'confuse' neat distinc-tions between identities. When asked by his wife, Kate, if there are savages in London, Goosequill replies that there are 'plenty' of savages and pagans in London, but that 'they wear clothes and hats like the rest of us' (*MA* 74).

Although this does not trouble the proletarian, comic Londoner, it does disturb the poet, who says elsewhere of the Catholics: 'They are not true Englishmen. They are merely painted ones, like the Indians' (*MA* 167–8). Again, Milton refers to the 'painted garbage they call the mass' (*MA* 180), and collapses all sense of cultural difference, when, speaking of the Catholic-Indian settlement, he imagines the 'vomited paganism of their sensual idolatry' (*MA* 172). If all this seems an unfair representation of Milton, and marked by reductive caricature, we would do well to remember the historical Milton who, in his 'Of Reformation touching Church Discipline', describes episcopacy as giving 'a Vomit to GOD himselfe' (Milton 1979, 86).

Painting the face and body clearly exercises Milton's imagination. It hints at transgression, corporeal transcoding and even possibly transvestism. Clothing and appearance are part of the carnivalesque in the text, as these confuse identities even further. The first is a description of Ralph Kempis:

> 'Fellow of sanguine humour. Face very large and ruddy like a bowl of cherries. Beard as red as the tail of a fox .... Frock-coat of blue, with a green band around his waist. And on his head, oh Lord, a hat of white felt with some feathers sticking from it.'
>
> (*MA* 165)

The bright colours of clothing and face suggest a figure of pagan revelry, a latter-day lord of misrule. But Kempis is not alone in presenting such an appearance. The Catholic settlers and Indians are described similarly:

> 'They are wearing clothes, sir, as brightly coloured as the drapers' livery. But it is not exactly London dress. Nor is it exactly Indian. It is somewhere betwixt the two'.
>
> (*MA* 165)

> The male inhabitants, Indian and English alike, were dressed in the strangest mixture of striped breaches, wide shirts and feathered caps.
>
> (*MA* 183)

> ... here at last were Englishmen who seemed to revel in the wilderness, who wore clothes as bright as the Indians.
>
> (*MA* 171)

Again, we hear Goosequill attempting to relate the image to the old world. That the dress, described by Susana Onega as 'colourful and disorderly' (1998, 75), is neither one thing nor the other suggests the extent of confusion.[21] Importantly though, the images are carnivalesque because, aside from their obvious playfulness and theatricality, they challenge notions of the appearance of an authentic body. Neither Indian nor Londoner, exactly, in appearance, yet both dressing similarly. There is a performative oscillation at work here, a ludic gesture of transgression and dissidence. In this confusion of dressing up, the individual body and identity is challenged by and dissolved into a festive, theatrical and communal body, the self collapsing into the multiple.[22] It is this carnivalesque dissolution which Milton fears. It is the communality of the excessive, 'inauthentic' body which his language and rhetoric, founded as it is on classical principles, cannot control or contain, and which leads to his description of them as a 'rabble ... of papists, fugitives and savages' (*MA* 171).

It is not only clothing which is colourful and confusing in *Milton in America*. When Mary Mount is first established, Kempis lives in a brightly coloured tent (*MA* 174). Perhaps most significantly, at the edge of the town a brightly coloured Maypole is erected (*MA* 173). As the symbolic locus of carnival, the Maypole attracts the town's performances, some of which have already been mentioned in passing. It is at the Maypole that the town is 'baptised':

> The baptism of Mary Mount, as Ralph Kempis had described it, was ordained as a day of revel. At first light a pair of antlers were brought forth from the forest with drums, guns and pistols being sounded for their arrival; they were carried in state by Ralph Kempis to the maypole, whereupon a native boy took the horns and climbed with them to the top of the pole. He bound them there with a rope, to the accompaniment of loud shouts from the crowd below, and at once the inhabitants of this new town began to drink each other's health with bottles of wine and flagons of brewed beer ....
>
> ...
>
> Goosequill ... was given some cordial of wine and honey in a clay pot, and he drank it down eagerly. Then his hand was taken by an Indian woman and he found himself following the settlers and natives as they formed a large circle around their maypole, skipping and leaping in the spring morning. Then they broke off and watched as the Indian men began their own separate dances; they danced alone, one beginning after another had ended, and Goosequill was delighted by the gestures they employed during the performance. One kept one arm behind his back, while another whirled on one leg, and a third jumped up and somehow danced in the air. Suddenly there was a strong smell of spice, or incense, which seemed to rouse them to even greater efforts. But then the loud ringing of a bell stopped the entertainment. From a canvas tent, painted light blue, two priests emerged carrying a statue of Mary between them. Everyone, English and Indian alike, knelt before the image. Even Goosequill fell upon his knees. But he watched with interest as the statue, painted in white and pale blue, was carefully placed in front of the maypole. The priests implored its aid in this vale of tears, and the boy heard

that it was blessd among women. There was something about fruit, and then the priests carried the Virgin slowly around the pole before returning to their blue tent. The revelry began again and, all that day, there was dancing and drinking and gaming.

(MA 175–7)

The scene is clearly one of carnival, as distinct events, Christian and pagan, high and low, sanctioned and impromptu, are combined to produce a communal, yet heterogeneous identity, in which no one ritual or performance is allowed precedence over another. Even the language of the description mixes discourse, as for example in the first line, where the 'revels' are 'ordained'. Symbolic territories and narratives overlap, co-existing in the same imaginative space. And, as the juxtaposition and cross-fertilization of cultural and symbolic practices makes clear, the scene is carnivalesque in its concentration on 'doubleness ... there is no unofficial expression without a prior official one or its possibility ... the official and unofficial are locked together' (Wilson 1983, 320, cit. Stallybrass and White 1986, 16). It is possible to locate this yoking precisely in that opening phrase, just mentioned.

A few months later after the baptism, on the 'feast day of the visitation of the Blessed Virgin' (MA 183), the play, The London Magician is performed. As quoted above, the nature of the settlers' and Indians' clothing is observed by Goosequill, and we are told that:

The play was to be performed that afternoon .... Goosequill arrived just as mass was being said on the open ground behind the tavern. He was intrigued by the silver and yellow vestments which the priests wore, but looked on in astonishment as the host was raised into the air; then the Indians and English, kneeling on the firm earth, bowed their heads as the bell rang three times and the incense mounted towards the sky. Eventually he left them and walked over to the tavern, with its sign of the seven stars swinging in the breeze ....

...

The London Magician was to be performed later that day, after a procession in honour of the Virgin .... The London Magician was played on a small wooden stage behind the tavern, in the same area where mass had been said that morning. It was a comedy of prose and verse, written at the beginning of the seventeenth century, which concerned the fortunes of a Cheapside conjuror .... Goosequill knew nothing of it, and, since stage plays had been banned during the sixteen years of Puritan rule, he had little real memory of any theatre. So he was intrigued by the play, just as he had been by the rituals of the mass.

(MA 183–5)

Once more, we witness the symbolic overlaying of events on a single ground, the performance of the mass and the performance of the play, both being connected to the tavern. If the ceremony around the maypole had its origins in rural ritual, it was nonetheless, a rite of passage, acknowledging the shift from rural space to urban sensibility as the memory of a certain continuity for the construction of shared identities. The memory of the rural and pagan is sanctioned by the official discourse of Catholicism which enters into the carnivalesque transaction by offering its own performances, on the ground around the maypole, and then on the land behind the tavern. But, as Stallybrass and White make clear in their history of the fair, it is a mistake to see such performances as simply festivals of rural life (1986, 35). Ackroyd marks an important transition in cultural history in connecting the revels to urban development in the new world. Moreover, he brings together competing discourses from within the same temporal moment, while also bringing back into the performance as part of its possibility older performative and cultural elements. Importantly, the social spaces around the maypole and tavern effect the production of a carnivalesque discursive space for the text; event thus becomes imaginatively re-enacted in and as text. Dissipation, disorder, comedy: all exist not merely alongside, but, significantly, *within* the same social and psychic locus as the rituals of religion. Like the chatter of *Chatterton*, carnival in *Milton in America* resists being ordered into some single discourse or identity which performs consistently. The performances of Mary Mount privilege forms of symbolic and semiotic spectacle, where 'languages, images, symbols and objects' (Stallybrass and White 1986, 38) meet and clash in an interanimating fashion, which precisely generates their significance as sites of complex resistance and confusion.

It is tempting, from the perspective of Ackroyd's Milton, to see in the celebrations of Mary Mount that which the historical John Milton describes in *Paradise Lost* as '... the barbarous dissonance / Of *Bacchus* and his Revellers ... ' (7: 27–33), or, otherwise, the 'luxurious, and ribald feasts of *Baal-peor*' (Milton 1979, 98). Certainly, in the second half of the novel, John Milton becomes increasingly intemperate, as we have seen. At one point early in the novel, however, Ackroyd's Milton appears more moderate in his views than either his historical counterpart or his later 'postlapsarian' self, saying that he is not 'undisposed to mix the poetry of history with its plain prose. I have never condemned the employment of mild and agreeable matter, as long as it be not wanton, among high and tragic stuff; there is no harm to be taken from jocose interludes within our epic theme, so long as they are not inclined to gratify a corrupt and idle taste' (*MA* 81). However, notice in this that, wherever a pairing of apparent opposites is offered, the 'low' or 'popular' term is almost immediately qualified, restricted, licensed in the limit to which it can go. *Milton in America* repeatedly tests such license, playing with the Miltonic limits through its carnivalesque disregard of the poles of binary definition. If the novel offers, in Tony Tanner's words, the 'reductive and schematic dichotomizing of Puritans and Catholics' (Tanner 1997), this is only so as to undo the very same binarism which is being established *through* the playfulness of the carnivalesque text.

Moreover, the Catholic/Puritan binarism is not the only pairing which is played out and connected. We have already indicated a small number of binary pairings and oppositions, but the list can be extended:

Puritan	Catholic
Propriety	Impropriety
Seriousness	Play
Blindness	Insight
Forgetfulness	Memory
Intolerance	Tolerance
John Milton	Ralph Kempis
John Milton	Goosequill
Christian	Pagan
Tragedy	Comedy
High	Low
Classical	Grotesque
Old World	New World
New World	Old World
Individual	Community

The list could be continued easily. What is noticeable, however, is that the pairs will barely stay still, once considered in the light of the text as a whole. I have deliberately complicated matters by introducing Milton twice and by juxtaposing 'Old World' and 'New World'. If there is any dichotomizing, reductive or otherwise in *Milton in America*, then it is merely an initial ludic strategy which deconstructs itself through a constant and effective sliding of categories, most notably, as the list above is meant to suggest, from right to left. The contamination and interanimation is relentless, as that which is symbolic of carnival always comes to inhabit the serious, the authoritative, the authentic. As we read here, and in other novels by Ackroyd to greater or lesser degrees, otherness and carnival are not simply forms or terms of opposition. They always already inhabit the self-same and any supposedly well-regulated sense of identity.

4

'Endless Variety': Writing the City in the Biographies, *The House of Doctor Dee* & *Dan Leno and the Limehouse Golem*

London holds a significant place in many of the texts of Peter Ackroyd, a significance which may well be brought to the fore in unexpected and unpredictable ways with the publication of Ackroyd's forthcoming *Secret London*.[1] Not merely the stage on which his narratives are enacted, the city of London is itself theatrical, a performative phenomenon more accurately described not as a place, but as that which takes place. There is an unending reciprocity between the city and the writing subject. As there is always one more undiscovered street, so there is always another story to tell. As one reviewer puts it, in a review of *Dan Leno and the Limehouse Golem*, 'The crepuscular atmosphere of industrial London ... meticulously evoked by the author ... is no mere backdrop for the action; it is the reason for it' (Meyer 1995). As Ackroyd himself asserts in his biography of Charles Dickens, the dark reality of nineteenth-century London determines the novelist's vision of the city, which vision in turn, as a response to that darkness, adds 'to the reality itself.... When we see London now, it is in part his own city still' (*D* 275). London is written by Ackroyd and it, in turn, writes his characters, whether those characters are the fictional Tim Harcombe, Goosequill, or Nicholas Dyer, or the figures of Charles Dickens, William Blake and Thomas More. The Act of writing the city, and the city's performative projection onto the condition of the subject, effectively dismantles any neat distinction between the word and the world, writing and reality.[2] This is not to suggest that the world, or what we call 'reality' does not exist. Rather, the point is, that Ackroyd's writing, and, specifically, his engagement with the urban space, unfolds the interwoven and essentially textual condition of the world and our perception or comprehension of it.

Inasmuch as the city is central to Ackroyd's imagination, Ackroyd may be said to be the latest in a line of London authors who write on the city, responding to its myriad personalities, its multiple masquerades, and its ability to shape and texture any writing responsive to the city. From the anonymous author of *London Lykpeny*, and John Lydgate, to Hogarth, from Blake and Dickens to Sam Selvon and Iain Sinclair, Ackroyd is that writer peculiar to London, who is capable of reading it as what Roz Kaveney has described as '[t]he city of possibilities [which] allows a perpetual reinvention of itself' (1994). Ackroyd allows for this in his description of both the young and the mature Dickens, who understood the 'reality' of his favourite novels' characters, seeing them, as it were, on the streets of the metropolis, so that, in Ackroyd's version of Dickens, the novelist makes no distinction as such between the world of fiction and the world of the city (*D* 66). It is this possibility of reinvention, a condition of London to which the novelist responds, which allows for the spectral possibilities that haunt Ackroyd's novels. Kaveney's definition acknowledges the intimate relationship between the performance of the city and the performance of identity. Like his predecessors and his contemporary Sinclair, Ackroyd finds, again to quote Kaveney 'a[n intertextual] language for describing the physical, emotional and ... spiritual landscape of London. It is intertextual because collage is the only way to represent all the Londons' mapped by the author (1994). The writing of London is, in Ackroyd's texts, 'polyphonic because he tries to do justice to all the London voices he can hear' (Kaveney 1994). The reviewer is describing Iain Sinclair's act of writing the city in *Radon Daughters*, but the same can also be said of Ackroyd's own urban inscriptions, even though they are frequently markedly different from those of Sinclair.[3]

That which Kaveney's review registers in both Ackroyd and Sinclair's writing, suggesting Ackroyd's relationship to those other writers of the city, is the idea that, for Ackroyd, the act of writing the city is not one of describing a stable and predetermined image or identity. Instead, as intimated above, writing the city involves responding to the dictations of London, hearing the London voices, to borrow Kaveney's phrase, or, perhaps more precisely, tracing or attempting to read the multiple and semi-legible, often cryptic inscriptions out of which the city is formed. The ghost of the city remains, even when the city is materially altered, changed even beyond recognition, as the opening pages of *English Music* attest, when Timothy Harcombe, searching for the 'Chemical Theatre', finds only a 'car-rental showroom and a Superdrug chain-store ... a Spar supermarket. Yet *something* remained the same ....The situation of the buildings, the disposition of everything, was familiar to me' (*EM* 1; emphasis added). That *something* is as close as the writer can come to naming the ineffable, giving it meaning indirectly and thereby acknowledging London's resistance to definition. This *something* is indescribably that which either you know and feel, or you do not. It is this response to the 'situation', where the subject comprehends the spectral return – by *intimation* rather than imitation – where the city takes place for the subject, which is explored in the temporal and spatial relationships of, for example, Dyer's churches in

Hawksmoor, or through the layered architectural structuring of Dr Dee's house. From the title of *London Lickpenny*, through oblique references in the poetry; from *The Great Fire of London*, through *Wilde* to a lesser extent and *Hawksmoor* to a much greater extent; from *Chatterton* and *English Music* to *The House of Doctor Dee* and *Dan Leno and the Limehouse Golem*; even to *Milton in America* and, of course the biographies of Eliot, Dickens, Blake, and, most recently, Thomas More. In almost all of Ackroyd's writing, London is always *there*, although difficult to approach. Its appearances and performances are multiple, differing from one another. Yet all occur and recur frequently, often in the same place. London is variously and provisionally camp, theatrical, gaudy, mystical, radical, threatening, melancholy and comic, but ultimately unknowable, for it rewrites itself and erases itself even in those moments of apprehension when its identity seems understood finally. However, this does not prohibit either the novelist or the reader's desire to trace the unreadable, in the effort to make connections.

Ackroyd's writing could then be said to belong, however tangentially, to a genre, if not a tradition, which defines itself even as it escapes definition through the exemplarity of its most singular texts: that of the London novel. This is described by Roz Kaveney as 'a novel of sensation, of chiaroscuro, of mysteries unravelled. At its best it offers a myth of connectedness' (1994). John Clute discusses this myth, in his review of *The House of Doctor Dee*, as the tracing of correspondences which the city makes possible. Clute writes, 'the London of some centuries ago lays its correspondences on the glass sepulchres of today ... frail modern man seems doomed to fade into a shadow and parody of a dead but more substantial figure' (1993). Once again, there is that sense of the possible relationship between place and the subject; or, rather, between what takes place between the place and the subject. As a result, London, 'in all its awful, teeming, endless variety ... erupts from Mr Ackroyd's overheated imagination with the hectic, insistent reality of a nightmare' (Martin 1995). We thus read a doubled metropolis, 'a London at once realistic and mythological' (Pettingell 1996). 'Street cries and street smells are depicted with fidelity', writes Eric Korn, and 'Ackroyd's London is crammed with paranormal apprehensions of something evil around the Isle of Dogs' (1993). Rhetorically, Korn's vague definition and firm topographical location hints economically at the way in which Ackroyd's urban writing manages to unsettle and affect. Ackroyd provides us with 'visions of alternative Londons' amounting ultimately to 'a timeless London' (Korn, 1993). Finally, Francis King suggests that, in writing the city and tracing its endless variety, Ackroyd relies on recurring, favourite metaphors for the relationship between time and the city (King, 1993). These are the architectural and the archaeological, where the city is both structurally and temporally composed, constructed and reconstructed of layers, strata, patchworks of masonry, plaster and timber.

These figures can be seen, as already suggested, most readily in *Hawksmoor* and *The House of Doctor Dee*, where figures of topography and structure overlay themselves in endless textual patterns. The temporal layering of place upon place, event upon event, is caught in *English Music* where the burial ground of Bunhill Fields, wherein are buried Bunyan and Blake, is connected to a dissenters' chapel, then to a working-class theatre (*EM* 1–2; typically, the connection here, between religion and theatre, is one of which Ackroyd is fond). The layering of *Dan Leno and the Limehouse Golem* is of another kind. While it insists on the cultural and psychic accretion of recurring and similar events over a period of time in the same location within the city – as with the example of murders on the Ratcliffe Highway – it also recognizes the textual aspect of this recurrence. Writers return repeatedly to particularly violent and shocking events, whether Thomas de Quincey, Karl Marx, or George Gissing, as *Dan Leno* suggests. The structuring of the city, its performance, is, at least in part, a response to the city's violent moments. Writing is thus shaped by London, and Ackroyd's text is written into this obsessive concern. Even as Ackroyd writes of those other writers, and, by intimation, the fascination with the mythology which has grown up around Jack the Ripper as part of his narrative (also partly the concern of Iain Sinclair's *White Chappell Scarlet Tracings* [1995]), then his own novel is readable as, once again, an act of writing the city as a response to and dictated by the city, and, at the same time, an act of writing the novel into the textual tradition of urban obsession and interest. *Dan Leno* knowingly invokes not merely history but also textual or literary history. Simultaneously, it acknowledges the generation of textual interest, by being structured from numerous textual layers and forms.

This layering, the already reciprocal delineation or tracing of textual and textural reciprocity, is at work ceaselessly in the texts of Peter Ackroyd, particularly as those texts fold themselves into, even as they unfold, the trace of the urban text. Such movement and rhythm of reading and writing become shaped according to London's dictation. We shall consider this briefly in the biographies of Charles Dickens, William Blake and Thomas More, and then in *The House of Doctor Dee* and *Dan Leno and the Limehouse Golem*.

Blake, More, Dickens: 'brief but vivid intimations'

> He would now be instructed in ... *prosopopoeia* ... the assumption of a character – fictional or real – to create a fluent and persuasive discourse.
>
> (*LTM* 30)

The biographies of Charles Dickens (1990), William Blake (1995) and Thomas More (1998) all make plain Peter Ackroyd's sense of the potential interconnectedness between the subject, the act of writing, and the city of London.

Indeed, in a certain sense the three biographies are as much biographies of the city and its intimate relationship with the Law and economic power, religion and dissent, narrative and fantasy, as they are biographies of the lawyer, states-man and martyr, the poet and visionary, the novelist and entertainer. The word 'biography' will not quite do, though. For the narrative of the city is fragmented and reiterative. It asserts itself in momentary surges, appearing, vanishing, and reappearing, intruding to interrupt and punctuate the writing of a life. The bio-graphical subject disappears into the textual movement of the city momentar-ily, as 'biography' unfolds itself from within, becoming temporarily other.

If Ackroyd is dissatisfied with the term 'biographer', as we claimed in the introduction, how might the expression of the city be understood as a break with the biographical? How might these texts be made to escape their identi-ties as biographies simply, through the act of writing the city? How might the response to London and the act of writing the city aid the writer in erasing, at least in part, the limits of biography? Furthermore, in what ways precisely can the writer's interest in the city be said to serve in questioning the identity of the biographical form? What manner of writing might the comprehension of the condition of London help to initiate?

Each of these questions is generated from the premise that London as event, as that which takes place, is refigured in writing not merely as description, any more than it is simply a stage for the subjects in question. Writing the city involves a performative gesture. The language used by the writer breaks away from the act of description or representation to become a performance of the city itself, in excess of the merely descriptive or supposedly secondary scene-setting function of London images in the form of the biography as a whole. Such an act in writing knowingly breaks with the function and law of the merely descriptive passage in biography, which authorizes the biographer to re-present his subject before the reader. We might even suggest that the act of writing the city sheds light on the act of writing the subject for Ackroyd, whether real or fictional, whether More or Dyer, Blake or Chatterton, Dickens or Wilde. In each example, the question of writing is not so much a documen-tary and subservient constative act of 'biography'. It is, rather, if we recall the epigraph above, taken from Ackroyd's description of More's education, the performative act of *prosopopoeia*. Whether fictional or real, Ackroyd's subjects are performative discursive structures, and not simply representations of some person. Similarly, the city's writing belongs to this gesture of 'fluent and per-suasive discourse', whereby the reader is seduced through the rhetorical device to comprehend the nature of the urban event. But it is the act of writing London which, when read in this fashion, can give the reader to comprehend why 'biography' is a word to be distrusted for Ackroyd.

Moreover, the reiteration of London scenes across the biographies, intimates both temporally and spatially a sense of London's reiterative and regenerative power, a power which in the performative inscription returns from biography to biography, thereby overflowing the limits of each particular narrative. Whether it is in the tracing of walks or routes through the city of More, Blake and Dickens; whether it is in the act of naming the streets, wards or boroughs; whether it is in displaying the life of the streets, the vendors, stalls, shops, marketplaces, or the countless anonymous figures who cross and recross the streets through which More, Blake or Dickens walk, writing London performs the condition of the city itself, whether in the fifteenth, the eighteenth, or the nineteenth century. Through such performance, Ackroyd's text returns to us a city which is simultaneously strange and estranged, and strangely familiar. Through the device of recurring scenes, which, however, retain their singularity and exemplary condition, a rhetorical device which spreads the writing of the city beyond the particular biography, Ackroyd structures a certain urban resonance, as well as a sense of urban continuity. London may change, but the city remains in some manner the same. It returns to itself, never quite as it was but always haunted by its previous forms, returning to disturb the present identity of the city, dislodging both it and our perception of London.

The biographies present the reader with powerful imaginary accounts of London in moments of crucial formation and transition. First *Blake*:

> Golden Square was just south of Broad Street; it had been finished in the 1670s and the square itself, with its grass plots and gravel walks and wooden railings (with a statue of King James in the centre), was a token of early eighteenth-century gentility. Like Broad Street, it was losing its former status; the houses of the nobility and the great merchants were now occupied by painters and cabinet-makers. Even wholesalers began to arrive in the 1770s, heralding the louche desolation that Charles Dickens would describe in the opening pages of *Nicholas Nickleby*. So, growing up in the 1760s, in the immediate area around his family home, Blake was exposed to some of the variety of London life.
>
> (*B* 30)

And now, *Dickens*:

> How much London had changed in just ten years .... Even the early nineteenth-century London of Nash was itself being destroyed in the course of the enormous transition through which the capital was now passing .... For inhabitants like Dickens ... it might well have seemed as if the old city were being extirpated and a new one erected in its place.... London was being transformed. It was no longer the city which he [Dickens] had known as a child and young man. This was now becoming the London of wide streets and underground railways, the orderliness and symmetry of the old Georgian

capital quite displaced by the imperialist neo-Gothic of Mid-Victorian public buildings. Something of the old compactness had gone for ever …. In its place rose a city which was more massive…

(*D* 939–40)

The two passages catch the sense fleetingly of transformation, which any major city is always in the process of undergoing. Both are marked by a certain rhythm of transition and animation, even if such movement is not necessarily either progressive or positive in any sense. The resonance of change passes across the passages, remarking a continual process across the biographies, peculiar to the city. Ackroyd, typically, installs possible connections, with that forward looking reference to Dickens in the passage from *Blake*, and, in the excerpt from *Dickens*, in the acknowledgement of Nash's structures and the Georgian capital, in which Blake would have wandered. The movement herein registered is, itself, a response to the movement of London, so that the writing traces the temporality of reinvention, even while the newer aspects of the city are grafted over the traces of its previous identity.

The installation of resonances such as those just mentioned can be read as performative inasmuch as the text builds allusion and reference, the acknowledgement of other structures, other texts, into its own structure as that structure's possibility. This in itself hints at the possibility of that urban continuity desired by Ackroyd, and given expression in both *Blake* and *The Life of Thomas More*:

… it is one of the features of London of this period that ruins were to be found among the modern buildings as a perpetual reminder of the city's past.

(*B* 33)

Londoners [of Blake's time] … were in fact like Londoners of all times and all periods.

(*B* 33)

[of Londoners' speech] … through such tags and apothegms it is possible to glimpse a true permanence of continuity within English culture … a tradition of speech enduring for almost a thousand years.

(*LTM* 20)

Between architecture in ruins and the recurring fragments of language which persist in the everyday speech of the city, Ackroyd traces that sense of 'tradition' or 'continuity' which is so often perceived in his writing in a more general manner and is assumed to be that which Ackroyd creates. As the constant return of catchphrases suggests, there is a textual continuity, if by continuity we can infer a fragmentary continuity, a continuity which transforms, which is translated and which changes. Continuity is not simply the unchanging presence of the same, which then would not be readable, but the constant resurfacing of particular traces, undergoing processes of translation, now more or less visible. This sense of continuity or connection may well be the expression of a desire for connection through an act of seeking to read the traces as in some way connected. As the first example of ruined architecture makes clear, the desire for the textual tracing is written into the very fabric of the city itself, as the space of the city knowingly alludes to its own resonant historical traces.

Writing's relationship to architectural structure and the topography of the city, its ability to trace in words the map and the space, mimes the city's own constant development and reinvention. At the same time, it performs the urban rhythm as Ackroyd weaves together architecture and text, topography and inscription. For example, as a means of placing ourselves in relation to both London and Ackroyd's own writing, we are informed that Dickens's godfather, Christopher Huffam, lived near to Nicholas Hawksmoor's Limehouse church (*D* 67). Although the Hawksmoor mentioned here is the historical figure and obviously not either Hawksmoor or Dyer from *Hawksmoor*, nonetheless the resonance between the historical and the fictional remains in place, as it does when the architect's words are cited to describe William Blake's education as belonging to the 'hidden tradition of "English Gothic" '(*B* 51). Nicholas Hawksmoor is as important a figure in this hidden tradition which the architect describes, a tradition always intimately connected to London (at least for Ackroyd, where Englishness and belonging to London are seemingly synonymous or, at the least, reciprocally resonant concepts), as is William Blake, Charles Dickens, John Stow (*LTM* 4, 8, 10, 25, 112, 116, 234, 326), Thomas More, and the author of *London Lykpeny*. This 'hidden tradition' is most expressly encountered in the acknowledgement of the city being filled with 'angels and prophets' for Blake (*B* 33), or the darkness of the city, which for Dickens, was integral to the being of the city, and to which he 'added' a 'further note of darkness'. When 'we see London now,' Ackroyd argues, 'it is in part his own city still' (*D* 274–5). Clearly, while the city may well determine the writer's response in ways which are not always in the writer's control, any sense we have of the city is always generated by the vast complex web of interconnections between text and space, between the traces of London and the discourse on the city. Our location, our interest in the urban structures of writing and mapping is the result of the echoes between texts. As Rainer Nägele puts it, '[e]ach encounter with any specific language or with any specific text is already determined by a structure of resonance' (1997, 3).

Such resonant configuration, pertaining particularly to the city, can be traced between *Dickens* and *Dan Leno and the Limehouse Golem*. In the former, Thomas de Quincey's textualized memory of his early years lost in the streets of London is cited in comparison with Dickens' own childhood experience of London around 'the thoroughfares of Oxford Street and Tottenham Street' (*D* 20). Importantly, it is the London passages of de Quincey's *Confessions of an English Opium Eater* which provide the resonating echoes for Ackroyd, rather than any historical detail. From these, Ackroyd remarks in a language resonant with echoes of nineteenth-century prose, that 'it would be a foolish person indeed who did not believe that the strange mysteries and sorrows of London did not in some way pierce or move his infant breast' (*D* 20).[4] De Quincey appears as an urban authority in *Dan Leno* also, particularly with regard to the Ratcliffe Highway murders.[5] In the novel, reference to De Quincey's essay, 'On Murder Considered as One of the Fine Arts', is given by George Gissing, whom Ackroyd places reading an article on murder of his own, in the British Library. For Gissing, his predecessor creates a 'wonderful Romantic hero' from the murderer John Williams (*DLLG* 37). Gissing's article is at pains to connect the murders, and the recurrence of murders on the same sites, to the condition of 'sinister, crepuscular London, a haven for strange powers, a city of footsteps and flaring lights, of houses packed close together, of lachrymose alleys and false doors. London becomes a brooding presence behind, or perhaps even within, the murders themselves .... It is not difficult to understand the force of De Quincey's obsession' (*DLLG* 38).[6] From this, Gissing continues, to consider De Quincey's depiction of the scene in 'the great thoroughfare, Oxford Street ... a street of sorrowful mysteries', before discussing how De Quincey's *Confessions* were believed at one time to have been written by Thomas Griffiths Wainewright, a 'critic and journalist' who championed William Blake, and who praised *Jerusalem* (*DLLG* 39–40). Wainewright, Gissing (Ackroyd) reveals, was also a murderer, who became fictionalized and 'celebrated by Charles Dickens in "Hunted Down"' (*DLLG* 40). Thus Ackroyd, recalling Gissing, recalling De Quincey, recalling Dickens, recalling De Quincey, recalling Ackroyd. It is not difficult, in this echo chamber which slips into the endless mirroring of the *mise en abyme*, to understand the force of Ackroyd's obsession. For here we have unfolding, between novel and biography and undoing the limits and identities of both, the structurality of the structure of resonance, and this occurs specifically through the obsession with London. It might even be suggested that the name for this structure is London.[7]

This structure of resonance is moreover readily apparent in Ackroyd's descriptions of Thomas More's birth in London and his early years in the city. Thomas More was born approximately seventy years after *London Lykpeny* was written. The city depicted in that poem and the city of *The Life of Thomas More* are not that dissimilar.[8] We cannot know for sure of course whether

Ackroyd drew on his knowledge of that poem, which is, in any case, only ever acknowledged directly by the title of the collection of poems and in a reference in the More biography. In this most obvious of correspondences there exists the undecidability which inhabits so much of Ackroyd's work. However, whether or not Ackroyd consciously borrows from the poem's descriptions of the city or from the poem's understanding of London as a city constructed on exploitative economic and legal principles is not the most immediately important point. The fact remains, to urge the point once more, that London, if comprehended at all, is always understood as text, as what Nägele calls an encounter determined by a structure of resonance. London is understood as composed of various traces, which are shared between texts. This is the case, whether it is a matter of this example of the possible relationship between the narration of More's life and *London Lykpeny*, or whether it is a matter of other influences, such as the importance of John Stow in the recording of the history of the city (*LTM* 4), or the effect of various novelists' depictions of London in the eighteenth century on Dickens's imagination (*D* 66). Ackroyd writes himself into the history of the city through the continual knowing connection to those other writers fascinated by the urban space.

More was born 'in the heart of London' (*LTM* 4). Ackroyd provides the reader with four densely illustrative paragraphs around the occasion of More's birth and baptism, naming churches, wards, boroughs and streets as the writing appears to assume a topographical function. The writing assumes the role of a performative cartography:

> [More] was born ... in the heart of London. Milk Street is in the ward of Cripplegate Within, bordering upon that of Cheap .... the churches closest to his house showed visible evidence of ... urban power. St Lawrence Jewry, a few yards to the north of Milk Street, near the Guildhall, was as ornate and as sumptuous as any parish church in London ....At the other end of Milk Street, just before the corner of Cheapside, stood the little parish church of Mary Magdalen .... More was born within an urban tradition as closely packed and as circuitous as the streets of Cripplegate or Cheap wards.

> (*LTM* 4–5).

The passage traces the map of the city around the location of More's birth, indicating the intimate relationship, albeit indirectly, between Church and wealth, if not Church and State. This act of mapping takes place in the other biographies also, and we will need to return to it. For now, however, it is important to note that, in the process of narrating the situation of More's birth and in tracing the web of discursive, ideological and economic interrelations, Ackroyd pauses:

If you walk down that narrow thoroughfare today, [Milk Street] between the banks and the companies which have their home in the 'City', you will see a small statue of the Virgin lodged about thirty feet above the pavement.

(*LTM* 4)

Breaking the narrative suddenly, almost before it is underway, Ackroyd addresses the reader, while bringing the reader somewhat peremptorily into the present day. Ackroyd's device stresses both the break with the past – streets and churches are 'now long destroyed or forgotten' (*LTM* 4) – and yet, also, a sense of continuity and architectural-cultural memory, by which it is possible to imagine, on the one hand, the pervasiveness of London's identity, while, on the other, the unknowability of that identity through its having been transformed irrevocably, now retaining only the echo of its past selves. The sense is that the city is composed from a series of palimpsests gathering one upon another, promising the imaginative connection between the London of Thomas More and the city of the present, via those Londons of Hawksmoor, Blake and Dickens. London survives as the grafting of successive temporal texts, evoked both by Ackroyd's own writing and, in this instance, through his citation of 'London chronicler and antiquarian John Stow' (*LTM* 4).[9] The city thus returns to us as a spectral writing and revenant text. This is described by Ackroyd in that already cited phrase, the 'urban tradition' (*LTM* 5), where the same site, though endlessly reinvented, continues through the grafting and serial process to cite and re-cite itself in its seriality as, constantly, the other of, within, itself. The suggestion of serial reinvention is of course everywhere in Ackroyd's writing, as seen above. In this case however, as if to strengthen the resonance of iterative correspondence, Ackroyd points to the coincidence of London's other Saint, Thomas Becket, having been born some centuries apart from More but only twenty yards from the latter's birthplace.

At the same time, the passage concerning More's birth provides an oblique explanation of Thomas More, of who he was to become. The intimation in Ackroyd's writing is that the place determines the subject and his role within the city. This is also suggested in both the Blake and Dickens biographies. In the former, the reader is told that Blake 'had a very strong sense of place, and all his life he was profoundly and variously affected by specific areas of London' (*B* 31). In *Dickens*, we read that 'it is a curious if perhaps accidental fact that for the rest of his life Dickens lived near this area of London; just like the characters in his own fiction who seem rooted to one part of the metropolis as if they had been created by it, as if the darkness of London had compressed itself into their tiny wandering forms' (*D* 62). The city writes the subject's identity, even as fictional characters define and are defined by their respective areas, even as their 'wandering' maps out the locations which, in turn, maps onto them who we read them as being. Ackroyd acknowledges topographical specificity in both passages, even as the hesitance of the sentence from *Dickens* suggests an uncertainty – from that 'perhaps accidental fact' to the semi-colon – about making the assertion too unequivocally. Even though Ackroyd does not spell out the correlative connection in *More* as he does in the other biographies, there is, as it were, a dim poetic echolalia between the city and the self, so that the echo of the city will not only speak in and through the subject, it will speak the subject's being.

Furthermore, the writing is performative in that the frequent inscription here of various proper names of streets, alleys, and churches assumes the structural and spatial proximity of the streets themselves (as it does in other passages, and as is acknowledged above; *LTM* 15–17, 25, 135). This takes place again in those same passages through the naming of professions and occupations, as in the descriptions of More's daily walks of a 'few hundred yards' to and from school, as we will see below (15–17, 25). As the performative mapping of the sentences in Ackroyd's passages on and through the City of London take effect, they are more than mere scene setting. To recall our earlier argument, they enact both the space or site of London, and also the events which take place in the late fifteenth-century city. As in the biographies of Dickens and Blake, the text of Ackroyd is moved by the rhythm of the urban encounter. This rhythm is then visible in the acts of listing and naming:

> The culture of London had other manifestations as well, none more colourful or more pervasive than that of the popular print.... These prints ... turned the city into a place of mystery and of intrigue. The city which Dickens in turn inherited. And so here is a further picture: the boy, really still only a child, surrounded by music, diverted by illustrations, entertained by songs, haunted by cheap fiction, the whole panoply of London entertainment ... The Adelphi arches. The Coal heavers. The Strand. The flaring gas.... the running patterers or 'flying stationers' as they were called, the coster girls, the oyster stalls, the baked potato men, the groundsel men, the piemen, the sellers of nutmeg-graters and dog-collars and boot-laces and lucifer matches and combs and rhubarb and crockery ware .... There were the street conjurors, the acrobats, the negro serenaders, the glee-singers; and there were the cries of London ...
>
> ...
>
> the rich tumult of voices ... which encircled him as he walked through the crowded thoroughfares ....The red brick of the City squares ... the weavers' houses of Spitalfields and the carriage-makers of Clerkenwell and the old clothes stalls of Rosemary Lane.
>
> (*D* 98, 99)

And when he [Blake] returned to the great city after his excursions north, he would come back to the footpaths thronged with people, the songs and the street cries, the hackney chair men and the porters, the thoroughfares crowded with carriages and dustcarts and postchaises, the dogs and the mud carts, the boys with trays of meat upon their shoulders and the begging soldiers, the smoke from the constant exhalation of sea-coal fires, the whole panoply of urban existence.

(*B* 33)

The old 'Chepe' had been crowded with street-stalls and street-sellers, but much of its atmosphere still survived in the late fifteenth century ... [with] the ancient and familiar cries of 'satin!', 'silks!', 'foreign cloth!', and 'courchiefs!'.... [More] passed ... among stone buildings with figures placed in niches, gilded and painted signs, timbers decorated with carved fruits or flowers, painted walls and gables, roofs of red tile, wrought iron poles bearing lamps, piles of dung and chips from firewood .... The whole quarter had once been the home of saddlers, tanners and tallow chandlers, but mercers had displaced them in one of those changes of commercial activity which are explicable only in terms of the city's own organic and instinctive growth.
...
He made his way among the pumps and springs and water conduits, past the gardens and the markets and the almshouses, along small lanes and even smaller footways, between the stables and the carpenters' yards and the mills, past brothels and taverns and bath-houses and street privies, under archways adorned with the images of saints or coats of arms, into courtyards filled with shops, beneath tenements crammed with the families of artisans, moving from the grand houses of the rich to the thatched hovels of mud walls frequented by the poor, hearing the cries of 'God spede' and Good morrow!', past nunneries and priories and churches.

(*LTM* 16, 25)

[More] wrote once, with some conviction, of the taverns and bathhouses, the public toilets and barbers' shops, used by servants, pimps, whores, bath-keepers, porters and carters, all of them swarming the streets.

(*LTM* 135)

There is in effect here what J. Hillis Miller, in defining the performative topography of Dickens's own writing, calls 'a way of doing things with words' (Miller 1995, 109). The streets, their noise, movement and general crowded busy-ness, impose themselves on us with what Peter Ackroyd is pleased to call in *Thomas More* 'brief but vivid intimations of London life...' (*LTM* 25; see below).[10] The key to understanding the performative element is perhaps in

Ackroyd's choice of the word *intimations*, which resounds with *imitations* but neatly side-steps the inference of mimesis in favour of a somewhat phenomenological apprehension, which his own writing mimics. The words, in their frequently furious, condensed rhythms, their celerity and velocity intimate the subject's experience. It is not a question of description, the city is not imitated or represented directly according to the devices of realist verisimilitude; for hardly is something, someone, named in its or their urban typicality, than off the passages rush again. Such a gesture repeatedly manages to respect the exemplarity of each scene according to its historical and cultural specificity – even street cries, while being a perpetual part of the urban scene, have a historicity – while, at the same time, intimating that sense of continuity peculiar to the subject's encounter with the metropolis. However, even as the writing performs the city, there is also a ludic displacement of the reality which is intimated. Such displacement calls our attention to the language, to the text of the city, to recall Miller once more (1995, 131). Thus the 'biography' overflows its merely documentary and descriptive, recording functions. There is the suggestion of the writing escaping or exceeding the writer or the viewing subject, so rapidly do details come to sight, and so apparently without any order, except that imposed by the city on the attempted acts of inscription and memory. Indeed, London resists ordering, whether in the memory, or in the writing of Blake, Dickens, More or Ackroyd. The return to lists, to names, to the most basic of identities, to architectural details, suggests that London begins, again and again, and yet there is never simply a single beginning. Furthermore, while each of these passages map the city, while they each belong to an urban discourse or language, they are all composed of more than one language. The language of the city is always radically heterogeneous, even to the extent that it can, in its resistance to order, appear improvisatory in its affirmation of the city's condition. Street cries jostle with figures of different kinds, architectural and structural features give way to stalls, shops and domestic residences. Colours, sounds and sights strain for our attention. There is no sense to the naming of items being sold being brought together, any more than there is to who or what the reader next encounters. The legal and illegal, the high and low, the proper and improper, all mix in the language of London. Even phrases such as 'the whole panoply' reiterate themselves, as the intimation is that the city, whether in song, print, text, utterance or structure, 'both is and is not the same' (*D* 679).

There are other lists and acts of naming in *Blake*, in *Dickens*, and in *The Life of Thomas More*. These are the lists of street names, the proper names of Churches and those of specific areas of London, about which Ackroyd, like Dickens before him, is very particular. In *The Life of Thomas More* we read of 'Milk Street ... Threadneedle Street ... St Mary Magdalen ... Cheapside ... the River Tybourn ... West Chepe ... the Standard ... St Mary-le-Bow ... Poultry

Lane ... St Laurence Lane and Ironmonger Lane ... Blossoms Inn ... St Martin
Pomary ... St Mary Colechurch ... Old Jewry ... the meeting of Broad and
Threadneedle Streets', all of which are within a 'few hundred yards' of one
another in the City, and as closely related in Ackroyd's prose (*LTM* 15–17). In
Dickens, street names and place names come thick and fast: 'Queen Victoria
Street cut through from Blackfriars to the Bank of England. Canon Street
extended. Farringdon Street. Garrick Street. New Oxford Street. Clerkenwell
Road. Southwark Street .... Westminster Bridge and Blackfriars Bridge rebuilt.
The Hungerford Suspension Bridge ... Hungerford Market ... Cannon Street
terminus. Victoria Station. St Pancras. Broad Street. The line from Shoreditch
to Liverpool Street' (*D* 939). At one moment, Dickens's London is described in
its rapid growth:

> For London was growing too fast. The 'Great Oven', as Dickens sometimes
> called it, was spreading through Bloomsbury, Islington, and St John's
> Wood in the North, and in the West and South, through Paddington,
> Bayswater, South Kensington, Lambeth, Clerkenwell and Peckham.
>
> (*D* 402)

The figure of the city 'spreading' implies both an organic sinuous quality and
also a disease, while those compass markers recall not so much the texts of
Dickens as they do lines from Blake's *Jerusalem*. Numerous locations are cited
with almost equal rapidity in *Blake*: 'Oxford Street towards Tottenham Court
Road ... St Giles High Street ... Hanway Street ... The Blue Posts Inn ... Percy
Street and Windmill Street ... Capper's Farm ... the New Road from Paddington
to St Pancras' (*B* 32–3). The area being mapped here in these three lists is no
more than a few square miles. Even the reader not familiar with the topography
of London will have, through the occasionally repeated location, a sense of
proximity, of routes in common or places connecting with one another, like so
many arterial threads. Moreover, the area is also, distinctly, three spaces which
take place through the double movement of memory and writing. Movement
through the city is traced even as the map is drawn, through the frequency of
proper names. In the place of description stands the inscription of the place, as
the city occurs through the rhythm of urgent or fragmented sentences.

Yet such lists, such acts of naming, do rely on what J. Hillis Miller describes
as 'topographical circumstantiality', which, he argues, is typical of Charles
Dickens's own 'exact naming of streets and hotels' (1995, 105). Miller continues, saying of Dickens and the route of Sam Weller that the author 'assumes
his readers will have a detailed map of London in their minds and will be able
to follow Sam's progress... Dickens assumes his readers will be streetwise ....
[The example from *Pickwick Papers*] is a good example of the way many novels
assume a shared topographical inner space in the community of their readers.

Many meanings are elliptically conveyed just through toponymy' (1995, 105). The assumption of community through the work of toponymy is equally in operation in Ackroyd, whether we are speaking of his novels or his biographies. Our sense of those texts is dependent to an extent on our familiarity with the metropolis, regardless of story or history. Our own urban memories and imaginations are tested as the performative toponymy takes us into its contours. The sense of community suggested by Miller is, for Ackroyd, a community composed of heterogeneous, protean, and surviving elements, whether textual, vocal, imaginary, real, or architectural. For the performance can only truly take effect if we comprehend or recognize the sense of the urban event. This sense is not mere apprehension. It is dependent, as Miller suggests of Dickens's writing, on the recognition of complex interwoven economic, cultural, historical traces. For the sense of community defined by Miller's reading of Dickens is akin to the desire for continuity so prevalent in Ackroyd's text. In this, community, a community of diverse and differing elements, is both that sense of belonging to both a place, to what takes place in that place serving to shape the identity of the location as well as its idiomatic, singular articulation, and to the history of what takes place, to the historicity of that identity. Part of that identity is its ability to reinvent itself, to exaggerate its delineations and to become excessive, extravagant, beyond identification. The shared sense of the city promoted by the lists of names, the streets and places, the types of people, the wares sold, exceeds mere definition. Each passage so far quoted extends itself into the other passages, across the biographies. In so doing, each passage in its performative rhythms plays with the community and continuity of urban identity, while overflowing the limits required of such descriptive passages within a single text. There is at work in such listing and naming what William Corlett calls a 'radical extension of spacing' which upsets any stable identification of either 'orderly principles' or 'meaninglessness' (1989, 157). Such spacing as the writing of the city enacts is, as we have suggested, both temporal and spatial. In its performance it confesses to its own flux, to its own 'extravagant monstrosity' (Corlett 1989, 162). The radical play of the city's writing draws us in different directions. Calling our attention to a rhetoric of catachresis, whereby the city transforms with every clause, every hiatus of punctuation and every pulse of naming, it estranges its identity even as it supposedly serves to help in the definition of an identity, that of the biographical subject. The structure of resonance, figured by the city's writing, far from closing upon itself, opens itself from within the very place where identity is sought.

Endless peripatetic acts belong to the urban experience, as figures trace and retrace routes across the city. Aleatory wandering, of the kind pursued by William Blake and Charles Dickens, are movements remembered in both their own texts as well as in those by Ackroyd, unfolding and tracing the structures of London. Lists such as those just discussed are generated in turn by, or otherwise help shape in the imagination, the memory of walking through the city, as we see in the following examples:

> It is characteristic of so lonely and separate a boy that Blake's principal childhood memory is of solitary walking ....And of course beyond the streets of his early childhood lay 'Infinite London', which is 'the spiritual Four-Fold London eternal' .... These are the streets through which Blake wandered as a child....He walked south, towards Dulwich and Camberwell and Croydon....But let us accompany him on one of his long walks...
>
> (*B* 30–32)

> Thomas More turned left and walked down [a] relatively wide thoroughfare of mud and cobbles towards Poultry and Threadneedle Street .... Thomas More then took the left-hand turning towards Poultry and the Stocks Market .... These were the streets and alleys among which More would spend most of his working life....So the young Thomas More walked by Poultry and the 'pissing conduit' at the south end of Threadneedle or Three-needle Street, passing several more parish churches ... until he came to a well at the meeting of Broad and Threadneedle Streets...
>
> (*LTM* 16–17)

> At the end of the day, after his release from school, it was a short journey from Threadneedle Street to Milk Street. The city surrounded More once again, and he noticed everything: his prose works are filled with brief but vivid intimations of London life...
>
> (*LTM* 25)

> It was here, then, that he [Dickens] sank into what he once described as 'a solitary condition apart from all other boys of his own age'. Alone, friendless, bereft of any possible future or any alternative life, he would sometimes walk down the little paved road of Bayham Street and look south towards the city itself .... The roofs, the chimneys, the churches, the light upon the river and there, towering above them, the great cross on the summit of St Paul's .... it is the cross which the young Dickens cannot take his eyes from even as he wanders lost through the streets of the metropolis, as recorded in his essay 'Gone Astray'. It is the very symbol of London, of its grimy and labyrinthine ways in which we might all lose our path.
>
> (*D* 64)

Recalling to the memory the act of the subject's perambulatory encounter is effectively to perform the city, through engaging the reading subject with the space through which the subject of the biography or narrative moves. At once, the city is both real and textual. In each example from the three biographies in question, Ackroyd provides the reader with the sense of the importance of walking in the city to the constitution of the subject while also hinting at the connection between his subject and the subject's own textual production. In each case the city serves to produce writing, projecting itself onto the texts of Blake, More and Dickens. These passages are not only responses to the reality of the encounter with the city. They are, as well, acknowledgements of prior textual records, traces, and networks. They hint for example at those lists of Blake's in *Jerusalem* of London locations, or the lists of items encountered randomly in so many of the texts of Dickens, where the city is composed through the movement of the walker responding to the aleatory and ungovernable taxonomy of phenomena, which have no other rhyme or reason than that they are of London.

London is thus poised between naming and meaningless. Playing with the discernible limits of both, the city in writing confronts the reader with the inadequacy of definition or the imposition of an identity. Knowing the name of a place does not necessarily serve to make that location any more familiar. Indeed, as we remarked above, tracing the city's topography may be read as part of an estranging process. The reader is given an injunction against familiarization at one moment: 'we must not see London as the city so familiar today' (*D* 402). Describing over four pages a 'landscape of filth and destitution, death and misery', Ackroyd reminds us that 'we have here glimpses of an urban life which is so alien to us as to seem almost incredible' (*D* 406). 'Westminster, Southwark, Bermondsey, Whitechapel, Rotherhithe, St Giles' comprise 'unknown and forbidden territory...a world within a world' (*D* 401). What this territory is remains ill-defined except by appalling squalor and violence. Violence as well as commercialism is stressed in *The Life of Thomas More* (15–17). Elsewhere, we read of the close proximity of four graveyards, all within Clement's Lane (*D* 404–5). In *Blake* the sound of workhouse looms echoes over the burial ground in Lambeth (*B* 30), while '[a]round the corner from Broad Street, in Carnaby Market, there was an abattoir which was famous for its female butchers' (*B* 31). In *More* once again, in being asked to envision the scene of the marketplace near to Broad Street, we are told that 'it is appropriate to imagine the surroundings of an eastern bazaar or *souk*; the fifteenth-century city was closer to contemporary Marrakesh than to any version of post-Restoration London' (*LTM* 16). Ackroyd's performative writing also estranges. It estranges both the possible representation of the city and our own possible familiarity with London. For, if the shared and overflowing sense of the city is one of community, it is a community of the performative, the strange, and the other. London is at all times never itself but always a series of masquerades, which challenge our knowingness concerning urban identity.

There is in this constant estrangement of the known from within itself, caught in that phrase 'a world within a world', the abiding sense of the inadequacy of description, the potential collapse of definition in the face of the continuous reformation of the urban event. Brief but vivid intimations can never settle into comforting patterns; we can never know the city finally, any more than we can understand the identity of a novelist, poet, or lawyer from the playful artifice of the biographical narrative.

The House of Doctor Dee

The House of Doctor Dee begins with the words, 'I inherited the house from my father' (*HDD* 1). In this line, it is possible to trace multiple writings, to hear countless voices, all of which belong to the texts of Peter Ackroyd.[11] Obsessions, concerns and interests are to be unearthed there. The sentence is the first uttered by Matthew Palmer, the narrator of one half of the novel, who, as that line tells us in part, inherits from his father a house, which we find is in Clerkenwell. The simple past tense of the sentence may be read as indicating a possibly endless tradition of inheritance, and thus allows for readings seeking thematic connections between this and other texts by Ackroyd, particularly those concerned with fathers and the possible break in filial continuity. The novel begins by recalling the past and the legacy of the past on or in the present, as the means by which the narrating subject seeks both to orient himself, to determine his identity in relationship to other identities, and to commence his narrative. Inheritance implicitly transforms a 'beginning' into a narrative moment *in medias res*, as the condition of self-identification. Self-awareness dawns as a condition of the recognition of temporal continuity. The first line retains an anonymity, however, despite the first person narrative, even while it has the capacity to seduce through the mystery of as-yet-unspoken narrative threads. It seeks to inscribe a double writing: that which is both intimate and, seemingly, universal, promising the story of both Matthew Palmer and, in a certain way, Everyman.

The House of Doctor Dee is formed from two narratives, which are told for the most part in alternating chapters. This structure resembles, at least superficially, that of *Hawksmoor*, even to the point where the narratives seemingly converge. The narrative strands are divided between Matthew Palmer and John Dee, between the twentieth and the sixteenth centuries. Palmer's chapters are numbered, as if to give his narration only the most fundamental of structures, barely an identity at all (which is appropriate to Palmer's own sense of himself initially). Dee's, on the other hand, are given titles, which are as follows: 'The Spectacle', 'The Library', The Hospital', 'The Abbey', 'The Chamber of Demonstration', 'The City', 'The Closet', 'The Garden'. In accordance with the importance given in this book to architectural structures (as suggested in the very title of the novel), each chapter title (with the exception of the first and final titles) names a formal architectural structure, whether a room or building. Arguably, even 'The Garden' may be said to name a formal structure. In the final chapter, also given a title ('The Vision'), moments of being and moments in time come together. In this last chapter there is a free flowing play between temporal locations, which, though distinct, are nonetheless over-laid on one another, in the same area of London. The more rigid imposition of formal structure is undone in the concluding chapter. At the same time, there is also a movement outside the times of Palmer's and Dee's narratives, when someone masquerading as the author steps forward to question what his responsibility is to his characters and to present his vision of London.

The idea of the house is itself important, as just suggested. As figural trope and imaginary architecture, it serves a purpose similar to that of the conceit of 'English music' in the novel of that name. *The House of Doctor Dee* is not par-ticularly concerned with real buildings, except as they may be said to mark sites in London which have significant narratives to tell, significant histories to convey, so that, in Ackroyd's London, a building such as a house or library, or an area such as Clerkenwell or Limehouse is formed through a structural resonance which is both temporal and spatial, and which therefore serves in an emblematic manner for the writer as a figure for the secret history and the spectral revenance of London as a whole, all traces of the city being interwo-ven. *The House of Doctor Dee* is not even concerned with the particular build-ing in which the historical figure of John Dee had lived in Barnes. Instead this is another house and with it another Dee, an imagined figure and one of several possible Dees, as Matthew Palmer suggests, unsure of himself, when he puts it to his friend, Daniel Moore, that 'every book has a different Doctor Dee ....The past is difficult, you see. You think you understand a person or an event, but then you turn a corner and everything is different once again .... It's like this house too' (*HDD* 136). The house, the inheritance, and, we feel, the city, is filled with inexplicable occurrences, chance encounters, possibly overheard voices, the fleeting glimpse of another reality. Matthew's acknowl-edgement of the ability to reinvent a historical figure also suggests that no past figure or moment of history can ever be wholly recuperated, even while it may resonate within the present. Interestingly, Palmer employs a structural, if not a topographical metaphor, when he notes how things are different once one 'turns a corner'. This metaphorical passage is given literal significance later, when Palmer, speaking of an area of London he believed he knew well, says: '...but I found myself turning down an unexpected and unfamiliar lane. That is the nature of the city, after all: in any neighbourhood you can come across a street, or a close, that seems to have been perpetually hidden away' (*HDD* 265). Whether the question concerns the city, an identity, a house, or a passage in a text, the question is one of what comes to light by accident, of chance illumination rather than of deliberate inquiry, as *The House of Doctor Dee* makes clear on a number of occasions and at different levels of the text. Matthew's remark to Moore tries to pursue a labyrinthine thread, to create connections. Beginning with reading, interpretation and identity, he moves through the question of time and historical narrative, to that metaphorical turn which implies the moment of wandering, to the often haunted, uncanny nature of the house. This labyrinth – which is implicitly architectural as well as formal, as are all labyrinths – is, for Peter Ackroyd, the condition of the city itself and all that it brings to bear on the urban writer and reader.

The connections are both visible and invisible. Palmer suddenly comes to recognize the hidden course of the 'old River Soken ... from Waltham Forest down through Bethnal Green and Shadwell' (*HDD* 179), where it will merge with the Thames. Later, Palmer thinks when looking at the flow of traffic down the Farringdon Road, that 'it seemed to me then that it would go on forever, in the various forms of various centuries, following in the direction of the old Fleet River' (*HDD* 261). Earlier in the novel, Matthew Palmer had heard running water in his house in Clerkenwell, and had imagined in that the sound of the Fleet River as heard by John Dee (*HDD* 126). Ackroyd chooses deliberately banal moments such as the flowing of water and the flow of traffic to make connections indirectly. In doing so he insists on the subjective perception of a possible thread, rather than defining the connection itself. Resisting the forcing of the mystical and hermetic, the novelist tentatively traces possible imaginative concatenations, thereby hinting at the city's identity whilst also suggestively retaining its ineffability in instances of tentative, provisional comprehension. In this way, 'a buried city had been discovered. *Something* from the past had been restored' (*HDD* 179; emphasis added). What that *something* is remains unspoken and unspeakable, and thus all the more potent. To put this in another way, what is most important for Ackroyd is the acknowledgement of the possibility of a certain movement or 'flow', rather than the act of deciphering what the flow might mean. This is acknowledged by Daniel Moore, early in *The House of Doctor Dee*, when he tells Palmer, '...all time has flowed here, into this house' (*HDD* 82). If we understand the connection between identity and house, between house and city, we begin to comprehend the haunting possibilities of connection with which Ackroyd plays.

Such moments of illumination serve to map alternative geographies, topographies and histories for the city, even as they make tentative topographical, temporal connections, so that, simultaneously, the city both is and is not the same, to recall a phrase of Ackroyd's from *Dickens*. This haunting of the other within the same is not a paradox for Ackroyd but is, instead, intrinsic to any acknowledgement of the urban condition. Ackroyd's interest is with spiritual or spectral topographies and architectural or architextural forms, reading the possible connections of which acknowledges the haunting trace of otherness and the past within present identity, whether that identity is that of Matthew Palmer or the city of London. Indeed Palmer might well be read as one more emblematic figure of London inasmuch as, by the end of the novel he has come to know how intimately connected his identity is to specific parts of the city. Earlier in the novel, however, he feels himself to have no particular significance, for he tells Daniel: 'I can't bear to look at myself. Or look *into* myself. I really don't believe that there is anything there, just a space out of which a few words emerge from time to time' (*HDD* 81).[12] Of course this sense of identity changes as Palmer discovers his connectedness, not only to the house, but also to the area of Clerkenwell,[13] and, through that, to the flow of London time, which flows within him and gives him a specific sense of himself. Matthew comes to discover, to speak in litotes, as does Daniel Moore so often, that '[i]dentity is a very strange thing' (*HDD* 82).

Connections are made between personal identity and the urban sense of self. At one moment, Palmer remarks that 'sometimes I feel as if I'm excavating some lost city within myself' (*HDD* 83). When visiting the National Archive Centre in order to pursue research in the parish records of Clerkenwell, Matthew senses the enmeshed relationship between the signatures of 'the long–dead' on the documents he handles and 'the true self' (*HDD* 89). Moreover, it is not merely a question of the signatures themselves and their ghostly traces, but also the paper on which they are written. 'I could feel the texture of the paper beneath my fingers,' remarks Matthew, 'and it was like earth baking in the heat of this modern city' (*HDD* 89). The library thus acts as the architectural form in which archives connecting past London lives to those of the present are maintained. Importantly, the parish records determine identity through the connection of signature and place. As parish records make clear, the giving of identity through the baptismal gift of the proper name, by which one is given one's identity, is intimately bound up with the place within which one gets one's identity. One's self is authorized according to locale, the inscription of one's identity is an event which takes place within a specific area and is recorded as belonging to that area. More than a moment of religious significance or the authorized establishment of familial connection, the gift of the name is the gift bestowed by and in the parish through the agency of the church, and this in turn becomes transcribed as an official textual form.

More generally, however, London libraries are important to Matthew, even though '[o]nce upon a time' he was afraid of them (*HDD* 129). They provide for him 'a world ... a sweet labyrinth of learning in which I could lose myself...' (*HDD* 129). Libraries provide a place where, Palmer imagines, books 'are forever engaged in an act of silent communion, which, if we are fortunate, we can overhear' (*HDD* 129). This passing, somewhat fanciful remark of the narrator's hints at that sense of nothing ever having been lost in the city, which Ackroyd seeks to convey. Begun with that invocation of the beginning of all narrative, a moment of lost origins, Matthew Palmer's discussion of the relationship between his identity and his sense of connectedness to libraries comes almost exactly at the structural middle of *The House of Doctor Dee*. It is as if Ackroyd has fashioned a textual labyrinth into the midst of which Palmer must probe – and the reader follow – before he can begin to emerge into an awareness of the connection between his sense of self and the city. The figure of the library provides an economical architectural matrix where temporal structures of resonance and spatial connections overlay one another, as archive and labyrinth overdetermine each other in a place where the present self and the texts of the other and of the past come together.

Ackroyd's description of one particular library, the English History Library, relies on the material condition of the library for its ability to hint at temporal passage and spatial significance. The library is, according to Matthew Palmer, 'of all London libraries ... the most curious and dilapidated; the passages are narrow, the stairs circuitous, and the general atmosphere one of benign decay. The books here are often piled up on the floors, while the shelves can hardly bear the weight of the volumes which have been deposited on them over the years' (*HDD* 129). Ackroyd's writing maps out and thereby constructs the imagined space of the library, reminiscent in its inscribed delineation of Piranesi's drawn text.[14] Like Piranesi, Ackroyd, both in his construction of the library and in his mapping of the city of various temporal moments, provides a blueprint for the urban labyrinth in that image of the decaying and dilapidated gathering of random, en-crypted scripts. The archival crypt of the library houses the countless scripts of the city, which promise to map out for us the city itself. Yet at the same time, and to borrow from Jennifer Bloomer's discussion of Piranesi's drawings, Ackroyd's writing of the library in particular and the city in general intimates an endless reciprocity between city and text, where the library, and, in turn, the city act as markers 'of something greater' while also being 'built and ordered [or, perhaps more appropriately *disordered*] upon collective mythmaking and, most significant ...its palimpsestic, [PATCH-WORK] like form' (Bloomer 1993, 72). We come to learn even as Matthew Palmer begins to apprehend, that the city, like the self, is 'an intricate network of sites of interpretation' (Bloomer 1993, 72).[15] Furthermore, the performative aspect of this passage in turn de*scribes* rather than represents the textual, structural enterprise of Ackroyd's novel and the desired correspondences and weavings of the text between identities of specific structures and the structure of identities. Ackroyd weaves the various strands of countless forms together which have their meeting place, and which, in turn, serve to define the eternal city of London. His writing retraces hidden elements in the city's identity, thereby promising to return to us the city, any number of cities, at any moment in the secret and submerged history of London.

Structural resonance and palimpsest, the insistence of place, recurring events on the same location, *genius loci*: all are important in *The House of Doctor Dee*, as are recurring images, figures, and traces of light, both literal and metaphorical, and enlightenment, all of which persist throughout the text. In this novel, light is made mention of in the most sustained and overt fashion since Ackroyd's poetry (with the possible exception of *First Light*). Light in the novel emanates from the city to make apparent the city's structures and topography, as well as the various temporal layers.[16] Matthew's father once asked his son whether he felt the light 'coming through the stone of this wonderful city' (*HDD* 7), while Matthew remarks of the house that 'the white walls seemed to be trembling with light' (*HDD* 80). Matthew, on coming to recognize something of his identity and its indebtedness to the city, remarks on the perceived connection amongst those who work with books, and who thereby travel back through the city's history as a disparate community connected to the past. He says of entering libraries that 'it is as if I were entering a place I had once known and forgotten, and in the same *light of recognition* had remembered something of myself' (*HDD* 12–13; emphasis added). John Dee remarks that light is 'the origin of wonders' (*HDD* 20), and that 'there must also be light within us to reflect … meaning' (*HDD* 74).[17] He comments later, in an echo of Matthew's own sentiments regarding texts that 'I concluded with myself that it was only in books and histories I might find the light for which I searched' (*HDD* 33), qualifying this further still, by recalling that 'I soon found myself bent towards other learning as towards a glorious light' (*HDD* 34). Indeed, while initially Matthew Palmer feels no connection to the world, to the house or the city (*HDD* 4), both men come to be connected apparently by a vision which offers to join them not directly in occult communion but through a shared enlightenment, this being an instance of light's projection from the city:

> 'About a year ago I was walking by the Thames. Do you know, near Southwark? When suddenly I thought I saw a bridge of houses. A shimmering bridge, lying across the river…. It was like a bridge of light.'
>
> (*HDD* 17)

These words, first spoken by Palmer to Daniel Moore, are heard by John Dee, as he witnesses the scene as if in a vision towards the end of the novel, shortly after having been enlightened as to his delusion concerning the making of an homunculus (*HDD* 273). Just prior to this moment, his house having been burnt and his library destroyed, Dee walks through London to find himself presented with a city of lights, 'a holy city where time never was' (*HDD* 272), to be informed by a vagrant (who has appeared both to Dee and Palmer, and is reminiscent, perhaps, of the tramps in *Hawksmoor*) that 'the spirit never dies, and this city is formed within the spiritual body of man' (*HDD* 273). This remark recalls Palmer's own conceit of excavating the city from within himself, already commented on, above (*HDD* 83). Thus Ackroyd traces resonant configurations throughout the structure of the text, foregrounding, often through the projection of light as the medium of enlightenment, the possibility of the revelation of connection. For Ackroyd nothing is ever lost in the city. Instead, its spectres play endlessly, serving to form and inform London, time and again. Such ghostly figures occasionally project themselves in such a manner that their resonance – that which Ackroyd has Palmer describe vaguely as 'some interior life and reality which glowed within all things' (*HDD* 42) – enlightens.

The city, the dual narratives, and the text in general, all are haunted by immanence and return, therefore, in an abyssal reciprocity. A constant folding, overfolding and unfolding takes place as if to bring to light or project the resonance of the interwoven and multiplying structures of a novel, where possible, if dissonant correspondence resounds.[18] Conceivable correspondence is recognized by Matthew in the opening chapter, when he acknowledges that, though the house 'was only a few yards from the Farringdon Road ....yet it was entirely quiet. I might just as well have entered a sacred room' (*HDD* 3). The correspondence is indirect, from the disturbance occasioned by the quietness, to the imagined architecture of the sacred room. He does not yet understand why the quiet disturbs and yet apprehends something about the room. The room itself is a metonymic figure for the house, and both in turn signify indirectly the city. The idea of the house itself is therefore structured as the locus of revenance, attempted communication and the temporal persistence of a shared, if barely recognized, identity. This house therefore, and to reiterate the point, figures both the condition of London itself, and those who are 'of London'. At the same time, it is also a figure for the construction of Ackroyd's novel in particular and the resonant structures of writing as comprehended by Ackroyd: 'the eighteenth–century façade of the ground floor had been designed as a casing or shell for the sixteenth–century interior' (*HDD* 16). Layer on layer and structure within structure, the house is figured by Ackroyd as a material, architectural approximation for writing the city, and speaking of a writing which can respond to the city in an appropriate fashion.

What I am describing here is termed by Eric Korn in his review of the novel, 'psychomorphic resonance' (Korn 1993). Korn is only describing the relationship between Palmer and Dee, however. (Indeed most of the reviews of *The House of Doctor Dee* focus on characterization to the exclusion of other concerns, as part of the humanist assumptions belonging to aesthetic analysis, along with questions of mimesis and verisimilitude.) He does not read this mutual resonance as part of the greater resonance of the city within both men. They do not connect to one another but are connected by the flow of

London through them both. There is that in both Dee and Palmer which is other than them. Of course, it is possible to read this in the title, inasmuch as the title of the novel directs us not to John Dee, but to the house. This is a seemingly obvious, yet important point, where the 'house' of Ackroyd's title is as significant to the text, potentially, as 'portrait' is in the title of James Joyce's first novel. Francis King, another reviewer, understands this. In suggesting that Ackroyd's favoured metaphors for time in the novel are archaeological or architectural (already mentioned at the beginning of this chapter), he is correct (King 1993), for these speak both to the condition of the city and that of writing.

However, Ackroyd is not merely concerned with sustaining the dual metaphors as a means of signalling the interpenetration of time past, time present and time future for their own sakes. He is also keen to pursue as far as possible the interanimation between the material condition of the city and its ghostly otherness, which may be glimpsed as the other within the city's material being. Such materiality is not simply a matter of seeking the appropriate language with which to represent architecture. It is a question of playing with the materiality of language itself, as a gambit for destabilizing temporally discrete moments. There is not, for Ackroyd, some facile distinction between the materiality of the world or 'reality' and the textuality of language. For Ackroyd understands language in all its material condition. As the biographies' acts of writing London show us, London is as much composed of the persistence of street cries, place names and proper names, their imprinting and the trace they leave on the topography and the city's inhabitants, as it is constructed by the incorporation and renovation of buildings and other sites. London's ghostly imprimatur is also signed in Ackroyd's choice of place and street names in *The House of Doctor Dee*. Matthew Palmer recalls or is used to alert the reader to street names, without necessarily understanding their general significance himself. In remembering the area in which he grew up, he recalls a number of street names, including the Anglo–Saxon names of Wulfstan and Erconwald (*HDD* 175). There is probably nothing important about these names other than their persistence and return as the counter–signatures of another London appearing as coincidental traces within the modern city. Another example of the manifestation of the past through the remnant of the proper name occurs when Palmer crosses 'Clerkenwell Green into Jerusalem Passage' (*HDD* 40), the name of the passage recalling a twelfth–century abbey 'of the Knights Templar' (*HDD* 40) which had stood in the area until the reformation.[19] The name clearly testifies to what remains, to the remains of an other city. It offers a fragmentary signature returning endlessly from some other location to speak of an excess beyond that which can be read.

In *The House of Doctor Dee*, the materiality of language is manifested in a number of other ways. There is of course the following admission towards the end of the novel:

And what is the past, after all? Is it that which is created in the formal act of writing, or does it have some substantial reality? Am I discovering it, or inventing it? Or could it be that I am discovering it within myself, so that it bears both the authenticity of surviving evidence and the immediacy of present intuition? *The House of Doctor Dee* itself leads me to that conclusion: no doubt you expected it to be written by the author whose name appears on the cover and the title-page, but in fact many of the words and phrases are taken from John Dee himself. If they are not his words, they belong to his contemporaries. Just as he took a number of mechanical parts and out of them constructed a beetle that could fly, so I have taken a number of obscure texts and have fashioned a novel from their rearrangement.

(*HDD* 275)

In what appears to be the voice of the author, there is the acknowledgement of the persistence of the materiality of language. The novel, it is insisted, is a patchwork construct. Neither simply a novel written in the latter part of the twentieth century nor merely a pastiche, this text is configured from multiple voices and multiple writings, from different places and different temporal instances. Dee's writing and the other inscriptions from the sixteenth century are worked into the fabric of the text, returning to make the form possible. Thus, anachronistically, language marked indelibly by the traces of its own historicity is materially returned to the reader, so as to allow the spirit of another moment, an other identity, to haunt the identity of the present text as a counter-signature. Although Ackroyd – or a particular performance of one possible Peter Ackroyd – is writing specifically about the composition of the text, this passage comes as an interlude in Dee's vision of the permanence of London.[20] Dee is apostrophized and conjured by the novelist: 'Oh, Dee, Dee, come out from *that passage* where I glimpsed you then for a moment, wandering through the eternal city of your own time and mine' (*HDD* 275; emphasis added). The emphasized phrase, in the context of the vision of the 'eternal city', is, arguably, equally a passage in the text of Dee or a passage in the city of London. In a material and textual, as well as a spiritual, fashion, the other is envisioned, even as the other of the text envisions the modern moment. The textual event of reinscription of the material text transforms the scene of encounter, and through this London's alterity – its places and people – haunts the structures of modern narrative.

Elsewhere in the novel the materiality of language is expressed and inscribed in yet another manner, and connected to the materiality of the city. Towards the end of the novel, Matthew Palmer and his mother find some indecipherable signs scratched into the brickwork of a garage (from the bricks of which there appears to emanate a dim light), once owned by Matthew's father (*HDD* 267). Matthew has no sense of what the marks might mean, although he does wonder aloud whether the stones before him are of the present or past, or both. This question connects to Dee's assertion that 'all that ever we were left is the London stone, which is a visible portion of the lost city' (*HDD* 156). Earlier, when Matthew and Daniel explore the house, they find other unreadable symbols scratched into the fabric of the building, in the basement, 'very little [of which] could now be traced' (*HDD* 14–15). Daniel speculates that the basement was never a basement at all but, originally, the ground floor, 'and it has slowly sunk through the London clay' (*HDD* 15). Elsewhere, John Dee has cause to notice the marks on an inn table, which he says seemed to 'boast cabbalistical scribblings' (*HDD* 30). Signs are thus found in various places materially embedded into the very fabric of the city, thereby becoming part of the city's materiality. However, and paradoxically, the more the materiality of the sign is made manifest – library shelves threaten to give way beneath the weight of accumulated books, stone and wood are transformed into text through the traces left upon them – and the greater the potential 'weight' or possible meaning, the harder it is to read the signs.

So embedded into the material texture of place and encrypted or buried by time, the materiality of the signifier affirms its otherness and historicity by resisting any interpretative mastery. Once more, Ackroyd plays with the potential for asserting meaning and making connections, even while he never wholly gives in to making the connection.[21] The city, like the signs inscribed in its material, is barely readable as a certain concatenation of palimpsests ineffably there, even while meaning and identity remain undecidable. We might suggest that we can only read the undecidable as what remains, from the remains, the ruins of the city's past inscribed into the present. All we can read is that we cannot read, and it is in this resistance that the city returns as the eternal city, as other than the city we believe we comprehend. In this manner, Ackroyd reveals how there is always another figure within the perceived structure. The other of an identity is maintained within, even as that identity, whether of a person, building, an area or, by extension, London as a whole, only comes to be traced by the persistent resonance and projection of the other. The chance recognition of alterity within the same makes it possible for Ackroyd to write the city as 'this wonderful city' (*HDD* 29), 'the entire mystical city', and 'the most wonderful city on the face of the globe, a mystical city eternal' (*HDD* 167, 168).[22]

The phrase 'the mystical city eternal' concludes *The House of Doctor Dee*, as though the reiteration of the phrase itself were somehow able to inscribe the condition of London, or as though, in the absence of definition, the phrase itself would speak of the city, albeit indirectly. If language and text, stone and structure leave their trace, what of the countless Londoners? Perhaps most poignantly in the act of writing the city, in seeking to return via language the sense of the eternal city, Ackroyd seeks to recall those whom he calls the 'forgotten inhabitants of London' (*HDD* 276). In a moment at the end of the final chapter the narrative voice once more appears to become that of a certain Peter Ackroyd – or, at any rate, neither Dee nor Palmer, for these are both named and observed from some other place – who speaks of shining his light in the 'dark streets of London' (*HDD* 276), the light falling on the faces of the forgotten. These are not only John and Katherine Dee, or the various fictional characters of Ackroyd's novels, such as Matthew Palmer or Nicholas Hawksmoor, the tramps or itinerant street vendors who appear, across the centuries and across the biographies; they are also 'the Moravians of Arrow Lane, the Ranters, the followers of Jakob Boehme', the Swedenborgians, the Huguenots, and other dissenting groups (many of whom are discussed in the biography of William Blake). In this attempt to bring to light so many anonymous figures, we read an act of responsibility on Ackroyd's part. The ethical gesture is sought in the effort to allow the other London voices to speak for themselves (often through the mediumistic act of pastiche), rather than to speak for them. It is perhaps as part of this gambit on Ackroyd's part, that he only ever traces the possibility of connection, rather than forcing the connections on his readers. It is in this way that we come to comprehend how, for the novelist, these forgotten inhabitants, 'and so many others, all of them still living within the city' (*HDD* 276) are 'all those with whom we dwell – living or dead' (*HDD* 277). In comprehending this, we come to understand how we, like all the others, 'will become the mystical city eternal' (*HDD* 277).

Dan Leno and the Limehouse Golem or, *The Trial of Elizabeth Cree: a Novel of the Limehouse Murders*

The play with/in the title/s, to begin.

If familiarity is implicitly expected in the writing of London's toponymy and the narratives which perform their acts of naming and mapping, what familiarity, or lack thereof, is assumed in the play between and within the two titles of Peter Ackroyd's ninth novel? How does that play concern the various narrative forms of the text? How are we to locate Dan Leno, Elizabeth Cree, Karl Marx, George Gissing and the other characters who inhabit the crepuscular space of London between fiction and history in relation to the titles? What do the two titles have to tell us? How might we read them or read between them, so as to comprehend, albeit indirectly, the assumption of either familiarity with or the strangeness of a particular urban moment in its own possible relationship with other moments in the violent history of the city? Why two titles at all? And why two titles, which, even within themselves, within their own identities as titles indicating indirectly some aspect of London, appear to have their attention divided? Why are the titles readable as directing the reader's attention in different directions, offering different and differing routes through the labyrinthine text?

Dan Leno and the Limehouse Golem is the British title. In the US the title is *The Trial of Elizabeth Cree: A Novel of the Limehouse Murders*. The former in its ambiguity appears to encourage play, while the latter can be read as wanting to limit that play. The only feature which the two titles have in common is that location in London: Limehouse. Already the issue of the reader's familiarity and sense of community is tested. For, one will be able only to anticipate in some fashion the content, the narrative, if one belongs to that community of readers identified by J. Hillis Miller, who are topographically, culturally and historically savvy. Otherwise, Limehouse has no greater particular significance than, say, Nethergate or Camden, Hoboken or Queen's. If we know how to read the location, we already know the location, at least in part; in thus knowing it, we find that reading is already underway and that we are already en route to mapping the place.

The British title also evokes a particular kind of text. It is redolent with echoes of the titles of stagey melodramas or silent sensational films, such as *Maria Marten or, The Murder in the Red Barn* (to which Ackroyd refers, as well as to a melodrama called *The Great Fire of London*; DLLG 162, 173) or *The Cabinet of Doctor Caligari*. The title plays with different kinds of cultural information, and only begins to unravel itself if the reader is familiar with either the stage history of Dan Leno or the mythology of the Golem.[23] In either case, there is a question of, if not mythopoesis exactly, then popular culture and folklore, certain urban legends, forms of entertainment, and the possible relationship – the tantalizing connection – between the two. The novel's title alludes to proletarian narratives of disguise and identity, to acts of invention and imagination; it speaks of the ability of an identity to pass into a common understanding which serves to define a community, and by which the community can define itself as a world within a world. The title intimates delights both comic and gothic, but always larger than life and always grotesque.

The North American title and subtitle is seemingly more down to earth than its British counterpart. The reader is not required to know as much at the mythological or doxical level as is implied by the title of the English publication. This title can be read as documentary in its promise. It hints at due legal process and the narrative recording thereof. Elizabeth Cree's identity is not important here, for this title, in promising the record of the trial, implicitly promises to reveal such things. Trials tell us all we need to know about a person, about the aspects of a person's life which have led to the moment of the trial. From reading this title we assume a relationship between the subject being named and the location identified. Thus this title does a little more work for the reader than the British version. The subtitle reveals more, and we read in the articulation of this title the guarantee of a tale of murder and subsequent legal punishment. The US title provides a more direct path through possibly uncertain information than does *Dan Leno and the Limehouse Golem*. The North American title is still ambiguous, however. For all its legal and documentary resonance, *The Trial of Elizabeth Cree: A Novel of the Limehouse Murders* plays between that factitious location for its narrative and a degree of potential prurience and voyeurism intimated in the subtitle which, in letting us in on the secret of this being a novel in fact, signs and certifies that it is a novel of a certain kind, belonging to a particular genre. In case we might have thought 'trial' too uncertain, referring possibly to a vague definition of life's trials, the subtitle appears to make it quite clear that we will be witnesses at a trial, and that we'll get to hear all the evidence, not in some dry juridical or forensic narrative, but in a narrative form wholly more enticing.

The change in titles is, of course, incidental. It indicates a curious decision between author and publisher occurring perhaps because of the US publisher's fears over the inaccessibility of a title, in a country where, in the 1990s, every novel has the phrase 'a novel' on its jacket, in case the bookstore browser should mistake it for something else, or otherwise be in too much of a hurry to get beyond the cover. Despite the possibly 'accidental' nature of the change, the choice of titles remains, nonetheless, tantalizingly readable. Moreover, such a promise of complicated acts of reading speaks not only in obvious ways about what we might call conventionally the 'principal narrative concerns' (supposing for the moment that we are able to identify these so easily, as though we were reviewers of the journalistic variety). Perhaps, more importantly here, the two titles address the immediate range of textual interests and folds, as these find themselves folded into the numerous textual forms through which Ackroyd structures his novel. Such a complex range of textual voices creates endless resonances, all of which are concerned intimately with the city of London, and with its various worlds within a world.

Put simply, the novel figures the city as being composed and asserting its identities as a resonant configuration of textual grafts, trace upon trace, fold upon fold. It chooses to make little if any apparent distinction between the 'evidence' of so-called 'real' texts and 'imagined' texts, those which, to clarify the distinction, are composed by Peter Ackroyd, and those identified as belonging, for example, to Thomas de Quincey (whether quoted by John Cree or George Gissing), Karl Marx, George Gissing or, occasionally, Oscar Wilde. Texts, whether those written by Ackroyd or those of other writers, belong to the city primarily; they compose and construct the urban space as much as the pages from the Bible pasted to the walls make up the room in which Elizabeth Cree lives as a child: 'Our two rooms were bare enough, except for the pages of the Bible which she had pasted to the walls. There was hardly an inch of paper to be made out between them, and from my earliest childhood I could see nothing but words. I even taught myself to read from them...' (*DLLG* 12). In this instance, pages come to define the architectural form. This single domestic instance provides the reader with a performative textual and synecdochic figure, for the comprehension of the city's composition which the novel advances. At stake through this novel are the ways in which particular texts belong to a greater textual network or structure, and the uses to which textual evidence is put in searching for meaning or framing the definition. If anything is 'on trial' before the reader as witness, it is the reliability of the city's texts, none of which are allowed any greater validity than any of the others in Ackroyd's performative and playful structure. In *Dan Leno*, the city, formed from endless replications and palimpsests (Preziosi 1986, 237), is performed as an already transformed series of texts, having always already become in Carol Bernstein's words 'the scene of writing' (1991, 172). In this, there are enacted equally endless 'correspondences between urban and verbal creation [in] a city now conceived of as text' (Bernstein 1991, 45), into and through which Ackroyd weaves his own act of urban inscription, as yet one more turn in the performance of London. 'Here we are again', the phrase uttered on various occasions by Elizabeth Cree, Dan Leno and John Cree, is readable as the city's own performative epigraph (*DLLG* 2, 191, 279, 280).

The novel is divided into at least four principal narrative strands: the journal of John Cree, Elizabeth Cree's 'autobiography' or 'monologue' (this narrative could as easily be staged as it is supposedly 'authentic'), mimicked contemporary documentary sources, including journalism of the period (Ch. 37) and court transcripts (which bear a marked resemblance to play-texts) and the third-person narrative, which spends time on a number of subjects, but mainly the murders, and the stories of Lizzie Cree and George Gissing.[24] Like *Chatterton* before it, *Dan Leno* seems to raise questions concerning authenticity and masquerade. Unlike that novel, however, *Leno* circulates its numerous texts not around the question of authenticity solely, even though it toys with knowable, verifiable history, but around the condition of the city, which, Ackroyd makes us aware is a double condition – of performance and textuality, transformation and interpretation. Among the four principal narrative structures, composing a four-fold London narrative structure, there are many more voices and texts at work, some of which have already been indicated. There are citations, and citations within citations. Ackroyd cites, or otherwise alludes to, Marx. He cites Gissing. The novelist cites Gissing citing De Quincey or Babbage, while Gissing is said to compare Babbage's understanding of London to that of Dickens (*DLLG* 117). In the discussion of Babbage's vision, William Blake is commented on, via a critical study of Swinburne's from the *Westminster Review* which Gissing had, allegedly, been reading, prior to his visit to the site of Babbage's experiments with the 'Difference Engine' and the 'Analytical Engine' in Limehouse (*DLLG* 118). The site is, coincidentally, adjacent to the church of St Anne's, designed by the architect Nicholas Hawksmoor. Ackroyd comments that Gissing is struck by the possible correspondence between Babbage and Blake, in that both men conceive of designs, the significance of which is obscure to all but themselves. Commentary within commentary, text enfolding text, the significance of the location cannot escape Ackroyd's readers. We might suggest that the phrase 'Difference Engine' speaks not only of the complex layering of coincidences, of textual and historical events within the city; it also names the differential structure, the temporal and spatial construct, which is the novel itself.

Elsewhere in Gissing's musings, the texts of the city are cited and coincide, bringing together topographical and architectural concerns. Gissing's article, 'Romanticism and Crime',[25] tells how Thomas de Quincey and Ann

> ... would meet in order to console each other among 'the mighty labyrinths of London'. That is why the city and his suffering within it became – if we may borrow a phrase from that great modern poet Charles Baudelaire – the landscape of his imagination ... it could be said that the old highway led him directly to those nightmares and fantasies which turned London into some mighty vision akin to that of Piranesi, a labyrinth of stone, a wilderness of blank walls and floors. These were the visions, at least, which he recounted many years later when he lodged in York Street off Covent Garden. (*DLLG* 39)

Ackroyd draws together writers for whom the urban and imaginary structures present similar possibilities of poetic imagination in this passage. He thereby appears to promise forms of connection which are linked not merely thematically, but, more importantly, structurally or architectonically. The urban imaginary is mapped through the occurrence of the proper name, which itself stands in for other texts, in an implied, potentially endless *architexture*. Furthermore, Ackroyd implies that the city, its streets and buildings, its localities and details, can only be known through textual form. The city can only be given form through the textual act, an act which is a response recognising the already textual condition of the city. The city can never be recovered except as the labyrinthine archive of textual memory. Endless replications and palimpsests are the only true forms of the city; there is no 'original', single identity for London, which can then be represented faithfully and unequivocally.

There are further weavings. Ackroyd writes John Cree's journal, which either alludes to De Quincey or else cites him. Karl Marx is witnessed reading Dickens (*Bleak House*). The third-person narrative oscillates between 'explaining' or 'dramatizing' what we might term a 'fictional' account of part of the life of George Gissing and presenting Gissing's own abiding fascination with

London through some of his texts. It also alludes to Oscar Wilde, to Robert Louis Stevenson and Conan Doyle. At one moment Elizabeth Cree recalls sleeping with another actress, saying 'I would press up against her nightdress to *get the beauty of her hot*' (*DLLG* 91; emphasis added). Her final phrase of course 'anticipates' a line from 'A Game of Chess' in Eliot's *The Waste Land* ('...they had a hot gammon,/And they asked me in to dinner, to get the beauty of it hot'; Eliot 1974, 69). However, in its comic transformation – a ham becomes an actress, even though the actress may well be a ham already – the line also acknowledges the idiomatic utterance of a working-class Londoner, as does Eliot's. What these and all the other texts share in common is London itself, fictional and real. Indeed, if, in the passage above, it is the proper name which both promises structure and a linking textuality which maps performatively the city space, whereby that space is always being reconstructed anew, then, as the proper name of the city, London both names and performs a similar endless and labyrinthine event: whereby, every time the city is named, it rewrites itself.

There is another effect at work through the third-person narrative. The narrative 'adopts' or assumes the role or persona of the writer of historical-sociological-critical discourse. It performs as a secondary critical text, already installed within the structure of the novel, yet displacing the novel's identity. Assuming a tone of distance and dead-pan restraint, it gives way on occasions to unexpected moments of camp. The opening line of the novel implies such a discursive context: 'On the 6th April, 1881, a woman was hanged within the walls of Camberwell Prison' (*DLLG* 1). The US title might well appear closer in tone to this than Ackroyd's British title. The chapter continues in this manner until its very end, when it details, in an equally dead-pan fashion, how the prison governor, 'Mr Stephens', takes home the white gown in which Elizabeth Cree has been hanged. Upon arriving home, which we are told is in Hornsey Rise, North London, for factual accuracy, 'he lifted it above his head and put it on. He was wearing nothing else and, with a sigh, he lay down upon the carpet in the gown of the hanged woman' (*DLLG* 3). So, the chapter concludes, a disconcerting moment in the identity of the chapter, as a figure of authority surrenders to an act of private transvestism.[26]

The second chapter resumes the historical-critical discourse, moving, however, from the purely factual account of a Victorian hanging, with some sociological commentary along the way, to introduce the story of the 'Limehouse Golem', detailing the myth and the meaning of the word 'Golem', which we are assured 'literally means "thing without form"' (*DLLG* 4; another possible translation could be 'matter without form'). Like narrative itself, the creature only comes to have shape as it is 'filled', so to speak, with details, descriptions, and actions. Form is the result of narrative, and each narrative will take on a different structure, as we come to understand through the multiple layerings of *Dan Leno and*

the Limehouse Golem. The Golem is compared to that other mythological creature, the homunculus, which had been Ackroyd's concern in his previous novel,
The House of Doctor Dee, before the reader is told that the secret of the 'revival' of
the Golem is 'to be found within *the annals of London's past*' (*DLLG* 4; emphasis
added). Once more, there is that sense of cautious, calm critical delineation in
process. The reader is then directed to the description of the first of a series of
murders, vaguely reminiscent of those of Jack the Ripper:

> The first killing occurred on the 10th September, 1880, along Limehouse
> Reach: this, as the name implies, was an ancient lane which led from a
> small thoroughfare of mean houses to a flight of stone steps just above the
> bank of the Thames. It had been used by porters over many centuries for
> convenient if somewhat cramped access to the cargo of smaller boats
> which anchored here, but the dock redevelopments of the 1830s had left it
> marooned on the edge of the mud banks. It reeked of dampness and old
> stone, but it also possessed a stranger and more fugitive odour which was
> aptly described by one of the residents of the neighbourhood as that of
> 'dead feet'.
>
> (*DLLG* 5)

Once more, as with the opening chapter, the discursive location of the
passage is, apparently, easily identified and assumed. The reader is engaged by
a performance of a particular kind and is asked implicitly to accept the
verisimilitude of the performance, to 'go along with' the truth of the identity
of this passage. Ackroyd sets up a structural resonance with a critical discourse,
here as throughout the text, especially when speaking of supposedly factual
and historical matters relating to London. However, what gives the reader
pause is that final definition of the 'strange and more fugitive odour'. The
tone, and, with it, the identity of the passage is unsettled through the attributed definition. Moreover, what is interesting about this playful effect is that
it works in a number of ways. The phrase, 'dead feet', is caught between a kind
of gothic cliché or the intimation of a sense of the uncanny which often
haunts texts of terror in the 1870s, 1880s and 1890s (this novel is set in the
1880s), such as *Dracula*, *The Picture of Dorian Gray*, *The Strange Case of Doctor
Jekyll and Mr Hyde* or *The Beetle*, and a comic, farcical effect more immediately
reminiscent of Charles Dickens. Furthermore, the phrase arrives as the punc-
tuating and defining moment from outside the critical-historical discourse
being mimicked here. For, as we are told, the phrase belongs to an
unidentified Londoner. A disembodied East-End voice displaces the authority
of the assumed discourse, bringing back the urban scene and its community
in a manner similar to Elizabeth Cree's choice of phrase, discussed above.
There is a connection also, in this rhetorical playfulness, to the moment of

cross-dressing from the opening chapter, which unsettles that narrative identity. For, in both examples, a certain authority is subverted, and this takes place, importantly in the form of a return, a certain haunting which, in each case, is given a specific London identity. In effect, the text is disjointed by the return of a trace always connected, however obliquely, to the city, and pertaining to irreverence, to performative and dissonant, even dissident identities. It is as though the city haunts any narrative which seeks to maintain distance from it, rising through the moment of stability, as if to remind us that 'here we are again'.

Hence the 'return' of violent acts, of serial killing and mass murder, as particularly violent traces of the city's disturbing identity, of which more below. Such traces are both indelible and spectral, and given particular, exemplary 'form' in the imagined shape of the Golem. As already suggested, the Golem never exists, as such. It is only a textual trace, a shared, communal memory, given life only through the articulation of its possibility. This possibility of resonance extends from the novel to the murders identified as those committed by Jack the Ripper. The resonance between Ackroyd's novel and the Ripper murders is enough to seduce certain readers into seeking further correspondences, even though these are not necessarily there. Indeed, as we have suggested elsewhere, given that the prostitutes, a Jewish scholar, Solomon Weil, and a family are murdered, it is as true to say that the scene of Ackroyd's novel in no way resembles the Ripper murders, other than in the coincidence that they occur in the East End of London. The Ripper murders occurred in Whitechapel, the victims being exclusively prostitutes, as is well known. Ackroyd's 'murders' have little in common with the events in Whitechapel.

The murders of the novel are all particularly staged, bloodily violent and melodramatic. Indeed, Cree persistently connects the murders to theatrical performance, seeing London as his stage (see n. 26). At one point, one of those moments in Ackroyd's writing where 'tone' doubles itself being, in this example both horrific and crassly comic, Cree recalls of one of his victims that, 'her head lay upon the upper step, just as if it were the prompter's head seen from the pit of the theatre' (*DLLG* 62). However, beyond this, there is no connecting meaning for the murders, unless it goes by the mystical and mystifying name 'Golem', which in itself tells us little about the identity of the murderer but is merely, in the context of the novel, a journalistic means for creating and constructing a narrative pattern pertinent to East End of London in general and to Limehouse in particular. While John Cree 'admits' to the murders of the prostitutes, Weil, and the family who occupy a house on the site of the Marr murders (those discussed by Thomas de Quincey) in his journal, there is no conclusive evidence in the novel that Cree did commit the murders. All the reader has to go on is textual evidence without any access to authenticity or any authenticating trace. Whether or not Cree did kill and butcher the various victims of the so-called Golem, the suggestion is never made that he is the Golem. Indeed, the Golem only 'exists' in writing, in the form of words on the page, at least as far as *Dan Leno and the Limehouse Golem* is concerned.

This in itself is appropriate both to the mythology of the Golem and to the narration of London. As mentioned before, 'Golem' can mean thing or matter without form. The *Oxford English Dictionary* renders the term from the Hebrew as 'shapeless mass'. The Golem can only be formed by giving it form, so that, each and every time the Golem is made, it must, of necessity, be formed anew and, perhaps, differently. Part of the formation of the Golem is the inscription on the Golem of the Hebrew word *emet*, meaning *true*. The word must be inscribed on the Golem's hand, in order that it come to life (at the same time, however, if the first character of Hebrew word is erased, what remains is not 'true' but the Hebrew for 'death'). Each Golem is therefore the true Golem, given identity by the inscription of the word. The 'truth' of the Golem is only found in its formulation, its truth embodied in itself. Writing, not the form, gives the Golem its being. Writing, if you like, writes the form on formlessness. The shapeless mass is effaced even as it is transformed in the act of inscription upon it, which changes its shape with every textual act. For these reasons, there is no Golem in Ackroyd's novel, even though there is Golem, Golem written or whispered everywhere.

We may therefore suggest, albeit provisionally, that Ackroyd implicitly acknowledges the truth of Golem's truth, in his writing about the Golem without representing it. The act of writing the novel gives the Golem shape. Or rather, shapes. For the Golem of the novel is multiple, assuming as many shapes as there are narrative and textual formulations in the novel, which is, moreover, a novel always acknowledging its indebtedness and the possibility of its form to prior acts of writing which allow it to take shape, and without which it would be a shapeless mass, matter without form. Indeed, the novel is itself Golem-like, formed in its various true shapes according to the forms of inscription. Furthermore, the Golem is, in a certain sense, London, though never restricted to this, anymore than London is restricted to a single definition. When Ackroyd, in critical-historical voice, suggests that the secret of the 'revival' of the Golem is 'to be found within the annals of London's past' (*DLLG* 4), he effectively dismisses the possibility of any pure or single origin for the Golem, by contriving its revival as an effect of place and what takes place. The city determines the identity of the Golem, but, more than this, the city assumes a form which determines the condition of the location throughout time, even though it becomes transformed. That 'something', grasped after by Timothy Harcombe, remains, though indefinable once again. London has no form, no shape, unless narrated, unless it takes place.

Elie Wiesel, in his version of the Golem legend, suggests that the 'whole picture' of the Golem was only obtained by piecing together various 'visions and memories ... everyone possessed a fragment of a tale; they had to be brought together to create a legend' (1983, 47). Inscription is not a solitary act, an original act of invention or genius, but a response to countless texts. The act of creating and narrating the Golem relies upon numerous voices, a community of voices. Once again, as Ackroyd shows us, the city, like the Golem, only comes into being through the multiplicity of enunciations and inscriptions, while never remaining the thing itself. These narrations, like the city itself, rely on previous narrations, previous structures and architectural forms, out of which both the narrations and the city grow. Thus London is both performative and transformative. Having no particular meaning as such, it must always be redefined, even though, in this, the city will always have escaped definition and the imposition of a definite identity. Such escape is, in part, due to the fact that the haunted layering of location and citation shapes the writer's response, rather than being defined solely by the writer. *Dan Leno and the Limehouse Golem* is, like both city and Golem, an act of multiple, heterogeneous swirling voices, constantly reinventing its selves. In this the novel enters into the condition of London, as, Golem-like, it is determined from countless other places, others' texts, both real and imagined.

This persistent babelian resonance is a favourite conceit of Ackroyd's, not only in his writing in general, as he militates against notions of originality, invention and solitary genius, in favour of pastiche and palimpsest, textual grafting and weaving, but specifically, in *Dan Leno*, where no voice is authentic or original. Indeed, even as the phrase 'here we are again' is reiterated, so too is a comment of Charles Babbage's, which, repeated and remembered by George Gissing in the novel, defines the Ackroydian conceit: 'The air itself is one vast library, on whose pages are forever written all that man has ever said or woman whispered' (*DLLG* 117).[27] Gissing later repeats this line to himself 'as he walked through the damp and misty streets of London', until he becomes lost in a labyrinth of streets which are thoroughly unfamiliar, even though they lay only 'a mile or so from his own lodgings' (*DLLG* 243). Encountering a number of poverty stricken Londoners in the 'maze of streets' (who are themselves reminiscent of those figures encountered in Henry Mayhew's account in *London Labour and the London Poor*), Gissing comes to realize that 'if the air indeed were one vast library, one great vessel in which all the noises of the city were preserved, then nothing need be lost' (*DLLG* 246). The idea is manifested earlier in Gissing's thoughts. When temporarily apprehended by the police for questioning over the murders, Gissing considers the stones of the cell in which he is held. He 'had read in a recent copy of the *Weekly Digest* that part of the ancient city of London had been found during the building of certain warehouses by Shadwell Reach. Some stone walls had been uncovered, and it occurred to Gissing that this cell might have been constructed from the remnants of them' (*DLLG* 146–47). Though not connected to Babbage's text, Gissing's thought hints at how nothing is ever lost, how the city is reinvented within itself, so that, even in the most basic architectural manifestations the city's past leaves its trace.

Gissing is thus used by Ackroyd as a medium for the city, for its traces and its textual reconfigurations. From Babbage's general comment, Gissing hypothesizes about the condition of London itself. Indeed, the partial reiteration and paraphrase of Babbage's conceit is performative in that it becomes part of the babble of London voices in the text, filtered via Gissing through Ackroyd's urban imagination. However, as if to resist the reader's assignation of the phrase either to Babbage or Gissing alone, Ackroyd denies that the image of the babble belongs to any one figure. The image of the vast library of textual traces and voices as a possible figure for the constant refiguring of the city is offered as a continuous anonymous generative and performative process in this description of the British Library. 'They were lost in their books,' we are told, 'as the murmuring of all the inhabitants of the Reading Room rose towards the vast dome and set up a whispering echo like that of voices in the fog of London' (*DLLG* 401). If the figure of Gissing is suggestively delineated as a kind of medium, he is not alone, for Ackroyd intimates that the process of communal articulation enfolds countless readers.

Ackroyd therefore establishes an endless reciprocity, a process of folding and unfolding, whereby any distinction between 'reality' and 'writing' becomes erased. This is seen in one passage where the scene is set in an apparently conventional manner. We read that 'the notorious pea-soupers of the period, so ably memorialised by Robert Louis Stevenson and Arthur Conan Doyle, were quite as dark, as their literary reputation would suggest' (*DLLG* 45). The line reads ambiguously, or appears to, at any rate. Beginning with a literary cliché, it moves to indirect citation of two London authors whose work is largely responsible for generating stock images of the late Victorian city. In that 'ably' there is readable a possible suggestion of these writers being damned with faint praise, as is perhaps appropriate when referring to such a cliché. Curiously, the sentence plays between the reality of the London smogs and fog and their literary representations, the curiosity of the line being in that hint that one turns to the 'literary reputation' primarily for verification. The 'reality' of the city is, it would seem, dictated by stock literary devices for staging the *grand guignol* urban experience. It is as if we cannot know London, without prior access to its canonical texts.

Another example of the city's history mediated through textual filters occurs in the citation of Gissing's article 'Romanticism and Crime' (already quoted): 'the house which had witnessed the immortal Ratcliffe Highway murders of 1812 ... [had been] preserved forever in the pages of Thomas de

Quincey' (*DLLG* 117). De Quincey's text, returning to us through a textual detour of nearly two hundred years, becomes the form by which one aspect of the city is given shape. This aspect or persona of the city is a particularly violent one, as already suggested, above. The historical reiteration of violence violently marks a locale such as Limehouse, which, in turn, becomes the focus of writers through the centuries who retrace the bloody scene of the location, thereby mapping the urban event, both temporally as well as spatially. It is as if the history of the city is written in the blood of its victims. Violence is part of any city and leaves its trace in a particularly indelible fashion on urban experience or memory. The legend of the Golem is of course a narrative response to acts of violence, and Ackroyd draws upon the urban legend as a means of approaching, or bearing witness to, that which is unrepresentable in any city's history. If the city's identity is theatrical, as Peter Ackroyd repeatedly suggests throughout his writing, then the theatricality is of a dark and often destructive kind. Theatricality is not an escape from the darkness of the urban spirit, but a grotesque manifestation of that spectre. It is this thought which leads the novelist, in his own masquerade as the critical voice of the text to remark that 'it would not be going too far to suggest, in fact, that there was some link between the murder of the prostitutes in Limehouse and the ritual humiliation of women in pantomime' (*DLLG* 171).

Whether or not we are to take this remark at face value is undecidable. The reciprocity of which we have already spoken is not discernible in terms of an originating point, for the textual configurations of resonant structures suggest the *mise en abyme* rather than the *mise en scène* of the gothic fictions of Stevenson, Wilde, Conan Doyle, Morrison, Richard Marsh, or even Joseph Conrad. Any sense of authenticity collapses due to the perpetual cross-contamination between supposedly distinct identities such as 'art' or 'life', 'history' or 'fiction', 'world' or 'word'. What remains, however, is a somewhat ineffable sense of the power of the city, of its violent, haunting trace, a trace which remains resistant to identification, as the following two passages imply.

> It was almost as if [Londoners] had been waiting impatiently for these murders to happen – as if the new conditions of the metropolis required some vivid identification, some flagrant confirmation of its status as the largest and darkest city of the world. This probably accounted for the eagerness with which the term 'golem' was taken up .... It was an emblem for the city which surrounded them as the search for the Limehouse Golem became, curiously enough, a search for the secret of London itself.
>
> (*DLLG* 88)

> Some dark spirit had been released, or so it seemed, and certain religious leaders began to suggest that London itself – this vast urban creation which was the first of its kind upon the globe – was somehow responsible for the evil.

Note the uncertainty, the staged indecisiveness if you will, of Ackroyd's prose, even as it strains to approximate the need for definition, for fixing the identity of London and thereby domesticating and making safe the formless mass of the city, become compliant through the act of determination. What London is remains a secret, but that there is a secret is apprehended. Ackroyd plays with the question of the secret and on it, the indecisiveness being part of the play. Size seems to matter, for, in part, it is size which makes definition or identification impossible, even as it is a question of massiveness related to formlessness which dictates the desire to determine meaning. Tellingly, Ackroyd defines attempted definition as 'flagrant confirmation', as though those who rush to give the city meaning and therefore make it knowable are in breach of the laws of the city's structure, which are as secret as the city itself. The city comes to be blamed as though it were, if not living exactly, then some manifestation of the undead or otherwise haunted by its own spectre, the spectres of all its violated and oppressed inhabitants, reaching back over the centuries.

To conclude, if familiarity is implicitly expected in the writing of London's toponymy and the narratives which perform their acts of naming and mapping, what kind of familiarity are we speaking of with regard to a novel which makes explicit the final unknowability of the city's identity? In the case of *Dan Leno and the Limehouse Golem*, familiarity with toponymy and narrative go hand in hand with another kind of familiarity: an acquaintance with strangeness and estrangement, an intimacy with play that disturbs identity, a familiarity with the limit which one's knowledge reaches of the labyrinth. What Peter Ackroyd strives to make us familiar with is that London remains ineffable. It resists definition, by being nothing other than the voices, the texts, the traces of itself, endlessly reconfigured and performed, time and time again. Ackroyd toys with the idea of the city being a golem-form, even as, finally, he rejects too facile a definition. For to name the city 'golem' and to come to rest on that identification, albeit one shrouded in mystery, legend and obscure cabbalism, as the *only* identity for the city would be to miss the ever-changing condition. The play in which Ackroyd engages is risky, to say the least. He engages playfully, time and again, with the very meaning he refuses to assign, even though he tempts his readers into slipping into the act of easy assignation, assuming the wrong kind of familiarity. For Ackroyd, the idea the Golem, its narrative potential, is more important than any cheap trick stage illusion of an urban monster. Playing with the suggestive possibility of a haunting return is but one way in which to approximate through indirection the condition of infinite London. The idea of the Golem provides merely one more textual trace. It is merely one more text, itself composed of numerous voices and inscriptions, put together piecemeal by the heterogeneous community of urban dwellers, who come to define the city as much as its architecture. We read this in the final paragraph of the novel:

> The audience filed out into the dark night after the performance was over, the young and old, the rich and the poor, the famous and the infamous, the charitable and the mean, all back into the cold mist and smoke of the teeming streets. They left the theatre in Limehouse and went their separate ways, to Lambeth or to Brixton, to Bayswater or to Whitechapel, to Hoxton or to Clerkenwell, all of them returning to the uproar of the eternal city. And even as they travelled homeward, many of them remembered that wonderful moment when Dan Leno had risen from the trapdoor and appeared in front of them. 'Ladies and gentlemen,' he had announced in his best mammoth comique manner, 'here we are *again!*'
>
> (*DLLG* 282).

Once more there is that implicit familiarity in the play of proper names, as the map of the city is reconfigured through the writer's toponymic gambit. At the same time, the play between the polar opposites of the audience is echoed in the play between the immateriality and materiality of the streets, alive with the movement of insubstantial vapours and nameless millions. The performance gathers its community, only to release them to the various areas of the city, to become themselves urban performers, traced through by the endless return of Leno's words. This final paragraph plays through a series of reiterated rhetorical and syntactical structures, even as it performs the movement away from the theatre, a movement in which the reader is caught up, as s/he prepares to leave behind the performances, the stagings, the dressings up, of *Dan Leno and the Limehouse Golem*. This serial play is itself one more variation on both the novel's construction and the comprehension of the city, which we read in the textual performance. Yet nothing is ever left behind quite completely, as the phrase 'eternal city' suggests. For, even as each member of the audience recalls Leno's words, so the past moment returns to the present moment of memory, caught in the present tense of the comedian's words, and oscillating through this structure as its own anticipated future return, where the eternal city will therefore have brought us together – *again.*

Have you got the time please he obviously wants the best price but he wants to sell as well I shall be off then shall I he never wants to hear the truth can you possibly tell me the time what to say when it's already too late, when now more than ever it seems a question of time, despite what I have before me? What to write, here, now, in this margin, after the book is supposedly finished, though while, as yet, it is not in print? (And yet – parenthesis, after the event – you will have read this in print that this is not yet in print; what's going on here?) What about that, three weeks or so before receiving the copy-edited typescript from the publisher, having just finished – I hardly dare to say for the first time – or having just begun *The Plato Papers*, by Peter Ackroyd? I know that there's no time (no time to lose, no time like the present, hurry up please, it's time, I imagine the publisher saying), not enough time to 'read' *The Plato Papers*, that is, to provide an exemplary analysis, and yet – here we are, *again*.

Indeed. Lights, children, the city, time. A novel? In ruins, in fragments. Dialogues, oration, performance (no don't laugh), dreams, witless misinterpretation (*caveat lector*) of the literary, ludicrous speculation, reconstruction, textual analysis, tentative definitions for an unfinished glossary, composed mostly of twentieth-century terms and idioms. Plato returns to us from the future, a ghost we cannot quite believe in, to speak in public of, amongst others, Poe or E.A.P. (Eminent American Poet), whose writings tell us all we need to know about Americans (*PP* 29–34); Charles Dickens, the author of *On the Origin of Species*, one of the wittiest and most savagely parodic novels of the nineteenth century (*PP* 5–8); Sigmund Freud, the comic genius with his blue bag of tricks, and his pantomimic sidekick, Oedipus (*PP* 59–61); George Eliot, the African singer, who has left behind scraps of a poem, with the words 'fragments' and 'ruin' being nearly all that's left (*PP* 78–9).

Where then, to begin? Or, for that matter, to end?

Hurry up please, its time

To embark upon a journey while remaining in the same place

Here we are, again

...the ghosts of the past come hurrying to greet me.
building ... breaking up into words

And this is the part that no one understands. It might be better to begin at the beginning.

'The literary text inserts itself into the set of all texts: it is a writing-response to (a function or negation of) another text or other texts. By writing while reading the anterior or synchronic literary corpus the author lives in history, the society writes itself in the text.'
Julia Kristeva

There appears to be a certain return, the question of what can return, how the return might be readable, when a spectral figure, the trace of someone who has never existed, returns and in doing so, appears to evoke 'the text of Peter Ackroyd'. Specifically, what returns is recognizable as figures already at work in the earliest published pieces, in the poetry; what returns also is a certain mocking relationship to knowledge, given voice in *Notes for a New Culture*. There is – to return to what I have already mentioned – the recurring interest in the city and, simultaneously, the impossibility of knowing the city, in lights, in the imagines of children, and in the playful comedy directed at the act of interpretation, analysis and translation.

As an example of the work or, rather, the pl(a)y of *The Plato Papers*, it is necessary to go back to the pages before the first. The text begins before the book, as a series of citations, grafts, all attributed as is proper, and yet not quite in place. The citations, most of which concern the 'holy' city, London, two thousand years in the future, are on unnumbered pages, while they also introduce, in the final citation, attributed to 'Anon.' (who, it appears is to be the voice reconstructing all the subsequent narratives and voices), the subject, Plato, and the question of his orations. These properly cited, improper citations return to the reader as the ghostly fragments of texts already underway and, equally, already lost. In a sense, though coming before the novel, they come after it, returning to haunt any act of reading, as an act of re-citation, of assembly, of memory, surrounding the novel with a 'filter of commentary', to recall an earlier phrase. By the articulation of this filter or mesh of phrases, we are given to comprehend the concerns of *The Plato Papers*, and from which we may seek to construct a certain reading, before reading can be said to have got underway.

There is thus through the various narrative voices of *The Plato Papers* a constant narrative recurrence, a rhythm of return which displaces and defers the

In returning to the origin of all things, we meet our destiny. Do you see our doubles, passing by us weeping? This is the nature of our world.
Proverbs of Restituta, guardian of London, 3640.
...it is constituted by the past of written literature

Sparkler: Impossible. I never know when Plato is telling the truth.
Sidonia: That is what he enjoys. The game. [...]
Sparkler: But who could be convinced by such wild speculations?

Now he had a theme – and it was London itself, wasn't it that?

Sidonia: They are moments of reappeaing, little gleams of time.

Hawksmoor stared at the page, trying to imagine the past which these words represented Thus do we see in every Line an Echoe, for the truest Plagiarism is the truest Poetry.

'For the writer, then, poetic language is a *potential infinity* ...: the unproblematic citation of an origin, a source, a moment of unquestionable beginning. Narrative voice, whether in the form of dialogues, in orations, in glossaries, in epigraphs and citations, posits a 'character of recurrence', in the words of Bernard Steigler, which suggests that 'access to ... [any sense of] future is only possible through access to its having-been: access to its having-being is access to its future. The origin is at the end, and the end at the origin – with this one différance that there is time (that of the return, time as deferral), that is, facticity (itself deferred: effaced, forgotten)' (Steigler 1998, 261).

Yet to return again to the citations which begin before the beginning, displacing the beginning and returning to us the 'future' of, that is, *The Plato Papers*, if I can put it in this fashion. How to cite these citations, 'properly' so to speak, given that there is no page number? How can I read from what are, already, fragments, existing in an apparently tangential relationship to either the beginning or, indeed, all of the book? Strictly speaking, this remains unanswerable, and all that can be acknowledged here is that the text inserts itself ahead of the game in the play between writing and reading, narrative and commentary. It (dis-)places itself between two times at least, its rhythms and movements always already caught within and acknowledging the temporal-spatial weave of différance.

Even as Ackroyd's text 'returns' to its earliest interests, placing itself in a form of conversation with them – if not a dialogue – , marked by the passivity of a discourse with the other; so these texts return to (or even, perhaps, as?) *The Plato Papers*, even while this is a novel wherein texts from the past return in virtually unrecognizable form. Moreover, there are other returns, establishing 'intricate patterns of movement' (*PP* 89). Plato claims to have returned to the past of London, to what is called Mouldwarp London, or London of the twentieth century. This is a city reconstructed

infinite set (of poetic language) is considered as a set of realizable possibilities.'
Julia Kristeva

It may seem peculiar to us that our earliest ancestors always looked back to some mythical point of origin...

'Coming to oneself from the future is a returning to the already ... this repetition is having-been'.
Bernard Steigler

'The fundamental reality of consciousness is temporality – a temporal flow or succession of perceptions (impressions and ideas) that perpetually and spontaneously glide away. This flow is characterized by immanent disconnection. It is a *system of differences.*'
Shaun Gallagher
Yes, I have returned to the past.

Plato: What if the past is all invention or legend? ... What if my interpretation of the books is false or misguided? 'This past of *mine* is only inherited insofar as it is not *my* past: it has to come "to be so".'
Bernard Steigler

in part through narrative from fragments of film, Hitchcock's *Frenzy* to be precise (*PP* 72ff.), while the city, visited by Plato, 'had no boundaries. It had no beginning and no end' (*PP* 91).

While Plato's return is as an invisible spirit, he notices that Londoners are sometimes capable of glimpsing 'images or ghosts of the spirit' (*PP* 92). Such spectral moments haunt the very texture of the writing itself. Of Plato, one of the incidental characters, Ornatus, taking part in a dialogue says: 'Then he put his hand across his face and mentioned that he had seen me in the race against the oarsmen of Essex Street' (*PP* 83). This instance of memory is haunted, disjointed from within the apparent straightforwardness of the statement, by the merest possibility of reading a translation of (the fragments and ruins of) Eliot. Undoubtedly fanciful, but it is precisely through such resonance that Plato is moved to ask, 'How can it be the same and always different?' (*PP* 94), even while such a ludic moment gestures towards the unconsciously parodic reassembly of texts and the past in which Plato is engaged. (And which, in turn, recall and return [to] us, those poems which playfully ply the dangers of interpretation [*DP* 7, 9, 11–12].)

What is left to us, ahead of any reading is a certain dissolution where '... the fabric of the old reality had dissolved or, rather, it had become interwoven with so many others that it could only rarely be glimpsed' (*PP* 52). Ackroyd's haunted text relies on the belief 'that everything, past and future alike exists eternally' (*PP* 66–7). There is no recuperable origin, a single moment of genesis for, 'creation occurs continually' (*PP* 67). And even these suggestions may be undermined, opened to undecidability. For there is always the possibility that, in the words of Plato's soul, 'you were meant to be wrong ... [what if] every age depends upon wilful blindness?' (*PP* 76).

Such a commentary gives the critic pause. Or it should do, at least. The figure of Plato evinces a naively literalist approach to the question of

it is as if I were entering a place I had once known and then forgotten ... If my work meant that I often viewed the past as my present, so in turn the present moment became part of the past.

'There I saw one I knew, and stopped him, crying: "Stetson! You who were with me in the ships at Mylae!"[...] Elizabeth and Leicester Beating oars'
The Waste Land

What do these words mean? ...
Try to explain in your own words how the writer felt...

most of the signals ... are so faint, and so complex, that they cannot yet be analysed.

interpretation, and it is easy to laugh, despite the fact that, on several occasions throughout the novel, during his orations Plato asks his audience – and us – 'no, please do not laugh', or words to that effect. The fact of apparent repetition seems to negate the command or request, while carrying in it a performative gesture which indicates that laughter is the desired response, despite the ostensible meaning. Reiteration attunes the phrase's oscillation as the phrase appears to take on the guise of a comedian's catch-phrase. Thus we catch a glimpse of the ludic in play. But this remains a tentative speculation. Through the dissonant resistance to unequivocal communication installed in the phrase, we glimpse – do we not? – the play with the possibility that while commentary may appear to make itself ludicrous, its articulation may serve some other purpose which remains to be read. How can we tell, how can we know, especially in a text where the phrase 'opening night' – 'the creation myth of Mouldwarp' (*PP* 20) – is interpreted as the emergence of the universe 'from darkness and chaos' (*PP* 20)? The theory of the 'big bang' becomes a theatrical moment, the scientific narrative of origin merely a performative instance.

Much remains to be read in the text of Peter Ackroyd, and I want to conclude with what is, admittedly a highly fanciful, playful (if not to be read by some as ludicrous) speculation on the title of Ackroyd's latest – as I write – publication.

Elsewhere in *Peter Ackroyd: The Ludic and Labyrinthine Text*, it has been observed that figures of fathers occur, albeit fathers who invariably fail, who have vanished, who disappoint. In *The Plato Papers*, a novel the very title of which names a heterogeneous collection of texts, gathered apparently anonymously while circulating around the figure of Plato, there appears to be no father – or, to put that another way, no father appears, directly. Plato is no father figure, but is referred to occasionally as child-like, as small: 'little Plato' (*PP* 37). It is Plato's mother, not his father

Little Victor's Daughter was the young virgin who said quite innocent things – how could she help it if she was open to misconstruction?

'Is this our ending?'

(who is never mentioned), who tells Plato tales and fables of London (*PP* 11–12).

There is perhaps a father for Plato, however, though nowhere to be found directly in the text. His appearance is fleeting and encrypted, barely a paraph, which returns the ghost of the author, lurking in the background, hanging around, dictating Plato's visions of the city, his literary analyses, his various commentaries. The paraph, that most minimal of signatures is simultaneously hidden and in plain view, signed throughout the book, everywhere the name of Plato is mentioned, but most immediately in that title: *The Plato Papers*. Every time the proper name *Plato* appears, Peter Ackroyd appears to sign himself, within that name: **Pla**to. Peter Ackroyd, the pa of this Plato at least, the spectral father, who returns to haunt the future even as he returns, the merest trace from the future he imagines to the multiple presents of writing and reading, though of course, never present as such. Possibly, we see this everywhere, as the playful text of Peter Ackroyd seems to authorize us to see this name and more than this name, a ghostly signature. 'Cleverly integrated into the texture' (Temple 1995, 54), readable everywhere and yet nowhere immediately obvious, the paraph dares me to read it, yet denies its inscription. (Brief, final parenthesis: when Plato discovers a statue in Finsbury, with the letters LO inscribed between her breasts, and concludes that this represents the city of London [*PP* 55], is this an intimation of how – or how not – to read?) But, perhaps you will object, I'm having a laugh, aren't I? It's all a bit of a joke, a game *en travesti* – isn't it? If this is not merely, simply, another ludic moment, is this then merely what Michael Temple has called, in his study of Stéphane Mallarmé, 'honest onomastic labour' (1995, 68), or [b]y thus actively participating in the elaboration of his signature', is the writer 'preparing his name for eternity' (Temple 1995, 4)? Who can tell? After all, I might be quite wrong. I might be half-wrong and half-right … Only the reader has the answer …

'Openly paradoxical and open to contradiction, the signature is the name writ deep and large. It has become a metaphor for reading itself.'

Michael Temple

'This is perhaps the moment to return to our starting point.'

Slavoj Žižek

5

Three Interviews with Peter Ackroyd

Interview between Jeremy Gibson and Peter Ackroyd
26 August 1989

JG: In your first novel, *The Great Fire of London*, you draw upon Dickens quite a lot, and now you're writing his biography. Just a general question: to what extent do you identify with Dickens as a writer?

PA: Not to a very large extent. Common elements would be the interest in London, obviously, and his affection for London life. I suppose I would share that. On a larger scale, without being pretentious about it, I would say that Dickens represented the one strand in the English novel which really interests me, which is what you might call the mythic quality in the English novel. Now that's a tradition which in recent years has been disparaged or rendered invisible by other traditions in English fiction. But my interest in Dickens stems from the fact that I'd like to go back to the wealth and richness of the English novel, which it certainly possessed in the middle of the nineteenth century.

JG: There are similarities between your style and Dickens', especially, I find, in terms of characterization and plot structure. Coming back to characterization later, you weave different plot strands together, often mixing high camp comedy with sincere tragedy, much as Dickens himself does. One reviewer found this lacking in taste, and it could be viewed as an uncomfortable coupling, rather than a complementary contrast. How would you defend this style?

PA: Well, it's just the way it happens really, it comes instinctively like that to me. It's not something that I deliberately engineer, or in any event wish to emphasize. What happened in the novel *Hawksmoor* was that it was all entirely in what you might call a serious or melancholy basis, and I thought at the time that it was rather lacking a large component of my own temperament which happens to be – for want of a better

221

word – 'comedy', high camp or otherwise. And I decided that I wasn't going to be either true to myself or true to what I wanted to do if I wasn't able to incorporate that kind of comedy into my – for want of a better word – 'work'. So it just started to happen, and of course the personal consequences – which some people find more palatable than others. I myself don't mind the combination of seriousness and farce or wit, or whatever you want to call it, because it strikes me as being perhaps the only valid way of responding to the world which I've tried to create in the fictions. Of course, you're better off asking other people what it all means than I am, it's no good asking me. But certainly in my own reaction to the world, whatever seriousness there may be, it's certainly meant to be a certain kind of humour, I suppose. And it's simply natural for me to transpose that into my novels as well.

JG: What kind of elements were you looking for in Dickens's text, and generally in other writers that you draw upon?

PA: I wasn't looking for anything in particular, I must say, in the Dickens novel. I was simply looking for any Dickens novel which I could use because it could easily be filmed, and one which … well, I suppose I was looking for something; I was looking for a novel which, to use at least in parts because it might be really inside my own preoccupations primarily, that's of course London and the London dispossessed, the poor. And of all Dickens's novels, [*Little Dorritt*] that's the one, for me, which most readily encompasses all of these various realities. When it comes to other writers, I don't think I look for anything in them in particular. I certainly don't read fiction for pleasure any more, if I ever did. And the only things that sort of strike me in novels, I suppose, are things which I would like to be able to do myself. So, I suppose, my own real reaction is one of envy. There is another point of course, which might be of interest. I've always believed that fiction, or rather all forms of writing, feed upon previous forms of writing. So, in a sense, all my novels tend to encapsulate other people's novels.

JG: To what extent do you identify with Oscar Wilde as a writer?

PA: Not at all. I have no particular interest in Oscar Wilde at the moment. Well, I suppose I have *some*. When you talk about this identification business, I presume you're talking about the fact that I used the language which Oscar Wilde uses, or I adopted his style …

JG: More actually in theoretical concerns I suppose, not so much in terms of style.

PA: Well, in that case I certainly shared Oscar Wilde's interest in the unreal. Artifice is more real than reality, and of course can shape reality, that's something which interests me in Oscar Wilde's case. In *Notes for a New Culture* you can see the seeds from which the novels and the poetry sprang. The poetry came before the fiction, and in a sense the fiction grows out of the poetry. So, there's three definite stages. One was the theoretical study, which came first of all, then poetry, then fiction.

JG: Are we to believe your representation of Wilde to be the historical figure as he might have been then, or is a vital part of the text the actual knowledge that the character is an imaginative construct in the present, drawn from historical sources?

PA: It's a bit of both. Certainly, I've used the fact that he was a historical figure in his own right to justify the existence of the book in the first place. But the very language of the book itself, and the way in which I tried to write it, was, I suppose, an attempt to interfuse the past and the present and suggest that the past can only really exist in the present, and the present in the past. I think that's rather abstract, but you know what I mean: I mean the sense that the language I have used in the book – it's a sort of adaptation of Wilde's own language – is really a modern version of Wilde. People reading that book ought to be able to see how twentieth-century language sprang out of nineteenth-century language, and how nineteenth-century language has received the twentieth-century language within it. So, in other words, it's sort of a double 'thing', a double 'phenomenon'. And the character of Wilde shows similar characteristics, a bit of the past and the present.

JG: More in terms of genre: your interest in Dickens and Eliot has resulted in biographies, presumably your study for Wilde could have turned out as a biography also. Instead you opted for fiction. What were the reasons for this and what do you see as the pros and cons of fiction and biography as genres?

PA: I think it's much the same activity in certain senses. I certainly don't believe there's any real or any *genuine* difference between the two activities. Certainly I approach them in the same spirit. For example, I always think of biography as being a form of fiction, and of course it is a form of fiction. All forms of history are forms of fiction. And in both cases, in both fiction and biography, you're trying to construct a narrative, and characters, and atmosphere. You're trying to tell a story, at least in another sense you're trying to tell a story. So, even on the very basic technical level, you're engaged in the same activity. But on a larger level, of course, on a more grandiose scale, it's certainly true that in biography you are creating fiction just as assiduously as you are in a conventional novel, because you rely upon interpretation. That's all you have to rely upon, and interpretation is a matter of acumen.

JG: This question of interpretation: do you feel a pressure to stick to the facts of history? Chatterton as a figure is plausible, but Hawksmoor obviously isn't, he is a fictional character. Especially in the book

Chatterton, the scenes with Meredith and Wallis draw on fact, whereas Amy Dorrit's presence in *The Great Fire of London* is not plausible.

PA: Well, it's difficult to draw any general conclusions from each novel. I certainly would say that I'm writing so-called biographies, I presume I have to rely on the facts to a certain extent. But, there again, they become twisted up and shaped in the act of interpreting them. I mean facts, such as they are, are rather neutral and, in most cases, rather uninteresting, 'he went to a certain place at a certain time', and so forth. And the only way they come alive is when they're placed within an interpretative framework, in other words, when they are fictionalized. I mean, fiction, in itself, in *Chatterton* and *Hawksmoor*, the process is, as it were, taken only one step further, or it's made more self-conscious, it's made more – what's going on is made more evident to the reader than it is in biography, although the same process is at work in both forms, if that makes any sense.

JG: It does, yes. We'll be coming back to a lot of these ideas actually, more specifically. One theorist I have been reading refers to the past as 'always already interpreted' – i.e.: it's like a semiotic system of texts as documents and other pieces of evidence that are carried through time to us now. Do you actually work from this more primarily intertextual basis, or do you try and break it – such a removed perspective – in order to achieve a more emotional ...

PA: Do you mean do I work from sources, textual sources?

JG: ... that you try to read into these sources an emotional atmosphere.

PA: Oh, sure. Well, in many cases I invent textual sources, so they don't really exist. So, that's one way of doing it. I've always been attracted by the reality which books or works create, so, in almost all cases, I think in the work I do the actual fiction depends to a large extent upon written texts of one form or another. In a very obvious sense, it depends upon the languages I create for the past. As for breaking them open for the emotional resonance, I presume that does happen, yes. It's not a conscious effort at all, it just happens that way. I use the texts as a sort of springboard for other things, on the whole.

JG: We were talking about the world you create in your texts. Louis Mink suggests that in creating structures for events we necessarily isolate them through giving them form from the chaos of reality, they enter a state of suspension from time. In citing past texts, in the character of Chatterton, or Wallis's painting, or Wilde, or *Little Dorrit*, it seems to me that you are trying to locate your fictions in some kind of historical perspective – trying to put them into a continuum.

PA: Sure, well, one of the basic ... one of the things that occurred to me after I'd written these books, although not at the time, is the extent to which all of them are concerned with the nature of history itself, the process of history or the nature of time. So, everything goes back to the larger question of what is time, what does the process of time amount to? Right? i.e.: what is history? And I suppose that if you wished to you could extract or elicit from these novels a philosophy of history, or a philosophy of time. I haven't done that myself, but it is possible for it to *be* done. So, to that extent, it is certainly the case that I am trying to take specific or various instances and relate them to larger processes.

JG: Now, as for this idea of abstracting art from reality, the modernists, for example Eliot, considered the aim of art to be to create autonomous creations, existing through their own internal systems. This is an aesthetic that postmodernist theory tries to break down. Would you say part of your allegiance is to the modernist aesthetic of creating this autonomous system?

PA: Yes, to a certain extent. Certainly my instinctive allegiance would be to modernism in the sense of self-referential works of art and all the rest of it. And yet, on the other hand, in the novels themselves the practice of modernism tends to break down, I'm afraid, and becomes something rather more diffuse, or at least more colourful. Presumably that's another aspect of this humour we were talking about before, how the seriousness of the books, such as it is, is something that is being undercut by the comedy. So, the comedy acts, as it were, as a realism. It's real life breaking into the modernist aesthetic. At least you could see it in those terms.

JG: Louis Mink, in his essay 'History and Fiction as Modes of Comprehension', writes that 'we do not dream or remember in narrative, but tell stories which weave together the separate images of recollection ... so it seems truer to say that narrative qualities are transferred from art to life'. In *First Light,* more than any of the other novels, you deal with this story-telling idea, including four stories in the narrative, and it is linked to the concept of historical continuity. Are you weaving together separate images of recollection and structuring life through artistry?

PA: I don't know. I think that's part of what it is, yes. But stories just come naturally. Well, I'll tell you what the stories are there for. One, they're just there to break up the narrative so that you can keep the reader's attention; it's a good way of, you know, spicing things up. But then, as you say, their central point is to throw a shaft of light upon a certain meaning in the book. So, whatever you said about this historical business, it's another way of getting at the same theme time and time again, getting at it in a more explicit or dramatic way than is possible in the narrative. Was that the answer to your question?

JG: We take images and form narratives from them ...

PA: Where do we do that?

JG: We take art and transpose it onto life ...

PA: Oh, yeah, yeah. Well, that's certainly true. The other thing – one thing I have done in the course of writing fiction, and it's something which I supposed I've learned directly after I'd written both the theoretical study and the poetry, is that most things come before me in terms of stories, in the shape of stories. The most recondite material can be exemplified in terms of stories. And, in fact, it's a natural and instinctive human activity to tell stories. This is where the modernists of course were wrong when they eschewed story-telling as a sort of corrupt art, Joyce and that. In fact, story-telling is at the heart of most forms of human activities, as far as I can see. History is a form of story-telling, obviously; science is a form of story-telling, which is one of the lessons of *First Light*. So, in that sense, telling stories in that book is just a way of re-emphasizing what is the central narrative point of that book, that everything is a story.

JG: Quite. Stories are very obviously constructed narratives, and all your novels characteristically display a carefully orchestrated structure. This lends the texts an air of artificiality in 'realist' terms. I'm not trying to say that a text *ought* to be realist or realistic, but should one recognize such stylized artifice in your texts as one would, say, in a play? Should we suspend our disbelief? Are you trying to convince us, or asking us to accept your formulation?

PA: Well, both I suppose. Sure, you have to lay aside your conventional expectations about realistic narrative; no doubt about that because I'm not interested in doing it, well, I can't do it to be quite frank, and also I don't want to do it, it's never interested me, it's only a passing phase in the history of modern fiction. No, the artifice is deliberate, because that's the way I see the world: I see all as artifice of one kind or another.

JG: So, do you then write along a rigidly formal basis?

PA: No. It just happens. It's quite instinctive.

JG: Do you find that you consciously don't want, in your writing, to try to include no, or as little as possible, superfluous or distracting material – sticking only to that material which actually engineers the narrative content?

PA: Well, it's a strange combination of doing it instinctively, as I said with the artificial, what you might see as artificial is what comes immediately to the pen. But, I certainly at a later stage do try to prune out all the stuff which doesn't strike me as being immediately interesting. So I remove a lot of what you might call the realistic stuff at a certain point because it doesn't play a part in what I'm trying to say.

JG: In *T. S. Eliot* you say that 'the major difficulty with *The Confidential Clerk* is that its techniques of stage action are so thoroughly and obviously conventional that anything Eliot cares to place within them is diminished'. It struck me, and some reviewers, that the climax of *The Great Fire of London* loses something of its vitality as the plot seems to be rapidly and almost cursorily wrapped up.

PA: Yes. That's the trouble with that book.

JG: Would you say that here form outweighs content?

PA: It's partly that, and partly also that I'm not very good at constructing endings in any case ...

JG: Well, the second part of the question is: are you a believer in the climactic ending, a conventional *finale*?

PA: I do like to have one, but I find it very difficult to do. The trouble with all my novels is ending, as it were, properly. But that's the part of the nature of the narrative of the fiction itself in most cases. Because in the case of *Hawksmoor*, *First Light*, *Chatterton*, where it's essentially cyclical, a parallel process, for an ending you need to go bang bang bang bang bang on the line. The trouble with those books is they round in circles, or they go up and down in parallels between periods ...

JG: So, where does one put one's ending?

PA: So, where does one put the ending on a circle, that's the problem. So, it's very important, I think you're right to emphasize that, because often the endings are the best clues to a writer's intentions. Because obviously when he or she is very tired, or think they've come to an end, then tend to let rip, you know, it's just sort of human nature. In my case, I just have extreme difficulty doing them. *The Great Fire of London*, my first novel, is a very obvious warning of how you can create a bad ending. In later years I've tried to correct my 'badness' slightly by having what you might call a 'mystical' climax ...

JG: Transcendent?

PA: Yes, exactly, I've tried for that. It's the only way of dealing with cyclical, parallel narratives.

JG: You say the narratives can move in parallel, up or down. Just a small question: were the elements of *Hawksmoor*, *Chatterton*, *First Light*, done separately, or were they worked out together?

PA: In the case of *Hawksmoor* they went side-by-side, there are only two stories, two time periods. I worked them simultaneously, one with the other. In the case of *Chatterton*, I can't remember exactly now what happened. I added the Wallis chapters at a later stage, they were all written separately. But the other twentieth-century and eighteenth-century parts were written at the same time. So, it's like a mixture of two things.

JG: Coming back to characterization now, mentioned earlier. As far as characterization goes, you say in the profile 'Aspects of Ackroyd' in the *Sunday Times,* that you are not interested in being realistic, as we said before. Do you see characterization more as representing, like in, say, a Greek drama, or even caricatures, is the reader supposed to identify with the characters as 'types' from reality?

PA: No, certainly not to identify with them, which would be fatal in most cases. I don't know what they are exactly, they're just words, they exist in words. I hear them talking first, and they start to exist after that. So, if anything, they're verbal representations. Like Harriet Scrope in *Chatterton.* She just started existing in language, I mean she started talking and I listened to her and wrote it all down.

JG: There seems to be a tradition of bitchy ladies through your books. We have Laetitia and Joan in *The Great Fire of London,* and Harriet Scrope and Sarah Tilt, Evangeline Tupper and Hermione Crisp; there's also Augustine Fraicheur and Cumberland. They seem to be a 'type' that tends to reappear.

PA: It's quite accidental on my part. I'm sorry, that's the way it happens. I can't do anything about it, it's just the way it works out. I don't do it deliberately. They seem to want to come into it, I can't really stop them.

JG: Lola Trout is a bizarre character, does she have consequence beyond offensiveness and outrageous humour?

PA: No, no, just ... sometimes you like to put something in to make people laugh, or *hopefully* to make people laugh. Of course, you can never legislate for people's sense of humour, and some people laugh, some people find it less funny than others. I find it funny. I just put it in for the sake of a laugh, you know, a little bit of light relief. But these other characters – they certainly seem to come in patterns of some kind. I can see them as, they're just aspects of myself emerging and re-emerging from time to time.

JG: It struck me that Little Arthur could be a perverted representation of Arthur Clennam, there's a very close parallel, only with a more distorted passion and Little Arthur has this obsession to save an innocent child.

PA: It's perfectly possible, I never thought of that. In fact, there was a review of that, of *First Light* I think, which went through *The Great Fire of London* and pointed out a lot of parallels which I'd missed. It's perfectly possible. It's completely unconscious on my part though.

JG: Your central characters all seem to experience a sense of dislocation from the world around them. Is there some kind of common thread of alienation or paranoia or something in their construction? We have characters like Audrey Skelton, Spenser Spender, Oscar Wilde, Detective Hawksmoor, Nicholas Dyer, Charles Wychwood, Damian Fall, Mark Clare .... All of these people seem alienated. Is there a thread?

PA: I presume so. Again, it's one of those things I wouldn't know about. But it certainly seems to emerge from time to time, I mean time and time again, but it's not something that I consciously *do*. It just comes out that way. It's difficult to ... I don't have any theory about this, certainly. You might find it explained in the poetry, it might be there, it's possible. If you think of the narrator of the poems as a fictional character, there might be ... you might find a secret there. I mean, if you think of the *writer* of the poems as a fictional character. There might be a useful parallel between the poetry and the fiction.

JG: Your biography of Eliot and the concern of Eliot with drama. You say that the 'world of "appearances" is the material for parody, drama, and wit'. Is this a philosophy animating your own style? Have you considered writing drama?

PA: No, I haven't considered writing drama, but it's certainly a philosophy I'd agree with. Because all we really have are appearances, and of course that was part of the thing with *Chatterton*. But I haven't considered writing drama, no. Does that answer your question?

JG: That's fine. Would you say that your juxtaposition of past and present employs the past in a nostalgic way or a more critically active way? I think here of the ancient peoples of *First Light*, and also the characters of Chatterton, Dyer, Wilde ...

PA: I think it's both aspects. There's a certain kind of nostalgia involved, I suppose, but on the whole – well, let's put it this way: there's some people who say that the search for the past is like the search for the lost father, or the search for the lost Deity. It's a way of trying to consolidate one's origins. But more than that of course, it's a way of – I would say – it's also a way of averting death, we dwell on the past in the same way that we dwell on death. So, both these possibilities are evident, I suppose. On a larger scale, what I was concerned with, in some of the fiction at least, is with the possibility that the past is penetrating the present, and it has a determining effect on the present. That's why I use several pastiches, like in *Hawksmoor*. It wasn't really pastiche, it was just a way of showing how the language of the past and the present are the same. So, to answer your question, it can be both nostalgic, in the sense that it can be a vehicle that overcomes death; and it can also be creative in trying to suggest that the past manifests itself in the present.

JG: In your essay, 'The Neo-Gothic Imagination and the Death of the Past', you say that anything of value in the past will have been carried over into the present. I have a slight quibble with this. Surely, (a) value is a subjective quality, and (b) to recognize such aspects of the past is merely to create their presence, rather than identify it. And, even if it were identification, is it not also a matter of what one is willing to recognize?

PA: I don't know. You're probably right about that.

JG: What do you think of the narrative style, in terms of historical distortion, employed by such writers as Doctorow, Rushdie, Fowles or D. M. Thomas?

PA: Never read them. There has been a definite revival of what you might call 'historical fiction', hasn't there?

JG: Yes, well, this is what this postmodernist aesthetic is all about.

PA: Is it?

JG: Writers are taking the past and, well, subverting it.

PA: Yes, I would say writers like Graham Swift are apparently doing much the same thing. It's certainly, I mean, I don't know, I haven't read the books. I imagine it's part of the same process. I just don't read these books.

JG: Brian McHale defines one of the features of postmodernism as – I must point out here that I'm not trying to say 'Peter Ackroyd is a postmodernist' or 'postmodernism is like Ackroyd'; I'm just using them to bounce off each other – I'm not trying to categorize or criticize things for what they're *not* ... Brian McHale defines one of the features of postmodernism as 'foregrounding the temporal distance between the act of narration and the objects narrated'. Although, in terms of theme, your novels could be seen as allied to postmodernism, in terms of narrative style and structure, it could not. The authorial voice is not a self-conscious feature of the narrative. Although you do display some textual tricks, like *Hawksmoor* suddenly being presented like the text of a play, and the reader being addressed by the characters, or snatches of narrative being dislocated as a preface to *Chatterton*, for the most part your fiction follows classical formulae. Would you see your texts somehow as being to some extent conventional or conservative, and how important and to what effect are the textual oddities employed?

PA: I don't know about them being conventional or conservative. I think that might go back to what we were talking about earlier, about the importance of story and how the idea of story was unjustly neglected by the modernists, and, presumably, postmodernists too. I'm very interested in story in any sense – so, to that extent, I presume it's conventional. As for the texts of the novels themselves, I'm not aware of them being *particularly* conventional. I mean, I don't mind if they are, but I don't think of them as being so. If I think of *Hawksmoor*, for example, in the parallel narrations, one in the twentieth century and one in the eighteenth.

JG: When I say conventional, what I mean is more in terms of structure rather than the actual narrative – the shaping, flowing, engineering of the story; the *narrative* can be more experimental …

PA: Yes, I never thought of that. I presume you're right about that, it's not something which has occurred to me. I don't know the answer to that. Again, you might find a clue in the poetry, in the formal shape of the poetry, because it's something which I try to transpose into the fiction, but it's difficult to answer in any other sense.

JG: Would you say that you shift authorial perspective within the narrative, or maintain an all-embracing, central control?

PA: I don't know about that. Again, that is something which is almost impossible to answer because it varies from day to day and mood to mood and book to book. I would have thought, on the whole, the language in the books themselves is more or less maintained at a certain level of articulacy, which would suggest one person, one perspective. I would have thought that if you pick up a novel of mine, you'd know – if you knew anything about modern fiction – you'd know it was by me rather than anybody else. So, to that extent, I would assume that the authorial voice was very important. How you define that, I don't know.

JG: Would you see it as a single source?

PA: Well it has to be because I'm sitting there …

JG: Well, actually, the postmodernists try to break this idea down. They try to destroy the personality of the author, try to make it seem as if there are different authors, or different authorial perspectives.

PA: Sometimes the author tends to be imperious. But they're all emanating from the same source, I presume, unless we have some theory about spiritual possession. Of course, I think one of the strange aspects of the books is that many of the characters seem to be possessed in the sense that voices speak through them, and I presume that's a reflection of my own unease about the fact that I'm creating a language which is not my own – like the eighteenth century – and characters have nothing to do with me. And to that extent I suppose I am invisible.

JG: Linda Hutcheon believes that if two, or more, different narrative genres are employed in a text, the two will always only ever play off each other, never actually merging. It seems to me that you appear to disagree with this viewpoint, by trying to work the texts to a unificatory closure of disparate elements. Would you say your texts display a disconnectedness, or work towards totalizing …

PA: The texts within each novel, or the novels as a whole do you mean?

JG: The texts within each novel.

PA: I presume they're reaching some kind of unity of purpose.

JG: This sort of transcendent …

PA: Yes, exactly. I presume that's what's happening, but how it happens and why it happens I simply don't know. I certainly see the eighteenth-century, nineteenth-century and twentieth-century texts as being related to each other in more than casual ways, they're all emanations of the same linguistic spirit.

JG: Hutcheon further states that intertextuality is manifest as ironical, in juxtaposing past and present, for instance, this is what happens to traces of the past when we put them in a present context. Bearing in mind Hardy, Dickens, Chatterton and eighteenth– and nine-teenth-century styles, would you say you employ such elements from a fundamentally ironic stance?

PA: No, I don't think so. Probably more adulatory than ironic, in the case of those people you've mentioned. But on the other hand, you can never resist sending up the things you most admire, so I assume it's a combi-nation of the two. So, you've got admiration and parody at the same time, which is quite a common thing to do. In fact, the early parodists only wrote parodies of the things they admired and mimics mimicked only people they rather respected. Does this make sense?

JG: In the profile 'Aspects of Ackroyd', there was a mention about 'cosmic plagiarism', as if all the books published filter down into a single text.

PA: I don't remember saying that. It could well be. It's like, walking in the library you feel that all the books are just one book, all the books are like part of the same reality. And, you know, once you've read one, you've read them all, to a certain extent. I never thought about it before, and I don't remember saying that. It's probably all made up by the person who wrote it anyway. I've often thought, by the way, that I'd like to write a novel in which someone enters various books. In fact, in *First Light* someone is so affected by books that he feels he wants to become a part of them.

JG: Was that not Kathleen?

PA: Was it? Oh yes, she becomes part of a Hardy novel. But there's someone else too – oh no, he was affected by rooms, I'm getting confused. But anyway, I thought of the idea of someone being so affected by books that he actually enters them and enters the plots, which was quite a good idea. And there's a similar scene in *Chatterton* where someone is standing in a basement library in London, in the basement of a library, and sees the shapes of the authors and is haunted by the ghosts of the authors. And I thought that was one interest which seems to recur from book to book as though books themselves had some phantom reality of their own.

JG: Some reviewers claim to have noticed a certain intertextuality with other novels, sentences recurring ...

PA: It's quite accidental on my part. There's only one exception: in the poetry. If you look at the poetry, two or three, a lot of phrases in the poetry recur in the novels. That's deliberate on my part. When I'm stuck I will read the poetry and see if there's a phrase I can use.

JG: Do you see your books as a family, and, if so, in what way are they related?

PA: They are related because they're all written by the same person. That's the only relationship I can think of. What do you mean?

JG: Well, I was thinking more thematically.

PA: Oh, thematically, I'm sure there's a family in some sense. In fact some people say I just write the same book over and over again – and to a certain extent that's true, it is the same book being re-written. But then, of course, so is everybody else's. What those family of concerns are I find it very difficult to describe; it's something which the reader is much more able to spot than I am. But I would certainly say that the narratives all seem to curve around certain magnets, as it were, however you would define the magnet – whether it's the actual history and the idea of time, or whether it's the combination of comedy and seriousness, I mean it's always the same ingredients which seem to be there from book to book.

JG: Fredric Jameson sees the use of parody and pastiche as an imprisonment of the text in the past, undermining originality and individual style: 'The disappearance of the individual subject along with its formal consequence, the increasing unavailability of the personal *style*, engender the well-nigh universal practice today of what might be called pastiche'. What do you think of this view?

PA: Not in the least. That rather contradicts what you said the postmodernists believed in, that the author should disappear.

JG: Yes, he claims that it just happens anyway through use of pastiche, and I'm proposing that I don't think it's true. Obviously there is a strong style in your books.

PA: There is a strong style. I think he's working on a very febrile idea of what originality consists of to start with. There's nothing original in the world, actually. The whole idea of *Chatterton* (if it had a whole point) was nothing original was ever written. The author relies on the language which came before us, and the words which came before us, phrases which came before us, so it seems an original voice, I would have thought, is an impossibility. Certainly the use of pastiche, parody and so forth, has become much more prevalent in the last twenty or thirty years, but again it's part of a historical cycle, in the 1890s pastiche and parody were quite common. So, I wouldn't say it's some new threat to the identity of the author, no. Quite the opposite. A good author should be able to use pastiche and parody just as readily as he can use so-called 'original' perceptions or original sentences. It's part of the same reality after all, we live in a world which is partly fake and partly real.

JG: So, you say that 'cosmic plagiarism' and the use of pastiche can result in an original style, for example in Eliot?

PA: Sure, I mean plagiarism's a form of individual art after all.

JG: Do you find similarities between Eliot's approach and your own, in terms of adopting voices, personae, styles? To what extent do you identify with Eliot.

PA: Presumably there are similarities, but again it's instinctive on my part. I didn't do it because Eliot did it, and I presume Eliot didn't do it because other people had done it. It's just the way that certain people's temperaments and so-called 'creative gifts' operate. Certainly, my imagination, as such it is, relies upon this use of mannerisms, techniques I've borrowed from other people, words I've picked up from other books, phrases I've picked up, tricks I've learned from other people, dramatic masks one might have to adopt: in short, the whole panoply of ordinary learning about anything. I presume in my case that because I've had a so-called literary education, and I presume I've done nothing more than read books for most of my life, it's inevitable that a few of my fictions should be derived from books in one way or another.

JG: You refer, in *T. S. Eliot*, to his desire to write poetry in colloquial speech – how people would speak if they spoke poetry – thereby maintaining a 'social purpose' in his work. Do you think this philosophy important, to write with a view to general, popular appreciation, i.e.: a non-élite audience.

PA: No, no, I don't care, actually, who reads the books.

JG: You don't write with any view to ...

PA: No, none at all. But I do know the young people read them more than anyone else, so I presume there's a large audience there. But I've no idea who the people are. I certainly wouldn't wish to characterize the readers.

JG: Presumably you'd care if nobody read them.

PA: Oh, I'd care about that. But I wouldn't – assuming people do read them – care in what category they place themselves. And the concept of élitism is of course not to the point, because fiction of all the arts is the most democratic, so I'm told. If people can afford to buy them, of course.

JG: Postmodernist texts and texts like yours seem to me to bridge the gap between élite and popular art, being both generally successful and receiving academic attention. Linda Hutcheon suggests that 'as typically contradictory postmodernist texts, novels like these parodically use and abuse conventions of both popular and élite literature'. Do you find you do this – a mixture of intellectual and popular, using and abusing conventions of both?

PA: No, I don't. I'm certainly not abusing them. I'm not even using them. Well, I suppose I am using them, but I never thought of it. Using and abusing what? Élite literature?

JG: Using and abusing the conventions of both popular and élite literature.

PA: I don't think so. I think conventions are meant to be abused, that's what they're there for. A convention, when it ceases to be abused, ceases to exist – if that makes any sense.

JG: It seems to me that your texts share the cerebral concerns of postmodernist theory, without indulging in the sort of intellectual masturbation of the experimental authors who perhaps alienate themselves and appeal only to an academic élite. Are you communicating a message of serious import concerning contemporary culture and art in a negligent society by presenting your ideas in a form at once both provocative and popular?

PA: Well, what do you think?

JG: I think you are.

PA: Well then, I am.

JG: I see, it's entirely up to the reader.

PA: Yes, exactly. And I honestly don't know what the books are about. I never know anything about them when they're finished. I never re-read them; I never understand them; I don't really appreciate them; and anything which is found in them tends to be introduced by the reader or the critic. The things you've been talking about, although quite valid and genuine, are only things which occur to me after the event and in a vacuum, as it were. At the time these things don't occur to me.

JG: So, the novels are like the result of a process just through your own general concerns anyway?

PA: Yes, partly that. The novels were written, as it were, after the event of theory, theory came first in my case. When I was in my very early twenties I wrote this study of theory, *Notes for a New Culture*, and then I wrote the poetry, and the novels didn't come until I was in my mid-thirties.

JG: How was *Notes for a New Culture* received?

PA: It got very bad reviews. It was published in 1976 and written in 1973, and it got very bad reviews because it was – it sounds rather clichéd to say this – it was rather before its time. It was before structuralism had been received in this country. The thing you have to remember is that the novels came after a period when I disabused myself of theory.

Interview between Peter Ackroyd and Jeremy Gibson
4 January 1995

JG: The first thing I was interested in was the poetry. I was looking at *The Diversions of Purley* and, to make a rather gross generalization, there seems a very objective approach to language, tying it in with *Notes for a New Culture*. Do you think that's an unfair generalization, because obviously not all of the poetry is like that at all?

PA: No, I don't think that's unfair. I think it's a perfectly fair generalization. What I would say is that the process of composition in the poetry is quite different from that of the prose. For one thing, it was done over a much more scattered period, so the poetry tended to be composed in terms of phrases which would occur, and then another phrase might occur two days later, and then another phrase might occur three days later, and they'd be put together in that way. So, there's no sustained intellectual work involved in that sense; so, it's a very different process from writing prose fiction. But I would say, as I've said to you before, that all the interests of the poetry emerge within the prose at a later date; so they're part of the same project as it were.

JG: Do, you still write poetry?

PA: No, as soon as I started writing prose the poetry sort of vanished, it simply transmigrated to the new form.

JG: So, you don't ever feel that it might be a way of expression that is lost in the poetry, the fiction is quite adequate ...

PA: Yes, I think fiction is as adequate as poetry for what I wished to say, or not wished to say. Certainly, in fact, in the prose itself you find scattered images throughout the novels which fulfil the same functions as in the poetry in a strange way. Do you want biographical stuff too?

JG: Yes, I do.

PA: I stopped writing poetry in around 1978 ... I wrote my first novel in 1982 I think it was, and I think I stopped writing poetry in exactly that period, so I was in my early thirties.

JG: Was that a conscious decision?

PA: No, it wasn't so much conscious, it was as soon as I started writing fiction or prose, I realized that it was just as amenable to me as poetry, and in fact might reach a larger audience than the poetry ever did. And I found it equally satisfying, in some ways more satisfying because it was a daily routine, rather than simply waiting for a phrase to emerge from time to time, which is what happened with the poetry. It was much more fulfilling than writing poetry ever was.

JG: Do you think that the end product becomes more routine?

PA: No, not at all, not at all. No, I think the end product becomes more interesting for me because it requires more use of one's powers, as it were, it requires more concentration, more ingenuity. You're not simply waiting passively for things to occur, for phrases to occur, you're actively involved in shaping them and connecting them together. And that for me was actually more satisfying in the long run than writing poems, which simply came when they wished to come. I had more control over the process, partly, but also the end result was more satisfying to the reader apart from to me.

JG: Have you explored any further the interfaces between fictional and biographical writing in *Blake.*

PA: Not so much. I think you might find *Blake* to be in a certain sense a rather straightforward biography, except to the extent that Blake himself did not lead a straightforward or easily visible life. So, you tend to rely much more on impressions, themes, intuitions, rather than upon a straightforward chronology. So, in that sense it is not at all straightforward, and I suppose it means that you bring to it the same kind of attention, and the same kind of rigorous concentration that you have to apply to fiction. Because Blake's life in a sense had to be manufactured, it had to be made up in a way because so little is known.

JG: Well, then, with *Dickens*, did you feel that you wanted to include the more experimental episodes because so much *is* known and so much has been written about Dickens?

PA: Yes, that's exactly right. The danger there would be simply to write a straightforward biography like any other, so I wanted to introduce elements of uncertainty, or elements of self-communing which would not be present in an ordinary biography. That problem never arose with *Blake* because Blake's life was so mysterious in the first place, it was never clear.

JG: So, in effect what happened with *Dickens* was that you felt you needed to set yourself more of a challenge to get into the writing of it?

PA: Yes, *Dickens* was a challenge to make something less straightforward than it need otherwise have been. With *Blake,* the challenge was to make something coherent which would not be otherwise coherent, so it was a different kind of challenge.

JG: Are there any surprises that a reader of conventional biographies might find in *Blake*?

PA: Well, it's difficult to say. I think that the problem is no one knows ... previous biographies of Blake haven't really ... put it this way, I don't think the general reader or any reader in particular knows very much about Blake or his vision, and I was just trying to make it clear in ways that it hadn't been made clear before. So, it is new in that sense, it is novel because it tries to be comprehensive. You'll find that, in most lives or accounts of Blake, they tend to dwell upon the antinomianism in separate compartments, and, I hope, for the first time I've brought everything together in a synthesis which hasn't been attempted before.

JG: Moving on from discussing crossovers between fiction and biography: in fiction, the use of language can be more 'free' than in biography. In *English Music,* for example, you plunder an entire fictional history. But, at the root of *English Music* is the theme of inheritance. To what extent for you was this a personal theme or a personal subject?

PA: Well, I think it must in the last resort be relatively personal, having come from a background which didn't have a sort of cultural atmosphere, and being brought up by my mother and grandmother, without having a father, I presume that there must be some sort of search for origins going on in a way. And I suppose what happened was that I decided I'd find my origins in literary history, rather than in genetics or genealogy.

JG: Can you expand on that at all?

PA: Well, I've always presumed that part of the interest in the past, or part of the interest in literary inheritance was really an attempt to find my own identity which was not otherwise necessarily very apparent to me. And I presume part of the reason I write in the way that I do is to sort of create an identity for myself which might otherwise not exist.

JG: Leading on from that, have any of the books been more autobiographical, to your own mind, than any of the others?

PA: That's very difficult to say – I think they're all equally autobiographical. For me they're sort of autobiographical exercises, on the whole, in the sense that I sort of create a character with whom I can identify, and then it helps create my own identity in the process. So, in a sense the autobiographical impulse is always very strong, in the biographies and in the fiction.

JG: Is it literal?

PA: Not, not literal. It's all transformed, obviously, by the subject or the medium that you're using. But I would definitely say that a biographical, or an autobiographical approach might be as fruitful as a critical approach, if you wanted to do it that way.

JG: Have you considered writing straight autobiography?

PA: I was thinking about it the other day, but I don't think it's very likely. But I think it would be a challenge, because of course then you'd be confronted with the real subject rather than with a variety of different subjects.

JG: What would the distinction between the real subject and a variety of different subjects be, in the context of what you were talking about earlier about creating an inheritance for yourself.

PA: It would be very difficult to know exactly until you began writing it, but I would assume there would be some ... I don't know, it's difficult to say ... one would not have the freedom which one otherwise might have, I suppose. But it's very difficult to explain, very difficult to think about at the moment – because I haven't got any reason to do so.

JG: Let me try and come at it from an alternative perspective with a different question then. Given that to one extent or another there will be an implicit autobiographical element in the novels, and given also that any reader, even yourself, might not be able to trust that element, how certain or uncertain do you feel about the product? Once you have written a character, and there are elements there that you might have drawn from your own past or tried to create from your own past, does that then become a certainty for you?

PA: I presume what happens is you borrow their history, or you borrow their vocabulary, or you borrow their sensibility and you make it part of your own, which it is anyway in the first place. So, to that extent you are sort of creating images of yourself, in some idealized way. As for the certainty at the end of the process, of course there is none once the book is finished, and you go on to another project, another image. So, yes, I suppose you're always involved in a rather frustrating and inconclusive search for yourself.

JG: Would you consider it to be a regeneration in the terms of *Dr Dee*? That book is very much about that.

PA: Yes, it is partly. It's partly the magical process of reinventing yourself, recreating yourself, and of course, recreating the world – whatever the world might be. But of course it's always in a sense doomed to failure because then you just go on to the next one and the next one and the next one.

JG: Is that a doom?

PA: Well, it's a fate I suppose. A self-chosen fate.

JG: That's an interesting choice of phrase, as a self-chosen fate is not the fate for all people then?

PA: I presume most people don't feel the same urgent need to reinvent themselves every time they, well most people don't write books in the first place, but most people don't feel that urgent need to reinvent themselves. Or the need to explore different possibilities of the self; I presume one has a very fluid self, you see, and it just takes different shapes.

JG: Do you think that that's very much influenced by one's immediate conditions, one's surroundings?

PA: It must be engineered almost entirely by origins and by a sense of one's life when one was a child, I presume.

JG: Can we be certain about this sense of origins?

PA: No you can't.

JG: Is that actually what we're reinventing?

PA: We're reinventing origins because we don't have any as such. We're attempting to make places for ourselves in the world; I mean, I'm using these pronouns very vaguely. But, you see, in the process of endlessly reinventing yourself, you're also creating conditions in which your idealized self might flourish. So, for example, I find – although you may not find the same thing – in the process of reinventing yourself, you reinvent the conditions in which your so-called self might flourish, so although you may not see it in the books as I see it, I'm always convinced, or I'm half-convinced, that a sort of vision is being created. We've talked about it, about a Catholic vision, a pantomimic vision. That's partly it. A vision of English inheritance, a vision of buried Catholic inheritance, a vision of a London topography, a vision of a London genius. All these things, which I presume I've, as it were, created for myself, I mean they're not necessarily there in the first place, are all part of the attempt to find a stable environment in which one can flourish.

JG: It's difficult for me to understand how important the Catholic sense of inheritance is.

PA: Yes, we've discussed this, haven't we? We've discussed the Catholic sensibility. I'm starting work on a life of Sir Thomas More, the Catholic martyr, and I'm very interested in the idea of a buried Catholic inheritance; a sensibility of civilization which was suppressed in the sixteenth-century, in England, by the Protestant Reformation. I have a feeling that there might be, I mean England was Catholic for fifteen centuries and Protestant for four, and I'm assuming that there is a Catholic sensibility which might be at work in the language and within the English people, which has not properly been brought to recognition. Catholic inheritance might be important, it might not, it might turn out to be a red herring. But I believe that there is a possibility that the things I'm interested in, like the music hall, like pantomime, a sort of baroque extravagance, is related to a sort of Catholic inheritance which as sort of remained underground for four centuries.

JG: I think this is very interesting. Do you actually believe that it has existed, but underground, and each time it comes up it is then reinventing itself; or is it actually an inheritance, or a continuity?

PA: I don't know, it might be a continuity, but here again I would have to … I just don't know enough about … I mean, I suppose it's a question of human social psychology or something, I don't know. But I assume there is some latent Catholicism within the English temperament, which emerges in things like pantomime. The new historical theory, of course, is that the Protestant Reformation, far from being a sort of upwelling of the masses against the Catholic monasteries and so forth, was engineered from above by some very noble men, by reformers, and was actively .... The people of England were actively oppressed by the Reformation, and their rituals and their beliefs were extirpated in the same way that the Americans extirpated native American Indians' religious belief, as it were, it was actually done by an élite, who decided for the purposes of control, State-craft Protestantism would be more successful. And that is possible, it may be there's that latent religious inheritance which may still survive. On the other hand, it may be that people like me, who, in order to acquire a proper identity within English culture, have decided to formulate it, to construct a culture.

JG: How much would you say it was connected to mainstream Catholic religion?

PA: That's a very difficult question to answer. I believe very little. I suppose it's much more concerned with certain kinds of paganism.

JG: Can you elaborate on that a bit?

PA Well, Dr Dee was interested in that. The old Catholic faith was of course an amalgam of native English paganism and superstitions which it used. And all that sense of life, whether it's maypoles, or whether it's mummers, or whether it's ritual, has its roots deep in every nation, but Catholicism was uniquely able to deploy that in the early centuries for its own purposes. And with the Protestant Reformation all that of course was destroyed, the images were destroyed, the theatres were closed, and so forth. And I think that may be true. On the other hand, it may just be me, as I've said, like Dr Dee, trying to create something, some lost past which never really existed. And in the end it doesn't really matter. If I can make it happen in the books then it might as well have existed in the first place.

JG: A rather straightforward question, well it might not be a straightforward question, but it's coming away from the more esoteric ideas: the de Quincey essay in *Dan Leno and the Limehouse Golem* – 'On Murder Considered as One of the Fine Arts' – is thematically very central, I think; can you tell me whether you select source materials at a later stage in the composition, or at an early stage? Do the source materials suggest the fiction, or does the fiction then suggest what you might then be able to seek in the sources?

PA: It works both ways. With the *Dan Leno* book, for example, I can tell you exactly what happened. It began as a straightforward nineteenth-century murder mystery, because I'd always wanted to write one. I was also interested in Dan Leno for a long time, and I was on a train and I suddenly realized that I could put Dan Leno in this vicinity, I could bring him into the story because I'd always wanted to do Dan Leno. De Quincey has always been one of my interests also, and I realized at that stage that de Quincey's rather purple prose would also be useful. So, you generally find that it's a case of beginning with an idea, and then another idea, and a further idea, bringing them all together at a late stage, and they all sort of inter-animate with each other.

Sources happen in a different way. Once you know that you're going to deal with a certain area, or a certain period, or a certain interest, what I tend to do is read as much as I can in areas which will impinge upon that interest, and one thing will lead to another. For example, Charles Babbage I'd vaguely remembered about, and I'd always been sort of half-interested, and he just suddenly emerged in it too. Then I read, I came across him when I was doing my book on Dickens because Dickens quotes Babbage in one of his essays. It's simply a question of, I don't know how to … it's rather like the poetry in that respect; you talk about the relation of the poetry to the prose. In the poetry stray phrases would emerge from time to time, in the prose stray themes emerge from time to time, and connect with each other at a later stage.

JG: So, you don't see it in terms of themes, you don't approach in an academic way, rooting out the themes saying I'm going to write about such and such, how can I fictionalize it and make it an interesting story.

PA: No, you do that, but then another theme emerges a few days later, or weeks later, and you think, how can I make that work in this context? And then another theme emerges, and it's a question of using things that have been in the back of your mind for a long time. And one little plot will sometimes serve as a catalyst for things which have lain in the back of your mind for a long time, and those will be added to it at a later date, and so it gets more complicated as you go along.

As for the actual source material, it's often used in a much more obvious way than people might think. For example, with *Dr Dee* or *Milton in America*, I will literally just quote or paraphrase passages from books of the period, because in almost all cases it works. It's simply the way I suppose my mind tends to work; whatever I borrow or steal from other people actually becomes part of a living narrative.

JG: I can see that people might criticize that approach to be a form of plagiarism.

PA: Well, you see I would go back to an earlier sense of narrative. You know, in Renaissance poetics it was considered *de rigueur* almost to use classical sources, to imitate rather than to originate; the whole theory of Renaissance aesthetics is that you are not a single lone creator, you're part of an inheritance and you simply use the inherited themes, use the inherited vocabulary and just play with it as it were, deploy it in a different way. And, I presume, again you could relate it to Catholicism because that's part of an earlier, a different sense of tradition, a different sense of authority. I would argue that I'm simply returning to an earlier sense of what it means to be a creator – so-called. Creation is not a self-inventing, self-originating process.

JG: Which is more of a Romantic-humanist ...?

PA: No, well the new one is, yes, I mean the idea developed over the last century or two, where it's always been assumed that the original genius is someone who works as it were from nothing. I would go back to, say, Philip Sidney or Edmund Spenser, or people who spent their lives translating Ovid, and who were considered just as creative as people who wrote so-called original poetry. Translation and imitation were the essence of what was considered to be a writer.

JG: But are you telling me that you will literally pick up a block of text and then replace it?

PA: Yes, but it will have to be changed, I mean, Renaissance aestheticians were very clear about that, you couldn't simply just take it and stick it in, you had to redeploy it and redefine it, and re-use it in ways which were decorous, which were effective.

JG: You regenerate it.

PA: You regenerate it, but you don't rely on something coming out of your own head all the time. You imitate the great originals.

JG: And do you think, then, that the idea of something coming out of your head as an autonomous creative product is a myth?

PA: Yes, it never has been the case, and I can't think of any writer who has managed to achieve that. But of course on the face of it, it would be an absurd proposition, because the language we use itself is completely drenched in inherited meanings and significances.

JG: To create something entirely original would mean it would be unreadable, wouldn't it?

PA: It would not exist.

JG: To talk about *Dan Leno* for a moment, I was interested to find Marx appearing. I have this feeling that all cultural and intellectual ideas are implicitly political all the time, and your inclusion of Marx seems to relate to what appear to be very important political themes in your work.

PA: I know. I'd have to part company with you there, not because I don't believe you, but because on my part they're instinctive and not theoretical. I mean, I didn't sit down and say I'm going to introduce this material because it's important, it's just the way the book happened to fashion itself.

JG: Would you then see any merit in an approach which suggests that the two themes of *Dan Leno* – the political and the theatrical – became so strong in Victorian England, and that, subsequently, the more creative music-hall attitude, if I can put it like that, was stamped out in the twentieth century, whereas the desire to regulate and order society has actually gained in ascendancy?

PA: Yes absolutely, you're absolutely right. I can see it now, but I didn't see it at the time I was writing. Let me refine that. I *was* interested in Babbage, for example, and I was interested in the proto-computer, as it was, and the ramifications of that only became clear to me as I finished the book.

JG: Were you surprised by those ramifications?

PA: Well, not surprised, because I assume they must have been somewhere within me, but ...

JG: I've never noticed such an explicitly socio-political line in any of the other fiction; it could be read into it, but I think that would be such a contrived effort that it would be missing the point.

PA: Well you didn't read it into it because it was definitely there. But that's not something that's easy for me to explain because it just happened. What I will say is that, well, there are two elements to this, and both are biographical. One is, when I was a kid I voted Communist, and I was very interested in Communism as a creed; and the other thing is that, being brought up as a Catholic, you are quite used to an authoritarian tradition in any case. And I would assume, if you were looking at the political ramifications of what I do, I presume you would say it was as conservative as you could get; because one is talking about authority and inheritance, and one is rarely talking about the possibility of individual action or individual liberty; we're talking almost always about a ritualistic society aren't we, whether it's magical or whether it's pre-humanist, there's no sense of political action being possible. I remember in *Dan Leno* I talk about Gissing, and Gissing writing a book called *Workers in the Dawn* and he seems rather passive, rather defeatist ...

JG: ... and almost welcoming that because it provides him with the angst with which he can create ...

PA: Yes, exactly. And I'd assume that, the Catholic thing here might be important or it might not, but I assume that being brought up in an authoritarian religion, it sort of reduces you, or allows you to submit much more readily to the laws of inheritance, the prescripts of authority, than might otherwise be the case.

JG: Do you carry any sense of value about this, that it's welcome, it's positive or negative?

PA: It's impossible to say, I mean there's no value ascribed to it as such. All you can say is that it gave me a propensity for receiving authority or literary inheritance with open arms, rather than rejecting it. Other writers as you know reject the past, as it were, of dead white males and all that sort of thing. People think they have new things to say, and new ways in which to say it. Now, I'm constitutionally and instinctively averse to that sense of life, because of my education, because of my upbringing, because of my interests, I assume I'm simply one more person in a line, which you could call authoritarian or not authoritarian, but a line which exists before me and which exists after me. So, in other words, I'm not an individual sensibility, I'm more of a medium, as it were.

JG: But, you speak of this line, and bring in the word 'authority' with respect to the line. How does this mix the sense of how one might be able to envisage that line *for* oneself and see that line continuing into the future with a sense of vision, and regenerating one's own position?

PA: The more difficult question is this, I think: how is it possible to have that sense of authority within and at the same time, also as I believe, deconstructing it or playing with it or almost destroying it by juxtapositions? And that again is a mystery to me, I don't see how it is one has such a reverence for, or interest in, the past, and yet, at the same time, this continual need to reinvent it, recreate it, almost destroy it, by making up stuff. So, in the biographies and fiction, one is involved in much the same enterprise. I assume it's part of that endless process of debate, which occurs to anyone who is brought up in an authoritarian tradition: you both need it and, at the same time, you seek to destroy it.

JG: This double-edged dilemma leads me back to your mention of Babbage and the proto-computer. I link the idea of the Golem with the proto-computer. Can you stick your neck out and tell me whether you think that our modern golems, the golems that were beginning to gain ascendancy in that period, the golems of ordering and regulating society, sucking the life out of the people of that society, are actually so powerful now that we are beyond regeneration?

PA: That's very difficult to say. It depends what you mean precisely, and I think not. I think part of the reason why I was interested in Dr Dee and part of the reason I was interested in Hawksmoor was the sense in which there are certain people who stand out against orthodoxies of the period, and I presume it's possible ... let's put it differently: you know in all the books I have this sense of place, this almost religious sense of place, and the way people are determined by a sense of place. I assume that that sensibility, such as it is, which has nothing to do with scientific orthodoxy as far as I know, that sensibility and other elements of it will, in the next millennium, become recognized as important. The scientific orthodoxies, the golems or our century, will slowly but steadily be destroyed.

JG: This is a tangent; I'm just reading at the moment J. K. Gailbraith's *The Culture of Contentment*. He's describing this culture, which is basically that a society is organized and ruled by the people who have the dominating interests in that society; and the people who are left out, in a sense, who don't bother to vote, don't bother to make an effort … well, he argues that this culture of contentment will inevitably implode upon itself.

PA: Yes, and you could put it differently, you could say scientific and technological contentment might also implode on itself. Certainly, I haven't read the book, but I assume he's right in saying that society is organized and arranged by people who have a vested interest in maintaining it, obviously, but you could extrapolate it to a different medium, a different sphere and say, well, isn't that true of scientists, isn't it true of those who rely on science as a form of knowledge. And most of us are left outside of that in one respect or another, and that might implode upon itself.

JG: Because, I would suggest, science is held up to be somehow abstract and autonomous, but at the end of the day it is invented by human beings and used by human beings, and misused by human beings. The human element is always going to override that abstract element.

PA: Yes, science has always been just a form of human knowledge, and it will be replaced by other forms of human knowledge. I mean, you can't say you're not going to reinvent penicillin or whatever, obviously that's ridiculous, but the forms of scientific knowledge I'm sure will be replaced by other forms.

JG: Let me come to that surety from another direction, in reference to *Dr Dee*. I find this a difficult book in the canon.

PA: Yes it is, it's very difficult, because it has a sense of redemption …

JG: … and faith …

PA: Yes. Well, that was written when the person I was living with was dying, as you know. And so for me it was a sort of fable of human relationships, which I wanted to write down when I had the chance. But you're right, it was much more born out of emotional experiences than … it wasn't instinctive in a certain way, it was deliberate.

JG: It is very different, and those passages where this comes to the surface are very powerful and beautiful …

PA: But it was a very deliberate book in that sense, it was quite out of the normal, I mean it's not the way, I mean it just – I can't describe it to you, but I determined to write it rather than just let it happen as it were. Which is not normally the case with me, I normally just let things happen.

JG: It's also one of the most visionary of novels, I find, in that Dee has these two major visionary experiences towards the end of the novel: one of a world without love and one of a world with love. And the emphasis of the book is very much on the world with love, it is this which must be aspired to and one mustn't give in to the world without love. And the crucial element in this is faith, Dee must stop putting so much faith in manufactured, artificial knowledge, and just in faith in the world as it appears to him at the time, having that value for that time then.

PA: Yes.

JG: Is this faith secular, religious, transcendental?

PA: Oh, God knows, God knows. I simply don't know the answer to that. In the case of *Dr Dee* I presume it was ... well I don't know, I simply don't know the answer to that.

JG: You've used the word 'faith', which for most people would be associated with a religious sensibility. I focus on this word in my research and it's not a faith – with regard to your books – which is transcendental in the sense of being universal and true for all time; it's a faith that is transcendental in the sense that you, in your immediate circumstances, see as symbolic for what is meaningful and valuable in your life at that time. It's not simply the material conditions of you life, but what you make of them, which of course is not universal for all people at all times. So, it's a faith that is neither religious, nor simply secular, but it is faith in that it doesn't rely on proof and veracity, or statistics.

PA: I don't know, you know. It's very difficult for me to talk about this because I don't understand it myself. I assume ... faith ... I can't describe it, ask me another question and I might get round to it another way, I can't get to it at the moment. Are you talking about ... I mean, let's put it differently, let's say ... there are certain people, we've had this discussion many times, but there are people who have a secular view of life, and there are people who have a religious view of life; in other words, people who believe this is no abiding city and there is something beyond, and there are some who believe this is it. I would try to reach some sort of point where both co-exist, as you were just saying, but you can only do it in fiction, you can't do it in real life.

JG: What then is the distinction between fiction and real life?

PA: You know, I find it more and more difficult to distinguish. The good thing about being a writer is that you can, if you get to a certain point, confuse the two. And you live in a world which is partly fictionalized, well obviously everyone is, everyone's life is, but you become more and more self-conscious about it, you realize what you're doing, and you still do it. So, you fictionalize your life and you bring your life into your fiction. And I suppose faith would be that everything has some significance, even if we don't understand what it is. I think you cease to fear things so much, once you have a faith in the possibilities of transcendence, not transcendence but the possibilities of something being larger than itself, then you cease to fear the world.

JG: Perhaps you can tell me something about the next novel?

PA: *Milton in America* is a story of Milton fleeing from Royalist persecution and founding a colony in New England.

JG: Which isn't true.

PA: No, he stayed in England until he died. It's difficult to explain ... it's a question of trying to put John Milton and that inheritance up against ... it's a question of putting a certain sense of values up against native Indian values and Catholic values and so forth, and seeing how they work together.

JG: Do you draw from American history?

PA: Yes, I've had to steep myself in the early history of America, and I've got to know how the Indians spoke, so I've got to get the vocabulary right, and the appearance right, and the tribes right, and so forth.

JG: This is quite a departure then, not only outside London, but ...

PA: Outside England. Also outside English civilization, as it were; but I suppose you might say it's a case of trying to place London or England in an alien context and see what happens.

JG: It's the perfect dramatic setting for the idea of re-evaluation and regeneration as well, isn't it? Actually uproot yourself, go somewhere else ...

PA: Yes, exactly, see what they'd make of you, and see what the Indian gods make of the English gods, and so on.

JG: One last question, then. How do you feel about having a critical study written about your writing?

PA: I think it's fun because it gives me a perspective on it which I would not otherwise have had. If I was working in a dark room by myself then the uncertainty would be profound, wouldn't it?

JG: You probably wouldn't have the possibility to be able to do that anyway. What would happen though, in conclusion, if what I came up with you thought was either nonsense or just obnoxious?

PA: It would still be valid. It would be very helpful, because it would help me understand what I'm trying to do. I don't have any fixed points of perspective, you see, it's just a question of going on and seeing what happens; and whatever people say about it, it will probably strike me as being very true indeed.

Interview between Peter Ackroyd and Julian Wolfreys
21 December 1997

JW: Whenever one reads your works, the novels, the biographies, there is always a sense that London is, insistently, of crucial importance to whatever you write so that, in a way, if one reads the biography of Blake or the biography of Dickens, to give just two very different examples, these are biographies of the city, of two distinct cities, also. London is central to most of the novels as well, it is imminent all the time. Could you say how you see or perceive the city, how you begin to write about it?

PA: Well, the interest in London came about, not exactly late in the day, it came after I began writing ... I suppose that I discovered it as a theme after I'd written *The Last Testament of Oscar Wilde*, after I'd begun writing *Hawksmoor*; then again, it was also very indirect because I didn't know I'd been writing about London, its presence hadn't become so palpable to me – and I suppose that it was only in the course of writing the biography of Dickens – or perhaps before – that I realized that this was the great theme, this was something which could be explored and embellished. But not until recently did I think of myself as being specifically a London novelist in that sense. I was much more interested in creating plot, certainly in *Hawksmoor* and *Chatterton*, as well as character. The city was a subdued subject, as far as I was concerned.

JW: Perhaps that is one of the reasons why the representations you construct of London are so diverse, because the city in *The Great Fire of London*, for example, is very much recognizable, it is a certain London that the reader comprehends, while *Dan Leno* offers us another city, which, while still recognizably London in literary terms, is nonetheless distinct...

PA: What would you say is the difference between them? *The Great Fire of London* provides a theatrical city as does *Dan Leno*, doesn't it? ...

JW: Yes, *The Great Fire* represents a much less ostensibly 'Dickensian' city, despite that novel's relationship to *Little Dorrit*, because, while it's theatrical, that is tempered because it's also more 'grubby', or maybe 'distasteful' is the right word.

PA: Ah yes, I see; well, certainly, I wouldn't like to say there was any definite development in the vision of London in each of the novels, because, for example, in the book I'm just finishing now, it's London 4000 years ahead, it's not the Dickensian or sentimental London of *Dan Leno*, it's another kind of city altogether – what is or would be a mistake would be to try and gothicise the city too much; I'm afraid I've run the risk of doing that too often because, as you've said to me, it's a disservice to London, it's a mistake to try and compartmentalize London too much, to try and turn it into a kind of gothic landscape...

JW: This leads me on to my next question. Your responses to the city rely, as you've said, on plotting and the central characters – Dan Leno, the Quilp-like character, Little Arthur, of *The Great Fire*, Nicholas Dyer and the detective Nicholas Hawksmoor in *Hawksmoor* – those characters are conduits, as it were, through which one sees the city in certain ways; character determines the shape of the city. However, in contradistinction to your work, and as we move not only towards the end of the century but also towards the end of the millennium, there is an increasing strain in writing, typified by the writing of Iain Sinclair, Aidan Dun, Alan Moore, and in films such as Patrick Keiller's *London*, where the emphasis is on what is called psychogeography, or what Blake scholar Morton Paley described with reference to *Jerusalem* as 'psychic cartography'.

PA: Yes, this is not an area which I have actually tended to explore, myself, although it is very important in the book which I am currently writing about London, you know, the sacred geography of druidic sites – I mean, I take it with a slight pinch of salt, I'm not a zealot of New Age interests; ley lines I can take or leave. But certainly such elements tend towards a powerful presence. Whether the writers you've mentioned are describing the city in terms which I would use is another matter; I suppose that Iain [Sinclair] also sees London in modern terms, doesn't he, really?

JW: Yes, and *Hawksmoor* is the novel in which you come closest to the incorporation of the psychogeography of the city ...

PA: Yes, that was directly inspired by a poem of Iain's called *Lud Heat*, as you know. I suppose what happened is that Iain Sinclair's poem opened my eyes to that vision of London in a way in which I had never experienced before, and this is going back years and years, when I first read it in the seventies, but it lay dormant for me and I never really thought about it. But I think that while there are elements of psychogeography about my writing (to a greater extent in *Hawksmoor*, and much less discernibly in other novels), there are also other elements such as historical research, the sheer act of wandering around the city. Yet I have never confronted the city head on, except at the moment when I am writing this book about the city, and I find I don't know what to say directly about the city, quite frankly ...

JW: ... well, it evades you if and when you attempt to do that, doesn't it ...?

PA: You've got to be enormously linguistically inventive in order to make it work properly, as we've said of our friend Dickens; I probably tend to see London obliquely, in the shadow rather than in the substance sometimes.

JW: You mentioned walking around London just now. Is that essential to writing about the city?

PA: I need to have a place, a definite place: Clerkenwell in *Dr Dee*, Limehouse in *Dan Leno*; I always try and focus on a specific locality as much as possible. I don't know why that is, I just have a predilection for that, rather than seeking to see the city as a whole; Dickens sees the city as a whole, doesn't he?

JW: To an extent; what he appears to do is to rely on a sense of a particular place, and then confound that sense by reinventing it; which I think is true of your work as well. I find that I think I know the place to which you refer, and, as I read the novels, I find I don't know exactly where the place in question is ...

PA: Yes, the houses, the buildings are made up, invented ...

JW: ... which, of course, is the very thing which many critics and reviewers missed about *Dr Dee* ...

PA: ... and I think the other thing we ought to mention in this argument is not just London, but the kind of people I tend to write about – magicians, occultists, mystics, visionaries, this is a side which is almost as important as the palpable presence of the city; each character always has a personal response to the city in a particularly – oblique's the wrong word – particularly magical way; all my characters are lost souls, aren't they? They make their own reality with spells and magic and in a sense what they're doing is creating London, each character creates his own London.

JW: And it is through this process, it is this process which allows you to write a different narrative, a different London each time, even though there are common factors.

PA: Yes, Dan has a vision of London, Oscar Wilde has a vision of London, and yet this is also true of the biographies, you see; the biographies and the novels are flung together in that sense; I tend to choose figures for the biographies and for the novels who create the city for themselves, so I suppose what I try to do is create a different character and then create a different London ...

JW: ... which leads to all sorts of fascinating and endless possibilities, as endless as the city itself ...

PA: ...Exactly, in a city of 7 000 000 people, one could write 7 000 000 novels, and that's just the initial number – the reason why London is so amorphous is because it is also so endlessly imaginable; as a physical city it is unimaginable, but for the visionary, or a particular type of person, his or her London becomes the world.

JW: Such a response on the part of the visionary is a passive response, such a person allows the city to dictate to him or her; this makes me think of certain remarks on architecture and cities by architect Bernard Tschumi, who comments that the structure is not a place but what *takes place*, it is an event; the city is constantly renewed, constantly reinvented, which is why, I think you'll agree, it is incorrect to talk of the end of a city such as London, as Roy Porter does in his social history of this city.

PA: Oh no, it has no end, it is limitless, it is infinite – there are other aspects of it too, as I try to show in my writing. The merging of biography with fiction is important in that respect, because when writing about London and London visionaries, in either case, you are, in a sense, mimicking the activities of the city, and merging both the real and the unreal.

JW: You mentioned just now that you are working on a book on London set in the future; do you have a title for it yet?

PA: Not yet...

JW: ... such works, when set in the future, run the risk of being predictive, would you say this is the case with the new work?

PA: No, nothing like that ...

JW: ... so will this London be a recognizable London in any sense?

PA: It will be recognizable only in that the old streams of London will have re-emerged, the Tyburn for instance, so I suppose you could say that I have taken the sacred geometry idea and just imagined it as only sacred geometry and nothing else ...

JW: I'm struck by what you say that, in allowing natural features to resur-face, you will be sharing certain concerns with another *fin-de-siècle* writer, Richard Jefferies, in his *After London* ...

PA: Well, partly that, but it is difficult to describe, but certainly in that book it is mainly the sacred landmarks which have survived, which I believe they will, in some sense. As an example of this we have not far from us Richard Rogers's Lloyd's building, which stands on the same spot as the biggest maypole ever erected; it's quite coincidental, obviously, in many respects, but I think that the city is much more powerful in that sense than people realize – there's a topographical power, a topographical spirit, and it has nothing to do with ley lines, nothing to do with any of that, but it does have to do with what happens on any one spot over and over again.

JW: Everyone has a different heart or centre for the city; Dickens in *Our Mutual Friend* says that the heart of the city is St Mary Axe, and I wonder if you have a particular centre...

PA: ...It's the City, it has to be the City, it has to be those few streets which have existed since Anglo-Saxon times around Bread Street, Cripplegate, Upper Thames Street, Lower Thames Street, Gracechurch Street, that area; it may be clichéd to say so, but that has been the most – I may be wrong about this, but I imagine that this has to have been the most – consistently inhabited portion of Europe. Now that may be wrong but we have evidence of occupation there since Celtic times, so those are the streets which are centre of London for me.

JW: Let's turn to the idea of the male city. You suggested the last time we met that the city is masculine, even though it's very hard to pin down why.

PA: Well, it's a city that is built on power, it's not a civilized or cultured city, it never has been, it has always been where the money and power are; money and power have until recently equaled men, so I suppose that this male persona has gradually developed over two thousand years; everyone thinks of London as just that, it's a question of commerce, it always has been: the Saxons used London as a market, as did the Romans, there's the Royal Exchange, the Imperial City, the banking industry – it's always been that sort of place, and it's an oppressive city for many people as a result.

JW: All of which, of course, is especially true in much of the writing of the city in the nineteenth century. In *Villette* there is a chapter dedicated to the City, where Brontë, through her principal character Lucy Snowe, makes the point that the rest of London may be the place where one gets one's pleasure, but the City itself is where real work is done, where men work, and Lucy...

PA: ... she wakes up, enamoured with the City, filled with excitement. I think Charlotte Brontë says something like it's the most exciting thing ...

JW: ...and this also relates to sexual power – the city is equated with men's ability to go to certain places where women cannot.

PA: The City has a very predatory quality and it has also been a very voracious city. As you know, for hundreds of years the mortality rate was so high, and in order to keep the City going, more people had to be brought in, because so many people were dying within it, and then we come to the question, which we mentioned to each other, the other day: do we belong to the City, or does the City belong to us? This is a difficult question to answer; theoretically, we are the city, but on another level, all of our characters and personalities are dominated by this huge ... *thing* ... which surrounds us.

JW: Yes, we define ourselves according to it or measure ourselves against it, and perhaps what that means is that one doesn't have to be born in London in order to consider oneself a Londoner; do you believe then, given what you've said, that, in a sense, the city writes us?

PA: Oh yes; Londoners are very thin on the ground because every generation has brought with it waves of immigration, whether from Ireland or France, Poland, or Holland, and once people are here, they become part of the city; it is that polyglot element that Wordsworth picks up on, and this has always been true, it is not new; there are no new phenomena in London, there are always persistent phenomena which are related to each other – people used to complain about immigrants in the fourteenth and fifteenth centuries, as they do now. If you think of the city as a body, as people always have done, it's always been seen as a sort of dropsical body, too heavy, always ill ... research prior to this century showed that people in London suffered from nervous fever, temperatures always too high, more than anywhere else in the country. The history of waves of mortality in London prove fascinating.

JW: All the while, however, we're talking of London as though we know what its boundaries are. Another fascinating aspect of London is the question of perimeters, boundaries, margins. Whenever I read your novels – and the same is true of the novels of Iain Sinclair – there is a sense in which I know and recognize this spirit of London, and I say 'yes, this is London, it's not the suburbs'; we all have our own ideas of where the suburbs begin and end, and everyone has their own particular view of this, so I wondered if you could say something on this matter of the border, of London, and not-London?

PA: This is a difficult question. Those places which try and retain their original identity, I call suburbs. When they have given up the struggle and have decided they are part of London, then they're London! Places which have 'High Streets', they attempt to retain an identity ... I was in Willesden the other day and the Council have tried to retain this myth of Willesden as a separate place; as a result of course it just becomes dreary and spiritless. When, say, a suburb almost as far out as Camberwell gives up the effort and says, OK, we are London, then it starts to become recognizably London. I still don't know what this is though ...

JW: ... it's a very curious thing, isn't it? One of the things that comes through in your writing is a shared quality across the novels, the biographies, of the city as a modern if not modernist location, with its qualities of ineffability, qualities of the sublime and of the inevitability dictated by that of surrendering oneself to this monstrous mass, which is oblique, shadowy, hard to define; but to return to this question of suburbs: a strange thing occurs in the representation of London at the end of the nineteenth century; most of those who write about London, about the 'centre' so-called, feel the need to transform and thereby limit it into what you've already described as the gothic city, to make it a 'city of dreadful night', of *grand guignol* effects ...

PA: ... yes, that's absolutely right ...

JW: ... but most of these writers are not from London, they're not English either – Stevenson, Wilde, Conrad, James, to name the most obvious.

All come into the city, attracted by it, to create a specific, limited vision of what the city is, while people who are from London write outwards, away from London, towards the suburbs, as though they can no longer say anything new about the city, and I wonder if you see London as the first 'modern' city.

PA: I'm not sure what you mean by 'modern city'.

JW: Perhaps what I want to suggest is that – and this is to continue the theme of the city as body – in being seen to be an 'organic' city, it is also seen as a city which outgrows itself very rapidly, always transforming itself from any stable identity. It doesn't remain contained or orderly, as does, for example, Hausmann's Paris.

PA: Oh I see, you're saying it's always like a megalopolis – that's certainly true, it has to be true, I mean, every period is a period of rapid expansion and change, certainly this is the case in the eighteenth century, and since then it has never stopped. But going back to your earlier point about the idea of a centre, and connecting that to the darkness at the centre, the material darkness of the fog in the nineteenth century, of course the other image of London which recurs endlessly is of London as a primeval wilderness or a swamp, and you find that, throughout the literature, there are continual images of strange creatures created by the mud; this always suggests that London is very old, and I think that writers throughout the history of literature are picking up on something about this site which is primeval.

JW: We've talked about the various images of London which recur through your work, and, specifically or implicitly, the works to which we've been referring have been your later works, your more recent works. Particularly, the biographies of Blake and Dickens are crowded with images of the London milieu. Yet, if one goes back as far as the T. S. Eliot biography, the importance of London is there also, albeit in another way; clearly *The Waste Land* is, at least in part, a poem concerned with what you called just now the megalopolis.

PA: I think the interest in Eliot and the city is more indirect; I think the main influence there, for me, was, as far as I was concerned, was his conception of time; I think only in London could Eliot have imagined the sense of time, of time past, time present and time future, in London; he couldn't have imagined that in Boston, so this raises for me the other element which we have not yet discussed is the theme of timelessness …

JW: So, for you, is this question of time/timelessness, dependent on, say, a cyclical rather than a linear model of time?

PA: No, I'd say, rather, that it is spiral; I used to believe in the cyclical theory of time, but it's much more complicated, the sense of time in

London is quite unlike any other place I've ever been, it's so specific that it's almost impossible to describe it, there's nothing with which to compare it.

JW: Does this give London the sense of being a haunted city?

PA: Yes. But, like the concept of time, it's not something I can really talk about. The question of time appears in my books without my having any real clue as to what it means; perhaps it's just the way in which my imagination works, but then it is a London imagination, whether that's good or bad, because it returns again and again in many texts; it's just one of those things. Partly, I have to admit, that it's characterized by the need to control a plot, and it's an easy way of creating a narrative; but on another level, it has to do with the need to write about and respond to this place, without even planning to. So, this quality of time in the city emerges and I don't understand where it comes from.

JW: There's this sense throughout your books of a certain return; something comes back, never quite as it was, to disturb, and create a rift, so that one can be in a place, and that place is haunted by its own palimpsest.

PA: That's true. If you look at the wall behind you, you'll see different views from different periods in the history of Clerkenwell. Constant reinvention is what London is.

JW: Which brings me back to an earlier point, which is that the most inventive and interesting London novelists are precisely so inventive, because they're not inventing at all; they are responding to the contours, the writing which is the city.

PA: Yes that's true, all over London, not just here in Clerkenwell, you see this, almost arcane, reverence of the past.

JW: And yet this is a very different kind of reverence, a different kind of remembering, from various governments' heritage projects ...

PA: ...absolutely, it's innate and ineradicable, there's an extraordinary sense of what went before on the part of the people who live here, who write themselves into this memory.

JW: This creates a certain tension; despite what you were saying earlier concerning the city as a place of power, yet there is this resistance to this power, so what survives about the city, is something which is affirmative and not about coercive or oppressive power ...

PA: ...yes, you're quite right and that's something which is always here, whether you call it the subversive or the radical or the underworld; this has always flourished here; there has always been that in and about London which has defiantly paraded its independence, against the crown, against government; for a number of reasons London has always been a place which has harboured dissent of many varieties, millenarian sects for example. This manifests repeatedly an egalitarianism against the city-structure, so that it resists single, imposed models or templates of what those with power think it should be.

JW: You mentioned earlier that you write about tricksters, magicians, alchemists, a whole gamut of marginal, shadowy figures …

PA: … Blake of course is the single greatest example of this …

JW: … yes, Iain Sinclair describes him in *Lights Out for the Territory* as the father of all psychogeographers …

PA: … yes, Iain belongs to that group of writers you mentioned earlier who come to London, he's Welsh, and he has the most extraordinary central London imagination. I think those who move to London take London and its phenomena more seriously than those of us who are born here. In Sinclair's books, he has created this extraordinary, almost malevolent force, maybe I'm wrong about that, but it seems that there is a darker side, even to the comedy. I think in my perception of the city there is more exuberance, more theatricality; as we've said the theatrical aspect to London – and to Londoners – is enormously important, the essential theatricality of the people. Now, why is this, is it because they know they're living in a city in which they have to perform …

JW: Perhaps it's because they're aware they live in what in the nineteenth century was perceived generally as the greatest city on the planet …

PA: The slang of the city is also important. Did you know that in the fifteenth century, Londoners spoke exactly as commoners do today? they dropped their 'h's, pronounced 'th' as 'v', 'brother' as 'bruvva', and so on.

JW: Language then remains a constant, part of the city itself, part of its theatrical element, and this, in turn, makes London such a fecund site for writers of all periods.

PA: Certain aspects of language remain the same, the catch phrases, the slang, the street cries, the songs; as you remember in Wordsworth's *Prelude*, he continually alludes to this intense theatricality as though everything were only there to be on show, everything *is* on show and the city becomes a harlequin figure for him, full of multicoloured and parti-coloured characters, and he longs for the silence and introspection inside himself, as a contrast to this elaborately stagey and theatrical world; and I suppose if you're talking about the theatricality in my books, it's exactly that, it is the same sort of staginess, campery, that sense of life; which, again, may have to do with the people who come from London and those who come to it and write about it. Maybe those from outside are more solemn about the city.

JW: You mentioned campery just now; is there a definite element to the city that is camp?

PA: There's always an element of campery about Londoners, they act constantly, and you find it in the pubs, in street stalls, there's an extraordinary gaiety, in the old-fashioned sense, which is just as powerful as the misery; think of the cockney music-hall.

JW: In many ways, a lot of music-hall songs, a great number of the lyrics are a comic take on the misery ...

PA: ... yes, absolutely. Now, whether all this is changing, whether we're going through some sea-change, I don't know. I really don't believe it, I believe that the personality of the city is too powerful, but I must admit that during the last few years there has been a slight change in the atmosphere.

JW: Is that possible to define?

PA: I just don't know. Perhaps it's becoming more violent; has it become more violent? I don't think so, it's become less violent.

JW: There was a moment I remember, moving away from Britain in the early eighties, and then coming back a few years later to find that there were far more homeless people than there used to be.

PA: Yeah, that certainly happened, but again, you might say that the city is simply reverting to its earlier state. It seems that shabbiness asserts itself continually; it refuses to be tarted up, shabby is the best word for it; in terms of vagrancy, I suppose until 1910 or so, the city was filled with vagrants, wasn't it?

JW: Yes, Engels is appalled by this in *The Condition of the Working Class*; but allied to this is the immensity of the city, which a number of nineteenth-century urban commentators comment on, you know the sort of thing: 'the city is immense, *therefore* it is appalling'; and yet for writers who are intensely involved with the city – even Dickens at his most ambivalent – there is the sense that London is not merely massive, but is, instead, a series of villages, such as Clerkenwell, which, as you've said, has a sense of its own identity...

PA: The other word which springs to mind is 'labyrinth' isn't it, you've always got the labyrinth of London. London seems to be all flow without any solidity, it is a mobile and fluid city; it's constantly being rebuilt and vandalized, there's no such thing as a fixed condition. And this is a constant complaint of Londoners, that nothing remains the same; it's been a constant complaint virtually since London came into being: nothing stays the same, it's getting too large; but the process of change, of tearing things down, is of the city, and it's better than the city's gentrification – at least the things which are cleaned up will become shabby again, it'll take a century and then these buildings will become tenements. But to go back to the theme of boundaries: I've always found boundaries completely artificial and this is true whether we're talking of the city or whether we're talking about writing – fiction, biography and so on. What I'd like to do eventually is to be able to write books which are neither fiction nor biography but which are a different type of descriptive writing. This London book I hope will be like that. I'm sure that the present forms of novel and biography are fading forms, like the three-volume novel; the biography is fading and has to be revived somehow.

JW: It's so difficult to break forms however. Does London allow you that possibility at all?

PA: Oh yes. Absolutely. I don't know how yet but I am certainly going to give it a good try. I would never – after the Thomas More biography – I would never want to write a so-called straight biography because one can see all its weaknesses, one can see all the constraints imposed upon you by the formal devices you're supposed to use, and of course the same is true of fiction, even the most – apparently – innovative fiction is dominated largely by early twentieth-century ideas and writing, so I would certainly like to try and reconcile several different forms of writing; how one does it of course is another matter. I suppose, thinking about the conversations in *Dickens*, that was my first little attempt to get out of the form. I suppose what you might say I was trying to do in the biography was to mimic Dickens's own attitude towards the city.

JW: Yes, I was very much taken by that on first reading the biography, especially in one of the earliest conversations in which you introduce Amy Dorrit who is, very much, a London character or type, isn't she?

PA: Yes, definitely, she's archetypal isn't she? And this goes back to what we had been saying the other day about de Quincey and the lost girl. Little Dorrit is quintessentially the lost girl. What that metaphor is in terms of London, I just don't know yet. The other image of course which Dorrit reminds me of, is the city as prison. That's been a constant amongst London writers at least since Thomas More, it emerges again and again. More has this long description of London as a prison in one of his religious tracts, and this is, as far as I can see, one of the first real, essential fictions of London or the world as prison, and, again, it's something to do with London which creates this metaphor. Clerkenwell is of course an area which Dickens knew better than any other, Snow Hill, Saffron Hill, where Fagin's shop was, so Dickens must have paced these streets quite often; and of course he invents; the book shop from which Oliver supposedly steals is here in Clerkenwell Green, where we are, but there never was a book shop here – Dickens always involves us in the most outrageous conflations of the real and the unreal.

On this very spot where we are now there used to be a dissenters' tavern, right next to Marx's place, the Marx library, one of the biggest collections of Communist and Marxist literature in Europe, and the place from where Eleanor Marx used to address the crowds from the balcony.

JW: Which brings us again to the subject of writing and which leads me to ask: is the city, then, more 'real' in the writing of the city, than it is in reality?

PA: Yes. Because it's a city which can only ever be imagined. It involves one in an endless quest for that which doesn't exist.

JW: Let's turn our attention briefly, if we may, to pastiche.

PA: Oh certainly. There's no such thing as an original idea. The idea of originality is quite a modern heresy. In the pre-Restoration period, the best poet was the one who used the found material and rearranged it most adeptly. Which is T. S. Eliot, which is any good writer, who takes the inheritance and changes it, just a tiny bit. In all my books I 'steal' people's writings, there are whole passages which I just rework. I find that immensely liberating, it's not imprisoning at all. In the novel I'm writing now, I'd gone to Plato, and I needed some crowd scenes, so I read Shakespeare's crowd scenes and someone else's crowd scenes, and retouched them. But that to me is just as interesting, just as much of the creativity as trying to invent something.

JW: I think that one of the important qualities of pastiche is that you let yourself into a particular style ...

PA: Absolutely. And not only a different style but also a different period. With *Hawksmoor,* for example, when I was imitating early eighteenth-century speech, I found it was the one sure way in which I entered the period fully, it came alive, I think for readers it made that period live in a way in which it would not have been by any other method. The speech was real, I had taken it from original sources, and that for me is writing. This absurd superstition about not using other plots, not using other characters, other stories, is just simply a modern heresy, it never occurred to people in the eighteenth century not to do it.

JW: Is London then a pastiche city, can we provisionally define it in those terms? I get the sense that it's always imitating itself, always mocking itself.

PA: That's difficult – it's always, as we said before, always theatrical, it's always stagey; look at the new buildings in the City of London, they're like Babylonian monstrosities, they've tried to create a new Babylon or new Egypt in the centre of London – those huge, monumental structures are very stagey.

JW: Which I think Sinclair is quite perceptive about – he sees it in *Lights Out for the Territory* as part of an attempt to invent a global city; it's Hong Kong, it's New York, it's everywhere. And the irony is that it's not London at all for Sinclair, because no one has bothered to try and understand what goes on there when you do this kind of thing ...

PA: ... yet which, of course, means that London remains exactly the same, paradoxically. We've always had gothic monstrosities in the centre of London, the first Roman mansion was a huge, gaudy affair. The one constant thing in London you have to think of as being gaudy is language itself. That's most evident in one of my earliest books, *Notes for a New Culture*, which is a history of modern European culture and is – to recall the theme of pastiche – very heavily derived from Saussure, Lacan, Derrida. A friend who read it just the other day said it had a polemical angle which my other books don't possess, and I imagine – this sounds pretentious – that everything I've written stems from that book in the strangest way.

JW: Given that you've said that you would like to see a breakdown of boundaries between fiction and biography, do you think that there is possible more exchange between academic critics and, say, novelists?

PA: Of course, of course. There's no reason why the disciplines shouldn't be disestablished and as quickly as possible. Writing is writing, regardless of the form you happen to want to use. It's part of the same process, to use that old-fashioned word again.

JW: Why then do you think that, when people read a novel, however 'experimental', they're perfectly prepared to work with the experimentation, the departure from or radicalization of form, or whatever, and yet when a critic writes in an experimental fashion, the readership can get very offended by the games they perceive the critic employing?

PA: That's just the usual folly, the idiocy of people who wish to stick to established forms. But at the end of this century, everything is breaking down, all formal narratives are breaking down, I'm sure of it.

JW: Is this a form of millenarianism? Is the questioning of form in writing, whatever form, field, or discipline an expression of our *fin de siècle*?

PA: Yes it could be, but I think it's more important than that. All narrative devices are breaking down. If I am still writing in 2030, and you are, we won't be writing novels or academic studies, we'll be writing something quite different, unrecognizable and unpredictable. I know the trouble with innovation is that there is never anything which is actually new, we both agree about that I suppose, but something recognizably different will emerge, I am sure of it. But I want to return to the gothic, which is very important in London; we've talked about the gothic, about *grand guignol*, the gothic as a form, which teeters between comedy and tragedy, you're never sure whether you should laugh or you should cry. And this is essential to the Cockney genius. In Blake's poems, for example, I discovered late in the day, that the scenery and characters in his poems are largely taken from the gothic melodramas he used to see in the Haymarket; this is very important, his great visions hinged upon stage effects. Almost every gothic author since Defoe has used gothic theatricality, pantomimic qualities, and there's this constant hovering between farce and seriousness, which is also a Cockney thing.

JW: It's also imbued with a certain camp quality as well, if one thinks of Michael Caine, who is most wonderfully camp when he's at his most serious ...

PA: ... yes, and Dickens is the campest creature in the world, calling himself the inimitable and all the rest of it, and never knowing whether he should laugh. There's always a performative element to camp, and vice versa. When people talk about London being a city of contrasts, which is absolutely true the very fact that London has so many contrasting qualities creates this sense of campery and irony, seriousness and farce, you can't dissociate these elements. Dickens embodies these qualities – the theatrical, the pantomimic, the camp – there's not one character in Dickens who is not risible at one level or another, whether it's Scrooge, or Little Nell. Dickens was an incredibly theatrical and camp man. He was also the most incredibly gothic figure, he was an incredible martinet, people were terrified of him. He was not an amiable man, he was an absolute monster, always very gay, high spirited, always had to be in charge, in control of everybody, marshalling everybody around with such a force of will that everybody just surrendered to him. I must say, though, that Dickens was the one person who I really enjoyed writing about. Blake was a puzzle in certain respects, but Dickens is absolutely transparent.

JW: And the biography of More is what you've just finished.

PA: Yes, it's out in the Spring, in March.* That was a very interesting book to write because the period is so remote, you know, pre-Reformation Catholic England. Which raises another of my theories, by the way. The gothic, the pantomimic, the camp and the theatrical aspect of the Cockney is a more or less direct inheritance from Catholic culture. There's a whole buried Catholic sensibility which emerges in very strange theatrical forms, lots of ritual, pageant, cruelty. All the fuss over Princess Diana was a ritualized attempt to create a saint or a modern day Virgin Mary. It seemed like a resurgence of the oldest ideas. But, then, London has always been a rebellious, violent and disrespectful city; antinomianism is one of the laws of London life. The rebelliousness of London goes back almost as far as the city itself.

---

* *The Life of Thomas More* was published in the United States in September, 1998.

There's always been a quality of egalitarianism about Cockney London, with its history of dissenting groups, the weavers, the Huguenots, and the sites of dissenting London are part of the secret history of the city, places where tourists hardly ever go, like Bunhill fields; Blake is buried there, Defoe is buried there, Bunyan is buried there. And it's such a difficult place to find, even if you've been there before. I mentioned earlier the Marx library next to here, on which site there used to be an old nunnery, near to which used to be the Priory of St John of Jerusalem, the Knights' Templars, and underneath us is a whole network of tunnels, possibly connecting the priory with the nunnery. This is so typical of the city. But you only ever find places in London when you're not looking for them. At the same time, there are resonances in the city, continuities which go on forever. I was reading Defoe's *Journal of the Plague Year*, a few months back, and he mentions a spot which was a huge plague pit and I said I've got to find this. So I found it and it's still as derelict as it always was, just a load of tarmac, with garages at one end, but the whole area has never been built upon, it just remains a waste land. In the book I'm writing at the moment about London, I talk about such continuities and, without exaggeration, I've found about 70 places in which an original event has changed the character of that place forever.

JW: I think, Peter, that, in conclusion, I'd like to say that your novels are truly London novels; they remain events at any rate which have changed my understanding of the city, and the character of London also, even as they are themselves marked indelibly with the spirit of London. I want to thank you for them, and for this interview.

Notes

Introduction

1. The only other book-length studies of Ackroyd published so far (at the time of writing) are Laura Giovannelli's *Le vite in gioco: le prospettiva ontologica e autoreferenziale nella narrativa di Peter Ackroyd*, and Susana Onega's *Peter Ackroyd* and *Metafiction and Myth in the Novels of Peter Ackroyd* (to which I have not been able to refer due to its having been published after the completion of this study). Full details are given in the Bibliography.

2. The title of *The Diversions of Purley* is taken from an uncompleted work, *Epea Pteroenta: or, The Diversions of Purley*, by John Horne Tooke (1736–1812). Two volumes were published, in 1786 and 1805 respectively. The work puts forward a theory of language, and is written as a discussion between four interlocutors which, often satirically and in anti-Lockean vein, takes philosophers to task for overlooking the fact that the basic purpose of language is to communicate ideas swiftly. Tooke further argues that philosophers, grammarians and philologists have frequently erred in misunderstanding the structure of thought and the structure of language as being similar. As part of his own playful practice, and as a gesture against Utilitarianism, Tooke speculates, often hilariously, about possible etymologies and verbal declensions, shit, shot and shut, for example, all being related.

   Laura Giovannelli mentions this source, suggesting that Ackroyd's use of the title foreshadows what she terms the 'bisogno quasi psicologico' [quasi-psychological necessity] on the author's part for finding precursors in the literary tradition' (Giovannelli 1996, 11 n.1). Susana Onega attempts to make a connection between Tooke's approach to language and that of Ackroyd's poetic practice (which is itself influenced by the 'language' poetry of John Ashbery and Frank O'Hara, amongst others), by arguing that Ackroyd's use of Tooke's title 'might be taken to function as a warning to the reader that he feels as free as John Horne Tooke to create his own wildly speculative and meaningless patterns' (1998, 22).

   London Lickpenny is the title of an anonymously authored poem (c.1405), which addresses questions of simony and the abuse of wealth. A satirical poem, its first-person narrative concerns a Kentish man who comes to court to regain his lost money, and attempts vainly to be heard in the judicial system. A critique of this system, the poem also offers a fascinating view of medieval London.

   Why these borrowings on Ackroyd's part? Fascinating as both works are in their own right, it is difficult to tell, given that the poetry seems to owe little to either in terms of direct intertextual reference. The subjects – the city and language – and the frequently satirical styles of both may be read as principal concerns in Ackroyd's writing but here the relationship ends, and, as we shall argue, it is precisely this kind of allusive game with which the author seduces the critic and reader.

   Full details of both works are given in the Bibliography.

3. Of text in its broader sense, Derrida has commented, 'a text ... is henceforth no longer a finished corpus of writing, some content enclosed in a book or its margins, but a differential network, a fabric of traces referring endlessly to something other than itself, to other differential traces. Thus the text overruns the limits assigned to it so far' (1991,

256–7). This is an important remark, even more so in the context of discussing Peter Ackroyd. It is important to understand Ackroyd's novels operating as a differential network and a fabric of traces, even as they themselves, in their performance of the city of London for example, perform the city as its own differential network. See the chapter on London, below.

4. The *Plato Papers* has subsequently been published (1999) and is discussed in brief between Chapters 4 and 5.

5. The epigram is that of a character from *Daniel Martin*; the narrator continues, appositely for the purposes, and in the context of, this introduction, to point out that '[i]t had been no good pointing out that all language, even the most logical and philosophical, is metaphorical in origin ...' (339).

6. I am borrowing knowingly from the conversation between academic Rowan Phillips and film-maker Spenser Spender in Peter Ackroyd's first novel, *The Great Fire of London* (89).

7. See the discussion below in Chapter 1.

8. I am borrowing here, playing on, certain formulae, opening gambits, used by Jacques Derrida in a recent publication (1997, 11), where the question being asked is not asked merely concerning a defined subject (for as the formula suggests the definition is not yet arrived at); instead, the question is being raised by the arrival of the subject. Play raises the question itself, as well as raising the stakes in the textual game.

9. Significantly – or not? – the number seven is a mystical number for Doctor Dee, as it is for Nicholas Dyer, in *Hawksmoor*. To what lengths do Ackroyd's labyrinthine patternings extend, or are we merely being led up the garden (of forking) path(s)?

10. Doing the police in different voices is, of course, Sloppy's particular talent, in *Our Mutual Friend*, and not, as is implied here, the ability of anyone from *Little Dorrit*. Interestingly, however, the line concerning mimicry is appropriated, not by Ackroyd, but, spookily enough, by the film of *Little Dorrit*, made a number of years after *The Great Fire of London* was written.

11. 'In fact' is, in fact, a playful phrase of Ackroyd's, as one reviewer has noted. When it appears, the reviewer tells us, you come to learn, almost instinctively, not to trust the alleged 'truth' you are about to be told.

12. See the discussion of Ackroyd's play with allusion and reference in the chapter on poetry which follows.

13. On the comedic dismantling of genre, and other comic effects, see James R. Kincaid, 'Throwing Pies at the Dean: Comedy, Power, and Institutional Practice' (1996, 5–12).

14. To what extent may it be said that the murders are based on the Jack the Ripper murders, when the murders in *Dan Leno* are those not only of prostitutes but also of a Jewish scholar and a family living on the site of the Ratcliffe Highway murders (a grisly event which, today, is equally 'historical' and 'literary', inasmuch as it is known principally through Thomas de Quincey's own highly gothic textualized account)? Keating's review typically – typically, that is, of reviews searching for the family likeness – seeks to suppress the most obvious of differences, if only so that it can push its theory of playful resemblance, precisely in order to become frustrated by the textual game.

15. A number of reviews of *Dickens* are worth mentioning in passing, specifically those by William H. Pritchard, Malcolm Andrews, Garry Wills and Kenneth S. Lynn (full details of which are given in the Bibliography). Lynn's is curious in that it hardly ever discusses Ackroyd's approach to his subject outright, giving tacit approval throughout to the biography, especially as he reads it countering the 'agenda' of

Marxist interpretations of Dickens's texts. For the most part, the reviewer decides to reiterate in précis form some of Dickens's habits and attitudes, while alerting the reader in a vague fashion to various aspects of Victorian life which Dickens's own life suitably exemplifies. Reading askew, it is as if Lynn does not know exactly what to say of this biography and so chooses to avoid saying much of anything, directly (1991).

Pritchard's review (1991) is ambiguously titled 'The Exaggerator'. The title is ambiguous because it may be that it refers either to Dickens or Ackroyd or, equally to both. A largely favourable review, it points to Ackroyd's 'boldness and extravagance' (1991, 301). While Ackroyd's fictional interludes are found to be intrusive, they nonetheless contain 'some revealing moments' (1991, 302). Ackroyd's accounts of the novels are, when compared with previous biographers' treatments (notably those of Edgar Johnson and Fred Kaplan), received favourably.

The stumbling block for Pritchard comes, however, over the (ab)uses of, for him as for Kincaid, the too-frequent, rhetorical question, and the 'disfiguring rhetoric … of sequences of terse, often one-word sentences sent out in unconvincing imitation of the opening page of *Bleak House*' (1991, 303, 304). The reviewer cannot believe that the use of rhetorical questions is accidental, but is at a loss to explain it. Both objections are levelled, then, at the aesthetic context and determination of particular writing practices. In both cases, it may be that a question of play, of parody, is involved. If no young writer should ever attempt to imitate Dickens, at least 'straight', then it may be that camp exaggeration may well be one way to engage and play with the Dickensian. Dressing up as a caricature of Dickens, or dressing Dickens up as one of his own caricatures, is not the same as trying to imitate Dickens, and pantomimic irony may well, in this context, be the sincerest form of flattery. Whatever the case may be, ultimately Pritchard's review is approving and there is no doubt sufficient generosity of spirit to overlook the perceived flaws.

Garry Wills finds little to like and demonstrates none of the ambiguous generosity of either Kincaid or Pritchard. The initial adjective used to describe the biography is 'unbuckled' (1991) and he is almost wholly annoyed by the text, despite that '[f]or long periods Ackroyd's breathless and accumulative approach works surprisingly well' (1991). He finds Ackroyd's guesswork exasperating, while the book itself is frequently 'sloppy, repetitive, coy, self-conscious … poorly written … [with] sententious asides, flip moralizing, [and] unearned generalizations'. Full of 'bloat and verbiage', the book is a 'baggy monster'. Unlike Kincaid, Wills finds the estranging suppositions about the Dickens-Ternan relationship unconvincing and weakly argued, and is annoyed – unreasonably it seems – by the fact that Ackroyd 'erases his own effort [to produce meaning] with the conclusion: "The fact is that in the end it [in this example the meaning of food in Dickens's texts] might be said to stand for anything or everything"' (1991). It is this very same uncertainty which Kincaid applauds in the biography. Though not as bad-tempered as a Martin Dodsworth, Wills is nonetheless so unambiguously disdainful of Ackroyd's ludic strategies that his review comes across as bad-tempered and lacking in any sense of what might be going on.

Finally, at the other end of the critical spectrum, is Malcolm Andrews's appreciative and positive review, from *The Dickensian* (1992, 43–5). Not finding the lack of dates a problem, Andrews admires the vivid, 'nearly seamless narrative' (403). He points out something observed by many of the reviewers, that the reader's 'stamina is severely tested', but then compares this with any attempt to keep up with Dickens's walks and suggests that the reader experiences 'a sense of the driving energy and restlessness of the book's subject' which 'is surely part of the book's purpose' (403). Ackroyd delivers details with 'almost Dickensian prodigality' (403). That 'almost' is telling, because it acknowledges the gap between the assumption of a role and naive imitation, which many of the reviewers either dislike or, as in the example of Wills, miss altogether. Unlike Pritchard, Andrews does not find the strange and estranging punctuation a problem but, instead, sees it as a formal device which reproduces and plays out Ackroyd's desire to eschew the conventional aspects of biography. He also admits to Ackroyd's 'zest for the innumerable and proliferating contradictions within his subject' (404), concluding with a generosity matched only by what he sees as Ackroyd's own spirit, that the complaints of other reviewers seem paltry in comparison with the achievement of *Dickens* (405).

More than anything, these reviews and others all reveal the deep division over the reception of this biography and the fact that the question of whether *Dickens* is to one's taste is, in the final analysis, the only question which can be raised. What is interesting is that, where the biography is castigated, the reviewer almost inevitably appears obliged to resort to criticism which verges on *argumentum ad hominem*; the singular exception to this is James Kincaid's review which is itself ambiguous, and which struggles so hard with *Dickens* that it deserves the space given to it in this introduction, partly because it is readable as assuming in part some of the qualities of the biography itself.

16. Once again, there is the sense of play here, because Ackroyd is playing with his own fictional recreations as well as with historical figures. There is a simultaneity of projection and invention, performance and mimicry at work, which is unsettling precisely because it seems to be effected so seriously, while playing for laughs at the same time. Such simultaneity of characterization is stressed by Ackroyd repeatedly in *Dickens* where Dickens is the most anxious *and* the most humorous of men, the most curmudgeonly and the most generous. A personality may contain such paradoxes of course. Inadvertently then, the reviews of the biography that are the most troubled have become pulled into the game in some fashion, by seeing it as the best of biographies and the worst of biographies, while not always seeing that Charles Dickens can be the best of writers and the worst of men.

17. See the discussion of camp in the following chapter on Ackroyd's poetry.

18. As mentioned before, seven has a mystical significance in both *Hawksmoor* and *Dee*. Whether the seven interludes are part of this mystical pattern, or merely seven interludes, is not for me to decide. Critics with an interest in numerology may wish to make something of this.

19. Other reviews by Ackroyd, which may be of interest, are those of *The Essays of Virginia Woolf. Volume Two: 1912–1918* (*New York Times* 27 March, 1988), *Lewis Carroll: A Biography* (*New York Times* 12 November 1995), *Perfume* (*New York Times* 21 September, 1986), along with a brief article, also from the *New York Times* (1 November 1987), entitled 'Oscar Wilde: Comedy as Tragedy'. Virginia Woolf is revealed as a rare kind of reviewer, one who, while seeking some version of herself in what she reads, nonetheless treats each work with the respect singularity demands, avoiding the imposition of some aesthetic theory (unlike Pound and Eliot, as Ackroyd points out), and demonstrating, in the process, that she not only loves literature but also has a 'comic spirit'. Morton N. Cohen's biography of Carroll has for Ackroyd 'a delightful oddity' about it, and the sentences have a Wonderland-like quality: 'a distressing but endearing habit of falling over one another like playing cards'. Patrick Süskind's novel, *Perfume*, is 'a genuine historical fiction ... primarily concerned with the contemporary world ... [it] is a meditation

on the nature of death, desire and decay'. This comment is itself worth remembering as a reflection, or meditation, on Ackroyd's own creative process, as is the following comment, also from the review of *Perfume*, and made, significantly enough, after Ackroyd has compared Süskind's work with *The Picture of Dorian Gray*: '... certain writers are drawn to the past precisely in order to explore ...[their] interests; history becomes, as it were, an echo chamber of their own desires and obsessions. But this cannot be conveyed by some easy trick of style: the generally debased standard of historical fiction springs from the fact that most novelists think it sufficient to create approximately the right "atmosphere." But the important things are the details.' The novel retains 'the strength of a fable'. Finally, the article on Oscar Wilde insists on the doubleness of Wilde, his Apollonian and monstrous qualities, which, Ackroyd argues, were the signs of the extent to which Wilde embodied the 'obsessions' of his age, and which, more dangerously, made him such a telling critic of that epoch. For Ackroyd, Wilde was a true 'modern'.

What is important in each of these reviews and commentaries is that Ackroyd responds to the complications and strangenesses of his subjects' identities, while bringing out even further the strangeness, so that not only do the books in question have powerful estranging features, but so too do their subjects, whether fictional or historical. Each piece of journalism provides a glimpse of a different Woolf, a different Dodgson, a different Wilde; the review of Patrick Süskind's novel offers the reader a fascinating insight into Ackroyd's own sense of the practice of historical fiction and its function, as well as suggesting a way of reading Ackroyd himself.

20. This remark is double-edged in its play; for, on the one hand, Ackroyd presents to us humour as the suspect package, ticking like a pantomime crocodile, while, on the other, he offers us wit as the bomb disposal expert, dismantling the technology of destructive force which is institutionally approved.

1.   The Poetry of Peter Ackroyd

1. 'Making is, in Greek, *poiesis*', as Heidegger reminds us in his ' "...*Poetically Man Dwells...*"' (1971, 214). From Heidegger's reading of Hölderlin's line which serves as the title of the essay, it is possible to indicate a direction for a reading of Ackroyd's poetry-as-archive. In such a reading, it can be suggested that the archive serves also as the construction of the dwelling of common identity, a shared identity whereby 'we' connect through the acknowledgement of the allusions as fragments of historical and cultural identity, handed down, transformed, communicated and translated. Ackroyd's poetry is therefore not merely playful for its own sake, but plays with the very conditions by which we seek to connect in order to transmit the sense of the constructedness of subjectivity. What Ackroyd's poetry 'makes' is the self as the ruined sum of its allusory references and excerpts.

2. See Susana Onega on this poem (1998, 8–10). She draws out convincingly the connections and allusions not only to Yeats, but also to Wordsworth's 'The Tables Turned'.

3. Connecting Ackroyd to Ashbery, to a certain Ashbery at least, is common among the reviewers and critics (as is referred to in this section of the chapter), and leads in part, through a misunderstanding of Ashbery as 'postmodernist' rather than as 'modernist', to the similar misreading of Ackroyd as also 'postmodernist'. However, if it is

necessary to trace such lineages, then perhaps it is worth reading Ackroyd's own account of Ashbery's modernist poetry, alongside that of Frank O'Hara in *Notes for a New Culture* (*NNC* 128ff.). Ackroyd's account reads Ashbery as a poet who, despite his modernism and the concern for a poetic language that ' "says" nothing' (130), still 'retains an overriding poetic voice' (*NNC* 133). In contrast to the adherence to 'voice' which Ackroyd reads in Ashbery's text, J. H. Prynne and Denis Roche are considered for their insistent interests in written language, in the employment of a multiplicity of discourses, and in the uses of fragmentation as an exploration of the surfaces of poetry (*NNC* 132–6). Whether one wishes to pursue family resemblances between Ackroyd and other poets or not, his readings of Prynne and Roche are suggestive of ways in which to comprehend his own poetry, rather than through the frequent comparison to John Ashbery.

4. Onega attempts to tease a reading of the poetry which places 'The Goldfish Sonata' from *Ouch* (later 'the hermaphrodite...'; *DP* 60) biographically in relation to Ackroyd and his father. The reference to the father is, she says, 'possibly a reference to Ackroyd's own father, the painter Graham Ackroyd, who separated Ackroyd from his mother shortly after his birth' (1998, 14). Whether or not this reading is convincing, the poem, with its images of gay fellatio, spilled semen, words as 'pillars of salt', dead art, the isolation of the poet and the desert station, all seem to suggest end-points, cul de sacs, the impossibility of continued or connected lineages.

5. See Alan Sinfield: 'Art is a space where femininity is permitted, and that permission limits its dissidence. The case may be different in camp, drag, and lesbian butch/femme role-playing, where categories of gender and sexuality are more provocatively juxtaposed' (1994, 198). Sinfield's sense of containment with regard to what art allows is important here, and in general for Ackroyd's work, at least as far as the negative criticisms of his writing go. For, it is as if, aware of the possibilities for disruptive play which the rule book of aesthetics allows, Ackroyd appears to push at the rules, to combine parody with camp, with irony and dead-pan, so that the reviewer or critic is never able to decide on what the text seems to be getting up to, or away with. Sinfield cites Andy Medhurst's argument that postmodernism's play with identity is merely a game that allows straights to catch up with camp (Sinfield 1994, 200). It is perhaps the other way round with Ackroyd, and one of the reasons for the constant misrecognition, mis-reading, of his work as postmodern. The use of this normative but outrageously vague academic label is a sly act of making Ackroyd safe, domesticating him and giving him an identity, albeit one which is multifaceted. For, 'postmodern' relies in its use as a definition on popular culture aestheticization, where citation and meaninglessness are the only available gambits, in a safely depoliticized arena of self-referential artistic endeavour.

6. On the subject of gender-identities and sexual confusion, Eliot's poem has as one of its principal characters, the hermaphrodite Tiresias, the 'old man with the wrinkled dugs' (l. 228), and, while little could be said to be directly camp in *The Waste Land*, from certain perspectives, much of 'Sweeney Agonistes' is markedly so, especially at the point when Krumpacker utters the following lines: 'Yes London's a little too gay for us / Don't think I mean anything *coarse*' (Eliot 1974, 129), when, of course, he does, doesn't he? It is this momentary dalliance with vulgarity and crassness which seems to play in Ackroyd's writing, and which is so frequently given voice in his comic characters in the novels, such as the Lenos, or Harriet Scrope, in *Chatterton*, or Augustine Fraicheur, in *First Light*.

The camp vulgarity is a quality belonging to many music hall artists and comedians connected to the music hall tradition, especially in London, as discussed in the body of the chapter, above, where campery and cross-dressing frequently go hand in hand, as in the example of Dan Leno, one of the characters in *Dan Leno and the Limehouse Golem*. The characters of Eliot's unfinished 'Sweeney' owe as much to music hall as they do to camp sensibility: on the influence of music hall on 'Sweeney Agonistes' see Ackroyd in his biography of Eliot (*TSE* 105, 145–8).

Also of interest of course is that, in the echo of the barmaid, Ackroyd is borrowing or alluding to a moment when Eliot 'performs' a female voice. Elsewhere in his poetry, Ackroyd has occasion to borrow another of Eliot's female impersonations, when, in 'the novel', the unidentifiable narrator remarks '...the self fades and flickers; we read novels late into the night' (*DP* 28), recalling Marie's comment in *The Waste Land* that 'I read, much of the night, and go south in the winter' (l. 18; Susana Onega elaborates on the complex web of allusions to Eliot in 'the novel' 1998, 17–18). And, as already mentioned in the discussion of 'among school children', Ackroyd gestures in the briefest of manners toward that other famous moment of female impersonation in English literature, Marvell's 'The Nymph Complaining for the Death of Her Fawn'.

A focus for a future study of Ackroyd, which discusses the possible connections between issues of sexuality, gender, class, theatricality, performance and masquerade in the context and setting of London presents itself through a complex of interrelated characters, some of whom have already been mentioned briefly in this note. In addition to these, in *The Great Fire of London* there is Sir Frederick Lustlambert, whose profile is reminiscent of Punch (*GFOL* 51), while there is also the character of Rowan Phillips, the gay Canadian Cambridge don and Dickens expert, who is asked to write the script for Spenser Spender's film of *Little Dorrit*, and who has a brief affair with working-class Londoner Timothy Coleman. Obviously, there are the interrelations of the issues of sexuality, class, masquerade and performance to be found throughout *The Last Testament of Oscar Wilde*.

Already mentioned from *First Light* is gay antiques dealer Augustine Fraicheur, who directs an amateur company's production of Eliot's *The Family Reunion*. Joey and Floey Hanover, once music hall favourites, bear close examination, especially Floey's often vulgar malapropisms, and Evangeline Tupper, a 'senior civil servant in the Department of the Environment' (*FL* 10), and caricature lesbian. In *Chatterton* there is the melodramatic Harriet Scrope, lesbian and novelist who screams exclamations while making a sandwich (*C* 37), the curious, theatrical Lenos, antique dealers, and Pat, the gay companion of Mr Joynson, who is first encountered wearing a leopard-skin leotard (*C* 51).

Goosequill is obviously developed from the music hall comedic Londoner (*Milton in America*), while the Catholic settlement of Mary Mount is highly theatrical. Most directly involved in the theatrical, along with issues of cross-dressing, is *Dan Leno and the Limehouse Golem*, while the darker sides of theatricality and ritual in London are explored in both *Hawksmoor* and *The House of Doctor Dee*. In *English Music*, the narrator Timothy Harcombe and his father, Clement, are both working-class 'theatricals'.

Music hall and working-class theatre in London are discussed in *T.S. Eliot* (particularly in relation to Eliot's composition of 'Sweeney Agonistes'; see above), throughout *Dickens*, in *Blake*, while *The Life of Thomas More* not only emphasizes the development of theatrical tradition in the city, but also the generally theatrical nature of London society in the early modern period, commenting also on the entertainments written by More, in which his family were forced to participate. As Ackroyd suggests in the final interview in this collection, there is not only an interrelated cultural history of camp and theatricality in London, London, and, more especially, Londoners, are all too frequently and inescapably camp *and* theatrical. There is always the element of masquerade and performance amongst the working class.

7. The extent to which this 'voice' has a particular London, if not, English currency, and that it has extended into the shared cultural consciousness, has recently been given coincidental expression in the *Sunday Times* (Robert Harris, 'Blair's third way to elected leadership', 20 September, 1998, no. 9082), in its coverage of what it refers to somewhat archly as *l'affaire Lewinsky* (which I would also argue is readable as delivered with a somewhat camp intonation). In four pages of coverage of the Clinton-Lewinsky investigation, one journalist, having recited some of the details of Kenneth Starr's findings, utters the remark 'titter ye not'. The phrase, as those with research interests in camp will no doubt recognize, comes from the patter of comedian Frankie Howerd, who would also, just prior to putting his own tongue quite firmly and literally in his cheek, comment in all apparent innocence on his audience's laughter: 'big titters, little titters'. Indeed.

8. See, for example, Ackroyd's own discussions in his *Dressing Up*, which pays particular attention to theatrical transvestism (see Ch. 5 'Transvestism as performance', 89–139). Masquerading and theatrical performative play with normative identities is discernible across his work, whether expressed through camp or 'stagy' characters in the novels, or through the interests of the various biographies' subjects, as is discussed in note 6, above.

9. On the subject of titles, see Susana Onega (1998). Reading the titles, she asserts that, on occasion, 'they obscure, rather than illuminate the meaning' of the poem, while, at other times, titles seem to be opposed ironically to the poem's content, as in the case of the poem 'Country Life', which, she argues, concerns itself with 'the alienation of life in the city' (7). Onega also points to the way in which Ackroyd will either drop titles or include them where none had previously been in successive reprintings of the poetry (8), and there is, she suggests, 'a willed unrelatedness and opacity' to Ackroyd's titular practice (8). Most frequently, however, Ackroyd will provide a title for a poem which previously had none in an earlier manifestation, by taking the first few words of the first line, and making these the title with a triple dot ellipsis.

10. These are: 'country life' (7–8), 'and the children ...' (11–12), 'This beautiful fruit ...' (13), 'my own ...' (15), 'only connect ...' (21–6), 'the cut in ...' (27), 'the novel' (28), 'In the middle ...' (30), 'there was no rain ...' (31), 'how did it ...' (34), 'out of the ...' (36–9), 'The extreme heat ...' (40), 'madness ...' (41), 'the room is ...' (43), 'opening...' (45) 'the secret is ...' (47), 'you do the best ...' (50), 'and then ...' (59) 'The great Sun ...' (64), 'The little tune ...' (65), 'watching the process ...' (67), 'love falls' (72). All page references are to the poems as they are reprinted in *The Diversions of Purley* and not to their earlier publications.

11. Those texts on which Vasseleu draws specifically are Derrida's 'White Mythology: Metaphor in the Text of Philosophy', in *Margins of Philosophy* (1982, 207–72) and Irigaray's *Speculum of the Other Woman* (1985). Irigaray, discussing Plato's cave, argues for the need to distinguish between artificial and natural light, on the distinction that the artificial light, in this case a fire, is a representation of the sun, a mime, translation or projection, always already a metaphor, a figure of detour and delay (245–6). Derrida also distinguishes between lights, forms of light, in 'On a Newly Arisen Apocalyptic Tone in Philosophy' (1993c, 147–8).

12. The Lacanian *point de capiton* is described by Slavoj Žižek as the 'theory ... of the phallic signifier as the signifier of lack' (1989, 154). Žižek discusses the Lacanian

reading of subjectivity as part of a response to what he describes as the poststructuralist critique of Lacan's theory, which he summarizes as arguing that Lacan, in positing such a theory, is attempting to 'master and restrain the "dissemination" of the textual process' (154ff.). The problem immediately is not so much whether Lacan's assertions or Derrida's responses (cited by Žižek) are more or less correct. I am interested here with the 'I-effect' and its reading or misreading, specifically as that concerns the performative 'I' in the text of Peter Ackroyd.

Bruce Fink provides a particularly lucid discussion of the *point de capiton*, translated by Fink as 'button tie' (1997, 93–5). Fink suggests how the arrest of the play of language, the play between 'language and meaning (reality as socially constituted), between signifier and signified, that will never break' (93), arises specifically as the child's response to the prohibition of the father. Significantly, however, Fink's discussion does not rely on the dialectical and polemical opposition in Žižek's assertion of the *point de capiton* against so-called poststructuralist objections. Fink argues that 'there is no true anchoring here, strictly speaking, since an anchor suggests an unmovable terra firma to which something is attached' (93). He continues: 'Rather, the result of the paternal metaphor is to tie a specific meaning to particular words ... without regard to an absolute referent' (93–4). Thus Fink makes available a textured or structural moment of meaning or stasis within the structure of language, which, while not being absolutely fixed or unshakable, is nonetheless foundational and operates within the textual structure or the structure of language because, on the one hand, it operates as though it were unshakable, absolute, and, on the other, and perhaps more importantly, is accepted as such by the addressee, in the Lacanian case, the child. The operation of 'I' is analogous, at least in terms of the reader's comprehension and misrecognition of it. 'I' is a moment of temporary, illusory fixity which reading teaches us is constant or has some signifying relationship to the signified of the speaking subject, the author or fictional character, whom we assume – or are taught to assume – is a more or less consistent unity.

13. On the play with authoritative status which the utterance or inscription of I effects, see Nicholas Royle on Derrida's use of 'I' (1995, 162–8).

2.   The Styles of Peter Ackroyd I

1. It is interesting to note Lodge's yoking together of two critical works, one from within the academy by Harold Bloom, about as far in as it is possible to get, and the other from outside. Ackroyd's 'polemical' work comes under attack for many aspects of style similar to Harold Bloom's work, notably its apparently overarching debt to the style of 'French structuralism' and its obscurantist prose (which Lodge often assumes as the sign of stylistic equivalence). Despite its being a polemic, *Notes* is castigated for, amongst other things, seeming to be a parody of structuralism, being selective in its historical examples, of playing fast and loose with language, and of being rhetorically sinister, whatever that may mean. Given Lodge's curiously, though predictably pedantic, Anglo-Saxon distaste and his efforts to pick Ackroyd up over his use of words, one wonders whether Lodge imagines Ackroyd quite literally writing the book with his left hand for the purposes of obscurity. Also telling of Lodge's native insecurity is the fact that he criticizes Ackroyd for suggesting an alternative beginning for modernism with the Age of Reason, historically prior to the then institutionally recognized beginnings of modernism at the end of the nine-

teenth century. Lodge's review is nothing so much as pompous in its pedantry and achieves a sort of middle-brow high-fallutin-ness (if such a paradox is possible, and with the English I've no doubt it is) which is telling about the degree to which Ackroyd's critique of Anglo-Saxon modernism provides a palpable hit, for all its selectivity and minor flaws. Had Lodge's pedantry been of a different sort, he might have given attention to the first word of the title: *Notes*. With its musical tenor, recalling the synesthesic effects of Ackroyd's poetry and anticipating *English Music*, the music of the spheres of Dr Dee, and the Music Hall songs of *Dan Leno*, the term also, and, most obviously, implies annotations rather than fully-fleshed – if Lodge will forgive me mixing my metaphors – prescriptions which, as that 'for' suggests, gesture towards, sketch out a possible route on the way to a 'New Culture'. The title itself of course reads parodically, and therefore politically, by seeming to invoke obviously T. S. Eliot's *Notes Towards the Definition of Culture* (1948). The *for* of the title is reminiscent also of translations from French of titles, where *pour* means both *for* and *towards*. Whichever way we choose to read it, *Notes for a New Culture* plays with critical and cultural expectations even before we open the book.

Not that Christopher Ricks bothers in his review to look at the cultural and critical expectations to any extent, happy as he is to criticize errors of fact (1976). Like Lodge, he gets greatly exercised over the essay, to the extent that he mixes his own metaphors (can an oasis in fact be buoyed up by a swell?) in criticizing the book's claims that its position is a somewhat isolated critical stance. However, this aside, Ricks never really engages the argument of the book, so annoyed is he at a number of egregious errors of fact and spelling. (Ackroyd was to correct these in the second edition.) Important, however, is the use to which the errors are put. For, as Brian Finney points out in his article on *Chatterton*, Ricks focuses on the mistakes as a way of avoiding a 'head-on' confrontation with Ackroyd's argument (Finney 1992, 242). What we can take away from this review is that, like Martin Dodsworth and David Lodge, Christopher Ricks is sufficiently disturbed by any challenge to English cultural assumptions. This is most tellingly shown when Ricks, criticizing Ackroyd's truly dreadful error concerning date correspondences between Tennyson and Mallarmé, recoils at 'that exclamatory put-down of my native land' (1976). This and Ricks's use of what he calls 'Anglo-French' are, quite possibly, intended to be funny; instead, these remarks sit there on the page like mother's cold rice pudding, unwanted at the Sunday dinner table.

2. T. S. Eliot's notion of 'Time present and time past' present in 'time future', and the latter contained in 'time past' (Eliot 1983, 189) may be said to be an important image for Ackroyd's own conception of time, as reviewers have, on occasion, noted. On the relationship between the text of Eliot and Ackroyd's work, see Onega (1998, 3, 9, 16–18, 20, 23).

3. Ackroyd has commented on a number of occasions on the importance of Catholicism as a submerged cultural trace in the construction of Englishness (as in the interviews in this book), most recently in the context of discussing London in an interview with Tim Adams, in 'A Life Sentence: London's Biographer', *The Observer* (1 March, 1998). See Onega on the significance of Catholicism, in her discussion of Ackroyd's *The Life of Thomas More* (1998, 77–9).

4. I take this term from a somewhat overlooked study by Leonard Orr, *Problems and Poetics of the Nonaristotelian Novel* (1991). The nonaristotelian novel is one which consciously avoids linear narrative progression and plays a variety of games with the temporal. It is not concerned primarily with organicist aesthetics, and neither is

it overly concerned with issues of strictly logical development centred on plot and/or character. A brief survey of some of more negative reviews of Ackroyd's fictions demonstrate an implicit focus on Aristotelian-derived aesthetics as the model by which to judge whether Ackroyd's characters are 'believable', whether his plots seem too 'contrived', whether the whole is organically convincing or not.

5. François Gallix's article on *English Music* begins by alerting the reader to the intertextual tradition to which Ackroyd belongs through a description of Jorge Luis Borges' short story, 'Pierre Ménard, author of *Quixote*', as, 'probably', 'la limite extrême de l'intertextualité' (1997, 218).

6. As the list of authors above shows, and as John Peck points out, 'the kind of novel' written by Ackroyd is equally, if not more so, the production of 'non-British authors' (Peck 1994, 442).

7. Not only does the label 'postmodernist' ignore the historical instance of similar forms of writing having existed prior to the moment of so called 'postmodernism', the 'question of whether or not Ackroyd is a post-modernist novelist is in the end irrelevant' (Peck 1994, 450). John Peck makes a convincing argument for seeing Ackroyd's saturation of his works with literary echoes and references as being closer, in its ironic and sceptical performativity, to Joycean devices (1994, 450).

8. See also Onega's discussion of Ackroyd's sense of the play in language (1998, 6–7).

9. Laura Giovannelli makes explicit certain of the connections between Ackroyd's *Notes* and T. S. Eliot's *Notes Towards the Definition of Culture*, which relationship she describes in terms of Harold Bloom's notion of the 'anxiety of influence' (1996, 12–13). Without going into the possible connections, it is perhaps important that we read the difference between the two titles. Ackroyd's is the more tentative of the two, speaking of 'a new culture'; Eliot's on the other hand, proposes to begin *the* definition, rather than one among many, of the existing culture.

10. How exactly should we read, for example, Spenser Spender's comment to his wife that, if a line could be drawn between the churches of Nicholas Hawksmoor, this would form a pentangle? (See Onega 1998, 43, 48.) Are we meant to believe that Spender has discovered this, or that he has read, like Peter Ackroyd, Iain Sinclair's *Lud Heat*? Or that Ackroyd, even at this point in his career, already had the idea of writing *Hawksmoor*?

11. Fires occur in a number of Ackroyd's novels. *Chatterton* and *Doctor Dee* both contain conflagration, as do *Hawksmoor*, which is generated partly and indirectly from the 'real' Great Fire of London, and *First Light*.

12. The family name and the alliteration of Spenser Spender also suggest Stephen Spender, but this is not to say that we can take this any further than noticing the chance resemblance. Fancifully, it might even be noted that the name sounds like 'suspense suspender'; playfully, it promises to reiterate itself partially, but suspends itself from doing so, even as it might be taken to be a definition of the halting work of a mysterious narrative! Susana Onega also suggests the echo of the name of 'the founder of evolutionist philosophy Herbert Spenser' (1998, 28).

13. T. S. Eliot, *The Waste Land*, in *Collected Poems 1909–1962* (1963) (London: Faber, 1974: pp. 61–86), p. 65. Eliot's phrase is, of course, well-known, virtually a cliché for defining the city. An interesting coincidence, and probably nothing more, is that, while Eliot's poem begins with April, the cruellest month (as is equally well known), the chapter from which the description of the set is taken (Ch. 19, Part II) begins with the arrival of Spring in London (*GFOL* 105). Further chance 'cross-fertilization' between Ackroyd and Eliot may be read in Eliot's own citation of

Edmund Spenser, in 'The Fire Sermon'. The arrival of Spring causes the city to appear to melt at the edges, anticipating the unreality, blurring the representation, and this is described through parodic simile on Ackroyd's part, like 'frozen food which is placed upon a warm plate' (*GFOL* 105). As much as Ackroyd's simile sounds as though it might be a parody of some Dickensian description of the city, updated to the late twentieth century, it also serves to remind us of the meal shared by the 'young man carbuncular' and the 'typist home at teatime'. These are, it has to be said, no more than echoes, intentional or otherwise; standard intertextual referentiality (perhaps). We do not wish to pursue these any further, but merely alert the reader to their possibility, as an example of the extent to which the text of Peter Ackroyd is traced densely with numerous other texts.

14. Compare, for example, the appearances of Amy in *The Great Fire of London* with those in *Dickens* (*D* 107–12), in which, for example, Little Dorrit and Maggie chance to meet with the celebrated author, and conduct him to an interview with the father of the Marshalsea. Ackroyd's interest in fathers who fail in some manner finds a felicitous connection in both Dickens's own life and the Dorrit family.

15. Fun City first appears in Ackroyd's prose poem 'Across the street...' (*DP* 42), in which the proprietor is not Arthur but Joe.

16. Travesty, in the sense of burlesque or parody, is also implied here, as is the now rare noun *travestiment*, which predates transvestism, and also carries a sense of the theatrical and performative. Originally an alteration of dress or disguise, travesty has of course come to mean a derisive or ludicrous imitation of a serious literary work, to quote the OED. But then, at what level is the serious separable from the ludicrous, either in Wilde or Ackroyd?

17. For the reader with an eye to the intertextual, Ackroyd not only has Wilde – who is later to appear in a cameo role seated in the British Library, alongside Karl Marx and George Gissing, in *Dan Leno and the Limehouse Golem* – refer to Chatterton (*LTOW* 67), but also to Dan Leno himself (*LTOW* 117), whose ability to mimic 'the voice of a washer-woman or the strange gait of a variety actress' strikes the fictive Wilde as 'quite alarming' (*LTOW* 117). The labyrinth of casual connections which Ackroyd traces is seen in this example to be without immediate semantic purpose, other than to evoke the 'truth' of a certain milieu or cultural moment. However, given that Wilde is used to comment on another London celebrity, one whose own life was defined by dressing up, cutting a caper and doing a turn, we can at least acknowledge a recurrent play of tropes within the urban setting which speak of performance and the assumption of identities.

18. Nicholas Hawksmoor worked for and with Wren, but the design of his churches is significantly different from those of the other architect. The 'Church Building Act of 1711 was responsible for six marvellous Hawksmoor churches – St Alfege in Greenwich, St Anne Limehouse, Christ Church Spitalfields, St George-in-the-East (Stepney), St George's Bloomsbury and the City church of St Mary Woolnoth' (Porter 1994, 124).

19. The theatrical metaphors used by Hollinghurst are an important acknowledgement of Ackroyd's performance, even though, arguably, the reviewer intends them as a criticism.

20. The effect I'm describing here is a little like the play between Jane Austen's knowing parody of Ann Radcliffe's gothic novels in *Northanger Abbey* and those elements of Radcliffe's own fiction which tend, all too readily, to lend themselves to a parodic reading ahead of Austen's efforts. The question that begs to be asked is: is it possible to parody that which is already available to parodic discernment?

21. Swope, Janik and Luc Herman each address the issue of mystery in their essays (Swope 1998, 222; Janik 1995, 173; Herman 1990, 122).

22. Even the critical effort is sometimes aimed at explaining the past, inadvertently making the past more believable because explained at greater length. In an exemplary reading, Susana Onega addresses the dualism of Dyer's time between scientific rationalism and hermetic tradition (1991, 117–38). She focuses on Dyer's knowledge of the 'Scientia Umbrarum', an 'occult science developed out of neolithic, hermetic, cabbalistic and gnostic elements' (Onega 1998, 45).

23. It is perhaps worth mentioning that Ned, in his previous identity, was a printer in Bristol. Bristol is also the home of printer Samuel Joynson, who printed the historical Thomas Chatterton's verse, and who, in the novel *Chatterton*, will fake documents supposedly written by Chatterton. There is no other discernible connection to be made, except to observe how Ackroyd's fictions, once again, not only conflate and disjoint the supposedly separate identities of fact and fiction, but also appear to connect to one another. See Richard Swope's essay (1998) which discusses the character of Ned.

24. In looking for other connections it has been noted by reviewers that Dyer's servant's name is Eliot, as one possible connection to the poet, while, in *Chatterton* , where other references to Eliot occur, the poet Charles Wychwood's wife is named Vivien, although the resemblance between her and the first Mrs Eliot ends with the name, as both Dennis Donoghue and David Lodge are quick to point out in their respective reviews of the novel (1988). The question is, once more, are we to make anything of this? Is Ackroyd being anything more than playful through such allusions? More importantly, how are we to distinguish between playful play and serious play? How, indeed are we to read 'play' at all as it resonates between its innumerable and undecidable registers? We cannot: play destabilizes, ahead of the effort to read, any identity which we might seek to assign it. In displaying its play, play displaces.

25. Jean-Pierre Audigier gives an interesting account of Ackroyd's use of nursery rhymes in his 'L'Apocryphe selon Ackroyd' (1994, 139–50). He suggests that the use of rhymes belongs to the process of the erasing the distinctions between fiction and history. Nursery rhymes, argues Audigier, are at the 'heart of hermetic semiosis', they serve an apparently oracular function even while they themselves are articulated at the 'limits of non-sense', and are inscribed with a certain 'thematic violence' which is both archetypal and primitive (142). Audigier goes on to suggest that, in the form of the nursery rhyme, we find nothing other than a textual form which, in its infancy figures the playful collapse between fiction and history which is Ackroyd's principal concern (143). Audigier continues by considering Ackroyd's use of citation, arguing that citation always ruptures and displaces the idea of continuity (145).

    The persistence of the nursery rhyme in the city echoes from *Hawksmoor* to *The House of Doctor Dee*, when Daniel Moore sings 'London Bridge is falling down, falling down, falling down' (*HDD* 17).

26. I have given the briefest paraphrase of Giovannelli's discussion, which runs as follows:

    'In *Hawksmoor* la congiunzione fra I due mondi risulta, insomma, prorogata fino all'ultimo e annunciata da una serie innumerevole di parallelismi, che coinvolgono la dimensione spaziale, il frasario (nonostante lo *spelling* e la sintassi arcaicizzianti delle sezioni dedicato al passato), la gestualità, la distribuzione dei ruoli e persino dei nomi all'interno delle narrazioni. Gli eventi più importanti hanno

luogo nel quartiere di Scotland Yard e nei dintorni di un gruppo di chiese londi-
nesi; frasi e dialoghi vengono spesso riecheggiati da voci anonime o individui
stranamente rassomiglianti agli interlocutori originali, e comunque sempre
accompagnati dalla riconoscibile 'musica' di sottofondo di ritornelli, proverbi e
children's rhymes, intonati perennemente nelle strade della città.' (1996, 107)

27. Dust may be read as a trace in the sense given the word by Emmanuel Levinas. The
trace is that signification of the other which is unconvertible into the same. The
trace seems to signify yet cannot be translated, made part of the same, part of self-
identity. The trace places us, Levinas argues, in a relationship with an immemorial
past. The trace 'signifies beyond being' and 'obliges us' to acknowledge this (1986,
356). We cannot develop a fully Levinasian reading of *Hawksmoor* here, although
we do gesture towards such a possibility at another time.

Interchapter

1. With the exception of the obvious citation from *The Waste Land*, and one other, all
the lines come from texts by Peter Ackroyd. The other quotation is from a recent
novel of Iain Sinclair's.

2. The discussion of the different aspects or interpretations of time owes much to
Peter Osbourne's reading of time, especially his discussions of Paul Ricoeur's analysis of temporality and narrative in the four volumes of *Time and Narrative* (1984–8),
in Osbourne's *The Politics of Time* (1995). Osbourne focuses specifically on Ricoeur's
consideration of 'historical' as opposed to 'fictional' time, and reads exclusively
from volumes 1 and 3. His discussion thus concerns itself primarily with 'philosophical' and not 'literary' issues. My interest here is with the perception of time
and Ackroyd's narrative unfolding of temporal ludics, which, as I shall suggest,
seeks to effect a collapse between the distinctions of historical and fictional time,
while still retaining the sense of the complex relationship between personal and
cosmological time as expressed through the act of narration.
   Equally important on the subject of narrative and time has been Mark Currie's
lucid and compelling analysis in *Postmodern Narrative Theory* (1998), particularly
'Narrative Time and Space' (73–113).

3. Compare the passages with those ending Chapters 11 and 12 of *Hawksmoor* (H 209,
217), where the speaking subject confronts time and eternity as the hiatus in the
narrative of the self.

4. See in the chapter following the discussion of the final pages of *English Music*,
which, in playing with figures suggesting circular closure and continuity, displace
those very same figures. See also the discussion of *First Light* below, on the desire for
narrative.

5. Marion Hobson's exemplary study, *Jacques Derrida: Opening Lines*, is one of the few
studies of Derrida's work to connect in a rigorous fashion issues of form and
content. In the sections from which I am quoting (75–88) she makes the convincing case for Derrida's subversion of phenomenology, and I gratefully acknowledge
my indebtedness to her discussion.

6. It is perhaps worth reiterating at this moment that Ackroyd is not a 'Derridean' or
'deconstructive' novelist, as Martin Dodsworth has claimed. As can be seen from a
careful reading of *Notes for a New Culture*, Ackroyd's comprehension of the condition of writing and subjectivity stems as much from his reading of continental
poetics and the modern tradition, from Mallarmé to Denis Roche, as does Derrida's.

3. The Styles of Peter Ackroyd II

1. Laura Giovannelli provides a brief, though thorough, biographical history of Thomas Chatterton and the fortunes of his publications (1996, 147–51).
2. 'The modern hero of Mr. Ackroyd's novel is a failed, doomed poet .... He has a precocious son and a splendid wife named, like [T. S.] Eliot's first wife, Vivien, but unlike that woman in virtually every respect' (Donoghue 1988).

   'The chief good guy is a youngish unpublished and unemployed poet, Charles Wychwood, with a wife, Vivien (the name of Eliot's neurotic first wife, though there the resemblance ends – Vivien Wychwood is a simple soul, with an uncomplicated devotion to her husband), and a young son, Edward' (Lodge 1988).

   'Charles sees nothing wrong with what he considers a perfectly natural act of literary appropriation. In fact he opens his preface to his planned book on Chatterton: "Thomas Chatterton believed that he could explain the entire material and spiritual world in terms of imitation and forgery ..." (126). How fitting that Charles's defence of plagiarism should itself be a double act of plagiarism. In the first place the opening of Charles's sentence has been lifted verbatim from the catalogue to the exhibition of Art Brut at the art gallery where Charles's wife, Vivien (cf. Vivien Eliot), works (109–10)' (Finney 1992, 253).
3. That 'Poor Tom' is a disguise for an illegitimate son has a number of complex resonances for Ackroyd's work as a whole, in the context of the constant return to the subject of fathers and sons, heritage and inheritance, whether culturally or biologically. This is not so much a case of standard intertextual referentiality as it is an acknowledgement that, to paraphrase Jacques Derrida's well known phrase, there is no outside-the-text.
4. We might perhaps ask, without too much impertinence, if the figure of Scrope is not one possible transvestitic performance of Ackroyd himself, dressing himself as his comic other, given that he readily admits to borrowing from other writers, other styles, other periods.
5. Meredith dresses up in the guise of another, although the transvestism is of an historical, rather than gender-bending variety.
6. Leno clearly can be read as anticipating Ackroyd's eighth novel, *Dan Leno and the Limehouse Golem* as Susana Onega points out (1998, 34), as well as the historical figure of Dan Leno (George Galvin), the cross-dressing comedic star of late Victorian music hall. The figure thus seems to suspend the seriousness of critical inquiry for the name inscribes an aporetic moment of undecidability between the possibility of intertextual meaningfulness, and yet one more chance example of random chatter. The oscillation here makes it impossible to decide, except on the undecidable.

   An important study of the perceived threat posed by music hall is that by Dagmar Kift (1996). Although it makes no mention of Dan Leno, it does provide an excellent study of the late Victorian context of music hall, especially in London, in Chapter 7 (135–54).
7. Derrida discusses the syntagm 'my death' in the essay 'Finis' (1993a, 1–42), beginning with the question: 'Is my death possible?' (21ff.)
8. The assumption that it should 'add up' is a reviewing assumption based on the kind of algebraic formula that if Peter Ackroyd = Peter Ackroyd, Peter Ackroyd is therefore not John Grisham; or Patricia Cornwall; or, to put that another way, Ackroyd is read as a 'serious' or 'weighty' or 'intellectual' novelist, one who writes the 'novel of ideas' (as opposed to the novel without ideas); therefore, Peter Ackroyd must add up

to something, or Peter Ackroyd is letting the reader down by not playing the game of being himself.

9. At one moment, Timothy Harcombe recalls how his father had always begun his shows at the Chemical Theatre by singing 'Jerusalem': '... and now whenever I hear "Jerusalem" the swelling voices take me back' (*EM* 3).

10. We have placed 'Leavisite' in scare quotes as a means of signalling that Leavis was, himself, merely one privileged agent in the discourse of a certain Englishness and not its originator. His articulation of an English tradition found a ready audience and gained ground so comparatively surely and quickly because the sense of Englishness articulated indirectly by Leavis through his criticism was, during the post-war period, a significant voicing of a desired construction of national identity. This sense of identity, and the qualities which inform the sense of self, predates the critic and which had suffered a series of assaults and uncertainties in a post-Victorian world. As a highly schematic sketch, we might provisionally suggest that, in a national cultural context, the isolation of the English self finds exemplary articulation in Matthew Arnold's 'To Marguerite – Continued' and 'Dover Beach' (Arnold 1979, 129–31, 253–7), the former stressing that isolation, the latter the desire for continuity, from Sophocles and the 'Sea of Faith' to the present moment of self-reflection; and both of which, in turn, are responded to, more or less indirectly, in at least two modernist instances: in E.M. Forster's longing desire to 'only connect', (1910; 1983), and in Eliot's *The Waste Land* (once more), when that cited voice remarks '"I can connect nothing with nothing"' (1974, 74). From Dover Beach to Margate Sands, this at least is a tentative 'connecting the dots' in the delineation of a particular Englishness, which it becomes the mission of English criticism to firm up and affirm, where 'only connect' becomes not an elegiac longing so much as an occasionally strident command.

11. Bunyan is more complicated than this suggests, even if his reception and interpretation is not. Ackroyd points to Bunyan as a figure of what he calls the 'first modernism' in English culture, in *Notes for a New Culture*. Bunyan is described as constructing a 'counter-mythology ... of the Word which counters the rational and transparent discourse of the first modernism' (*NNC* 41). As Ackroyd goes on to suggest, Bunyan, like Blake after him, conceived of himself as a traditionalist, 'more profoundly orthodox than [his] contemporaries' (*NNC* 41).

12. As a measure of Timothy's selectiveness and Englishness, the reader may choose to compare it with a list offered by T.S. Eliot in *Notes Towards the Definition of Culture*: 'It includes all the characteristic activities and interests of a people: Derby Day, Henley Regatta, Cowes, the twelfth of August, a cup final, the dog races, the pin table, the dart board, Wenslydale cheese, boiled cabbage cut into sections, beetroot in vinegar, nineteenth-century Gothic churches and the music of Elgar. The reader can make his own list. And then we have to face the strange idea that what is part of our culture is also a part of our *lived* religion' (1948, 30). There is a selectivity at work here which seeks to present a unified national cultural identity, which begins and ends with 'highbrow' events and tastes, while neatly containing working-class tastes and entertainments. As Ackroyd points out in his biography of Eliot, it is difficult to tell from *Notes* whether Eliot is using the term 'culture' in a neutral sense or whether it is a diagnostic tool (*TSE* 292). This ambiguity is similar to the dual impulse of liberalism and conservatism identified above in the work of F. R. Leavis, and may well be yet another marker itself of Englishness. The point is that Timothy's selectiveness is wholly predictable within various versions of cultural definition.

13. 'La bambina rincuorata dalla musica melodiosa del nuovo *bird* (O, per meglio dire, *Byrd*) non può, naturalmente, chiamarsi altro che Cecilia' (1996, 238).

14. *First Light* also plays with the possibility of meaning, but rejects this as anything other than the reader's desire to find a pattern in its final page: 'Once this region was thought to form the outline of a face in the constellation of Taurus. He smiled at his shadow. But the Pleiades contains three hundred stars in no real pattern' (*FL* 328). Even this comment is not stable, however, for, recounted by the narratorial voice in the final chapter, these words first appear as a remark of astronomer, Damian Fall, in the opening chapter (*FL* 4). See the following chapter on this novel.

15. Phrases concerning beginnings and ends can be found in most of Ackroyd's novels, not to mention the more general concern with questions concerning genesis and eschatology, and their narrative interchangeability.

16. Milton's experience or vision may be compared, not too fancifully, with that of Kurtz in *Heart of Darkness*. Milton's moment of revelation leads him to the desire to 'exterminate all the brutes', to recall Kurtz once more (Conrad 1995, 84). Interestingly, – no more than chance perhaps? – there are readable other possible connections. Marlow's description of the Russian looking like a harlequin (1995, 87), escaped from a 'troupe of mimes' (1995, 90) and being dressed in motley, in 'particoloured rags' (1995, 90), is comparable partly with the description of Ralph Kempis' and the Catholics' dress:

> His clothes had been made of some stuff that was brown holland probably, but it was covered with patches all over, with bright patches, blue, red, and yellow, – patches on the back, patches on the front, patches at the elbows, on knees; coloured binding round his jacket, scarlet edging at the bottom of his trousers; and the sunshine made him look extremely gay and wonderfully neat withal, because you could see how beautifully all this patching had been done.
>
> (Conrad 1995, 87)

> 'Fellow of sanguine humour. Face very large and ruddy like a bowl of cherries. Beard as red as the tail of a fox .... Frock-coat of blue, with a green band around his waist. And on his head, oh Lord, a hat of white felt with some feathers sticking from it.'
>
> (*MA* 165)

> 'They are wearing clothes, sir, as brightly coloured as the drapers' livery. But it is not exactly London dress. Nor is it exactly Indian. It is somewhere betwixt the two.'
>
> (*MA* 165)

> The male inhabitants, Indian and English alike, were dressed in the strangest mixture of striped breaches, wide shirts and feathered caps.
>
> (*MA* 183)

It may also be worthwhile remembering that Conrad's novel was the original source for an epigraph for T.S. Eliot's *The Waste Land*. While Pound on that occasion dissuaded Eliot, the poet would use the line 'Mistah Kurtz – he dead' as the epigraph for the later poem, 'The Hollow Men' (1974, 87). On clothing as part of the carnivalesque aspect of *Milton in America* see below.

17. On the subjects of *anamnesis* and the blindness of memory, see Derrida's *Memoirs of the Blind* (1993, esp. 45f.)

18. While Ackroyd's Milton no doubt intends to use 'vulgar' in a wholly pejorative sense, the original meaning of the word was simply 'the common people' or the 'common tongue', the vernacular.

19. See Barker's discussion of Milton's *Areopagitica* (1984, 41–55), which, as Barker points out, is a key text in the shift from the essentially collaborative production of play-texts, to the 'individual production' (50) of the written text, signed in the name of the author. Also, as Barker suggests, Milton's text, despite its overt expression against censorship, speaks decisively on self-discipline as a controlling factor in the formation of modern subjectivity (46–7). Ackroyd's Milton may not be the John Milton who wrote *Paradise Lost*, but he is somewhat similar, albeit in a highly schematized form, to the Milton who wrote the *Areopagitica* in 1644. As an expression of the 'privacy' of communion between the individual and God, and also as a rejection of otherness, given specific form in the examples of Judaism, Catholicism, and Paganism, see Milton's anti-episcopal essay 'Of Reformation Touching Church-Discipline' (1641; 1979, 77–111). Both this and *Areopagitica* were written, ironically for this discussion of *Milton in America,* while the historical John Milton could still see. However, while the historical Milton does describe Rome as the 'womb and center of Apostacy' in 'Of Reformation', thereby holding certain views in common with Ackroyd's Milton, he differs significantly from the novelist's creation, not least in his understanding of the necessity – at least in principle – for heterogeneity in the body politic, as this remark shows: 'And because things simply pure are inconsistent in the masse of nature, nor are the elements or humors in Mans Body exactly *homogeneall*, and hence the best founded Common-wealths, and least barbarous have aym'd at a certaine mixture and temperament, partaking the severall vertues of each other State ...' (1979, 105–6). That Ackroyd's Milton is then a 'cartoon Milton', to recall John Clute's definition, and markedly dissimilar from the historical Milton is not in doubt. It would be well, however, not to measure the possible similarities and differences as a means of assessing the 'reality' of Ackroyd's Milton, but, rather, to read him as a figure through whom Ackroyd addresses particular issues.

    Chance connections allow the reader to speculate that one of the shaping influences on Ackroyd in the composition of his Milton was Ezra Pound's view of the poet, whom the latter disliked for 'his asinine bigotry, his beastly hebraism, the coarseness of his mentality' (Pound 1954, 238).

20. From this definition of carnival as mobile in its intermixing effects, it is possible to suggest that Peter Ackroyd's work is, generally, carnivalesque, in its combinations of high and low, of profundity, erudition and camp comedy. Certainly it is the deformity of form's purity in Ackroyd's texts which causes the most problems for any number of his reviewers.

21. Onega usefully compares the settlers' and Indians' clothing, with the descriptions of dress in Thomas More's *Utopia* (1998, 75).

22. On the distinction between the classical and grotesque bodies, see Stallybrass and White (1986, 21–22).

4. Writing the City

1. Unfortunately, none of *Secret London*, which is due to be published in 2000, was available at the time of writing this chapter.

2. On the unstable and ineffable nature of the city in writing, see my *Writing London: The Trace of the Urban Text from Blake to Dickens* (1998), in which London's resistance

to comprehension and its determination of the shapes of writing in the nineteenth century are discussed.

3. Sinclair's writing on, and of, the city is shaped within a more restricted range of concerns than is Ackroyd's. Principally, Sinclair's comprehension of the city is that of the 'psychogeographer', the writer or artist whose work is shaped according to the understanding of the psychic or spiritual persistence of similar events which recur on the same sites within the city. Ackroyd's writing may be said to belong on occasions to the pyschogeographical, as, most obviously, with *Hawksmoor*, which, Ackroyd acknowledges, is informed and influenced by Sinclair's *Lud Heat*. Also, the psychogeographical element is evident in novels such as *The House of Doctor Dee* and *Dan Leno and the Limehouse Golem*, where, in the latter, violent, often ritualized murders occur, again and again over the centuries, within a few square miles of London. However, Ackroyd's writing does not restrict itself to the psychogeographer's interests, and is, arguably, just as concerned with issues of economic power in the city or the importance of popular entertainment in the psychic and material history of London. Almost all Sinclair's novels deal extensively with the city's occult history in one form or another, but the least oblique of his publications, and the one which directs the interested reader to other psychogeographers, is *Lights Out for the Territory* (1997). On the relationship between writing, the city, and spectrality, see my 'The Hauntological Example: The City as the Haunt of Writing in the Texts of Iain Sinclair' (1998, 138–58).

4. The phrase 'pierce or move his infant breast' echoes, arguably, with resonances of Blake's *Songs of Innocence and Songs of Experience*. Similarly, the concluding words – 'landscapes of his imagination' (*D* 21) – of the chapter from *Dickens* cited above, recalls the line from *Jerusalem*, 'My Streets are my, Ideas of Imagination' (Ch. 2, Plate 34).

5. Of course, Ackroyd adds to the urban grafting in *Dan Leno and the Limehouse Golem*, by having the murder of a family take place on the same site as the 'real' Ratcliffe Highway Murders. One might also add to this potentially endless equation 'The Cadaver Club' by Iain Sinclair, which cites both Ackroyd's novel and De Quincey's essay on 'Murder', as well as managing to include John Dee, T. S. Eliot, and Oscar Wilde (Sinclair 1997, 331–71).

6. Ackroyd's Gissing chooses the term 'crepuscular', which is echoed in Nicholas Meyer's review of the novel, quoted in the first paragraph of this chapter. Far from suggesting any possible connection between the two journalists, the recurrence does indicate in a simple manner the way in which the city dictates the acts of writing concerning it.

7. We might note one further brief resonance between *Dickens* and *Dan Leno*. One of the early literary influences on Dickens is noted as being George Colman's *Broad Grins*, 'a rather ghastly collection of verse stories' (*D* 65), in which there was one story, 'The Elder Brother', a London narrative which so struck Dickens in its description of Covent Garden, according to John Forster, that Dickens was compelled to compare Colman's verse with the reality of the market. In *Dan Leno and the Limehouse Golem*, one of Elizabeth Cree's most successful transvestite performances is as 'The Older Brother' (*DLLG* 151f.)

8. Readers might compare the descriptions of London street life in the biography of More, with the following stanzas from *London Lykpeny* (Ackroyd cites l.66 in the biography, as an authority for his own depiction), noting particularly, the author's use of street traders' cries, acknowledgement of which can be found not only in *More* but also in *Blake* and *Dickens*. Also worthy of note, in the first stanza, are the

exotic mix of fruits and spices, which support Ackroyd's contention in *Thomas More* that medieval London would have born a greater resemblance to a *souk* or middle eastern bazaar, than to the modern day city (see the discussion of this in the chapter):

> In to London I gan me hy;
> Of all the lond it bearethe the prise.
> 'Hot pescods!' one gan cry,
> 'Strabery rype, and chery in the ryse!'
> One bad me come nere and by some spice;
> Pepar and saffron they gan me bede, Clove, grayns, and flowre of rise.
> For lacke of money I might not spede.
>
> Then into Chepe I gan me drawne,
> Where I sawe stond moche people.
> One bad me come nere, and by fine cloth of lawne,
> Paris thred, coton, and umple.
> I seyde there-upon I could no skyle,
> I am not wont there-to in dede.
> One bad me by an hewre, my hed to hele:
> For lake of money I might not spede.
>
> Then went I forth by London Stone
> Thrwghe-outy all Canywike strete.
> Drapers to me they called anon;
> Grete chepe of cloth, they gan me hete;
> Then come there one, and cried 'Hot shepes fete!'
> 'Rishes faire and grene,' an othar began to grete;
> Both melwell and makarell I gan mete,
> But for lacke of money I myght not spede.
>
> Then I hied me into Estchepe.
> One cried, 'Ribes of befe, and many a pie!'
> Pewtar potts they clatteryd on a heape.
> There was harpe, pipe and sawtry.
> 'Ye by Cokke!' 'Nay by Cokke!' some began to cry;
> Some sange of Jenken and Julian, to get themselves mede.
> Full fayne I wold hadd of that mynstralsie,
> But for lacke of money I cowld not spede.

(1996, ll. 65–96)

9. As if to suggest the never-ending process of writing the city, each year a new quill is placed in the hand of the statue of John Stow.
10. This phrase is also chosen as the subtitle of this section of the chapter on the biographers as a definition of Ackroyd's own writing of the city. Ackroyd might thus, once again, and in a different fashion, be understood as writing himself into the 'tradition' of urban writing.
11. See, for example, the words put teasingly in Dee's mouth: 'I take up the pages which the canting beggar gave to me in the garden, but can see only a certain kind of curious writing in the English tongue. There are the words "house" and "father",

all closely inscribed, but in the gathering darkness I can read nothing more. So I light my candle and watch its fire. As the darkness is lifted the wax is consumed: the substance does not die but is transformed into flame. This is the final lesson. By means of that fire the material form of the candle before me rises into its spiritual being. It has become a light and a shining within this poor shambling room, my library' (*HDD* 79). Arguably, it is possible to read this passage as a certain gathering or a pulling together of numerous threads throughout the novel, some of which are discussed in the body of the chapter. Although Dee lights his candle, what remains of the text is left unread, as the two words in proximity, reproduced in Dee's discourse, are left to resonate. Ackroyd plays with the reader here in a number of ways, as he has Dee consider the transformation of material into flame, or light, or, perhaps, spirit which, in turn, illuminates. So, we might say, the material of the past comes to illuminate the identity of Matthew Palmer, the text of Peter Ackroyd, and the perception of the city. However, light not only emanates from some other place, it illuminates the self, as Palmer comes to recognize that which is projected onto him and that which is within him.

12. It is tempting to read this remark of Palmer's in the light of the critics' shared sense of flatness in the character of the policeman Hawksmoor, and that of his part of the narrative in *Hawksmoor*, already discussed. As suggested above, Hawksmoor is flat because he is such a literary cliché trapped within a genre notable more for its adherence to formula than for form-breaking departures. Palmer is a researcher of course, and so the statement has a certain local sense, in that he does produce a few words from within himself from time to time. But, importantly, he is also inscribed, his being or identity is written, not only by Ackroyd, but also by the city, its histories and narratives, to which he belongs. His identity is formed by the city, as is that of John Dee, who says 'I am of London though I was born elsewhere' (*HDD* 96).

13. For information about the 'peculiar' history of Clerkenwell, see the final interview with Peter Ackroyd in this volume (conducted in Clerkenwell), in which Ackroyd discusses the area, some of the details of which are also to be found in *The House of Doctor Dee*.

14. Piranesi is cited or otherwise mentioned in both *Dan Leno and the Limehouse Golem* (see in this chapter below) and in *The House of Doctor Dee* (*HDD* 43–4).

15. A useful future study of *The House of Doctor Dee* might consider the possible relationship between the Piranesian elements in Ackroyd's descriptions of buildings and the city and his adoption of the text of Paracelsus as a discourse on the construction of the body, put into the mouth of John Dee.

16. On the figure of light, and for an example of a certain play on Ackroyd's part between the figural and the literal, see note 11, above, and the passage quoted there.

17. Light is central to Dee's hermetic, alchemical discourse, and figures of projection and illumination recur throughout his thoughts on hermetic practice, often in relation to questions of spirit and being (*HDD* 75–8).

18. The correspondences hinted at by Ackroyd are dissonant because, as suggested elsewhere in this book, connections and symmetries are never exact in the novelist's writing, only apparently so. Connections are hinted at but fall into ruin, or are otherwise always already broken, fragmentary. Apparently mirrored images are only approximate, and there is always a degree of distortion in Ackroyd's play of structural resemblances.

19. The name of the passage allows Ackroyd to provide the reader with historical material pertaining to the area, while also hinting at possible imaginative links across

the centuries. In this passage and the one which follows, Matthew speculates that, although the Priory of St John of Jerusalem had long since vanished, the stones had been reused to build houses in Clerkenwell, and might even have been used to build his house. Then, looking at a neon clock, he recalls how sadastra, a stone greatly prized in the fourteenth century, would glow momentarily upon being broken open, likening the glow to that of the neon. This begins his meditation on the history of the area, leading to a memory of 'a multitude of voices' being heard in a telephone, and a dozen television screens glowing in a shop window, all with the same picture (*HDD* 40–1). In what is one of the more remarkably unsettling passages in an often disorienting novel, Ackroyd weaves together the haunted sense of the city which merges the significance of the proper name and the spectres who return via its inscription, while connecting this concern with the question of materiality. While Matthew dismisses the technology as 'all delusion, a trick of the cinematographer' (41), there is a sense here that Ackroyd is toying with possible connections between spectrality and tele-technology, which have been opened to discussion by Derrida in a number of texts, not least *Specters of Marx* (1994) but also in passing in 'Faith and Knowledge: the Two Sources of "Religion" at the Limits of Reason Alone' (1998), and in a more sustained fashion with Bernard Steigler in *Échographies: de la télévision. Entretiens filmés* (1996). Iain Sinclair also connects spectrality to technology and, in particular, the technology of surveillance in London, in *Lights Out for the Territory* (1996).

20. Prior to Ackroyd's apostrophe, Dee, having heard the words of Matthew and Daniel concerning the 'bridge of light', follows the two men until they enter 'a great house', which from its description we know to be the house inherited by Matthew Palmer (*HDD* 274). At this moment he encounters a 'child [who] stood on the threshold', who speaks of the projection of a light lasting a thousand years (*HDD* 274). Compare this image of the child standing on the threshold of the structure with the closing image of *Hawksmoor*: 'and I am a child again, begging on the threshold of eternity' (*H* 217).

21. On the limits of reading and the movement between materiality and the question of spirit, see note 11 above, and the passage cited there.

22. The phrase 'mystical city eternal' is doubly resonant. It echoes with the sound of Blake's 'four-fold city eternal', and thus suggests Ackroyd's biography of Blake, while it also catches at the phrase 'the Eternal City', which is commonly used to name Rome. As Jennifer Bloomer points out in passing, Freud has recourse to the phrase 'the Eternal City', with the archaeological and architectural layers of Rome in mind, when he seeks to describe the structure of the mind (and not, as Bloomer says, the brain; 1993, 72). Freud also draws on this phrase in seeking to analyse the persistence of Rome in his dreams (1991, 282–6; esp. 285, where Freud says he discovered the way in which his 'longing for the eternal city had been reinforced by impressions from my youth'). Freud's analogy between the structure of the mind and that of the eternal city or, as Ackroyd has it in a more Blakean manner, the city eternal, suggests the possibility of a more sustained reading of *The House of Doctor Dee* in which it would be possible perhaps to pursue the structural correlations between the question of human identity and that of the city in relation to the idea of the unconscious. If the folds and weaves of the city figure various repressed narrative strands spatially and, especially, across time, their return to Matthew Palmer is significant, in as much as they come to provide Matthew with a sense of self-awareness. As Juliet Flower MacCannell has pointed out to me, and for which I am most grateful, Lacan also alludes to both the Eternal City and Freud's analogy in 'The Function and Field of Speech and Language in Psychoanalysis' (1977, 30–113).

As one final note on the question of the eternal city, and perhaps as a pun on Ackroyd's part, an anonymous tramp asks Matthew Palmer, 'Do you bing Romewards?' (*HDD* 267).

23. The legend of the Golem has it that the creature was created of clay in 1580, in the city of Prague, by Rabbi Yehuda Lowe, or Judah Loew ben Bezalel. A creature brought to life by inscription, only ten letters were needed for its formation. Elie Wiesel provides a narrative account of the Golem in his *The Golem: The Story of a Legend* (1983), to which I am indebted.

24. For the purpose of reference, there are fifty-one chapters in *Dan Leno and the Limehouse Golem*, which have the narrative strands divided amongst them as follows:

Third-Person	Trial extracts from the *Illustrated Police News Law Courts and Weekly Record*	Elizabeth Cree	John Cree British Museum Ms. Ms. 1624/566
Ch. 1	Ch. 3	Ch. 4	Ch. 7
Ch. 2	Ch. 8	Ch. 13	Ch. 14
Ch. 5	Ch. 10	Ch. 17	Ch. 18
Ch. 6	Ch. 12	Ch. 20	Ch. 22
Ch. 9	Ch. 16	Ch. 25	Ch. 27
Ch. 11	Ch. 23	Ch. 31	Ch. 29
Ch. 15	Ch. 26	Ch. 38	Ch. 33
Ch. 19	Ch. 32	Ch. 40	Ch. 46
Ch. 21	Ch. 47	Ch. 42	
Ch. 24	Ch. 44		
Ch. 28			
Ch. 30			
Ch. 34			
Ch. 35			
Ch. 39			
Ch. 41			
Ch. 43			
Ch. 45			
Ch. 48			
Ch. 49			
Ch. 50			
Ch. 51			
The Morning Advertiser			
Ch. 37			

There appears to be no discernible significance to the division of the chapters.

25. The article 'Romanticism and Crime', attributed to Gissing by Ackroyd, appears to be invented. Attempts to locate it in any of the existing published bibliographies, either in print or on website, have failed. This approximates Ackroyd's invention of Wilde's journals in *The Last Testament of Oscar Wilde*, so that the reader is confronted with a fictional article, which is journalism and not a work of fiction, supposedly written by a fictional version of an author whose 'reality' is not in question, in which an equally 'real' work by another historical figure is cited. Thus, as a figure for the condition of the city's textuality, we recognize how a text can appear within an imagined text which itself is cited in a novel, the existence of which we can

verify because we have it in our hands. Such a labyrinthine and ludic gesture is indicative of the lengths to which Ackroyd goes in attempting to convey the spirit of London as he understands it, while also placing him in a textual tradition from Cervantes (at least) and Sterne, to Borges and beyond.

26. Questions of gender and the disturbance of identity are raised, either directly or obliquely, throughout *Dan Leno and the Limehouse Golem*. Solomon Weil is literally dis-membered, his genitals cut off and placed in the *Talmud*. 'Dressing up' in one form or another is a persistent interest in this novel, to the extent that most identities are read as being staged. As with the example just given, the court is viewed as a form of theatricality, while connections are made between stage and Roman Catholic church ritual. The detective inspector in charge of the case is revealed, late in the narrative and quite incidentally, to live in private with his gay lover. Both Elizabeth Cree and Dan Leno dress as men and women respectively when on stage (Elizabeth carrying on the practice of cross-dressing when off-stage), and there is much discussion throughout the novel by Elizabeth of the theatrical tradition of cross-dressing. At her trial, Lizzie corrects her impression of the judge, from thinking he looked like 'Pantaloon in the pantomime', to arrive at the judgement that the only part fit for him to play would be the Dame (*DLLG* 209). John Cree frequently draws on theatrical metaphors in his journal to describe both the murders and the city: 'I was a mere tyro, a beginner, an understudy who could not appear on the great stage without rehearsal. I had first to perfect my work in a secret hour, stolen from the tumult of the city ...' (*DLLG* 26; see also 60, 62). Elizabeth, upon first entering a theatre, finds a greater 'truth' in the staged representation of London, than in its reality: 'eventually the curtain was pulled aside ... it revealed a London street scene which, in the flickering gaslight, seemed ...the most wonderful sight in the world ... here was a picture of the Strand ... but how much more glorious and iridescent ...' (*DLLG* 18–19). The difference between John Cree's journal and Lizzie's impressions is that, in the former's accounts, theatricality always remains merely metaphorical. For Elizabeth Cree, however, theatricality, dressing up, the assumption of staged personae and the event of masquerade are the truth of the city and its inhabitants. Identity, Elizabeth recognizes, is assumed and not essential.

27. The remark of Babbage's is taken from *The Ninth Bridgewater Treatise: A Fragment*, 2nd ed. (1838). The treatises were 'sponsored by the will of the eighth Earl of Bridgewater, the Rev. Francis Henry Egerton FRS' (Campbell-Kelly 1989, 5). Despite its title, Babbage's was not one of the 'official' treatises, but a response to William Whewell's *Astronomy and General Physics*. The passages from which Babbage's remark is extracted are instructive:

> If man enjoyed a larger command over mathematical analysis, his knowledge of these motions would be more extensive; but a Being possessed of unbounded knowledge of that science, could trace every minutest consequence of that primary impulse. Such a Being, however far exalted above our race, would still be immeasurably below even our conception of infinite intelligence.
>
> But supposing the original conditions of each atom of the earth's atmosphere, as well as all the extraneous causes acting on it be / given, and supposing also the interference of no new causes, such a Being would be able clearly to trace its future but inevitable path, and He would distinctly foresee and might absolutely predict for any, even the remotest period of time, the circumstances and future history of every particle of that atmosphere.

Let us imagine a Being, invested with such knowledge, to examine at a distant epoch the coincidence of the facts with those which His profound analysis had enabled him to predict. If any slightest deviation existed, He would immediately read in its existence the action of a new cause; and, through the aid of the same analysis tracing this discordance back to its source, He would become aware of the time of its commencement, and the point of space at which it originated.

Thus considered, what a strange chaos is this wide atmosphere we breathe! Every / atom, impressed with good and with ill, retains at once the motions which philosophers and sages have imparted to it, mixed and combined in ten thousand ways with all that is worthless and base. The air itself is one vast library, on whose pages are forever written all that man has ever said or woman whispered. There, in their mutable but unerring characters, mixed with the earliest, as well as with the latest sighs of mortality, stand for ever recorded, vows unredeemed, promises unfulfilled, perpetuating in the united movements of each particle, the testimony of man's changeful will.

(Babbage 1989, 36)

Taken as a general statement of principal, it is tempting – is it not? – to read in this statement not only Ackroyd's comprehension of temporality, but also his approach to the construction of narrative, at least certainly with regard to the majority of his novels. Babbage's emphasis on the invisible, written record of the air, as opposed to the possible echo of voices, allows us to speculate, albeit tentatively, on Ackroyd's playful admixture of 'historical reality' with fictional narrative, of word and world. Furthermore, Babbage's comment on the ability to 'read' future events sheds light on temporal movement in more than one direction in novels such as *Hawksmoor*, *The House of Doctor Dee*, *First Light*, *Chatterton* and, of course, *Dan Leno*. Finally, Babbage's speculative fancy predates any notion of the postmodern, thereby allowing us once more to challenge the definition of Ackroyd's text as postmodernist in its playfulness.

Bibliography

Selected works by Peter Ackroyd
(including selected reviews and lectures)

Ouch. London: Curiously Strong Press, 1971.

London Lickpenny. London: Ferry Press, 1973.

Notes for a New Culture: An Essay on Modernism. London: Vision Press, 1976. New York: Barnes and Noble, 1976. Revised edition, London: Alkin Books, 1993.

'Three Poems by Peter Ackroyd'. In John Ashbery, ed., 'New English Poets'. *Partisan Review*. 44: 2 (1977): pp. 245–67.

Country Life. London: Ferry Press, 1978.

Dressing Up: Transvestism and Drag. The History of an Obsession. London: Thames and Hudson, 1979. New York: Simon and Schuster, 1979.

Ezra Pound and His World. London: Thames and Hudson, 1981. New York: Scribners, 1981.

The Great Fire of London. London: Hamish Hamilton, 1982. Chicago: University of Chicago Press, 1988. Rpt. London: Penguin, 1993.

The Last Testament of Oscar Wilde. London: Hamish Hamilton, 1983. New York: Harper, 1983. Rpt. London: Penguin, 1993.

T. S. Eliot: A Life. London: Hamish Hamilton, 1984a. New York: Simon and Schuster, 1984a.

'The Dark Forest'. Review of *The Company of Wolves*. *Spectator* (29 September 1984b).

(ed.) *PEN New Fiction II* London: Quartet Books, 1984c.

(ed.) *The Picture of Dorian Gray*. London: Penguin, 1985.

Hawksmoor. London: Hamish Hamilton, 1986. New York: Harper, 1986. Rpt. London: Abacus, 1986.

'Two Cultures, One Transplanted'. Review of *Milk and Honey*. *New York Times Book Review* (15 June 1986).

'Notes of an Investigative Son'. Review of *Family Secrets: A Writer's Search for His Parents and His Past*. *New York Times Book Review* (13 July 1986).

'A Killer Haunted by Smells'. Review of *Perfume*. *New York Times Book Review* (21 September 1986).

The Diversions of Purley and Other Poems. London: Hamish Hamilton, 1987. Rpt. London: Abacus, 1992.

'Under the Spell of Rawul'. Review of *Three Continents*. *New York Times Book Review* (23 August 1987).

'Oscar Wilde: Comedy as Tragedy'. *New York Times Book Review* (1 November 1987).

'Introduction'. In Piers Dudgen, *Dickens' London: An Imaginative Vision* (1987). London: Headline, 1994: pp. 7–20.

Chatterton. London: Hamish Hamilton, 1987. New York: Grove, 1988. Rpt. London: Penguin, 1993.

'The Knots and Loops of Literature'. Review of *The Essays of Virginia Woolf Vol. 2: 1912–1918*. *New York Times Book Reviews* (27 March 1988).

First Light. London: Hamish Hamilton, 1989. New York: Grove Weidenfeld, 1989. Rpt. New York: Grove, 1989.

Dickens. London: Sinclair-Stevenson, 1990. New York: Harper Collins, 1990. Rpt. London: Minerva, 1991.
Introduction to Dickens. London: Sinclair-Stevenson, 1991. New York: Ballantine, 1991.
'The Plantation House'. *New Statesman and Society Christmas Supplement* (December 1991): pp. 26–32.
English Music. London: Hamish Hamilton, 1992. New York: Knopf, 1992. Rpt. London: Penguin, 1993.
The House of Doctor Dee. London: Hamish Hamilton, 1993.
'London Luminaries and Cockney Visionaries'. *The LWT London Lecture*. Victoria and Albert Museum, 7 December, 1993. Edited version published as 'Cockney Visionaries'. *Independent* (18 December 1993).
'A Biographer's Biography'. *Los Angeles Times* (28 August 1994).
Dan Leno and the Limehouse Golem. London: Sinclair-Stevenson, 1994. Republished in the United States as *Elizabeth Cree: A Novel of the Limehouse Murders*. New York: Doubleday, 1995.
Blake. London: Sinclair-Stevenson, 1995.
'Blake and London Radicalism'. *TLS Talk*. Royal Festival Hall, 28 October 1995.
'A Tale of the Expected'. *Guardian* (22 December 1995).
Poems of William Blake. Selected and introduced by Peter Ackroyd. London: Sinclair-Stevenson, 1995.
'The Englishness of English Literature'. In Javier Pérez Guerra, *Proceedings of the XIXth International Conference of AEDEAN*. Departmento de Filoloxia Inglesa e Alemana, Universidade de Vigo, 1996: pp. 11–19.
Milton in America. London: Sinclair-Stevenson, 1996.
'My Interpretation of Dreams: A Time Machine'. *The Times* (21 August 1996).
The Life of Thomas More. London: Chatto and Windus, 1998.
The Plato Papers. London: Chatto and Windus, 1999.
Secret London. London: Sinclair-Stevenson, 2000 (forthcoming).

Criticism, interviews, and biographical articles

Adams, Tim. 'A Life Sentence: London's Biographer'. Interview in *Observer* (1 March 1998).
Anon. 'Peter Ackroyd'. *Current Biography* 54:5 (May 1993): pp. 3–7.
Anon. 'Peter Ackroyd'. *Contemporary Authors: New Revision Series, vol. 51*. Detroit: Gale Research, 1996: pp. 2–7.
Appleyard, Bryan. 'Aspects of Ackroyd'. *Sunday Times Magazine* (9 April 1989).
Audigier, Jean-Pierre. 'L'apocryphe selon Ackroyd'. Max Duperray, ed., *Historicité et Métafiction dans le roman contemporain des Iles Britanniques*. Aix: PU de Provence, 1994: pp. 139–50.
Bernard, Catherine. 'Peter Ackroyd entre plagiat et élégie'. *Études Britanniques Contemporaines* 5 (1994): pp. 13–22.
Billen, Andrew. 'Printed Melancholy, Unpublished Giggles'. *Observer* (15 May, 1992).
Cavaliero, Glen. 'Reversions to Type'. In *The Supernatural and English Fiction: From 'The Castle of Otranto' to 'Hawksmoor'*. Oxford: Oxford University Press, 1995: pp. 224–8.
Costa, Dominique. '*Chatterton*: An Analysis of Peter Ackroyd's Fictional World'. *Actas do XVI Encontro de A.P.E.A.A.* Villa Real: Universidade de Trás-os Montes e Alto Douro (March 1995): pp. 317–26.
Finney, Brian. 'Peter Ackroyd, Postmodernist Play and *Chatterton*'. *Twentieth-Century Literature* 38: 2 (Summer, 1992): pp. 240–61.

Fokkema, Aleid. 'Abandoning the Postmodern? The Case of Peter Ackroyd'. Theo D'haen and Hans Bertens, eds., *British Postmodern Fiction*. Amsterdam: Rodopi, 1993: pp. 168–79.

Gallix, François. '*English Music* de Peter Ackroyd. De l'autre côté du tableau'. *Études Anglaises* 50:2 (1997): pp. 218–31.

Giovannelli, Laura. *Le vite in Gioco: Le prospettiva ontologica e autoreferenziale nella narrativa di Peter Ackroyd*. Pisa: ETS, 1996.

Gregson, Ian. 'Epigraphs for Epigones: John Ashbery's Influence in England'. *Bête Noire* 4 (Winter 1987): pp. 89–94.

Herman, Luc. 'The Relevance of History: *Der Zauberbaum* (1985) by Peter Sloterdijk and *Hawksmoor* (1985) by Peter Ackroyd'. Theo D'haen and Hans Bertens, eds. *History and Post-War Writing*. Amsterdam: Rodopi, 1990: pp. 107–24.

Hotho-Jackson, Sabine. 'Literary History in Literature: An Aspect of the Contemporary Novel'. *Moderne Sprak* 86: 2 (1992): pp. 113–19.

— 'Peter Ackroyd'. *Post-War Literatures in English* 7 (March, 1990): n.p.

Janik, Del Ivan. 'No End of History: Evidence from the Contemporary English Novel'. *Twentieth Century Literature* 41: 2 (Summer 1995): pp. 160–89.

Johnson, Glen M. 'Peter Ackroyd'. *Dictionary of Literary Biography vol. 155*. Detroit: Gale Research, 1996: pp. 3–12.

Lange, Adriaan M. de. 'The Complex Architectonics of Postmodernist Fiction: *Hawksmoor* – A Case Study'. Theo D'haen and Hans Bertens, eds., *British Postmodern Fiction*. Amsterdam: Rodopi, 1993: pp. 145–65.

Lord, Geoffrey W. *Postmodernism and Notions of National Difference: A Comparison of Postmodern Fiction in Britain and America*. Unpublished doctoral dissertation, University of Texas, Austin.

Mackenzie, Susie. 'Portrait of an Artist Behaving Badly...' *Arena* (7 September, 1994).

Massie, Allan. *The Novel Today: A Critical Guide to the British Novel 1970–1989*. London: Longman, 1990

McGrath, Patrick. 'Peter Ackroyd'. *Bomb* 26 (1988–89): pp. 44–7.

Miller, Karl. 'Long Live Pastiche'. *Authors*. Oxford: Clarendon Press, 1989: pp. 85–95.

Onega, Susana. 'Empiricism and the "Scientia Umbrarum" in *Hawksmoor*'. In Francisco Collado-Rodriguez, ed., *Science, Literature, and Interpretation: Essays on Twentieth-Century Literature and Critical Theory*. Zaragoza: Servicio de Publicaciones de la Universidad de Zaragoza, 1991: pp. 117–38.

— 'Pattern and Magic in *Hawksmoor*'. *Atlantis: Revista de la Asociacion Espanola de Estudios Anglo-Norteamericanos* 12:2 (November 1991): pp. 31–43.

— 'British Historiographic Metafiction in the 1980s'. In Theo D'Haen and Hans Bertens, eds., *British Postmodern Fiction*. Amsterdam: Rodopi, 1993: pp. 47–61.

— 'British Historiographic Metafiction'. In Mark Currie, ed., *Metafiction*. London: Longman, 1995: pp. 92–103.

— 'Interview with Peter Ackroyd'. *Twentieth-Century Literature* 42: 2 (Summer 1996): pp. 208–220.

— *Peter Ackroyd*. London: Northcote House, 1998.

— *Metafiction and Myth in the Novels of Peter Ackroyd*. New York: Camden House, 1999.

Peck, John. 'The Novels of Peter Ackroyd'. *English Studies* 5 (1994): pp. 442–52.

Robbins, Ruth. '"Judas always writes the biography": The Many Lives of Oscar Wilde'. In Ruth Robbins and Julian Wolfreys, eds., *Victorian Identities: Social and Cultural Formations in Nineteenth-Century Literature*. Basingstoke: Macmillan, 1996: pp. 97–115.

Ross, Walter B. 'CA Interview'. *Contemporary Authors Vol. 127*. Detroit: Gale Research, 1989: pp. 3–5.

Schnackertz, Hermann Josef. 'Peter Ackroyd's Fictions and the Englishness of English Literature'. Günther Blaicher and Brigitte Glaser, eds., *Anglistentag 1993 Eichstatt: Proceedings*. Tübingen: Niemeyer, 1994: pp. 493–502.

Shiller, Dana. 'The Redemptive Past in the Neo-Victorian Novel'. *Studies in the Novel*. 29:4 (Winter 1997): pp. 538–60.

Smith, Amanda. 'Peter Ackroyd'. *Publishers Weekly* 232: 26 (1987): pp. 59–60.

Swope, Richard. 'Approaching the Threshold(s) in Postmodern Detective Fiction: Hawthorne's "Wakefield" and Other Missing Persons'. *Critique* 39: 3 (Spring 1998): pp. 207–27.

Taylor, D.J. *After the War: The Novel and England since 1945*. London: Chatto and Windus, 1993.

Selected reviews and commentaries

Abel, Betty. 'Quarterly Fiction Review – *First Light*'. *Contemporary Review* 255: 1482 (July 1989): pp. 45–8.

Adams, Phoebe-Lou. 'Brief Reviews: *Chatterton*'. *Atlantic* 261: 2 (February 1988): p. 86.

Adams, Robert M. 'The Poet and His Angels'. *Wall Street Journal* (9 April 1996).

Alford, Steven E. 'Poetic Vision'. *Houston Chronicle* (5 May 1996).

Allen, Bruce. '"Dickens": A Crowded Curiosity Shop'. *USA Today* (21 March 1991).

Andrews, Malcolm. *The Dickensian*. 88.1: 426 (Spring 1992): pp. 43–5.

Anon. 'Cold Comfort'. *Times Literary Supplement* (3 May 1974).

Anon. 'Fiction – *First Light* by Peter Ackroyd'. *Virginia Quarterly Review* 66: 3 (Summer 1990): p. 96.

Anon. 'Charles Dickens: Load Every Rift with Ore'. *Economist* (8 September 1990).

Anon. 'Slumdon'. *Economist* (23 May 1992).

Anon. 'In Paradise'. *Economist* (11 November 1995).

Anon. 'Recommended Reading – *The Trial of Elizabeth Cree* by Peter Ackroyd' (*Dan Leno and the Limehouse Golem*). *New Yorker* (21 August 1995).

Anon. 'Fiction of the Year'. *Guardian* (21 November 1996).

Baker, Kenneth. 'Investigating Blake's Visions'. *San Francisco Chronicle* (14 April 1996).

Banville, John. 'Working Man's Art'. *Los Angeles Times* (19 May 1996).

Barnacle, Hugo. 'Let's Not Be Puritanical'. *Sunday Times* (25 August 1996).

Barrell, John. 'Make the Music Mute'. *London Review of Books* (9 July 1992).

Battersby, Eileen. 'Maybe It's Because He's a Londoner'. *Irish Times* (20 August 1994).

Bayley, John. 'Even Old Ocean Smiled upon Him'. *The Times* (29 August 1996).

Beerbohm, Nonie. 'A Dickensian Encounter'. *Contemporary Review* 257: 1499 (December 1990): pp. 334–5.

Behrendt, Stephen C. Review of *Blake: A Biography*. *Criticism*. 39: 3 (Summer 1997): pp. 447–50.

Bemrose, John. 'The Nation Within – *English Music* by Peter Ackroyd'. *Maclean's* (10 August 1992).

— 'Burning Bright – *Blake* by Peter Ackroyd'. *Maclean's* (6 November 1995).

Bergonzi, Bernard. 'Exploring the Heart of Artistic Creation'. *Tablet* (8 September 1990).

Bering-Jensen, Helle. 'Seeing Life as Dickens Did'. *Insight* (4 March 1991).

— 'A Biography about Dickens that Raises and Fulfills Great Expectations'. *Washington Times* (11 February 1991).

Bernstein, Richard. Review of *Elizabeth Cree: A Novel of the Limehouse Murders*. (*Dan Leno and the Limehouse Golem*) *New York Times* (21 August 1995).

— 'For Milton in the New World, Trouble in Paradise'. *New York Times* (14 May 1997).

Birmingham, Stephen. 'History and Fiction Blur in Victorian Murder Tale'. *Washington Times* (14 May 1995).

Biswell, Andrew. 'Blind Justice'. *Guardian* (5 September 1996).

Blom, J. R., and L. R. Leavis. Review of *First Light. English Studies* 71:5 (October 1990): pp. 426–38.

Boland, Eavan. 'Confidence Tricked'. *Observer* (29 August 1993).

Bovenizer, David. 'Mound of Mystery'. *National Review* 41:19 (13 October 1989): p. 53.

Bradley, Richard. 'Reviews – *First Light* by Peter Ackroyd'. *Antiquity* 63: 240 (September 1989): pp. 636–7.

Brodsky, Alyn. 'Verbose Bio can be a "Dickens" of a Bore'. *Detroit News* (13 March 1991).

Broughton, Trev. 'The Poet Crying in the Wilderness'. *Times Literary Supplement* (30 August 1996).

Brown, Dennis. 'Great Writer from Humble Expectations'. *St. Louis Post-Dispatch* (7 April 1991).

Buchan, James. 'The Relics of Learning'. *Spectator* (30 May 1992).

Bull, Malcolm. 'Liberty Boy-Genius'. *Times Literary Supplement* (20 October 1995).

Burgess, Anthony. 'The Master of all Hearts in a Dissolute Age'. *Independent* (9 September 1990).

Busch, Frederick. 'The Best of Writers'. *Los Angeles Times* (20 January 1991).

Byatt, A. S. 'Dickens and his Demons'. *Washington Post* (10 February 1991).

Cantor, Paul. 'William Blake, Capitalist'. *Weekly Standard* (22 April 1996).

Carey, John. 'Paper Tyger'. *Sunday Times* (2 September 1990).

— 'The Life of Thomas More by Peter Ackroyd'. *Sunday Times* (22 February 1998).

Caryn, James. 'The Characters are Real, the History isn't'. *New York Times* (4 January 1989).

Clements, Denney. 'We're Poorer for Not Knowing that Art and Life Intertwine'. *Wichita Eagle* (28 February 1993).

Clute, John. 'Conjurors of Clerkenwell'. *New Statesman and Society* (3 September 1993).

— 'Pastures New'. *New Statesman* (27 September 1996).

Cohen, Morton N. 'Sketching God … from Life'. *Insight on the News* (3 June 1996).

Colinson, Patrick. 'Defined by His Death'. *Times Literary Supplement* (13 March 1998).

Condini, Ned. 'A Touch of the Poet Survives Any Poet Touched – *Chatterton* by Peter Ackroyd'. *National Catholic Reporter* (1 July 1988).

Conrad, Peter. '*Notes for a New Culture*: An Essay on Modernism'. *Times Literary Supplement* (3 December 1976).

— 'The Third Sex'. *New Statesman* (30 November 1979).

Cook, Bruce. 'Double Dose of Tradition in the Works of Peter Ackroyd'. *Daily News of Los Angeles* (25 October 1992).

— 'Another Paradise Lost'. *Washington Post* (15 June 1997).

Cosh, Mary. 'Oscar Winner'. *Times* (14 April 1983).

Cropper, Martin. Review of *First Light. Daily Telegraph* (15 April 1989).

Crowley, John. 'Something Vengeful and Ancient'. *New York Times Book Review* (17 September 1989).

Cumming, Laura. 'Time Trick'. *Guardian* (31 August 1993).

Danson, Lawrence. 'To Catch a Thief'. *New Republic* (22 February 1988).

Davenport, Gary. Review of *English Music. Sewanee Review* 102: 2 (Spring 1994): pp. 326–33.

Davie, Donald. 'The Modernist *malgré lui*'. *Times Literary Supplement* (21 September 1984).

Dean, Paul. 'How to See the Blind Poet'. *Wall Street Journal* (6 May 1997).

Dieckmann, Katherine. 'Brief Encounters – *English Music* by Peter Ackroyd'. *Village Voice* (8 December 1992).

Dinnage, Rosemary. 'The Ideal Husband'. *New York Review of Books* (20 December 1984).

Dirda, Michael. 'William Blake's Immortal Hand and Eye'. *Washington Post* (12 March 1996).

Disch, Thomas M. 'The Day of the Living Dead'. *Washington Post* (10 September 1989).

Dodsworth, Martin. 'Existing in Order to Exist'. *Times Literary Supplement* (11–17 September 1987).

Donoghue, Denis. 'One Life Was Not Enough'. *New York Times Book Review* (17 January 1988).

Dyer, Geoff. 'Clear-sighted'. *New Statesman* (27 September 1985).

Dyer, Richard. 'Ackroyd's Inventive "English Music"'. *Boston Globe* (9 December 1992).

Eder, Richard. 'A Coarsened Caricature of "Literature"'. *Los Angeles Times* (7 September 1989).

Edmiston, John. 'Tales of Two Writers bring them to Life'. *Houston Post* (16 February 1992).

Ellis, Steve. 'The Incoherent Curriculum'. *Times Literary Supplement* (28 August 1981).

Ewart, Gavin. 'In the Wrong Gear'. *Times Literary Supplement* (7 December 1979).

Fenton, James. 'A Life Behind Our Aloof Poet'. *Times* (27 September 1984).

— 'Time Present and Time Past Horrors'. *Times*. (26 September 1985).

Fertile, Candace. 'Ackroyd's Milton Teaches Lesson'. *Calgary Herald* (4 January 1997).

Firchow, Peter. 'English – *Chatterton* by Peter Ackroyd'. *World Literature Today* 63: 4 (Autumn 1989): p. 681.

Fisher, Barbara. 'Blake'. *Boston Globe* (31 March 1996).

— 'Milton in America'. *Boston Globe* (13 April 1997).

Ford, Mark. '*The Diversions of Purley*'. *Times Literary Supplement* (20–26 November 1987).

Fraser, Kennedy. 'Piper pipe that song again'. *New Yorker* (27 May 1996).

Games, Stephen. 'But What Does It All Mean, Mr Ackroyd?' *Guardian* (14 April 1989).

Garfield, Leon. 'Great Expectations Realised'. *Times Educational Supplement* (14 September 1990).

Giffen, Peter. 'Mass Killing and Chaos'. *Maclean's* (17 February 1986).

Gilbert, Francis. 'Citizen of Utopia'. *Guardian* (26 February 1998).

Gill, Stephen. 'The Key to a Continent'. *Times Literary Supplement* (31 August 1990).

Glastonbury, Marion. 'Body and Soul'. *New Statesman* (29 January 1982).

Glazebrook, Philip. 'Watching What Makes Us Tick'. *Spectator* (22 April 1989).

Glendinning, Victoria. 'Past and Present'. *Times* (3 September 1987).

Glover, Michael. 'Can't Get No Satisfaction'. *Books* (September 1993): p. 8.

Goodrich, Chris. 'Shadow Play'. *Los Angeles Times* (25 October 1992).

Graham, S. Keith. 'Tome on Author as Long, Boring as the "Dickens"'. *Atlanta Journal Constitution* (20 January 1991).

Gray, Paul. 'Old Stones'. *Time* (18 September 1989).

— 'Elementary my Dear Marx'. *Time* (29 May 1995).

Grossman, Ron. 'Thriller Poses Big Questions of Life'. *Chicago Tribune* (13 September 1990).

Grove, Valerie. 'How I Lost my Fear of Dying'. *The Times* (23 August 1996).

Guenther, Charles. 'A New Vision of William Blake'. *St Louis Post-Dispatch* (28 April 1996).

Gurley, George. 'Illuminating the Visions of William Blake'. *Chicago Tribune* (23 April 1996).

Haffenden, John. 'What the Life Leaves Out'. *Times Literary Supplement* (23 February 1996).

Hall, Richard. 'The Stars Circle over Ancient Grave'. *San Francisco Chronicle* (17 September 1989).

Harrison, Carey. 'Laying Bare the Evil in the Heart of Victorian London'. *San Francisco Chronicle* (21 May 1995).

— 'Milton vs. the Indians'. *San Francisco Chronicle* (30 March 1997).

Heller, Amanda. Review of *First Light. Boston Globe* (1 October 1989).

Heyward, Michael. 'Tradition and a Highly Individual Talent'. *Washington Post* (18 October 1992).

Hislop, Andrew. 'An Imitation Game'. *Times Literary Supplement* (15 April 1983).

Hollinghurst, Alan. 'In Hieroglyph and Shadow'. *Times Literary Supplement* (27 September 1985).

Hughes–Hallett, Lucy. 'Relishing the Disgusting'. *Sunday Times* (18 September 1994).

Hunter, Jefferson. 'In Dickens' Style, a Look at Dickens'. *Philadelphia Inquirer* (17 March 1991).

Jardine, Lisa. 'Milton Agonistes'. *Los Angeles Times* (27 April 1997).

Jenkins, Alan. '*The Diversions of Purley*'. *Observer* (22 March 1987).

Julius, Anthony. 'Lord and Martyr'. *Observer* (1 March 1998).

Kaganoff, Penny. Review of *The Great Fire of London*. *Publishers Weekly* (24 February 1989).

Kakutani, Michiko. 'Britain's Writers Embrace the Offbeat'. *New York Times* (5 July 1990).

Kanfer, Stefan. 'The Poet as a Young Corpse'. *Time* (18 January 1988).

Kaplan, Fred. 'Life is Long and Full of Surprises'. *Independent on Sunday* (2 September 1990).

Kaveney, Roz. 'Turn and Turn Again: Sinclair, Ackroyd and the London Novel'. *New Statesman and Society* (9 September 1994).

Keates, Jonathan. 'Creaking Floorboards'. *Observer* (22 September 1985).

Keating, Peter. 'Here We Are Again'. *Times Literary Supplement* (9 September 1994).

Keller, Johanna. *Antioch Review* 54: 4 (Fall 1996): pp. 487–8.

Kemp, John. 'Prodigiously Clever, Of Course'. *Literary Review* (May 1992): pp. 36–8.

Kemp, Peter. 'The Big Snooze'. *Sunday Times* (24 May 1992).

Kendrick, Walter. 'Past Master. Peter Ackroyd's Tales from the Crypt'. *Village Voice Literary Supplement* 78 (1989): pp. 23–4.

— 'Chuck Amuck'. *Village Voice* (12 February 1991).

Kincaid, James R. 'The Sum of His Oddities'. *New York Times Book Review* (13 January, 1991).

King, Francis. 'Lusty Début'. *Spectator* (30 January 1982).

— 'A Voice from the Past'. *Spectator* (28 September 1985).

— 'The Older the Better'. *Spectator* (11 September 1993).

Kirstein, Lincoln. 'Ezra Pound and his World'. *New York Review of Books* (30 April 1981).

Klinkenborg, Verlyn. 'Peter Ackroyd's Music'. *New Yorker* (23 November 1992).

—- Review of *Dickens*. *Smithsonian* 23: 10 (January 1993): pp. 131–2.

Kogan, Bernard. 'Prodigious Dickens'. *Chicago Tribune* (20 January 1991).

Korn, Eric. 'Evil in EC1'. *Times Literary Supplement* (10 September 1993).

Lannon, Linnea. 'Biography of Dickens Test Reader's Stamina'. *Detroit News and Free Press* (20 January 1991).

Lawson, Mark. 'Nothing Personal'. *Guardian* (31 August 1995).

Lee, Hermione. 'The Man Who Didn't Sleep'. *New Republic* (10 June 1991).

Lehmann–Haupt, Christopher. 'An Entertainment for the Literary'. *New York Times* (9 November 1992).

Leithauser, Brad. 'Thrown Voices'. *New Yorker* (8 February 1988).

Leivick, Laura. 'Following the Ghost of Dickens'. *New York Times* (22 December 1991).

Lerner, Laurence. 'The Long and the Short of It'. *Spectator* (20 July 1991).

Levenson, Michael. 'Tradition and the National Talent'. *New Republic* (18 June 1993).

Levi, Peter. 'The Hidden Eliot'. *Spectator* (29 September 1984).

— 'Is this the Region, this the Soil, the Clime?' *Spectator* (7 September 1996).

Levy, Paul. 'Borrowed Bras'. *Observer* (16 December 1979).

Lewis, Peter. 'The Truth and Nothing Like the Truth: History and Fiction'. *Stand Magazine* 27: 2 (1986): pp. 38–44.

Lewis, Roger. Review of *The Last Testament of Oscar Wilde*. *American Spectator* 17: 3 (1984): pp. 39–41.

Lindop, Grevel. 'The Empty Telephone Boys'. *PN Review* 15: 6 (1989): pp. 43–6.

Litz, A. Walton. 'The Invisible Poet Begins to Appear'. *New York Times Book Review* (16 December 1984).

Lodge, David. 'Mine of Course'. *New Statesman* (19 March 1976).

— 'The Marvelous Boy'. *New York Review of Books* 35: 6 (1988).

Longford, Frank. 'Oscar'. *Spectator* (16 April 1983).

Lynn, Kenneth S. Review of *Dickens*. *American Spectator*. 24: 5 (May 1991): pp. 45–6.

Lurie, Alison. 'Hanging Out with Hogarth'. *New York Times Book Review* (11 October 1992).

Mallon, Peter. 'A Music with Too Many Notes'. *USA Today* (27 November 1992).

Mallon, Thomas. 'Author's Latest Celebration of English Literature Needs a Bit More Spontaneity'. *Houston Post* (13 December 1992).

Manguel, Alberto. 'Untrue Confessions: The Many Moods of Thomas Chatterton'. *Village Voice* 33: 15 (29 March 1988): p. 68.

Martin, Valerie. 'A Victorian Nightmare'. *New York Times Book Review* (16 April 1995).

Matros, Michael. 'Sing a Song of England's Culture: Dreamy Visits by Old Masters Threaten to Drown Out Story'. *Columbus Dispatch* (1 November 1992).

Mattingly, Stacy. 'Acid and Poetry: Blake's Visions'. *Atlanta Journal Constitution* (21 April 1996).

Maves, Carl. 'The Duality of Dickens'. *San Francisco Chronicle* (27 January 1991).

McAleer, John. 'Peter Ackroyd Hymns "the Forms of Eternity"'. *Chicago Tribune* (1 November 1992).

McClatchy, J. D. 'Masks and Passions'. *Poetry* 64: 1 (April 1989): pp. 20–48.

Merle, Rubin. 'From Nebulae to Noah's Ark'. *Christian Science Monitor* (10 January 1990).

Meyer, Nicholas. 'Goings-on in Old London'. *Los Angeles Times* (25 June 1995).

Miller, Karl. 'Poor Toms'. *London Review of Books* 9: 15 (1987).

— Review of *Milton in America*. *Observer* (1 September 1996).

Miller, Nolan. '*Chatteron*'. *Antioch Review*. 46: 2 (1988): pp. 267–8.

Mitchison, Amanda. 'Sky Larks'. *New Statesman and Society*. (21 April 1989).

Monnickendam, Andrew. 'Peter Ackroyd: *Chatterton*'. *Anauri d'anglès* 11/12 (1990): p. 107.

Montaut, Mary. '*The Last Testament of Oscar Wilde*'. *Irish University Review* 14: 1 (1984): pp. 136–9.

Montrose, David. 'Unvarnished'. *New Statesman* (12 October 1984).

Moore, Charles. 'Enthusiasm Moves the World'. *Spectator* (23 September 1995).

Moore, George. 'Novel Angle on Murder Mystery Books'. *Sunday Star-Times* (14 January 1996).

Morton, Brian. Review of *First Light*. *Times Educational Supplement* (2 June 1989).

Motion, Andrew. 'A Passionate Dissent'. *Guardian* (1 September 1995).

Mysak, Joe. 'A Dickensian Life'. *National Review* (1 April 1991).

Neve, Michael. 'The Living Dead'. *History Today* 38 (January 1988): pp. 53–4.

Nichols, Ashton. Review of *Blake*. *Southern Humanities Review* 31: 3 (Summer 1997): pp. 284–9.

Nye, Robert. 'His Mind on His Sleeve'. *Times* (19 February 1987).

Oates, Joyce Carol. 'The Highest Passion is Terrour'. *New York Times Book Review* (19 January 1986).

O'Regan, Gerard. 'Ackroyd Keeps the Veil Drawn'. *Irish Independent* (3 September 1994).

Orent, Wendy. 'Search for a Killer reveals Dark Heart of Victorian London'. *Atlanta Journal Constitution* (20 August 1995).

Parini, Jay. 'A Thriller – But about Thinkers'. *Boston Globe* (4 June 1995).

Paulin, Tom. 'Oscar and Constance'. *London Review of Books* (17–30 November 1983).

Pettingell, Phoebe. 'The Immortal Adolescent'. *New Leader* (21 March 1988).

— 'Two Cockney Visionaries'. *New Leader* (3–17 June 1996).

Phillips, Alice H. G. 'Dreams, Literary Conceits Collide in Artistic Pastiche'. *Philadelphia Inquirer* (15 November 1992).

Porter, Peter. 'Hearts and Sleeves'. *Observer* (27 January 1974).

— 'Signs of Greatness'. *Observer* (19 November 1978).

— 'Mixing with the Great'. *Times Literary Supplement* (14 September 1990).

Porter, Roy. 'Boz's Great Expectations'. *Evening Standard* (30 August 1990).

Powers, Katherine A. 'Of Hoaxes and Hoaxers, and the Pleasures they Provide'. *Boston Globe* (6 October 1996).

Prescott, Peter S. 'In Lieu of "Chatterton"'. *Newsweek* (4 September 1989).

Pritchard, William H. 'London Forms'. *New Republic* 201: 10 (1989): pp. 39–41.

— 'The Exaggerator'. *The Hudson Review* 44: 2 (Summer 1991): pp. 301–8.

Prynne, J.H. '*London Lickpenny*'. *Spectator* (19 January 1974).

Quinn, Anthony. 'The Wizardry of Boz'. *New Statesman and Society* (7 September 1990).

Rabaté, Jean-Michel. 'À la recherche de Chatterton'. *Quinzaine littéraire* (1988): pp. 517–18.

Raine, Craig. 'Odds and Ends of a Great Life'. *Observer* (2 September 1990)

Raphael, Lev. 'Dazzling Trip in the Victorian Underworld'. *Detroit News and Free Press* (21 May 1995).

Rawson, Claude. Review of *First Light*. *Times Literary Supplement* (28 April–4 May 1989).

Reverand II, Cedric D. 'Review of Peter Ackroyd's *Hawksmoor*'. *Eighteenth Century Life*. 11: 2 (1987): pp. 102–9.

Richmond, Dick. 'The Trial of Elizabeth Cree'. *St Louis Post-Dispatch* (12 September 1996)

Ricks, Christopher. 'The Craft of Criticism'. *Sunday Times* (7 March 1976).

— 'The Braver Thing'. *London Review of Books* (1–14 November 1984).

Rifkind, Donna. 'Clever Mimicry Impersonates Genius'. (25 October 1992).

Roberts, Michele. 'Hampstead Made him Sick'. *New Statesman and Society* (8 September 1995).

Robinson, Peter. 'Literary Fantasy in an English Boy's World'. *San Francisco Chronicle* (10 January 1993).

Rogers, Pat. 'Street Wise'. *London Review of Books* 7: 17 (1985).

Rubin, Merle. 'Revisiting Dickens (and Friend)'. *Christian Science Monitor* (25 February 1991).

Rykwert, Joseph. '*Hawksmoor*'. *Art in America* (July 1986): pp. 11, 13.

Sexton, David. 'Spooks do Furnish a Room'. *Punch* (21 April 1989).

— 'Thereby Hangs a Tale'. *Spectator* (10 September 1994).

Shippey, T.A. 'From the National Pool'. *Times Literary Supplement* (22 May 1992).

Shore, Miles F. Review of *Chatterton*. *American Journal of Psychiatry* 145: 12 (December 1988): p. 1587.

Sinclair, Iain. 'The Cadaver Club'. *London Review of Books* (22 December 1994).

Smardz, Zofia. '*English Music* Celebrates England and its Arts'. *Baltimore Morning Sun* (22 November 1992).

Spilka, Mark. 'The New Yuppie Dickens'. *America* (14 December 1991).

Spurling, Hilary. 'From a Bridge of Tears'. *Weekend Telegraph* (8 September 1990).

— Review of *Dickens*. *London Review of Books* (27 September 1990).

Stanford, Peter. 'Church of Past Times'. *Independent on Sunday* (1 March 1998).

Stasio, Marilyn. 'Murder Most Fogbound'. *New York Times* (19 October 1997).

Stephen, Katherine. 'Glimpsing Eternity in Blake Biography'. *Christian Science Monitor* (23 April 1996).

Strawson, Galen. 'Failing to Connect'. *Times Literary Supplement* (29 January 1982).

Sutherland, John. 'Generations'. *London Review of Books* (4–17 March 1982).

— 'A Terrible Bad Cold'. *London Review of Books* (27 September 1990).

Talese, Nan A. 'A Death in London: But Was It Murder?' *Newsday* (2 May 1995).

Tanner, Tony. 'Milton Agonistes'. *New York Times* (6 April 1997).

Taylor, D. J. Review of *First Light*. *Independent* (15 April 1989).

— 'Fogey Heaven'. *New Statesman and Society* (5 June 1992).

Tehan, Arline B. 'Ackroyd Discards Facts About Milton, to No Good End'. *The Hartford Courant* (18 May 1997).

Thomas, Keith. 'Utopia and Beyond'. *Guardian* (12 March 1998).

Thomson, David. 'A Life that's Written like the Dickens'. *Boston Globe* (3 February 1991).

Tolson, Jay. Review of *Blake*. *Wilson Quarterly* 20: 3 (Summer 1996): pp. 96–7.

Updike, John. 'Eliot without Words'. *New Yorker* (25 March 1985).

Walsh, John. 'Confessions of a Monopolylinguist'. *Sunday Times* (17 May 1992).

Wheeler, Edward T. 'Charles the Great'. *Commonweal* (14 June 1991).

— 'Off-key'. *Commonweal* (26 March 1993).

Wills, Garry. 'The Angels and Devils of Dickens'. *New York Review of Books*. 38: 9 (16 May 1991): pp. 8–11.

Wolfe, Peter. 'Scholarly Dreams'. *St Louis Post-Dispatch* (7 February 1993).

Wood, James. 'A Prisoner in the Circle of Fiction'. *Guardian* (6 September 1990).

— 'English Primer all Blotted and Blurred'. *Guardian* (21 May 1992).

— 'Little Guignol'. *New York Review of Books* (21 September 1995).

Wood, Michael. 'Looking Away'. *London Review of Books* (18 May 1989).

Yardley, Jonathan. 'New Twist on Dickens'. *Washington Post* (29 July 1992).

Other critical and literary works

Anon. 'London Lykpeny'. In James M. Dean, ed. *Medieval English Political Writings*. Kalamazoo: Medieval Institute Publications, 1996: pp. 222–6.

Arnold, Matthew. *The Complete Poems*. Second Edition. Ed. Miriam Allott. London: Longman, 1979.

Babbage, Charles. *The Works of Charles Babbage. Volume 9: The Ninth Bridgewater Treatise, A Fragment*. Second edition. 1838. Ed. Martin Campbell-Kelly. New York: New York University Press, 1989.

Barker, Francis. *The Tremulous Private Body: Essays on Subjection*. London: Methuen, 1984.

Barthes, Roland. 'The Reality Effect'. (1968) In Tzetan Todorov, ed. *French Literary Theory Today: A Reader*. Cambridge: Cambridge University Press, 1982: pp. 11–18.

— *The Pleasure of the Text* (1973). Trans. Richard Miller. New York: Farrar, Strauss and Giroux, 1975.

Bennington, Geoffrey. 'Derridabase'. In Geoffrey Bennington and Jacques Derrida. *Jacques Derrida* (1991). Trans. Geoffrey Bennington. Chicago: University of Chicago Press, 1993. pp. 3–316.

Bernstein, Carol L. *The Celebration of Scandal: Toward the Sublime in Victorian Urban Fiction*. University Park, PA: Pennsylvania State University Press, 1991.

Blake, William. *The Complete Poems*. Ed. Alicia Ostriker. Harmondsworth: Penguin, 1977.

Bloomer, Jennifer. *Architecture and the Text: The (S)crypts of Joyce and Piranesi*. New Haven: Yale University Press, 1993.

Campbell-Kelly, Martin. 'Introduction'. In Charles Babbage, *The Works of Charles Babbage: Volume 9: The Ninth Bridgewater Treatise*. New York: New York University Press, 1989. pp. 5–7.

Carroll, Lewis. *The Annotated Alice: 'Alice's Adventures in Wonderland' and 'Through the Looking Glass'*. Revised edition. Ed. Martin Gardner. Harmondsworth: Penguin, 1970.

Cohen, Tom. *Anti-Mimesis: From Plato to Hitchcock*. Cambridge: Cambridge University Press, 1994.

Conrad, Joseph. *Heart of Darkness*. Ed. Robert Hampson. London: Penguin, 1995.

Corlett, William. *Community Without Unity: A Politics of Derridian Extravagance*. Durham: Duke University Press, 1989.

Currie, Mark. *Postmodern Narrative Theory*. Basingstoke: Macmillan, 1998.

De Quincey, Thomas. 'On Murder Considered as One of the Fine Arts'. In George Douglas, ed., *Selected Essays of De Quincey*. London: Walter Scott, Ltd. 1894.

Derrida, Jacques. *Positions* (1972). Trans. Alan Bass. Chicago: University of Chicago Press, 1981.

— *Margins of Philosophy* (1972). Trans., with additional notes, Alan Bass. Chicago: University of Chicago Press, 1982.

— 'Des Tours de Babel'. Trans. Joseph F. Graham. In Joseph F. Graham, ed. *Difference in Translation*. Ithaca: Cornell University Press, 1985: pp. 165–208.

— *A Derrida Reader: Between the Blinds*. Ed. Peggy Kamuf. New York: Columbia University Press, 1991a.

— 'Télépathie'. *Furor* (February 1991b): 5–41.

— *Acts of Literature*. Ed. Derek Attridge. London: Routledge, 1992.

— 'Finis'. In *Aporias*. Trans. Thomas Dutoit. Stanford: Stanford University Press, 1993a.

— *Memoirs of the Blind: The Self-Portrait and Other Ruins*. Trans. Pascale-Anne Brault and Michael Naas. Chicago: University of Chicago Press, 1993b.

— 'On a Newly Arisen Apocalyptic Tone in Philosophy' (1984). Trans. John Leavey, Jr. In *Raising the Tone of Philosophy: Late Essays by Immanuel Kant, Transformative Critique by Jacques Derrida*. Ed. Peter Fenves. Baltimore: Johns Hopkins University Press, 1993c: pp. 117–72.

— *Specters of Marx: The State of the Debt, the Work of Mourning, and the New International*. (1993). Trans. Peggy Kamuf. Int. Bernd Magnus and Stephen Cullenberg. New York: Routledge, 1994.

— *Points ... Interviews, 1974–1994* (1992). Trans. Peggy Kamuf et al. Ed. Elisabeth Weber. Stanford: Stanford University Press, 1995.

— '"As if I were Dead": An Interview with Jacques Derrida'. In John Brannigan, Ruth Robbins and Julian Wolfreys, eds., *Applying: to Derrida*. Basingstoke: Macmillan, 1996: pp. 212–26.

— and Bernard Steigler. *Échographies: de la télévision. Entretiens filmés*. Paris: Galilée-INA, 1996.

— and Anne Dufourmantelle. *Anne Dufourmantelle invite Jacques Derrida à répondre: De l'hospitalité*. Paris: Calmann-Lévy, 1997.

Dickens, Charles. *Bleak House* (1853). Ed. Nicola Bradbury. London: Penguin, 1996.

— *Hard Times* (1854). Ed Paul Schlicke. Oxford: Oxford University Press, 1989.

Dollimore, Jonathan. *Sexual Dissidence: Augustine to Wilde, Freud to Foucault*. Oxford: Oxford University Press, 1991.

Doyle, Brian. *England and Englishness*. London: Routledge, 1989.

Easthope, Antony. *Englishness and National Culture*. London: Routledge, 1999.

Eliot, T. S. *Notes Towards the Definition of Culture*. London: Faber and Faber, 1948.

— *Collected Poems 1909–1962*. London: Faber and Faber, 1983.

Evans, Dylan. *An Introductory Dictionary of Lacanian Psychoanalysis*. London: Routledge, 1996.

Fenves, Peter. *'Chatter': Language and History in Kierkegaard*. Stanford: Stanford University Press, 1993.

Fink, Bruce. *A Clinical Introduction to Lacanian Psychoanalysis: Theory and Technique*. Cambridge, MA: Harvard University Press, 1997.

Forster, E. M. *Howards End* (1910). Ed. Oliver Stallybrass. Harmondsworth: Penguin, 1983.

Fowles, John. *Daniel Martin*. Boston: Little, Brown, and Company, 1977.

Freud, Sigmund. *The Interpretation of Dreams. The Penguin Freud Library Volume 4* (1900). First published in *The Standard Edition of the Complete Psychological Works of Sigmund Freud*, Vols. IV and V. Trans. James Strachey. Ed. James Strachey, asst. Alan Tyson. London: George Allen and Unwin, Ltd. Present Ed. Angela Richards. Harmondsworth: Penguin, 1991.

Gallagher, Shaun. *The Inordinance of Time*. Evanston: Northwestern University Press, 1998.

Genette, Gérard. *Palimpsests: Literature in the Second Degree* (1982). Trans. Channa Newman and Claude Doubinsky. Foreword Gerald Prince. Lincoln: University of Nebraska Press, 1997.

Gregson, Ian. *Contemporary Poetry and Postmodernism: Dialogue and Estrangement*. Basingstoke: Macmillan, 1996.

Griffin, Susan M. *The Texture of the Visual in Late James*. Boston: Northeastern University Press, 1991.

Harris, Robert. 'Blair's Third Way to Elected Dictatorship'. *The Sunday Times* (20 September 1998): 9082.

Hartman, Geoffrey H. *Saving the Text: Literature/Philosophy/Derrida*. Baltimore: Johns Hopkins University Press, 1981.

Heidegger, Martin. '" ... Poetically Man Dwells ..."' (1951). Trans. Albert Hofstadter. *Poetry, Language, Thought*. Trans. and int. Albert Hofstadter. New York: Harper and Row, 1971: pp. 211–229.

— 'The End of Philosophy and the Task of Thinking' (1966). Trans. Joan Stambaugh. Rpt. in David Farrell Krell, ed., *Basic Writings: Martin Heidegger*. Revised and expanded edition. London: Routledge, 1993: pp. 397–449.

Hejinian, Lyn. 'The Reflection of Closure'. In Peter Baker, ed. *Onward: Contemporary Poetry and Poetics*. New York: Peter Lang Publishing, 1996. pp. 27–40.

Hobson, Marion. *Jacques Derrida: Opening Lines*. London: Routledge, 1998.

Hutcheon, Linda. *A Poetics of Postmodernism: History, Theory, Fiction*. London: Routledge, 1988.

— *The Politics of Postmodernism*. London: Routledge, 1989.

— *Irony's Edge: The Theory and Politics of Irony*. London: Routledge, 1994.

Hyppolite, Jean. *Logic and Existence* (1953). Trans. Leonard Lawlor and Amit Sen. Albany: State University of New York Press, 1997.

Irigaray, Luce. *Speculum of the Other Woman* (1974). Trans. Gillian C. Gill. Ithaca: Cornell University Press, 1985.

Jameson, Fredric. *The Political Unconscious: Narrative as a Socially Symbolic Act*. Ithaca: Cornell University Press, 1981.

Kearns, Katherine. *Psychoanalysis, Historiography, and Feminist Theory: The Search for Critical Method*. Cambridge: Cambridge University Press, 1997.

Kift, Dagmar. *The Victorian Music Hall: Culture, Class and Conflict* (1991). Trans. Roy Kift. Cambridge: Cambridge University Press, 1996.

Kincaid, James R. 'Throwing Pies at the Dean: Comedy, Power, and Institutional Practice'. *Imprimatur: A Journal of Criticism and Theory* 2: 1–2 (Autumn 1996): pp. 5–12.

Krell, David Farrell. *Archeticture: Ecstasies of Space, Time, and the Human Body*. Albany: State University of New York Press, 1997.

Kristeva, Julia. 'Towards a Semiology of Paragrams'. Trans. Roland-François Lack. In *The Tel Quel Reader*. Ed. Patrick ffrench and Roland-François Lack. London: Routledge, 1998: pp. 25–49.

Lacan, Jacques. *Écrits: A Selection*. Trans. Alan Sheridan. New York: Norton, 1977.

La Capra, Dominick. *Rethinking Intellectual History*. Ithaca: Cornell University Press, 1983.

Larissey, Edward. *Reading Twentieth-Century Poetry: The Language of Gender and Objects*. Oxford: Blackwell, 1990.

Levinas, Emmanuel. *Totality and Infinity: An Essay on Exteriority* (1961). Trans. Alphonso Lingis. Pittsburgh: Duquesne University Press, 1969.

— *Time and the Other (and Additional Essays)* (1947). Trans. Richard A. Cohen. Pittsburg: Duquesne University Press, 1987.

— 'The Trace of the Other'. In Mark C. Taylor, ed., *Deconstruction in Context: Literature and Philosophy*. Chicago: University of Chicago Press, 1986: pp. 345–59.

Light, Alison. *Forever England: Femininity, Literature and Conservatism Between the Wars*. London: Routledge, 1991.

Maclachlan, Ian. '*Musique-rythme*: Derrida and Roger Laporte'. In Julian Wolfreys, John Brannigan, and Ruth Robbins eds., *The French Connections of Jacques Derrida*. Albany: State University of New York Press, 1999: pp. 71–85.

Melberg, Arne. *Theories of Mimesis*. Cambridge: Cambridge University Press, 1995.

McCorkle, James. *The Still Performance: Writing, Self, and Interconnection in Five American Postmodern Poets*. Charlottesville: University of Virginia Press, 1989.

Miller, J. Hillis. 'Thomas Hardy, Jacques Derrida and the "Dislocation of Souls"'. *Tropes, Parables, Performatives: Essays on Twentieth-Century Literature*. Hemel Hempstead: Harvester, 1990: pp. 171–80.

— *Topographies*. Stanford: Stanford University Press, 1995.

Milton, John. *Selected Prose*. Ed. C. A. Patrides. Harmondsworth: Penguin, 1979.

— *Paradise Lost*. In *John Milton: Complete Poems and Major Prose*. Ed. Merritt Y. Hughes. New York: Macmillan, 1985: pp. 173–470.

Morton, H.V. *In Search of London*. London: Methuen, 1951.

Nägele, Rainer. *Echoes of Translation: Reading Between Texts*. Baltimore: Johns Hopkins University Press, 1997.

Nancy, Jean-Luc. *The Sense of the World* (1993). Trans. and Foreword Jeffrey S. Librett. Minneapolis: University of Minnesota Press, 1997.

Newman, Robert D. *Transgressions of Reading: Narrative Engagement as Exile and Return*. Durham: Duke University Press, 1993.

Orr, Leonard. *Problems and Poetics of the Nonaristotelian Novel*. Lewisburg: Bucknell University Press, 1991.

Osbourne, Peter. *The Politics of Time: Modernity and Avant-Garde*. London: Verso, 1995.

Picard, Michel. *La Lecture come jeu: essai sur la littérature*. Paris: Éditions de Minuit, 1986.

Porter, Roy. *London: A Social History*. London: Hamish Hamilton, 1994.

Pound, Ezra. *Literary Essays of Ezra Pound*. Ed. T. S. Eliot. London: Faber and Faber, 1954.

Preziosi, Donald. 'Between Power and Desire: The Margins of the City'. *Glyph Textual Studies 1* (1986): pp. 237–52.

Rajchman, John. *Constructions*. Foreword Paul Virilio. Cambridge, MA: MIT Press, 1998.

Rodowick, D. N. *Gilles Deleuze's Time Machine*. Durham: Duke University Press, 1997.

Ronen, Ruth. *Possible Worlds in Literary Theory*. Cambridge: Cambridge University Press, 1994.

Rose, Margaret A. *Parody: Ancient, Modern, and Post-Modern*. Cambridge: Cambridge University Press, 1993.

Roth, Michael. *The Poetics of Resistance: Heidegger's Line*. Evanston: Northwestern University Press, 1996.

Royle, Nicholas. *After Derrida*. Manchester: Manchester University Press, 1995.

Ruthrof, Horst. *Semantics and the Body: Meaning from Frege to the Postmodern*. Toronto: University of Toronto Press, 1997.

Sinclair, Iain. *Lights Out for the Territory*. London: Granta, 1997.

— and Dave McKean. *Slow Chocolate Autopsy*. London: Pheonix House, 1997.

Sinfield, Alan. *Literature, Politics, and Culture in Postwar Britain*. Berkeley: University of California Press, 1989.

Stallybrass, Peter and Allon White. *The Politics and Poetics of Transgression*. Ithaca: Cornell University Press, 1986.

Steigler, Bernard. *Technics and Time, 1: The Fault of Epimethius*. Trans. Richard Beardsworth and George Collins. Stanford: Stanford University Press, 1998.

Temple, Michael. *The Name of the Poet: Onomastics and Anonymity in the Works of Stéphane Mallarmé*. Exeter: University of Exeter Press, 1995.

Tooke, John Horne. *Epea Pteroenta: or, The Diversions of Purley*. 2 vols. (1829). Int. Roy Harris. London and Tokyo: Routledge/Thoemmes Press/ Kinokuniya Company Ltd., 1993.

Vasseleu, Cathryn. *Textures of Light: Vision and Touch in Irigaray, Levinas and Merleau-Ponty*. London: Routledge, 1998.

Weber, Samuel. *Return to Freud: Jacques Lacan's Dislocation of Psychoanalysis* (1990). Trans. Michael Levine. Cambridge: Cambridge University Press, 1991.

Wiesel, Elie. *The Golem: The Story of a Legend*. Illustrated by Mark Podwal. Trans. Anne Borchardt. New York: Summit Books, 1983.

Wilde, Oscar. *Complete Works of Oscar Wilde*. Second edition. Ed. Merlin Holland. Glasgow: HarperCollins, 1994.

Wolfreys, Julian. *Writing London: The Trace of the Urban Text from Blake to Dickens*. Basingstoke: Macmillan, 1998.

— 'The Hauntological Example: The City as the Haunt of Writing in the Texts of Iain Sinclair'. In *Deconstruction • Derrida*. Basingstoke: Macmillan, 1998: pp. 138–58.

Wordsworth, William. *Wordsworth's Poems of 1807*. Ed. Alun R. Jones. Atlantic Highlands: Humanities Press, 1987.

Žižek, Slavoj. *The Sublime Object of Ideology*. London: Verso, 1989.

— *The Ticklish Subject: The Absent Centre of Political Ontology*. London: Verso, 1999.

Index of Titles by Peter Ackroyd

'Across the street...', 275 n.15
'among school children', 37, 38, 40–1
'and the children...', 37, 38, 42, 51–2, 271 n.10
'and then...', 271 n.10
'the beautiful fruit...', 271 n.10

Blake, 173–88, 237–8, 270 n.6, 282 n.8

Chatterton, 1, 12, 17, 20, 21–2, 25, 74, 84, 112–13, 123–34, 147, 148, 158, 168, 172, 224, 227, 228, 229, 230, 232, 233, 249, 269 n.6, 270 n.6, 274 n.11, 276 n.23, 288 n.27
Country Life, 1, 35, 39, 61
'country life', 37, 38, 39–40, 41, 47–8, 51, 52, 55, 271 n.9, 271 n.10
'the cut in...', 59–60, 271 n.10

Dan Leno and the Limehouse Golem, 1, 19, 20–1, 68, 84, 170–2, 173, 178, 119–20, 198–211, 241–2, 243–4, 249, 250, 265 n.14, 270 n.6, 275 n.17, 278 n.6, 282 n.3, 282 n.5, 282 n.7, 284 n.14, 286 n.24, 287 n.26, 288 n.27
'the day...', 37
Dickens, 2, 16, 24–30, 32, 173–88, 190, 237, 259, 265–7 n.15, 267 n.16, 270 n.6, 275 n.14, 282 n.7, 282 n.8
The Diversions of Purley and Other Poems, 1, 35, 43, 51, 61, 236, 264 n.2, 271 n.10
Dressing Up – Transvestism and Drag, 1, 5, 18, 32, 271 n.8

English Music, 1, 134–47, 156, 158, 171, 172, 173, 238, 274 n.5, 277 n.4
'the extreme heat...', 271 n.10

First Light, 1, 3, 11–12, 112–13, 114, 147–55, 193, 225, 226, 227, 228, 229, 232, 269 n.6, 270 n.6, 274 n.11, 277 n.4, 280 n.14, 288 n.27
'Foolish Tears', 36

'The Goldfish Sonata', 269 n.4
The Great Fire of London, 1, 11, 19, 67–8, 77–84, 172, 199, 221, 224, 227, 228, 249, 250, 265 n.6, 265 n.10, 270 n.6, 275 n.14
'the great Sun', 63, 271 n.10

Hawksmoor, 1, 11, 17, 20, 21, 22, 68, 72, 78–9, 84, 92–104, 107, 109–10, 112, 117–19, 125, 172, 173, 177, 188, 195, 221–2, 224, 227, 229, 230–1, 249, 250, 260, 265 n.9, 267 n.18, 270 n.6, 274 n.10, 274 n.11, 276 n.25, 276–7 n.26, 277 n.27, 277 n.3, 282 n.3, 284 n.12, 285 n.21, 288 n.27
The House of Doctor Dee, 1, 10, 11, 20, 35, 72, 112–14, 117, 147, 172, 173, 188–98, 204, 239, 246–7, 250, 267 n.18, 270 n.6, 274 n.11, 276 n.25, 282 n.3, 284 n.13, 284 n.14, 284 n.15, 285 n.22, 288 n.27
'how did it...', 271 n.10

'in the middle...', 58–9, 271 n.10

The Last Testament of Oscar Wilde, 1, 72, 84, 85–92, 107–9, 127, 172, 270 n.6, 286 n.25
The Life of Thomas More, 4, 173–88, 270 n.6, 273 n.2, 282 n.8
'The little tune...', 271 n.10
'London Lecture', 70–3
London Lickpenny, 1, 264 n.2
'love falls', 271 n.10

'madness...', 271 n.10
Milton in America, 1, 72, 127, 147, 155–69, 270 n.6, 280 n.16, 281 n.19
'my own...', 271 n.10

'The Neo-Gothic Imagination and the Death of the Past', 229–30
Notes for a New Culture, 1, 5, 9, 22, 30, 31, 33, 41, 45, 69, 75–7, 141–2, 143, 214, 222–3, 235, 236, 261, 269 n.3, 272–3 n.1, 274 n.9, 277 n.6, 279 n.11
'the novel', 37, 61, 62, 271 n.10

'Only Connect...', 36, 53–4, 55,
    271 n.10
'opening...'
'Oscar Wilde: Comedy as Tragedy', 267
    n.19
Ouch, 1, 35, 269 n.4
'out of the...', 271 n.10

The Plato Papers, 213–18, 265 n.4
'the poem', 60–1, 62
'the room is...', 64, 271 n.10

'The secret is...', 55–6, 57, 271 n.10
Secret London, 170, 281 n.1
'the small girl...' 47

'there are so many...', 38, 41, 42
'there was no rain...', 64, 271 n.10
T. S. Eliot, 227, 234, 270 n.6

'watching the process...', 271 n.10

'you do the best...', 271 n.10

Index of Other Titles

After London, 252
Alice's Adventures in Wonderland, 146
The American Spectator, 86
'Among School Children', 40
'L'Apocryphe selon Ackroyd', 276 n.25
Areopagitica, 281 n.19
Astronomy and General Physics, 287 n.27

The Beetle, 204
Blast, 144
Bleak House, 24, 95, 127, 202
Broad Grins, 282 n.7

'The Cadaver Club', 282 n.5
Candle in the Wind (Goodbye English Rose),
    145
The Company of Wolves, 31, 33, 84
The Condition of the Working Class in
    England, 258
'The Confidential Clerk', 227
Confessions of an English Opium Eater, 178
The Culture of Contentment, 246

The Daily Telegraph, 148
Daniel Martin, 265 n.5
The Dickensian, 266–7 n.15
Dictionary of Literary Biography, 28
Dombey and Son, 26
'Dover Beach', 279 n.10
Dracula, 204

Échographies: de la télévision. Entretiens
    filmés, 285 n.19
Epea Pteroenta: or, The Diversions of Purley,
    264 n.2

'Faith and Knowledge: the Two Sources of
    "Religion" at the Limits of Reason
    Alone', 285 n.19
The Family Reunion, 148, 153–4, 270 n.6
'Finis', 278 n.7
The French Lieutenant's Woman, 149
Frenzy, 216
'The Function and Field of Speech and
    Language in Psychoanalysis', 285
    n.22

A Game at Chess, 203
Games with Time, 111
The Golden Bough, 149
The Golem: The Story of a Legend, 286 n.23
'Gone Astray', 186
Great Expectations, 142
The Guardian, 7

Hamlet, 146
Hard Times, 142
'The Hauntological Example: The City as
    the Haunt of Writing in the Texts of
    Iain Sinclair', 282 n.3
Heart of Darkness, 280 n.16
'History and Fiction as Modes of
    Comprehension', 225
'The Hollow Men', 41, 280 n.16

Jacques Derrida: Opening Lines, 277 n.5
'Jerusalem', 139
Jerusalem, 178, 184, 187, 250, 282 n.4

King Lear, 127

'A Life Sentence: London's Biographer',
    273 n.3
Lights Out for the Territory, 257, 260–1, 282
    n.3, 285 n.19
Little Dorrit, 27, 77–84, 107, 222, 224,
    249, 265 n.10, 270 n.6
London, 250
London Labour and the London Poor, 207
London Lykpeny, 171, 177, 178–9, 282–3
    n.8
The Los Angeles Times, 137
Lud Heat, 250, 274 n.10, 282 n.3

Margins of Philosophy, 271 n.11
Maria Marten or, The Murder in the Red
    Barn, 199
Memoirs of the Blind, 280 n.17
Metafiction and Myth in the Novels of Peter
    Ackroyd, 264 n.1

New York Review of Books, 7, 21
New York Times Book Review, 24, 138

New Yorker, 138
Nicholas Nickleby, 175
The Ninth Bridgewater Treatise: A Fragment, 287 n.27
Northanger Abbey, 275 n.20
Notes Towards the Definition of Culture, 273 n.1, 274 n.9, 279 n.12
'The Nymph Complaining for the Death of Her Fawn', 41, 270 n.6

The Observer, 273 n.3
'Of Reformation Touching Church Discipline', 165
The Old Curiosity Shop, 25
'On a Newly Arisen Apocalyptic Tone in Philosophy', 271 n.11
'On Murder Considered as One of the Fine Arts', 178, 241–2
Our Mutual Friend, 82, 252, 265 n.10

Paradise Lost, 156, 168, 281 n.19
Perfume, 267–8 n.19
Persuasion, 149
Peter Ackroyd, 264 n.1
Peter Pan, 36
The Phenomenology of Spirit, 111
The Pickwick Papers, 184
The Picture of Dorian Gray, 204, 268 n.19
'Pierre Ménard, author of *Quixote*', 274 n.5
The Pilgrim's Progress from This World to That Which is to Come, 146
The Pleasure of the Text, 56
'"…Poetically Man Dwells…"', 268 n.1
Poetry, 44
The Politics and Poetics of Transgression, 155
The Politics of Time, 277 n.2
The Portrait of Mr W. H., 91
A Portrait of the Artist as a Young Man, 23
Postmodern Narrative Theory, 277 n.2
The Prelude, 257
Problems and Poetics of the Nonaristotelian Novel, 273–4 n.4
Publishers' Weekly, 2

Radon Daughters, 171
Reading Twentieth-Century Poetry: The Language of Gender and Object, 46
'The Rejection of Closure', 57
The Rocky Horror Picture Show, 29

Scrutiny, 41, 141

Songs of Innocence and Experience, 282 n.4
The Spectator, 94, 138
Specters of Marx: The State of the Debt, the Work of Mourning, and the New International, 285 n.19
Speculum of the Other Woman, 271 n.11
The Strange Case of Dr Jekyll and Mr Hyde, 204
The Sunday Times, 22, 228, 271 n.7
'Suzanne', 55
'Sweeney Agonistes', 269–70 n.6

'The Tables Turned', 268 n.2
'Télépathie', 58
Tel Quel, 6, 7
The Tempest, 156
Textures of Light: Vision and Touch in Irigaray, Levinas and Merleau-Ponty, 52
'Thomas Hardy, Jacques Derrida and the "Dislocation of Souls"', 58
'Throwing Pies at the Dean: Comedy, Power, and Institutional Practice', 265 n.13
The Time Machine, 37
Time and Narrative, 111, 277 n.2
The Times, 36, 94
Times Literary Supplement, 6, 7, 44, 140, 157
'To Marguerite – Continued', 279 n.10
'The Torn Letter', 58
Two on a Tower, 12, 149
Under the Greenwood Tree, 148–9

Utopia, 281 n.21

The Village Voice, 94
Villette, 253
Le vite in gioco: le prospettiva ontologica e autoreferenziale nella narrativa di Peter Ackroyd, 264 n.1

'Wakefield', 97
The Waste Land, 37, 47, 69, 81, 203, 255, 269–70 n.6, 274 n.13, 276 n.1, 279 n.10, 280 n.16
Weekly Digest, 207
Westminster Review, 201
White Chappell, Scarlet Tracings, 173
Workers in the Dawn, 244
Writing London: The Trace of the Urban Text from Blake to Dickens, 281 n.2

Index of Proper Names

Ackroyd, Graham, 269 n.4
Adams, Tim, 273 n.3
Andrews, Malcolm, 266–7 n.15
Arnold, Matthew, 76, 144, 279 n.10
Ashbery, John, 5, 37, 44, 45, 64, 77, 264
    n.2, 268–9 n.3
Attridge, Derek, 4, 137
Audigier, Jean–Pierre, 95, 276 n.25
Austen, Jane, 149, 275 n.20

Babbage, Charles, 68, 201, 202, 207, 208,
    242, 287 n.27
Barker, Francis, 108, 110, 162, 281 n.19
Barnes, Julian, 140
Barthes, Roland, 56, 57, 69
Beckett, Thomas, 180
Bemrose, John, 139, 140
Bennett, Arnold, 25, 144
Bernard, Catherine, 34
Bernstein, Carol, 201
Blake, William, 136, 139, 170, 172, 173,
    174, 175–6, 177, 180–1, 183, 184,
    185, 187, 202, 237–8, 257, 263, 279
    n.11, 285 n.22
Bloom, Harold, 272 n.1, 274 n.9
Bloomer, Jennifer, 192, 285 n.22
Borges, Jorge Luis, 73, 274 n.5, 287 n.25
Bradley, A. C., 144
Brontë, Charlotte, 253
Broughton, Trev, 157, 158
Buchan, James, 138
Bunyan, John, 136, 142, 173, 263, 279
    n.11

Caine, Michael, 262
Carlyle, Thomas, 73
Carroll, Lewis, 65, 136, 142, 267 n.19
Cervantes, Miguel de, 73
Chatterton, Thomas, 124, 130, 174, 232,
    276 n.23
Chesterton, G. K., 25
Christie, Agatha, 95, 96
Clute, John, 157, 172, 281 n.19
Cohen, Leonard, 55
Cohen, Morton N., 267 n.19
Coleridge, Samuel Taylor, 76, 144

Colman, George, 282 n.7
Conan Doyle, Arthur, 136, 153, 203, 209
Conrad, Joseph, 209, 254
Corlett, William, 185
Cosh, Mary, 85
Currie, Mark, 277 n.3

Davies, W. H., 37
De Lange, Adriaan, 93, 96, 98
De Quincey, Thomas, 173, 177, 200, 202,
    205, 209, 241–2, 265 n.14
Dee, John, 68, 245
Defoe, Daniel, 136, 263
Derrida, Jacques, 8, 11, 23, 43, 52, 53, 65,
    72, 75, 76, 77, 80, 93, 118, 133, 261,
    264–5 n.3, 265 n.8, 271 n.11, 272
    n.12, 277 n.5, 277 n.6, 278 n.3, 278
    n.7, 280 n.17, 285 n.19
Dickens, Charles, 20, 25–6, 28, 29, 77, 78,
    81, 82, 83, 84, 136, 142, 170, 172,
    173, 174, 175–6, 177, 178, 180–1,
    182, 183, 184, 185, 187, 201, 202,
    213, 221–2, 223, 232, 237, 242, 249,
    252, 258, 259, 262, 266 n.15, 267
    n.16, 275 n.14, 282 n.7, 282 n.4
Dieckmann, Katherine, 143, 144–5
Dodsworth, Martin, 3, 17, 21–3, 30, 44,
    65, 70, 104, 266 n.15, 273 n.1, 277
    n.6
Dollimore, Jonathan, 46, 48, 49, 56
Donoghue, Denis, 130
Dun, Andrew Aidan, 250
Dyer, Geoff, 94

Eliot, George, 213
Eliot, T. S., 37, 41, 47, 81, 148, 172, 203,
    223, 225, 227, 234, 255, 260, 269–70
    n.6, 273 n.2, 274–5 n.13, 279 n.10,
    279.12, 280 n.16
Engels, Friedrich, 258
Evans, Dylan, 63

Fenton, James, 94–5, 96
Fenves, Peter, 129, 131, 132, 134
Fink, Bruce, 272 n.12
Finney, Brian, 12, 75, 77

Firbank, Ronald, 37, 77, 136
Forster, E. M., 37, 53, 54, 279 n.10
Forster, John, 25, 282 n.7
Fowles, John, 6, 149
Freud, Sigmund, 213, 285 n.22

Galbraith, J. K., 246
Gallix, François, 274 n.5
Galsworthy, John, 144
Genette, Gérard, 14, 80
Giovanelli, Laura, 2–3, 85, 102, 264 n.1,
    264 n.2, 274 n.9, 276–7 n.26, 278
    n.1
Gissing, George, 25, 173, 200, 201, 202–3,
    207–8, 244
Glendinning, Victoria, 20
Golding, William, 140
Goodrich, Chris, 137
Greene, Grahame, 37
Gregson, Ian, 44, 45, 46, 47
Griffin, Susan M., 74

Hardy, Thomas, 12, 21, 58, 148–9, 150,
    153, 232
Hartman, Geoffrey, 55, 56
Hawksmoor, Nicholas, 79, 93, 177, 180,
    202, 245, 274 n.10, 275 n.18
Hawthorne, Nathaniel, 97
Hegel, G. W. F., 111
Heidegger, Martin, 87, 100, 110, 268 n.1
Hejinian, Lyn, 57
Herman, Luc, 3, 97, 276 n.21
Hislop, Andrew, 86
Hitchcock, Alfred, 216
Hobson, Marion, 118–19, 277 n.5
Hogarth, William, 136, 171
Hogg, James, 73
Hollingshurst, Allan, 95, 275 n.19
Home, Daniel, 144
Hopkins, Gerard Manley, 37
Howerd, Frankie, 48, 271 n.7
Huffam, Christopher, 177
Hutcheon, Linda, 97, 231, 232, 235
Hyppolite, Jean, 111–12, 114, 118, 153

Idle, Eric, 48
Irigaray, Luce, 52, 271 n.11
Izzard, Eddie, 48

James, Henry, 21, 74, 254
James, P. D., 96
Jameson, Fredric, 109, 233

Janik, Del Ivan, 93, 276 n.21
Jefferies, Richard, 252
John, Elton, 145
Johnson, Glen, 2
Jordan, Neil, 31, 33
Joyce, James, 23, 37, 73, 226, 274 n.7
Joynson, Samuel, 276 n.23

Kaveney, Roz, 171, 172
Kearns, Katherine, 9, 16
Keating, Peter, 20, 21, 265 n.14
Keiller, Patrick, 250
Kendrick, Walter, 94
Kift, Dagmar, 278 n.6
Kincaid, James R., 24–6, 28–30, 34, 265
    n.13, 266 n.15, 267 n.15
King, Francis, 18, 20, 94, 172
Klinkenborg, Verlyn, 24, 138, 139, 143
Korn, Eric, 20, 172, 194

La Rue, Danny, 48
Lacan, Jacques, 63, 76, 77, 261, 271–2
    n.12, 285 n.22
Larissey, Edward, 46, 47, 49
Leavis, F. R., 21, 141, 279 n.10, 279 n.12
Led Zeppelin, 36
Lehmann–Haupt, Christopher, 139–40,
    141
Leno, Dan (George Galvin), 278 n.6
Levi, Peter, 158
Levinas, Emmanuel, 103, 104, 277 n.27
Lewis, Roger, 86
Lewis, Wyndham, 144
Lodge, David, 7, 17, 23, 30, 69, 70, 75,
    272–3 n.1
Lurie, Alison, 138–9
Lydgate, John, 171
Lynn, Kenneth S., 265–6 n.15

MacCannell, Juliet Flower, 285 n.22
Maclachlan, Ian, 49, 57, 62
Mallarmé, Stéphane, 118, 218, 277 n.6
Mallory, Thomas, 136
Marsh, Richard, 209
Marvell, Andrew, 37, 41, 77, 270 n.6
Marx, Eleanor, 260
Marx, Karl, 173, 200, 201, 202, 243
Mayhew, Henry, 207
McClatchy, J. D., 44, 45, 51, 64
McCorkle, James, 48
McHale, Brian, 230
Medhurst, Andy, 269 n.5

Meredith, George, 124
Miller, J. Hillis, 38, 58, 60, 182, 183,
    184–5, 199
Miller, Max, 70
Milton, John, 68, 281 n.19
Mink, Louis, 224, 225
Moore, Alan, 250
More, Thomas, 170, 172, 173, 174, 175,
    177, 178–81, 183, 187, 240, 259, 262,
    270 n.6, 281 n.21
Morrison, Arthur, 209
Myer, Nicholas, 282 n.6

Nägele, Rainer, 177, 179
Nancy, Jean-Luc, 65–6
Nye, Robert, 44

O'Hara, Frank, 45, 77, 264 n.2, 269 n.3
Oates, Joyce Carol, 20, 94
Onega, Susana, 40–1, 44, 45, 48, 75, 77,
    85, 95, 98, 138, 165, 264 n.1, 264 n.2,
    268 n.2, 269 n.4, 271 n.9, 273 n.2,
    273 n.3, 274 n.8, 274 n.10, 274 n.12,
    276 n.22, 278 n.6, 281 n.21
Orr, Leonard, 273–4 n.4
Osbourne, Peter, 111, 277 n.2
Ovid, 243

Paracelsus, 284 n.15
Peck, John, 11–12, 33, 95, 132, 148, 149,
    150, 153, 274 n.6, 274 n.7
Picard, Michel, 87
Piranesi, Giambattista, 192, 284 n.14
Plato, 271 n.11
Poe, Edgar Allan, 65, 213
Pope–Hennessy, Una, 30
Porter, Roy, 252
Pound, Ezra, 280 n.16, 281 n.19
Priestley, J. B., 25, 144
Pritchard, William H., 265–6 n.15, 267
    n.15
Proust, Marcel, 37, 73
Prynne, J. H., 43, 45, 49, 269 n.3

Quiller–Couch, Sir Arthur, 41, 140, 142,
    143, 144

Radcliffe, Ann, 275 n.20
Rajchman, John, 33
Rawson, Claude, 11
Ricks, Christopher, 70, 75, 273 n.1
Ricoeur, Paul, 111, 112, 277 n.2

Robbins, Ruth, 85, 86–7, 88, 92
Roche, Denis, 45, 49, 269 n.3, 277 n.6
Rodowick, D. N., 109
Rogers, Richard, 252
Royle, Nicholas, 39, 44, 272 n.13
Ruthrof, Horst, 5, 9

Saussure, Ferdinand de, 261
Schnackertz, Hermann, 136, 138, 144
Selvon, Sam, 171
Sexton, David, 18, 149
Shippey, T. A., 140
Sidney, Philip, 243
Sinclair, Iain, 171, 173, 250, 254, 257,
    260, 274 n.10, 282 n.3
Sinfield, Alan, 47, 141, 269 n.5
Spenser, Edmund, 243, 275 n.13
Stallybrass, Peter, 155, 156, 168, 281
    n.22
Starr, Kenneth, 271 n.7
Steigler, Bernard, 215, 285 n.19
Sterne, Lawrence, 20, 73, 287 n.25
Stevenson, Robert Louis, 203, 209, 254
Stow, John, 177, 179, 283 n.9
Strawson, Galen, 78
Süskind, Patrick, 267–8 n.19
Sutherland, John, 24, 25
Swift, Graham, 230
Swinburne, Algernon Charles, 201
Swope, Richard, 95, 97, 276 n.21,
    276 n.23

Tanner, Tony, 156, 157, 158, 169
Taylor, D. J., 137–8
Temple, Michael, 218
Tooke, John Horne, 264 n.2
Trollope, Anthony, 24
Tschumi, Bernard, 252

Vasseleu, Cathryn, 52, 271 n.11

Wainewright, Thomas Griffiths, 178
Wallis, Henry, 124
Weber, Samuel, 46, 53, 62
Wells, H. G., 25, 37, 144
Whewell, William, 287 n.27
White, Allon, 155, 156, 168, 281 n.22
Wiesel, Elie, 286 n.23
Wilde, Oscar, 85–92, 107, 174, 200, 203,
    209, 222–3, 224, 254, 275 n.16, 275
    n.17
Williams, Kenneth, 48

Wills, Garry, 265–6 n.15
Windsor, Barbara, 158
Woolf, Virginia, 267–8 n.19
Wordsworth, William, 41, 139, 257, 268
    n.2

Wren, Christopher, 93, 275 n.18

Yeats, W. B., 37, 40, 268 n.2

Žižek, Slavoj, 271–2 n.12